Islam

Islam

Second Edition

FAZLUR RAHMAN

University of Chicago Press
CHICAGO AND LONDON

The University of Chicago Press, Chicago 60637
The University of Chicago Press, Ltd., London

 Published 1966
Second edition 1979
Printed in the United States of America

08 07 06 05 04 03 02 01 00 99 10 11 12 13

LCN: 78-68547
ISBN: 0-226-70281-2

♾ The paper used in this publication meets the minimum requirements of the American National Standard for Information Sciences—Permanence of Paper for Printed Library Materials, ANSI Z39.48-1992.

PUBLISHER'S NOTE

In dating, Muslims naturally use their own era, dating from the *Hijra* or flight of the Prophet Muḥammad to Medina in 622 AD, sometimes called *Anno Hegirae*. Since the Muslim year is lunar it is impracticable to convert dates from the Muslim to the Christian era, and vice versa, by a simple formula. The publishers have therefore decided to give all dates—except for a few in the present century—in the Muslim style as well as in the familiar Gregorian calendar; this style of dating is in conformity with modern scholarly practice in the Islamic field.

The Muslim date is always given first, the Gregorian date following after an oblique stroke: thus, 287/900, 787/1385, 1287/1870–1, etc. Occasionally a Muslim year will fall entirely within one Christian solar year, but usually there will be some overlapping between the years of the two eras. The same system is also applied to centuries: 8th/14th century, early 12th/late 17th century, etc.

CONTENTS

Preface ix

Introduction 1

1 MUḤAMMAD 11

Muḥammad and the Revelation – Muḥammad's Struggle – Muḥammad's Strategy – Jews and Christians – Conclusion

2 THE QUR'ĀN 30

What is the Qur'ān? – The Qur'ānic Teaching – The Qur'ānic Legislation – Commentaries on the Qur'ān

3 ORIGINS AND DEVELOPMENT OF THE TRADITION 43

Preliminary – The State of Western Scholarship – The Nature of the Prophet's Authority – Ḥadīth and Sunna, or the Verbal and Practical Tradition – Classical Opposition to the Ḥadīth – Development of the 'Science of the Ḥadīth'

4 THE STRUCTURE OF THE LAW 68

Preliminary – Early Developments: Qur'ān and Sunna; Qiyās; Ijmā' or Consensus – Al-Shāfi'ī and After – The Law and the State – Formation of the Legal Schools – Conclusion

5 DIALECTICAL THEOLOGY AND THE DEVELOPMENT OF DOGMA 85

The Early Phase – The Mu'tazila – Ash'arism and Māturīdism – Philosophy and Kalām

6 THE SHARĪ'A 100

Preliminary – Development of the Concept of Sharī'a – The Traditionalist Reform: Ibn Taymīya – The Sharī'a and the Law

7 THE PHILOSOPHICAL MOVEMENT 117

The Philosophical Tradition – Orthodoxy and Philosophy – Philosophic Religion

8 ṢŪFĪ DOCTRINE AND PRACTICE 128

Rise and Early Development of Ṣūfism – Beginnings of Institutional Ṣūfism – The Ṣūfī Way – The Emergence of Orthodox Ṣūfism – The Ṣūfī Theosophy

9 ṢŪFĪ ORGANIZATIONS 150

Ṣūfism and Popular Religion – The Ṣūfī Orders – Sequel

10 SECTARIAN DEVELOPMENTS 167

The Khawārij – The Shī'a – Sub-sects of the Shī'a

11 EDUCATION 181

The Schools – The Character of Medieval Islamic Learning – Curriculum and Instruction

12 PRE-MODERNIST REFORM MOVEMENTS 193

Tensions within Pre-Modernist Islam – The Wahhābīs – The Indian Reform Movements – The African Reform Movements

13 MODERN DEVELOPMENTS 212

Preliminary – Intellectual Modernism – Political Modernism – Modernism and Society

14 LEGACY AND PROSPECTS 235

Faith and History – The Legacy to be Reformulated: The Political Dogma; The Moral Principles; The Spiritual Ideals – The Present and the Future

Epilogue 255

Notes to the Chapters 267

Bibliography 275

Index 281

PREFACE

This book seeks to give to the reader the general development of Islam throughout the approximately fourteen centuries of its existence. It is, therefore, primarily informative. But since it aims at presenting, as far as possible, a coherent and meaningful narrative rather than a series of disjointed descriptions of seemingly isolated phenomena or aspects of the development of Islam, the work had to become interpretative in character and could not remain just informative. Indeed, because of its interpretative character, the book assumes, to some extent, that the reader is already acquainted with some of the general literature on Islam that already exists in English.

The second point to be kept in mind is that although the book is basically descriptive and, therefore, necessarily seeks to be objective, in certain parts it is interpretative, not just in a historical sense but in an Islamic sense. This is particularly true of the first two chapters on Muḥammad and the Qur'ān, and of the last chapter. The writer is of the view that it is impossible simply to 'describe' a religion and particularly his own faith and fail to convey to the reader anything of that inner intensity of life which constitutes that faith. This book is, therefore, meant equally for Western and Muslim readers. The Muslim should learn to look more objectively at his religious history, particularly at how Islam has fared at his hands, and the non-Muslim should learn to know something of what Islam does to a Muslim from the inside.

My thanks are due to many colleagues and friends at Karachi and McGill who have given me valuable suggestions and criticisms. I am particularly thankful to Mr. A. S. Bazmee Ansari of the Institute of Islamic Research, Karachi, for reading through the proofs and suggesting improvements.

Karachi
2 December 1965

FAZLUR RAHMAN

INTRODUCTION

Professor H. A. R. Gibb, in his admirable book *Muhammedanism*, in its latest edition of 1961, puts the number of Muslims in the world at approximately one-seventh of its total population, i.e. 300 million (it would be now about 400 million). As against this, the figures issued by the World Muslim Congress at its fifth world meeting in Baghdad in 1962, as amended to date, give the estimate at certainly over 600 million and in the neighbourhood of 650 million people. Confessedly, all these figures are conjectures for lack of reliable total statistics and particularly because the number of Muslims in China is shrouded in mystery and information about several other outlying regions of the Muslim world is also incomplete. At the end of this Introduction, we give figures showing the distribution of the Muslim population in broad outlines. These figures appear to show that the Muslim population of the world cannot be, in any case, less than 500 million.

Yet the question of the actual number of Muslims inhabiting the world is perhaps of secondary importance compared to the phenomenon of the growth of the Muslim world community during the past fourteen centuries or so, and even more important is the nature of this growth which illuminates the character of the inner structure of the Muslim Community. It is to this question that we shall address ourselves here before undertaking a detailed description of the religious history o
Islam in the subsequent chapters. Already, before the death of
Prophet, Islam had developed its major characteristic: the esta
ment of the Community (*Umma*) of the Faithful expressing th
and spiritual quality of its faith through a variety of institutio
by a governmental organization. But at the same time, ir
complex, the Community remained as something mo
either the state organization or, indeed, the institut
What constitutes the Community is the conscious
status as the primary bearer of the Will of God,
God for man' – the Sharī'a (see Chapter VI); this t
be implemented through its governmental and co
The Sharī'a is the constitution of the Muslim Comm

It is this basic constitution that gave to the

outside Arabia their proper character which distinguished them both from the lawless tribal expansions which the Arabs had been experiencing before Islam and from the destructive conquests of the Central Asian Mongols many centuries later. This strength and an unyielding quality exhibited in its outward expansion, together with a strong faith in a higher moral order which kept this expansive thrust on a definite moral plane, had, as we have pointed out, already been bequeathed by the Prophet himself. It was conducive to the expansion of Islam outside Arabia during an astonishingly rapid series of conquests which within a century put Muslims in charge of a vast territory from Spain in the West, across deep into Central Asia and up to the River Indus in the East, and later confirmed it.

There is little doubt that the inner weakness of the gigantic empires of Byzantium and Persia, exhausted by incessant mutual wars and corroded from within by a spiritual and moral stagnation, hastened the progress of the spectacular Muslim advance. Yet this phenomenon of dazzling expansion cannot be explained entirely by this factor and due importance must be assigned to the fresh and virile character of the Islamic movement. A great odium of controversy has hung around the real character of this expansion and the issues have been clouded by the critics of Islam and, it must be owned, by the apologetic of the modern Muslims themselves. Whereas it is a travesty of facts to insist that Islam was propagated 'by the sword', it is also a distortion of facts to say that Islam spread in the same way as, say, Buddhism or even Christianity, despite the fact that from time to time the latter used the arm of the state. The real explanation lies in the very structure of Islam as a religious and political complex. Whereas the Muslims did not spread their faith through the sword, it is, nevertheless, true that Islam insisted on the assumption of political power since it regarded itself as the repository of the Will of God which had to be worked on earth through a political order. From this point of view, Islam resembles the Communist structure which, even if it does not oblige people to accept its creed, nevertheless insists on the assumption of the political order. To deny this fact would be both to violate history and to deny justice to Islam itself. To us there is little doubt that this fact, coupled with the inherent Islamic features of egalitarianism and broad humanitarianism, hastened the process of Islamization among the conquered peoples.

With the expansion of the Arab Empire outside Arabia, the Muslims t themselves the task of elaborating a system of law and administration herein they assimilated Byzantine and Persian institutions and other al elements into an Islamic framework. It is this system (of which the iled development will be elaborated in the subsequent chapters of this book) which conferred upon the Islamic civilization its distinctive character and which, expressing the fundamental moral ethos of Islam, has provided the real constitution, as it were, of the Muslim state and defined its limits. Within a century of Muslim conquests the Muslims were thus able to develop their peculiar intellectual life and had founded the specifically Arab Islamic sciences of tradition, law and history. This immensely rapid intellectual development, which was a result of the interaction of the Hellenistic tradition in Syria and the basic structure of ideas supplied by the Arabic Qur'ān, remains one of the marvels of the intellectual history of mankind.

This development was facilitated by the shift of the capital of the Islamic Empire from Medina to Damascus in the year 660 AD and by the fact that the Umayyad Caliphs at Damascus employed at their court certain eminent Hellenized Christian Arabs such as John of Damascus. At the same time, however, by this change a shift occurred in the relationship between the religion and the state. Although it would not be correct to say that the Umayyad state had become secular and that a full cleavage had occurred between religion and state, nevertheless it is true that the state life no longer possessed that kind of relationship with religious developments which it had had hitherto. Whereas previously the Caliph had enjoyed a religious and moral pre-eminence and his political decisions had been subservient to a religious end, the Umayyads, though their state basically retained the Islamic framework, were largely lay rulers who exercised political authority but lost a large measure of religious prestige. As a result, the specifically religious disciplines developed largely outside the state and, in a certain measure, out of harmony with it. The centre of the religious developments remained Medina, 'The home of the Prophet's Sunna' (for Sunna, 'model pattern of behaviour', see Chapter III).

One important result of the interaction of Islam with foreign cultural currents, particularly Hellenism and Hellenized Christianity, was the sudden eruption of conflicts of opinion on matters of theology and theological ethics and the emergence of a large number of heresies and early sects in Islam. This fact and the smouldering opposition to the Umayyad rule on the part of the non-Arabs, notably the Persians, subsequently resulted in the overthrow of the Umayyad Caliphate and the installation of the 'Abbāsids in Baghdad with the help of the Persians in 750 AD. The Umayyad régime had seen the growth of the early Arab religious sciences of Islam and the eruption of the heresies but it had not lasted long enough to see the full-fledged development of the lay intellectualism of Islam.

The 'Abbāsid Caliphate witnessed two mutually somewhat inconsistent developments both of which were results of deliberate policy.

On the one hand, the ʿAbbāsids sought to meet the claims of the dissatisfied religious leadership under the Umayyads and implemented the results of the religious achievements through the state machinery, thus removing the gulf which had largely separated religion from the Umayyad state; on the other hand, they hastened the process of the intellectual awakening of Islam by officially patronizing wholesale translations of Greek philosophy, medicine and science into Arabic and al-Maʾmūn set up an academy known as the Hall of Wisdom for this very purpose. The pure intellectualism that resulted from this activity reacted on the religion of Islam and produced the famous rationalist religious movement of the Muʿtazila.

Under the ʿAbbāsids, whose civil service was chiefly recruited from the Persian intelligentsia, the Persians regained their national self-consciousness. A long and bitter polemical movement arose between the Arabs and the Persians in a bid to show up their respective spiritual, intellectual and cultural superiority. The protagonists on the Persian side were known as the *Shuʿūbīya* (the nationalists) whose activities were undoubtedly encouraged by the secretarial classes within the Government. During the 4th/10th and 5th/11th centuries the Persian language reinstated itself as a vehicle of literary expression and satisfied Persian national aspirations, even though religious and other intellectual literature continued to be written in Arabic.

The impetus given to the Arab mind by the impact of the outside cultures worked itself out during the 2nd–4th/8th–10th centuries by the creation of a prosperous and brilliant religious intellectual and material culture. Muslims built up an opulent commerce and industry and, for the first time, scientific skill was harnessed for the actual material development of mankind and put to a practical use. Intellectually, the original Arab sciences of history and literature expanded vastly into general history, geography and *belles-lettres*. Objective history, including the history of religions, reached a remarkable level of development. Difficult and delicate matters like unbiased description of non-Islamic religions had developed so much that the famous al-Bīrūnī complains in the introduction to his work on India that while the Muslims had been able to produce fairly objective works on such religions as Judaism and Christianity, they had been unable to do so with regard to Hinduism and that, therefore, he was going to attempt the task. Muslims excelled in geography and, although the contributions of Muslims in this field have begun to be appreciated by modern scholars, full justice has still to be done to their originality and adventurousness in this field. The first social and cultural study of history, i.e. the working of natural historical forces, is also by a Muslim, the celebrated Ibn Khaldūn.

This entire development could not fail to react on religious intellectualism as well, and during the 2nd/8th and 3rd/9th centuries the Mu'tazila Movement developed rapidly and was in full swing. An account of it will be given in a later place in this work, but it may be said here that it had generally developed under the influence of Hellenic rationalism, thereby creating the first major tension in the religious history of Islam. The leaders of Muslim orthodoxy, representing the old tradition, at first suffered at the hands of this rationalist movement which was raised to the position of a state creed during the time of the Caliph al-Ma'mūn but subsequently, by mustering political strength and by borrowing the very weapons of Greek dialectic, effectively gained the upper hand. Gradually, the orthodox 'Ulamā' brought almost all education under their control, and worked out and implemented curricula to realize their own intellectual and spiritual ideals.

The orthodox system of education became so effective that the movement of religious rationalism lost all its strength and its organic entity, although it bloomed still further during the 4th–6th/10th–12th centuries in the works of outstanding individual philosophers whose thought, in turn, reacted on orthodox tradition. Under this new impact, the orthodox created a certain amount of room for intellectualism within their educational disciplines but thereby also effectively checked the development both of a systematic rational philosophy and of sciences.

This relative narrowness and rigidity of education in the *madrasas* (theological schools) was, indeed, mainly responsible for the subsequent intellectual stagnation of Islam. Particularly unfortunate was the attitude of the 'Ulamā' towards 'secular sciences', which seemed to stifle the very spirit of enquiry and with it all growth of positive knowledge. The 'Ulamā', however, were able to enforce and realize uniformity of mind and bring about a cohesiveness of the Muslim community which, in its own right, is an amazing achievement. The mainstay of this entire system was Islamic Law backed by dogmatic theology. Islamic Law, particularly, thanks to its all-embracing character, dominated the entire outward life of Muslims; and this system, more than anything else, made for Islamic solidarity, despite tremendous differences in the cultures of the lands through which Islam continued to spread throughout medieval times. Since Islamic Law comprehended all facets of human life and individual, social and political conduct, it ensured the unity of the Muslim body social even when the political unity of Islam disintegrated after the savage attacks of the Mongols who sacked Baghdad, the seat of the Caliphate, in 656/1258.

The 'Ulamā' system, and particularly the development and status of law, however, did not fail to generate a new and a much more far-reaching tension within Islam than the rationalism of the Hellenizing elements. This was the emergence of Ṣūfism or Muslim mysticism which began in the cultural centres of Iraq and Persia during the 2nd/8th and 3rd/9th centuries as an ecstatic method of realizing the spirituality of Islam. Confined in the beginning to a purely ecstatic ideal of moral purification and asserting itself as an internal reaction to the legalistic developments and the worldliness of the political forces, Ṣūfism soon developed the goal of communion with the divine. Until the 4th/10th century, Ṣūfism had remained confined to urban life constituting a somewhat peculiar and individual expression of a form of spirituality which, although it was foreign to the roots of original Islam, nevertheless expressed a type of refinement of spirit which might still be accommodated in the Islamic framework. From the 5th/11th century, however, certain outward developments took place within the Muslim world which changed the character of Ṣūfism and turned it into a religion of the masses, thereby accentuating the tension between this form of spirituality and the orthodox system of the ʻUlamā'.

With the weakening of the Muslim political centre in Baghdad, the Muslim world witnessed during the 10th/16th and 11th/17th centuries a resurgence of the Bedouin nomadic tribes in North Africa and an infiltration of Turkish barbarian tribesmen from Central Asia into the centre of Islam. The Turkish tribesmen were converted to Islam not through the activity of the ʻUlamā', as had been the case with the spread of Islam in its first phase through Iraq, Persia and Egypt, but through the activity of the Ṣūfīs. In order to make Islam acceptable to the mental horizon and the spiritual *milieu* of the new converts, and, above all, to mellow the harshness of the tribesmen, Islam was administered to them in Ṣūfistic terms. Orthodox Islam for them served largely as an outward symbol, but they were influenced by a type of spirituality which converted Ṣūfism from a way of life of the selected few in the cities into a vast network of Ṣūfī brotherhoods. Henceforth, the spread of Islam in India, in Central Asia and Anatolia and in Africa was carried on through Ṣūfī brotherhoods, and Ṣūfism in all these zones made compromises with the spiritual *milieu* already existing. The new challenge before the ʻUlamā' was this massive tension between the orthodox system and between Ṣūfism as popular religion.

With this fresh injection into Islam of Ṣūfism, the domain of Islam expanded far beyond what it had been since the middle of the 2nd/8th century. Particularly through the reconciliation of orthodox religion with Ṣūfī spirituality brought about by the monumental work and personality of al-Ghazālī (d. 505/1111), a fresh vitality was infused into the Muslim Community. Orthodoxy itself experienced a revival and a new strength, and Bāṭinism, an important subversive heresy, suffered a great loss, while even the Shīʻa following shrank palpably in numbers. On the other hand, vast areas of pagans and even of semi-Christianized tribes were won for Islam. The story of the rhythm of the interplay of tensions between Ṣūfism and orthodox religion will be fully told in the body of this book.

The weakening of the central political control of the Caliph in Baghdad, and the growth of semi-independent Amīrs and Sultans, more or less coincided with the growth of Ṣūfism as a ubiquitous phenomenon in the Muslim world. The Turkish Sultans, although outwardly zealous patrons of orthodoxy, nevertheless paid real homage and honour to the Ṣūfī shaykhs. In general, while the work of the propagation of Islam was henceforth carried on by the Ṣūfīs, as we have indicated earlier, orthodoxy provided the broad legal and dogmatic framework within which the state itself functioned. By the 10th/16th century the two new powerful, gigantic and highly centralized states of the Ottomans, and of the Mughals in India, had established themselves. These states, with their highly skilful and efficient administrative complex, bestowed a new stability on large sections of the Muslim Community. This encouraged the blossoming of newer Islamic culture which may be described as Perso-Islamic. In Iran itself the Ṣafavid rule presently established itself which, however, had the effect of isolating Iran both culturally and in religion, from the rest of the Muslim world by deliberate policies of antagonizing other Muslim powers and by raising Shīʻism to the position of the state creed. While the outward framework of this new culture remained the orthodox law represented by the 'Ulamā', its content, largely constituted by the new Islamic Persian art and poetry, represented a liberal trend shot through with the Ṣūfī structure of ideas, and in, more or less, conscious opposition to classical orthodox culture. This culture enveloped the Mughal empire as well as the Ottoman court until the impact of modern Western forces.

During the 12th/18th century both the Mughal and Ottoman empires declined. While the Mughal power was replaced by British power in India, the Ottomans managed to resuscitate themselves by adopting Western military techniques and other reforms until their defeat in World War I. The whole nineteenth and early twentieth centuries witnessed the political disintegration of the world of Islam. But Islam as a religious and social force remained not only alive but experienced a revitalization which has, in the past decades, substantially helped its political rehabilitation as well. In culture and identity, however, the impact of the modern forces is still felt in Muslim society which is in a transition stage at present.

During the 7th/13th and 8th/14th centuries Islam spread to the

Malay Archipelago largely through Arab traders. After its extension into Sumatra and Java by peaceful penetration, it also spread into the Malay Peninsula. But Islam had hardly established its nascent kingdoms in this region when it came under the military and administrative onslaught and control of Western Europe. Islam in Indonesia has, therefore, to a large extent remained as a kind of overlay on a social and cultural substructure which is still pagan in certain important aspects. However, during the present century there has been fresh influence from the Middle East, first from the Arabian Peninsula and then from Egypt, resulting in the formation of active groups of orthodox 'Ulamā' engaged in the Islamization of society.

It cannot yet be said with certainty how and when Islam spread into China, but it is believed by scholars to have secured firm footholds during Mongol times, although the Chinese assert that the entry of Muslims into China dates back to the very earliest times of Islam. This question can be settled only by a closer and deeper study of the documents pertaining to Chinese history and an actual analysis of the evolution of Chinese Muslim society. We have already remarked that it was through the Ṣūfī movement that Islam had spread into Central Asia and into Anatolia. The story of the penetration of Islam into Black Africa, south of the Sahara, also awaits a connected and comprehensive treatment. In East Africa it seems that Islam was able to make little headway primarily because of the slave trade, but as soon as slavery was banned Muslim missions became active in the interior. In West Africa, again, the active spread of Islam through various *jihād* movements occurred during the nineteenth century. One outstanding characteristic of the spread of Islam into Africa has been the combination of Ṣūfī missions with the orthodox concept of *jihād*, possibly because of the tribal organization of African society. At present, Islam appears to make rapid progress among Black Africans in opposition to the Christian missions, partly because of political feelings against the Christian West. In South Africa Islam is largely represented by immigrants from the Indo-Pakistan subcontinent, but it is at present making progress among the Negro population because of the sharp racial policies of the White South African Government. There are also sizeable Muslim communities in Eastern Europe. In Western Europe and America Islam has entered in the form of Muslim emigrants, while there is also a growing White Muslim population through conversion. An interesting and astonishing development of the recent decades is the growth of an active Negro Muslim population in the United States known as the 'Black Muslims'. Originally a reaction to social and political conditions, this movement seems to be partly influenced by the spread of Islam in Negro Africa itself.

We shall sketch out the interaction of modern Western education and ideas and traditional Muslim culture in the lands of Islam, and the results of this interaction, in the last two chapters of this work; it is important to notice here that, after the recent political emancipation of the Muslim countries from the domination of the West, there seem to be emerging various regional groupings of Muslim states for purposes of joint economic and cultural development and political action. The Arabs of the Middle East, although they have so far been unable to form any definite cohesive unity, nevertheless seem to be heading towards some community of purpose. Although the existence of Israel is a factor in this process, nevertheless the process itself seems to be the result of internal forces. The recent Istanbul Pact (June 1964) between Pakistan, Iran and Turkey known as 'Regional Co-operation for Development' is an important step in this direction. We may well witness in the very near future the coming into existence of other similar zonal or regional groupings. In the heart of the Muslim all over the earth there is an undeniably strong desire for a united Muslim world. Only time can reveal whether this can become possible and in what form. It is obvious enough that any such development would have very great importance for the whole world.

TOTAL MUSLIM POPULATION OF THE WORLD

Independent Muslim countries	380,846,000
Muslim majority countries under non-Muslim rule	182,214,000
Muslim minorities	30,926,000
Total	593,986,000

The most interesting factor in this picture is the number of Chinese Muslims. In his *'Alāqāt al-'Arab wa'l-Sīn* (Cairo 1370/1950) Badr al-Dīn al-Ṣīnī asserts that Muslims constitute 10 per cent of the total Chinese population. In the Bandung Conference, the Chinese Prime Minister, Mr. Chou En-lai, stated that the Muslims in China are 12 per cent of the total population and hence outnumber the Muslims in India. However, the Chinese official census figures put the Muslim population at 10 million. It should be pointed out, however, that since religion is not counted as a factor in the distribution of population in Communist China and the distribution is classified on a tribal basis, only those tribes are listed as Muslim, particularly the 'Hui' tribes, which are 100 per cent Muslim.

CHAPTER ONE

MUḤAMMAD

Muḥammad and the Revelation – Muḥammad's Struggle – Muḥammad's Strategy – Jews and Christians – Conclusion

Muḥammad and the Revelation

Muḥammad, son of 'Abd Allāh, was born into a respectable but relatively poor family of the Quraysh at Mecca about the year 570 AD; his father had predeceased his birth and he lost his mother in infancy. He was brought up by his uncle Abū Ṭālib who, although he never accepted Islam, nevertheless defended his nephew unflinchingly against the vehement opposition of the Meccans to the new Faith of Islam. Little is known about Muḥammad's life before his Call at about the age of forty, except that he was an honest man of unusual moral sensitivity and that Khadīja, a rich widow fifteen years senior to him in age, who had put him in charge of her trade, was so impressed by his honesty and other moral qualities that she offered herself to him in marriage. Muḥammad, who was then twenty-five, accepted the offer and did not re-marry until after her death when he was fifty years old. We also know that Muḥammad's moral sensitivity drove him to retire periodically to the cave Ḥirā' outside Mecca where he spent long stretches in contemplation, and this inner process of religio-moral experience culminated in his Call during one of these deep contemplative moods.

Modern writers on the genesis and nature of Muḥammad's mission have provided much speculation. Many point to the historical fact that before the emergence of Islam, Arabia had been going through a process of religious fermentation due to Judaeo-Christian influences and that in this fermentation some people, dissatisfied with Arabian paganism, had arrived at an idea of monotheism, and conclude that Muḥammad's contribution lay in an insistent emphasis on this idea. Others, carrying the argument further, tell us that Muḥammad, having borrowed some other elements besides monotheism from the Judaeo-Christian tradition, erected a national religion for the Arabs as the catalyst of a new, organized and massive expansionist wave after the previous outward movements of the Arabs that had been taking place for a long time due to the desiccation of the Arabian Peninsula. Still another theory, which has almost a romantic attraction, finds the origin of the absolute monotheism of the Qur'ān in the 'utter monotony of the desert life'! This last theory may be dismissed at once by pointing out that Muḥammad's message was inspired, as will be shown in this and the following chapters in closer detail, not in a Bedouin atmosphere but in the commercial *milieu* of Mecca, and that the Qur'ān was, indeed, severely critical of the Bedouin character.

The two arguments about the religious developments in Arabia before Islam as a factor preconditioning the latter and its providing an occasion for the vast and amazing Arab expansion are much more serious since they appeal to certain historical facts. They are not wrong in what they state but are not true explanations of either the genesis or the nature of Islam. It is true that some had arrived at a monotheistic conception of religion; but there is absolutely no reason to believe that their One God was exactly the One God of Muḥammad. For Muḥammad's monotheism was, from the very beginning, linked up with a humanism and a sense of social and economic justice whose intensity is no less than the intensity of the monotheistic idea, so that whoever carefully reads the early Revelations of the Prophet cannot escape the conclusion that the two must be regarded as expressions of the same experience. The Qur'ān says (CVII):

Did you see the one who repudiates the Faith? He it is who maltreats the orphan and does not exhort (others) to feed the poor. Woe betide those who (although they) pray, are (yet) neglectful of their prayers; those who (pray for) show and (even) refuse (the use of) utensils (to needy people).

It was this *élan* which subsequently resulted in the founding of Islamic society in Medina. Indeed, the commentators on the Qur'ān tell us that the first two sentences of the above quotation were revealed in Mecca and the rest in Medina. But so constant had remained this basic original thrust, both in intensity and volume, that it is impossible to detect the difference between the two parts. The Prophet seems to insist: One God – one humanity. Whereas, therefore, the contention that a religious ferment and some kind of vague monotheism existed before Muḥammad is undoubtedly correct, there is no trace of historical evidence that this monotheism was connected with any movement for social reform. This account also clearly shows that Muḥammad's monotheism and his movement had *nothing* to do with the desert life of the Bedouins but presupposes a city environment with a long commercial and religious tradition. The contention that Islam was, in its genesis, a 'national' religion of the Arabs, providing a sheet-anchor for their solidarity and expansion, will be dealt with later in this chapter.

Here we wish only to underline the fact that neither monotheism nor a feeling for socio-economic justice is peculiarly Meccan or Arab: indeed, on the contrary, the egalitarianism it presupposes transcends, by its very nature, any 'national' ideal.

According to tradition, the first time the Prophet had his revelatory experience, the following verses were communicated:

Read in the name of your Lord Who created; Who created man from congealed blood. Read, for your Lord is most generous Who taught by the Pen; He taught man what he did not know. Nay, man is, indeed, rebellious for he deems himself not responsible (i.e., law unto himself) – but to your Lord is the Return (Qur'ān, XCVI, 1–8).

The earliest accounts of Muḥammad point to the fact that this experience had occurred in or was accompanied by a state of vision or quasi-dream, for the Prophet is reported to have stated after narrating the experience, 'Then I woke up'.[1] As time passed and Muḥammad launched a fierce struggle based on his convictions, these experiences became more frequent, and tradition makes it clear that these revelatory experiences of Muḥammad (when he used to sink into the deeper strata of consciousness) were usually accompanied by certain physical concomitants. From this, some modern historians have conjectured that he suffered from epileptic fits. On a closer examination, however, the epilepsy theory faces objections which seem to us fatal. To begin with, this condition begins only when Muḥammad's Prophetic career starts at about the age of forty, there being no trace of it in his earlier life. Secondly, tradition makes it clear that this condition recurred only with a revelatory experience and never occurred independently. This is, indeed, a strange form of epilepsy which is *invariably* associated with the deliverance of guiding principles for such a powerful and creative movement as the Prophet's and never occurs by itself. We are not, of course, denying the possibility of someone suffering from epilepsy and *also* being endowed with spiritual experiences, but the point is that *at least sometimes* the former should be capable of occurring independently of the latter even if the latter may not occur without the former. Lastly, it is incredible that a distinct malady such as epilepsy should not have been identifiable clearly and definitely in a sophisticated society like the Meccan or Medinese.

This story also presupposes a picture of the Prophet that represents him in an otherwise normal state of psycho-physical life during the experience, for epilepsy, after all, occurs in and supervenes on a normal state. Now the view of the Prophet and the Prophetic Revelation, that his level of consciousness was 'normal', was something encouraged and, indeed, explicitly formulated by orthodoxy much later. This was supposed to guarantee the externality of the Angel or the Voice in the interests of safeguarding the 'objectivity' of the Revelation. The attempt may seem to us intellectually immature, but at the time when the dogma was in the making, there were compelling reasons for taking this step, particularly the controversies against the rationalists. A great deal of Ḥadīth ('tradition'; see Chapter III), commonly accepted later, came into existence portraying the Prophet talking to the Angel in public and graphically describing the appearance of the latter. Despite the fact that it is contradicted by the Qur'ān which says '. . . We sent him (the Angel) down upon your *heart* that you may be a warner' (XXVI, 194, cf. II, 97) this idea of the externality of the Angel and the Revelation has become so ingrained in the general Muslim mind that the real picture is anathema to it.

The same is the case with the rest of the religious experiences of the Prophet. The Qur'ān refers to an important transforming experience or perhaps a series of such experiences of Muḥammad in several Sūras of the Qur'ān (XVII, 1; LIII, 5–18; LXXXI, 23). In all these places, the Qur'ān alludes to the fact that the Prophet saw something 'at the farthest end' or 'on the horizon' and this shows that the experience contained an important element of the 'expansion' of the self. In LIII, 11–12, the Qur'ān says: 'The heart has not falsified what it has seen; shall you doubt what it has witnessed?' But the spiritual experiences of the Prophet were later woven by tradition, especially when an 'orthodoxy' began to take shape, into the doctrine of a single, physical, locomotive experience of the 'Ascension' of Muḥammad to Heaven, and still later were supplied all the graphic details about the animal which was ridden by the Prophet during his ascension, about his sojourn in each of the seven heavens, and his parleys with the Prophets of bygone ages from Adam up to Jesus. We may first concede the fact, which is rarely realized by the opponents of 'orthodoxy', that a religion cannot live on purely 'spiritualized' dogmas and that reification is necessary even if only to serve the purpose of a 'vessel' for the spirit. We may further insist that it is really impossible to hold that something should occur of a purely spiritual nature without a physical concomitant, and we might even assert that a single event may be called spiritual or physical according to its setting or context, yet in either case the doctrine of a locomotive *mi'rāj* or 'Ascension' developed by the orthodox (chiefly on the pattern of the Ascension of Jesus) and backed by Ḥadīth is no more than a historical fiction whose materials come from various sources.

Muḥammad's Struggle

The Prophet's preaching evoked strong opposition from the Meccans, especially from the oligarchy that controlled the very life of the city. The Meccans not only feared Muḥammad's challenge to their traditional religion based on polytheism but they felt that the very structure of their society, commercially vested interests, was being directly threatened by the new teaching with its emphasis on social justice which, as time went on, became more and more specific in its condemnation of usury and its insistence on the *zakāt* or poor-rate. All sorts of accusations were laid against the Prophet, that he was a man possessed, that he was a magician, that he had become unbalanced in mind. As the opposition grew, it became fiercer: it changed from anger to ridicule, from ridicule to denunciation. 'What a queer sort of Prophet,' they said, 'who goes about in the market-place.' And, 'Why could God not choose a bigger man with better means (and a bank balance) at his disposal to be the Prophet rather than this orphan-prodigy?' The struggle became hot, and relentless persecution its characteristic feature.

As the struggle proceeded, Muḥammad's faith became gradually more and more definitely formulated both by making explicit its implicit metaphysical assumption, i.e. a fundamental theology, through a strategy of argument, and by a process of crystallization of specific duties laid on his followers, both among themselves and *vis-à-vis* the opposing forces. Chronologically, the first belief that the Qur'ān inculcated after monotheism and socio-economic justice was that of judgment or final answerability. Man is not only rebellious, but is a hardened and obdurate rebel. There must, therefore, be a moral reckoning where dire punishment awaits the disbelievers and the evil-doers while immense recompense will be bestowed on the righteous. In the meantime, the Prophet's task is to preach his message and to warn unflinchingly, 'perchance they may return'. Along with warnings against the impending doom for the unrighteous, which the Qur'ān graphically points with great force, the saying of prayers is enjoined upon Muslims as a cardinal duty. We shall trace the development of these doctrines more fully in the next chapter. Here we only wish to make the point that the development of regular congregational prayers and the levying of alms for the poor, besides the spiritual benefit that they bestowed on an individual, contributed enormously towards producing that cohesiveness and spirit of solidarity which is especially necessary for a young struggling community and which is still a palpable characteristic of the Muslim community to this day.

Connected with the warnings about the judgment and as a historical support against the persecution of the Prophet and his followers, the Qur'ān also repeatedly recites the stories of earlier Prophets – Abraham, Noah, Moses, Jesus, etc., men who had also met with opposition, whose message had equally been treated with obduracy on the part of the majority of people. As time passes, these stories become fuller and fuller and the images of the earlier Prophets take on more definite shapes. The question of the 'historicity' of these details, i.e. of the extent of their conformity to earlier, pre-Islamic, stories and legends is in itself interesting but is beset with difficulties. Nor is the question of the 'material sources' of the Qur'ānic prophetology very meaningful for assessing the real originality and import of the Prophet's message which must be located in the purpose in which these materials were turned and the service in which they were pressed. On the other hand, the Muslim need not fear and reject the historical approach to these materials. The Qur'ān certainly says about these stories that they are revealed truth: but, surely, what is revealed is what they are meant to convey and the import with which they are invested. Indeed, if Muḥammad had not known 'historically' (as distinguished from 'through revelation') the *materials* of the Prophets' stories, he would himself have been at a complete loss to understand what the Revelation was saying to him.

Despite frustrations, however, and despite the Qur'ānic protestations that he was only a warner, Muḥammad neither really lost the hope of success nor, indeed, the dire and stark realization that he was *duty-bound* to succeed. It is surprising that none of his innumerable biographers, whether Muslim or non-Muslim, appreciates this last fact adequately, although it stands abundantly revealed in the Qur'ān and in the relevant traditional material. People seem to have placed too much emphasis on the discrete external events of his biography and not attended sufficiently to his vicissitudinous inner spiritual history which still remains to be reconstructed in full. Before his Call, the Prophet's mind was tormented by problems concerning the situation and destiny of man; this drove him into periodic retirement and contemplation. From the throes of this agonizing search, Revelation emerged and to this the Qur'ān points (XCIV, 1–3), 'Did We not open up your breast and relieve you of the burden which broke your back?' (Later on, tradition wove around this a whole legend of the physical opening of the Prophet's breast by Gabriel and cleansing his heart!) But after the Call, a new burden was laid upon the Prophet's shoulders, the burden of successfully executing the Call, and to this the Qur'ān refers when it says, 'We are, indeed, putting upon you a burdensome Call' (LXXIII, 5). The whole subsequent inner history of the Prophet is thus set between the two limits, i.e. the frustration caused by the attitude of the Meccans, which was outside his control, and the endeavour to succeed, for it is a part of the Qur'ānic doctrine that simply to deliver the Message, to suffer frustration and not to succeed, is immature spirituality.

So strong was the Prophet's anxiety to be effective that the Qur'ān returns to this subject again and again both in the Meccan and the Medinese periods of his career. 'We have not sent the Qur'ān to you that you may live in anguish' (XX, 2); 'Are you, then, going to melt away your soul in sorrow for them that they do not believe in this Teaching?' (XVIII, 6). That the Prophet's care and anxiety for the Jewish and the Christian communities in Medina was essentially the same as that he had displayed towards the Arab pagans in Mecca is clearly seen in the following verse: 'Say: "O People of the Book! you have nothing to stand on until you implement the *Tora* and the *Evangel* and what has been sent to you from your Lord": But what has been sent to you (O Muḥammad) from your Lord is, indeed, going to increase many of them in rebellion and disbelief; wherefore *do not feel sorry for the disbelievers*' (V, 68). The strongest illustration of this trait of the Prophet occurs in the following Meccan passage: 'We know, indeed, that it grieves you what they say, but it is not you they are repudiating: the wicked ones are rejecting the signs of God. Messengers have been repudiated before you; but they bore with patience their repudiation and their persecution until Our succour came to them: none can alter the judgment of God, and some news of the Prophets has already come to you. If their non-acceptance weighs so heavy upon you, then if you can seek out a hole in the earth or a ladder to the heavens and bring them some miracle (do so). . .' (VI, 33–35).

The Prophet considered it of capital importance that the Message should be effectively implemented and, in fact, that only then could it really become the true Message; therefore it is not surprising that the Prophet lost no opportunity that offered itself for putting his plan through. His opponents, both in Mecca and later in Medina, knowing the Prophet's anxiety for this human cause, offered him certain tantalizing opportunities in exchange for concessions; but the Qur'ān constantly warned him against any possible compromise and made the distinction clear between compromise and strategy.

They wish you would compromise so they would compromise also (LXVIII, 9). They nearly seduced you from what We revealed to you into attributing to Us something else, in which case they would have befriended you. If We had not made you firm, you were going to yield some ground. In that case We would have given you a double punishment in this life and a double punishment in the hereafter, and you would have been helpless against Us (XVII, 73–75).

Exactly the same story is repeated in Medina:

Those people (i.e., the Jews and the Christians) who inherited the Scripture from them (their forefathers) are in a great confusion about it. So invite (people) to it, be firm as you have been commanded and do not follow their wishes. Say: 'I believe in the Scriptures that have been revealed and I have been commanded to do justice among you; God is our Lord and yours...' (XLII, 15–16).

The Prophet's biographers also tell us that once, early in his career in Mecca, he was holding a parley with an influential person in order to enlist the latter's support for his cause when a blind man called on him. The Prophet was irritated and did not see the blind man at the time. This provided the celebrated Qur'ānic verses, 'You frowned and turned away because the blind man came to see you? How do you know perchance the blind man has a pure heart? . . . The one who feels independent, you seek him out on purpose . . . but the one who comes running and fearing God, you do not heed him' (LXXX, 1 *et seq*).

Muḥammad's Strategy

The instances quoted above at length throw into bold relief the spiritual dilemma of the Prophet. In Mecca he had gathered with him a small but devoted band of followers, yet it was obvious after thirteen years of ceaseless preaching and struggle that his movement had reached deadlock and there seemed little hope of any early victory against the obdurate opposition. It was at this juncture that the people of Medina (called Yathrib in pre-Islamic times) came into contact with the Prophet and invited him to move to that city as its political and religious head. For this reason, it would not be possible to hold that the Prophet had reached an absolutely forlorn stage or had been utterly rejected in Mecca, even though his work had shown very slow progress and, as we have just said, seemed to reach an immediate deadlock. If his mission had been progressing satisfactorily he would not have left Mecca, for to take that city, the religious centre of the Arabs, was his primary objective. But neither had he been completely rejected in Mecca, for otherwise, obviously, the Medinese would have never invited him to be their religious and political head if his prestige had been low in his own native place: nobody chooses leaders out of pity for them. It is absolutely certain, therefore, that the moral prestige and the statesmanlike ability of the Prophet must have already won the Medinese. For they were on the lookout for someone who could save them from the deadly feuds that had gripped the town for a very long period and had sapped the life of the people. After carefully negotiating with the Medinese, the Prophet left Mecca for Medina with his small but devoted band of followers. The *hijra* or the Emigration to Medina marks the beginning of the Muslim calendar.

In Medina the Prophet promulgated a charter guaranteeing the religious freedom of the Jews as a community, emphasizing the closest possible cooperation among the Muslims, calling on the Jews and the Muslims to cooperate for peace and, so far as general law and order was concerned, ensuring the absolute authority of the Prophet to decide and settle disputes. He succeeded in the quickest time in establishing a real and effective brotherhood between the Meccan immigrants and the Medinese Muslims, a phenomenon at which both old and modern historians marvel equally. This achieved, the Prophet turned to the task that was the crux of his Prophetic mission: to bring Mecca to accept Islam and through the religious centre of Mecca to spread Islam further. All his efforts thenceforward are directed to this end. He had tried his hardest in Mecca itself but he seemed to fail. In his anxiety he wanted to try strategies and measures that sometimes threatened to verge on compromises: the Qur'ān warned him and required him to wait 'till Our succour comes'. Was it not the time to go ahead? Who will say it was not? And yet it is exactly at this point that the Prophet has been most misunderstood, especially by Western critics. They say they fail to understand the Prophet at this juncture: how can a preacher become pugnacious? We must confess we fail to understand this failure, prejudice apart, except on the hypothesis that so addicted are these writers to pathetic tales of sorrow, failure, frustration and crucifixion that the very idea of success in this sphere seems to them abhorrent. We have made abundantly clear, however, that, so far as the Prophet was concerned, there was *absolutely no* change in him from Mecca to Medina, except that in Medina external circumstances were favourable to him, something that he had longed for in Mecca.

This is the point where we may appropriately resume consideration of the argument in that in Islam Muḥammad produced a national religion for the Arabs. We have previously pointed out that monotheism and a social and economic moral order, the essential impulse of the Qur'ān, had nothing peculiarly Arab about it. But at this stage the specific evidence urged for the thesis of the 'nationalization' of Islam is that Muḥammad, having been disappointed by the Jews who refused to follow him in Medina, turned against them and took concrete steps to 'Arabize' Islam by replacing Jerusalem by the Ka'ba at Mecca as the direction (*qibla*) of worship and declaring pilgrimage to the Ka'ba to be an obligatory duty for Muslims.[2] Normally, a Muslim would say that these steps were taken not by the Prophet by himself but were ordered by God through the Qur'ān. We shall outline our own view about the relationship between the Prophet and the Qur'ān at the beginning of the next chapter. Here, without prejudicing the other issue and for the purposes of discussion, we will not distinguish between the Prophet and the Qur'ān.

That the Prophet had soon come into conflict with the Jews in Medina who bitterly opposed him and his religion is an obvious historical fact, and we shall examine more closely the development of Muslim-Jewish relations especially in religious matters in the next section. But the argument as stated by the generality of Western historians simply exaggerates the rôle of Medinese Jewry on Islam's development and on this point particularly fails to distinguish cause from effect. The evidence of the change of the *qibla* to the Kaʿba would have carried more weight (although it would still not have been a decisive argument) had it been the case that the Prophet had appointed Jerusalem as the *qibla* on his arrival in Medina in order to woo the Jews. But this is certainly not the case. The change to Jerusalem seems to have been effected in Mecca and most probably at the time when the Muslims, under persecutions, were not allowed to offer their prayers in public, and, therefore, not allowed to go to the Kaʿba for worship. Moreover, for the Medinese, as for all Arabs, the centre of religious activity was the Meccan sanctuary and not Jerusalem. It follows that when the original change was made in Mecca in favour of Jerusalem, it was made under duress, as it were, in order to emphasize the distinction between the pagans and the Muslims. This is precisely what the Qur'ān itself tells us: 'We had only appointed the *qibla* on which you *were before* in order to distinguish those who follow the Prophet from those who turn back on their heels' (II, 143). If the idea had been to keep Jerusalem permanently as the *qibla*, this could have been plausibly done while at the same time dissociating Jerusalem, on the religious plane, from the actual Jewish claims just as the Qur'ān did with Moses and, indeed, Abraham whom it declared to be neither a Jew nor a Christian. As for the establishment of pilgrimage to Mecca, this has nothing to do even remotely with the attitude of the Medinese Jewry to the Prophet and his mission. The remarkable point is that both these steps were taken in close temporal proximity to each other, about eighteen months after the *hijra*, and a little before the first and important battle of Badr where the Prophet faced and defeated the Meccans.

The truth is that the active strategy of the Prophet in Medina, as indeed had been the case when he was in Mecca, had as its initial target to win Mecca itself for the cause of Islam and from Mecca to work outwards. Two overriding factors dictated this policy: first, Mecca was the religious centre of the Arabs and it was through the consolidation of the Arabs in Islam that Islam could spread outwards. Secondly, if Muḥammad's own tribe could be won over to Islam, Islam could get a great amount of support, for the Quraysh, through their own standing and their inter-tribal pacts, wielded great power and influence. Even in the early Meccan period, the Qur'ān had categorically asked the Prophet to approach first of all 'your nearest relations' and 'your tribe'. There is nothing 'national' about this but a simple manipulation of the actual forces and *matérieux* of history for the moral cause. The historian Ibn Khaldūn has clearly perceived this fact and has commented upon the importance and rôle of the actual power and strength (*'aṣabīya*) that was necessary for the initial launching of Islam.[3] The eighteenth-century thinker of Delhi, Shāh Walī Allāh, has argued on the same principle and said that 'Arabian conditioning' was absolutely necessary if Islam was to develop as an effective religion in the world.[4] The most fundamental point, however, is what we have also expressed already in different ways: That a God to whom it is, in the final analysis, indifferent whether He is effective in history or not is certainly not the God of Muḥammad and the Qur'ān. If history is the proper field for Divine activity, historical forces must, by definition, be employed for the moral end as judiciously as possible.

But, besides all this, the most urgent and immediate reason for the Prophet's measures against the Meccans was the hostility of the Meccans themselves against the Muslims even when these latter had emigrated to Medina. The Meccans had not only seized the properties of these emigrants whom they had virtually expelled from their homes, but they could not even look with equanimity upon the fact that the Prophet and his Meccan followers had joined another tribe in Medina. It was, therefore, natural for the Meccans to threaten Medina, as they did, and on the part of the Medinese, especially the immigrants, to do whatever they could to forestall an actual realization of the threat. In other words, a state of war existed between the two. The Qur'ān itself bears the most eloquent historical testimony to this when it says referring to a skirmish that took place without the Prophet's explicit permission between a Meccan caravan and a group of emigrants during the 'forbidden months' (when fighting was not allowed by Arab inter-tribal law) in 2/624. 'People ask you about fighting in the forbidden month. Say: "Fighting in it is a grave matter, but more grave than this is blocking the path of Allāh and rejecting Him, and (preventing) people from the Holy Sanctuary and their expulsion". Sedition is more grave than killing – (*the Meccans*) *still continue to fight you in order that they should turn you back from your Faith if they can . . .*' (II, 217).

It is, therefore, obvious that the Prophet's measures in terms of militaristic operations from Medina were not unprovoked, as the generality of Western writers think, since an actual state of war did exist. On the other hand, it is not necessary that for every measure taken by the Prophet a specific aggressive act of the Meccans should exist, as the recent Muslim apologists contend. It is open to a party, in a state of general war, to plan and effect its specific operations. What must be admitted is that the Prophet had certainly no desire to resort to war if he had not been fought against and if he could achieve the purpose peacefully. Even when attacked, the Muslims were ordered originally only to retaliate, 'while patience is still better' (XVI, 126). Only when fighting was inevitable did he fight. But it also must be remembered that he did fight wherever he had to and was able to do so. This is because the Islamic purpose must be achieved, as an absolute imperative, and for this not only preaching but the harnessing of social and political forces is necessary. That is precisely why the Medinese career of the Prophet, far from being a compromise of Islam with politics, is the inevitable fulfilment of Muḥammad's Prophethood. And we have brought evidence from the Meccan part of the Qur'ān to show why Muḥammad's actions were inevitable.

The strained relations and the early skirmishes led to the first pitched engagement between the Muslims and the Meccans who, after reports of a threat to their rich caravan from Syria had reached them, decided to join a major battle. In Ramaḍān 2/March 624 about a thousand Meccans met about three hundred Muslims at Badr but suffered a heavy defeat with some of their leaders slain. Soon after, the Prophet concluded a pact with some powerful Bedouin tribes who, seeing his rising power, were desirous to link themselves up with him but who, as subsequent events and the Qur'ānic criticisms of the Bedouins show, worshipped power only. Immediately after Badr, the Prophet also attacked and forced to emigrate to Syria the Medinese Jewish tribe of Qaynuqā' who had been found conspiring with the Meccans against the terms of their pact.

But the Meccans, chafing under the humiliation they had suffered at Badr, prepared in 3/625 an army of three thousand men and were met by the Muslims near the foot of the Uḥud hill outside Medina. The Meccans at first suffered a heavy reverse despite their great superiority in numbers and arms. But the Muslim archers, posted on the hill by the Prophet to cover the flank, left their posts against his express orders and joined in the battle for fear lest they be excluded from the booty. The Meccans attacked the exposed flanks and the Muslims were thrown into utter confusion and suffered heavy losses. The rumour spread around that the Prophet, who had been wounded, had been killed. Later, the Muslims recovered but the Meccans left the battle and marched back home. The Qur'ān partly criticized, partly consoled and partly sought to revive the morale of Muslims by saying that one hundred of them could really successfully face one thousand of the unbelievers but that their weakness now stood exposed in the sight of

God although they could still defeat double their number.[5] The Jews, who had made no secret of their delight at the defeat of the Muslims, were attacked once again and the tribe of Naḍīr received the same treatment as its sister tribe a year earlier. The Bedouins, watching the Muslim reverse, did not show themselves in a friendly mood any longer. Two years later (5/627) a greater calamity menaced Medina: the Meccans, at the instigation of the Jews of Khaybar and with the help of other Bedouin tribes, raised an army of ten thousand men with a view to occupying Medina. The Prophet had ditches dug in front of the exposed parts of the city. The Meccans and the Bedouins laid siege to the city. As the siege was prolonged, dissensions appeared among the besiegers who gradually lost heart and finally withdrew. The 'ditch' proved the final grave of the Meccan efforts to thwart Muḥammad's movement. Immediately after the withdrawal of the siege, the last big Jewish tribe of Qurayẓa in Medina was attacked: it was absolutely clear that Jews there could not be relied upon in any pact. But this time the Muslims were sharply divided as to the treatment to be meted out to them. One group, said to be headed by Sa'd ibn Mu'ādh, successfully insisted on the direst possible measures in view of the unfailing Jewish treachery. The men were largely ruthlessly massacred. The most sinister and heartless rôle in the whole drama was played by the 'Hypocrites' who were no doubt always in league with the Jews but who, after encouraging them, always left them in the lurch.

At last, the Prophet's strategy was drawing to its central aim, the taking of Mecca without bloodshed to serve as the pivotal point for the spread of Islam. Towards the end of 6/early 628 the Prophet dealt a decisive diplomatic stroke, based on a carefully calculated risk, by ordering his followers to march to Mecca in order to perform the rite of *'umra* or the lesser pilgrimage. A very large part of opinion in Mecca had by now swung over to his side. But there still remained a group of diehards who wanted to oppose his entry by force. The Meccans eventually sent a delegation to negotiate a pact with him, celebrated in Islamic history as the 'Pact of Ḥudaybīya'. According to this pact, the Prophet had to postpone the performance of *'umra* until next year, a condition which caused some immediate indignation among the Muslims. But the fact that the Meccans saw themselves forced to negotiate a pact was in reality a great diplomatic victory for the Muslims. The Prophet and his followers duly performed *'umra* next year (7/628). In 8/629 the Meccans were party to a conflict in which their opponents had an alliance with the Muslims who, therefore, had to move into action. The Prophet encamped outside Mecca: the Meccans negotiated for a peaceful surrender. The Prophet proclaimed a general amnesty for all his foes except for the idols in the Ka'ba which had to vacate their seats. Almost all Mecca turned Muslim. In that hour of absolute triumph and glory when the whole of Arabia lay within his power, his head bowed in humility and prayer: 'Now that the succour of God and victory have come and you see people embracing the religion of God in swarms, glorify and praise your Lord and seek His pardon, indeed, He returns (to the repenter)' (CX).

During the next two years, most of the rest of Arabia joined Islam largely voluntarily while the city of Ṭā'if and the Hawāzin tribes did so after stiff resistance. The Prophet made Medina his permanent seat from which in 9/630 he also conducted a campaign against the northern Christian Arabs of Transjordania. He died, however, on 13 Rabī' I 11/8 June 632 after a brief and what seemed to be an ordinary spell of fever, but not without ordering about a month before his death another expedition to the North. It is obvious that the Prophet would not have kept Islam to the confines of Arabia. A large section of modern Western opinion, however, strongly contends, basing itself on the argument that Islam was intended to be the 'national' religion of the Arabs only, that the Prophet's idea was only to bring the Arabs who were under Byzantine and Persian rule within the pale of Islam. We have found, in the foregoing, strong reason to reject this argument. The whole drift of the Prophet's career and of the Islamic movement under him seems to leave little doubt that its logic was fulfilled by the expansion of Islam outwards.

It is also on the basis of this logic that we are led to accept on principle the authenticity of the Prophet's alleged letters to the Ethiopian King, Muqauqis (the governor) of Egypt, and the Byzantine and Persian emperors inviting them to accept Islam, even though the actual texts of these documents may not have been faithfully reproduced and need to be examined. Many modern Western scholars have rejected or questioned the whole story of Muḥammad having written letters to these potentates on the most general ground that it is incredible that Muḥammad, an Arab, would dare such a step, especially when he had no means to compel these men to embrace Islam, or that Muḥammad, the sober politician, would have gone to such fantastic lengths. But is it not even more fantastic that a posthumous child whose mother died in his infancy, who was without worldly means, especially in a society where these things matter most should, after his claim to Prophethood, bring the whole of Arabia to submit to Islam? And did the Arabs not actually demonstrate a decade after the Prophet's death that far from being fantastic it was the most natural thing to put an end to these spent and tottering régimes? The Prophet had not been unaware of the course of the war between the two feuding empires. When one adds to all this the fact that Muslims had received sympathy in an hour of great difficulty and trial from the Ethiopian King when they had migrated to his land from Mecca under the pagan persecution; that Muqauqis, governor of Alexandria, had been friendly to the Prophet and had, in fact, presented to him the slave-girl, Mary the Copt, who bore to the Prophet his infant son Ibrāhīm (who, however, predeceased the Prophet); and finally that the Muslims themselves had come to harbour expectations from the Christians in general, the letters to the Christian rulers at least not only become understandable but appear to be a kind of logical consequence. But if to the Christian potentates, why not to the Persian ruler? The Prophet seemed determined that Islam should venture out of Arabia. To invite rulers was the most effective and reasonable method.

Before the Prophet died, he had created the conditions for a universal brotherhood on the basis of faith, a principle which he vigorously substituted for the old blood-ties and tribal loyalties of the Arabs. Thus, the *umma muslima*, the Muslim Community as a fabric of society, with its principles of internal solidarity, was brought into being under his own hands even though it underwent further important developments later, including *actual* incorporation within Islamic society of the non-Arabs which far outnumbered the Arabs themselves in course of time. In his remarkably effective 'Farewell Pilgrimage' address, the Prophet enunciated and formally pronounced those principles which succinctly summed up all the developments that had underlain the Islamic movement in its actual progress and towards which it had tended as its goal. These are the principles of humanitarianism, egalitarianism, social justice, economic justice, righteousness and solidarity. The text of this sermon, towards the authenticity of which modern scholarship has also extended its general scepticism, must, nevertheless, be accepted as being reliable on the whole. Internal evidence, including the strenuous denunciation of usurious exploitation which had been equally emphatically condemned in the Qur'ān, and the long preparation after which it came (in the previous year the Prophet himself did not join in the pilgrimage but remained in Medina where missions from Arab tribes were pouring in), render it basically impregnable. In some of its later versions, however, some interpolations have most probably been made, among them the sentence, 'An Arab has no privilege over a non-Arab except on the basis of righteousness'. This idea undoubtedly logically follows from the Qur'ān and the Prophetic teaching, but it is highly doubtful whether the Prophet would have actually mentioned the Arabs and the non-Arabs since this problem did not actually exist in his time and the sentence seems to reflect later developments in Islamic society.

Jews and Christians

From the very start of his Call, the Prophet was convinced that his message was a continuation or, indeed, a revival of the earlier Prophets, and in an early Meccan Sūra, the Qur'ān speaks of the 'recorded revelations of Abraham and Moses' (LXXXVII, 19). This attitude is, however, on a purely theoretical or ideal religious plane and has no reference to the *actual* doctrine and practice of the 'People of the Book' and the two must be distinguished. Much confusion has, indeed, arisen and persisted by an identification of the Qur'ān's attitude to ideal personalities such as Abraham, Moses and Jesus and its critique or appreciation of the actual Jews and Christians. At the practical level, especially in the Qur'ān's dealings with the Jews, political pacts and their violations come into the picture, although with regard to the Christians the stand remains essentially theological and religious. On the purely theological plane, however, the problem of the historical 'sources' of the Prophet's knowledge of the *materials* of the Judaeo-Christian tradition still remains an enigma. The following consideration will bring out the nature of the problem. While the Qur'ān had, since a very early date, accepted Jesus as God's Prophet, it had also rejected, again fairly early in Mecca, the claim of the divinity of Jesus (e.g. Sūra XIX). To urge against this fact, as Christian scholars of Islam universally do, that the idea of the Trinity presented to Muḥammad by the Christians was a very crude one, i.e. that Christians had portrayed Christ as a physical or quasi-physical son of God and that if a more sophisticated or 'spiritualized' view had been set forth before the Prophet, he might not have rejected it, is not at all convincing. Even the polytheism of the Meccans, as can be gathered from the Qur'ān, was not really crude and grossly physical. The Qur'ān certainly accuses the pagan Arabs of calling their gods 'daughters of God' but this term was not used in its banal sense for these gods were regarded as 'parts' of God (XLIII, 16).

To solve the enigma, it seems, therefore, imperative that a distinct Christian (or Christianized = the Arab Ḥanīfs?) tradition be postulated in Arabia which did not subscribe to the Trinitarian belief, and had probably only a loose connection with the Christian Church. But for some such postulate, the problem becomes still more insoluble as we proceed. For if the Qur'ān has categorically rejected the Trinity and the divinity of Jesus in Mecca and goes on doing so in Medina, why should it still continue to say, 'Those who have believed, and the Jews, the Christians and the Sabaeans, whosoever believe in God and the Last Day and act righteously, they shall have their requital from their Lord and shall neither fear nor grieve' (II, 62; V, 69)? But perhaps the clearest passage is V, 82–83, 'You shall find that the most relentless enemies of the Believers are the Jews and the Associationists while the nearest to the Believers in friendship are those people who say they are Christians. This is because among them are God-fearing men and monks and because they are not proud. When they listen to the revelations sent down to the Prophet, you see their eyes flowing with tears because of the Truth they have recognized in it. . . .'

The same argument must apply to Jews and Judaism. That, theologically speaking, there is Judaic content in the Qur'ān, far from surprising anyone, is insistently confirmed by the Qur'ān itself from first to last. Similarly, the Qur'ān refers to Palestine as the 'blessed land' more than once. But from this it does not follow by any logic that, but for the Prophet's bitter experiences with the Jews in Medina, Mecca would have been religiously subordinated to Jerusalem. Indeed, if, as we have shown above, the taking of Mecca was the master-plan with the Prophet, this already must assume the paramount place of the Ka'ba in Islam. If Jerusalem had *ab initio* occupied this permanent position, the opposition to Islam of the Jews in Medina could not have changed it, just as they could not change the place of their religious personalities in Islam. These Jews could have been exiled or crushed – as, indeed, they were – and yet the place of Jerusalem could have been retained after being *religiously* dissociated from them as were the personalities of Abraham, etc., dissociated from them.

This religious dissociation of Abraham and other religious personalities from the main body of Jews and Christians was an inevitable consequence of two strands among Jews and Christians. The Qur'ān continuously praises the one strand, and condemns the other, e.g., 'From among them (i.e., the People of the Book) there is an upright group but most of them perpetrate misdeeds' (V, 66). They were asked to live up to the *Torah* and the *Evangel* (V, 68), but, like the proprietors of all organized religious traditions, Jews and Christians quarrelled among themselves and each claimed that the keys of salvation were firmly in their exclusive grasp: 'The Jews say the Christians have nothing to stand on and the Christians say the Jews have nothing to stand on, and they both read the Book' (II, 113); 'Neither the Jews nor the Christians will ever be pleased with you until you follow their faith. Say: Guidance is the guidance of God' (II, 120). The inevitable result of this state of affairs was for the Qur'ān to proclaim that Abraham was neither a Jew nor a Christian and that those with most claim to him were those who really followed him (III, 67–8). This was done not only in the case of Abraham but with all the other religious leaders and Prophets down to Moses and Jesus (II, 135–6; 140). Having thus dismissed the pretensions of those who claimed proprietary rights over truth and divine guidance, the Qur'ān also told the Muslims in no unclear terms, 'If you turn your back (on this mission), God will replace you with another people who will not be like you' (XLVII, 38; cf. also V, 57).

At the political level, the Prophet's experiences with the Jews were certainly bitter, as outlined briefly in the last section. On his arrival in Medina, the Prophet had signed a pact with them, the celebrated Charter of Medina, whereby they were given religious autonomy provided that they joined the Muslims in the defence of Medina when it was attacked. But the Jews proved to be a very unhappy and unreliable partner in the alliance. They not only jeered at the Prophet and his new religion, but in all cases of conflict with the Meccans they threw their sympathy and even active support on the side of the Meccans and constantly conspired with the 'Hypocrites' in Medina itself. It is remarkable that after every major conflict against the Meccans, the Prophet ordered operations against Medinese Jewry which became gradually exiled and crushed out. Indeed, even the Jews of Khaybar, a prosperous oasis in the Ḥijāz, had made tangible contribution towards the Meccans' campaign to raise an army of ten thousand men against Medina. Khaybar was conquered and the *jizya* (poll-tax) imposed upon it in 9/630. This became the standard Muslim treatment for Jews and Christians, and was subsequently extended to other Faiths.

Conclusion

Nobody who studies the life of the Prophet can fail to be impressed both by its spiritual character and by a political and administrative acumen that has been so unusual in the religious leadership of mankind but which was wholly subservient in the Prophet's case to a spiritual vision that he was able to realize. Indeed, once we have acknowledged this fact, we have appreciated both the uniqueness of the Messenger of God, who would not claim anything else for himself but that he is the organ of this message, and also in a vital sense accepted the central theme of Islam. There have been invectives against his personal character chiefly from Christian missionaries and Western scholars (the latter have recently exhibited a considerable change in their attitude) on the score of his polygamy. It has been often pointed out by the Muslims that these marriages could hardly have been for the sake of pleasure: the Prophet married Khadīja, who was many years senior to him in age, at her own initiative and until she died – he was then fifty – he did not marry anyone else. A person who did not marry at the age of twenty-five for the sake of pleasure, long before his Call, cannot be expected to indulge in it at the age of fifty, especially after he had launched a most serious and grim struggle where he is not just a preacher, giving Caesar's things to Caesar and God's to God, but the creator of a spiritual system in the flesh and blood of history.

But even if the Prophet had married a number of women, as a normal Arab of his day did, there would be nothing morally repugnant about this provided a sense of proportion was kept. We must remember, for one thing, that neither monogamy nor polygamy can be regarded as the unique and divinely ordained order for every society in every season and that either institution may apply according to social conditions prevailing, although, given the right conditions, monogamy is certainly the ideal form. We shall discuss this general question in the next chapter: here it should be pointed out that in the Arabia of those days (as to some extent was the case in some countries of the contemporary West after World War II) conditions were such that monogamy could not be enforced immediately. The Qur'ān, therefore, laid down monogamy as the moral law for long-term achievement, but permitted polygamy immediately as a legal solution of the situation. Indeed, in Arabia conditions were in a way even worse than in the post-war West, the common factor being a disproportionate decrease in the number of men as compared to women chiefly due to wars, for in the West the woman is economically independent and in any case there is some form of social insurance.

But the real achievements of Muḥammad are to be judged, in the long run, not on the basis of how many times he married, not even on the basis of his personal achievements in a most brilliant career – he himself was so self-effacing that he referred every bit of it to God – but on the basis of what he bequeathed to mankind: both a set of ideals and a concrete way of achieving those ideals, which still constitute the best solution for mankind's ills.

CHAPTER TWO

THE QUR'ĀN

What is the Qur'ān? – The Qur'ānic Teaching – The Qur'ānic Legislation – Commentaries on the Qur'ān

What is the Qur'ān?

The Qur'ān is divided into Chapters or Sūras, 114 in number and very unequal in length. The early Meccan Sūras are among the shortest; as time goes on, they become longer. The verses in the early Sūras are charged with an extraordinarily deep and powerful 'psychological moment'; they have the character of brief but violent volcanic eruptions. A voice is crying from the very depths of life and impinging forcefully on the Prophet's mind in order to make itself explicit at the level of consciousness. This tone gradually gives way, especially in the Medina period, to a more fluent and easy style as the legal content increases for the detailed organization and direction of the nascent community-state. This is certainly not to say either that the voice had been stilled or even that its intensive quality had changed: a Medinese verse declares 'If We had sent down this Qur'ān on a mountain, you would have seen it humbly submit (to the Command) and split asunder out of fear of God' (LIX, 21). But the task itself had changed. From the thud and impulse of purely moral and religious exhortation, the Qur'ān had passed to the construction of an actual social fabric.

For the Qur'ān itself, and consequently for the Muslims, the Qur'ān is the Word of God (*Kalām Allāh*). Muḥammad, too, was unshakeably convinced that he was the recipient of the Message from God, the totally Other (we shall presently try to discover more precisely the sense of that total otherness), so much so that he rejected, on the strength of this consciousness, some of the most fundamental historical claims of the Judaeo-Christian tradition about Abraham and other Prophets. This 'Other' through some channel 'dictated' the Qur'ān with an absolute authority. The voice from the depths of life spoke distinctly, unmistakably and imperiously. Not only does the word *qur'ān*, meaning 'recitation', clearly indicate this, but the text of the Qur'ān itself states in several places that the Qur'ān is *verbally revealed* and not merely in its 'meaning' and ideas. The Qur'ānic term for 'Revelation' is *waḥy* which is fairly close in its meaning to 'inspiration', provided this latter is not supposed to exclude the verbal mode necessarily (by 'Word', of course, we do not mean sound). The Qur'ān says, 'God speaks to no human (i.e. through sound-words) except through *waḥy* (i.e. through idea-word inspiration) or from behind the veil, or He may send a messenger (an angel) who speaks through *waḥy*. . . . Even thus have We inspired you with a spirit of Our Command. . .' (XLII, 51–52).

When, however, during the second and the third centuries of Islam, acute differences of opinion, controversies partly influenced by Christian doctrines, arose among the Muslims about the nature of Revelation, the emerging Muslim 'orthodoxy', which was at the time in the crucial stage of formulating its precise content, emphasized the *externality* of the Prophet's Revelation in order to safeguard its 'otherness', objectivity and verbal character. The Qur'ān itself certainly maintained the 'otherness', the 'objectivity' and the verbal character of the Revelation, but had equally certainly rejected its externality *vis-à-vis* the Prophet. It declares, 'The Trusted Spirit has brought it down upon your heart that you may be a warner' (XXVI, 194), and again, 'Say: He who is an enemy of Gabriel (let him be), for it is he who has brought it down upon your heart' (II, 97). But orthodoxy (indeed, all medieval thought) lacked the necessary intellectual tools to combine in its formulation of the dogma the otherness and verbal character of the Revelation on the one hand, and its intimate connection with the work and the religious personality of the Prophet on the other, i.e. it lacked the intellectual capacity to say both that the Qur'ān is entirely the Word of God and, in an ordinary sense, also entirely the word of Muḥammad. The Qur'ān obviously holds both, for if it insists that it has come to the 'heart' of the Prophet, how can it be external to him? This, of course, does not necessarily imply that the Prophet did not perceive also a projected figure, as tradition has it, but it is remarkable that the Qur'ān itself makes no mention of any figure in this connection: it is only in connection with certain special experiences (commonly connected with the Prophet's Ascension) that the Qur'ān speaks of the Prophet having seen a figure or a spirit, or some other object 'at the farthest end' or 'on the horizon', although here also, as we pointed out in section I of the last chapter, the experience is described as a spiritual one. But orthodoxy, through the Ḥadīth or the 'tradition' from the Prophet, partly suitably interpreted and partly coined, and through the science of theology based largely on the Ḥadīth, made the Revelation of the Prophet entirely through the ear and external to him and regarded the angel or the spirit 'that comes to the heart' an entirely external agent. The modern Western picture of the Prophetic Revelation rests largely on this orthodox formulation rather than on the Qur'ān, as does, of course, the belief of the common Muslim.

The present work is not the place to elaborate a theory of the Qur'ānic Revelation in detail. Yet, if we are to deal with facts of Islamic history, the factual statements of the Qur'ān about itself call for some treatment. In the following brief outline an attempt is made to do justice both to historical and Islamic demands. We have explicitly stated in the preceding chapter that the basic *élan* of the Qur'ān is moral, whence flows its emphasis on monotheism as well as on social justice. The moral law is immutable: it is God's 'Command', Man cannot make or unmake the Moral Law: he must submit himself to it, this submission to it being called *islām* and its implementation in life being called *'ibāda* or 'service to God'. It is because of the Qur'ān's paramount emphasis on the Moral Law that the Qur'ānic God has seemed to many people to be primarily the God of justice. But the Moral Law and spiritual values, in order to be implemented, must be known. Now, in their power of cognitive perception men obviously differ to an indefinite degree. Further, moral and religious perception is also very different from a *purely* intellectual perception, for an intrinsic quality of the former is that along with perception it brings an extraordinary sense of 'gravity' and leaves the subject significantly transformed. Perception, also moral perception, then has degrees. The variation is not only between different individuals, but the inner life of a given individual varies at different times from this point of view. We are not here talking of an intrinsic moral and intellectual development and evolution, where variation is most obvious. But even in a good, mature person whose average intellectual and moral character and calibre, are, in a sense, fixed, these variations occur.

Now a Prophet is a person whose average, overall character, the sum total of his actual conduct, is far superior to those of humanity in general. He is a man who is *ab initio* impatient with men and even with most of their ideals, and wishes to re-create history. Muslim orthodoxy, therefore, drew the logically correct conclusion that Prophets must be regarded as immune from serious errors (the doctrine of *'iṣma*). Muḥammad was such a person, in fact the only such person really known to history. That is why his overall behaviour is regarded by the Muslims as Sunna or the 'perfect model'. But, with all this, there were moments when he, as it were, 'transcends himself' and his moral cognitive perception becomes so acute and so keen that his consciousness becomes identical with the moral law itself. 'Thus did we inspire you with a Spirit of Our Command: You did not know what the Book was. But We have made it a light' (XLII, 52). But the moral law and religious values are God's Command, and although they are not identical with God entirely, they are part of Him. The Qur'ān is, therefore, purely divine. Further, even with regard to ordinary consciousness, it is a mistaken notion that ideas and feelings float about in it and can be mechanically 'clothed' in words. There exists, indeed, an organic relationship between feelings, ideas and words. In inspiration, even in poetic inspiration, this relationship is so complete that feeling-idea-word is a total complex with a life of its own. When Muḥammad's moral intuitive perception rose to the highest point and became identified with the moral law itself (indeed, in these moments his own conduct at points came under Qur'ānic criticism, as is shown by our account in the second section of the preceding chapter and as is evident from the pages of the Qur'ān), the Word was given with the inspiration itself. The Qur'ān is thus pure Divine Word, but, of course, it is equally intimately related to the inmost personality of the Prophet Muḥammad whose relationship to it cannot be mechanically conceived like that of a record. The Divine Word flowed through the Prophet's heart.

But if Muḥammad, in his Qur'ānic moments, became one with the moral law, he may not be absolutely identified either with God or even with a part of Him. The Qur'ān categorically forbids this, Muḥammad insistently avoided this and all Muslims worthy of the name have condemned as the gravest error associating (*shirk*) a creature with God. The reason is that no man may say, 'I am the Moral Law'. Man's duty is carefully to formulate this Law and to submit to it with all his physical, mental and spiritual faculties. Besides this, Islam knows of no way of assigning any meaning to the sentence, 'So-and-so is Divine'.

The Qur'ānic Teaching

In the foregoing we have repeatedly emphasized that the basic *élan* of the Qur'ān is moral and we have pointed to the ideas of social and economic justice that immediately followed from it in the Qur'ān. This is absolutely true so far as man and his destiny are concerned. As the Qur'ān gradually worked out its world-view more fully, the moral order for men comes to assume a central point of divine interest in a full picture of a cosmic order which is not only charged with a high religious sensitivity but exhibits an amazing degree of coherence and consistency. A concept of God, the absolute author of the universe, is developed where the attributes of creativity, order, and mercy are not merely conjoined or added to one another but interpenetrate completely. To Him belong creativity and 'ordering' or 'commanding' (VII, 54). 'My mercy encompasses everything' (VII, 156). Indeed, the 'Merciful' (Raḥmān) is the only adjectival name of God that is very frequently used in the Qur'ān as a substantive name of God besides Allāh. It is of course, true, as modern research has revealed, that Raḥmān was used as name for the Deity in South Arabia before Islam, but this fact of historical transportation from the South is obviously irrelevant from our point of view. If we leave out man, for the time being, i.e. his specific spiritual-moral constitution, and consider the rest of the entire created universe, the interpretation of these three ultimate attributes is that God creates everything, and that in the very act of this creation order or 'command' is ingrained in things whereby they cohere and fall into a pattern, and rather than 'go astray' from the ordained path, evolve into a cosmos; that, finally, all this is nothing but the sheer mercy of God for, after all, existence is not the absolute desert of anything, and in the place of existence there could just as well be pure, empty nothingness.

Indeed, the most intense impression that the Qur'ān as a whole leaves upon a reader is not of a watchful, frowning and punishing God, as the Christians have generally made it out to be, nor of a chief judge as the Muslim legalists have tended to think, but of a unitary and purposive will creative of order in the universe: the qualities of power or majesty, of watchfulness or justice and of wisdom attributed to God in the Qur'ān with unmistakable emphasis are, in fact, immediate inferences from the creative orderliness of the cosmos. Of all the Qur'ānic terms, perhaps the most basic, comprehensive and revelatory at once of divine nature of the universe is the term *amr* which we have translated above as order, orderliness or command. To everything that is created is *ipso facto* communicated its *amr* which is its own law of being but which is also a law whereby it is integrated into a system. This *amr*, i.e. order or command of God, is ceaseless. The term used to indicate the communication of *amr* to all things, including man, is *waḥy*, which we have translated in the previous section as 'inspiration'. With reference to inorganic things it should be translated as 'ingraining'. This is because with reference to man, who constitutes a special case, it is not just *amr* that is sent down from high, but a 'spirit-from-*amr*' (*rūh min al-amr*), as the Qur'ān repeatedly tells us.

With reference to man (and possibly also to the *jinn*, an invisible order of creation, parallel to man but said to be created of a fiery substance, a kind of duplicate of man which is, in general, more prone to evil, and from whom the devil is also said to have sprung), both the nature and the content of *amr* are transformed, because *amr* really becomes here the moral command: it is not that which actually is an order but that which actually is a disorder wherein an order *is to be* brought about. The actual moral disorder is the result of a deep-seated moral fact to remedy which God and man must collaborate. This fact is that coeval with man is the devil (*shayṭān*) who beguiles him unceasingly.

The Qur'ān portrays the moral dualism in man's character which gives rise to the moral struggle, and the potentialities man and man alone possesses, by two strikingly effective stories. According to one, when God intended to create man as his vicegerent, the angels protested to Him saying that man would be prone to evil, 'corrupt the earth and shed blood', while they were utterly obedient to the Divine Will, whereupon God replied, 'I have knowledge of that which you do not know' (II, 30). The other story tells us that when God offered 'The Trust' to the Heavens and the Earth, the entire Creation refused to accept it, until man came forward and bore it, adding with a sympathetic rebuke, 'Man is so ignorant and foolhardy!' (XXXIII, 72). There can be hardly a more penetrating and effective characterization of the human situation and man's frail and faltering nature, yet his innate boldness and the will to transcend the actual towards the ideal constitutes his uniqueness and greatness. This fact of the devil creates an entirely new dimension in the case of man. God 'has ingrained in it (i.e. the human soul) a discernment of good and evil' (XCI, 8); but so artful and powerful is the devil's seduction that men normally fail even to decipher properly this eternal inscription of God on the human heart, while some who can decipher it fail to be moved and impelled by it sufficiently strongly. At times of such crisis God finds and selects some human to whom he sends the angel 'the spirit of the Command' that is 'with Him'. The Command that is with Him is so sure, so definite in what it affirms and denies that it is, indeed, the 'Invisible Book' written on a 'Preserved Tablet', the 'Mother of (all) Books' (LVI, 78; LXXXV, 21–22; XIII, 39). Men charged with these fateful messages to humanity are the Prophets. The Qur'ān 'sent' to Muḥammad is the Book that reveals the Command: Muḥammad is the final Prophet and the Qur'ān the last Book that has been so revealed.

With this background, therefore, the Qur'ān emerges as a document that from the first to the last seeks to emphasize all those moral tensions that are necessary for creative human action. Indeed, at bottom the centre of the Qur'ān's interest is man and his betterment. For this it is essential that men operate within the framework of certain tensions which, indeed, have been created by God in him. First and foremost, man may not jump to the suicidal conclusion that he can make and unmake moral law according to his 'heart's desire' from the obvious fact that this law is there *for him*. Hence the absolute supremacy and the majesty of God are most strikingly emphasized by the Qur'ān. On the other hand among all creation, man has been given the most immense potentialities and is endowed with the 'Trust' which entire creation shrank back in fear from accepting. Again, the idea of justice flows directly from that of the supremacy of the moral law, an idea equally emphasized by the Qur'ān. But with the same insistence the Qur'ān condemns hopelessness and lack of trust in the mercy of God, which it declares to be a cardinal infidelity. The same is true of the whole range of moral tensions, including human power and weakness, knowledge and ignorance, sufferance and retaliation, etc. While the potentialities of man are immense, equally immense, therefore, are the penalties which man must face as a result of his failure.

In pursuance of this picture, belief in one God stands at the apex of the Muslim system of belief derived from the Qur'ān. From this belief is held to follow belief in angels (spirits of the Command) as transmitters of the Divine message to man, in the Prophets, the human repositories of the Divine revelation (the last in the series being Muḥammad), in the genuineness of the messages of the Prophets, the 'Book', and in the Day of Reckoning.

The Qur'ān emphasizes prayer because 'it prevents from evil' and helps man to conquer difficulties, especially when combined with 'patience'. The *five* daily prayers are not all mentioned in the Qur'ān, but must be taken to represent the later usage of the Prophet himself, since it would be historically impossible to support the view that the Muslims themselves added two new prayers to the three mentioned in the Qur'ān. In the Qur'ān itself the two morning and the evening prayers are mentioned, and later on at Medina the 'middle' prayer at noon was added. But it appears that during the later part of the Prophet's life the prayer 'from the declension of the sun unto the thick darkness of the night' (XVII, 78) was split into two and similarly the noon prayer and thus the number five was reached.

The fact, however, that the prayers were fundamentally three is evidenced by the fact that the Prophet is reported to have combined these four prayers into two, even without there being any reason. It was in the post-Prophetic period that the number of prayers was inexorably fixed without any alternative at five, and the fact of the fundamental three prayers was submerged under the rising tide of the Ḥadīth which was put into circulation to support the idea that prayers were five.

One month's fast, a considerably strenuous total abstention from eating and drinking from dawn till sunset, is prescribed by the Qur'ān (II, 183 ff.). Those who may be sick (or experiencing difficulties) on a journey may postpone the fast until a more favourable time. The Qur'ān is believed to have been first revealed in the month of Ramaḍān.

So long as the small Muslim Community remained in Mecca, almsgiving, even though very recurrently emphasized, remained a voluntary donation towards the welfare of the poorer section of the Community. In Medina, however, the *zakāt*, or welfare tax, was duly ordained for the welfare of the Community and tax-collectors were appointed. So strong is the emphasis of the Qur'ān on this point that even prayer is seldom mentioned without being accompanied by *zakāt*. The ban on usury, the moral condemnation of which also started in Mecca, came in a series of pronouncements – one threatening war from God and His Prophet against those who practised usury – on the ground that it rendered the debt 'several-fold' of the original capital and was opposed to fair commerce (*bay'*).

Pilgrimage to Mecca (see Chapter I) was made obligatory for every Muslim once in a lifetime for 'Those who can afford it', i.e. who can not only pay their way to Mecca and back but can also provide for their families during their absence. The institution of pilgrimage has been a very potent vehicle of furthering Islamic brotherhood and a pan-Islamic sentiment among Muslims of diverse races and cultures.

The Qur'ān calls upon believers to undertake *jihād*, which is to surrender 'your properties and yourselves in the path of Allāh'; the purpose of which in turn is to 'establish prayer, give *zakāt*, command good and forbid evil' – i.e. to establish the Islamic socio-moral order. So long as the Muslims were a small, persecuted minority in Mecca, *jihād* as a positive organized thrust of the Islamic movement was unthinkable. In Medina, however, the situation changed and henceforth there is hardly anything, with the possible exception of prayer and *zakāt*, that receives greater emphasis than *jihād*. Among the later Muslim legal schools, however, it is only the fanatic Khārijites who have declared *jihād* to be one of the 'pillars of the Faith'. Other schools have played it down for the obvious reason that the expansion of Islam had already occurred much too swiftly in proportion to the internal consolidation of the Community in the Faith. Every virile and expansive ideology has, at a stage, to ask itself the question as to what are its terms of co-existence, if any, with other systems, and how far it may employ methods of direct expansion. In our own age, Communism, in its Russian and Chinese versions, is faced with the same problems and choices. The most unacceptable on historical grounds, however, is the stand of those modern Muslim apologists who have tried to explain the *jihād* of the early Community in purely defensive terms.

The Qur'ānic Legislation

The Qur'ān is primarily a book of religious and moral principles and exhortations, and is not a legal document. But it does embody some important legal enunciations issued during the community-state building process at Medina. Some of the economic enactments we have noted in the previous section. The ban on consumption of alcohol affords an interesting example of the Qur'ānic method of legislation and throws light on the attitude of the Qur'ān to the nature and function of legislation itself. The use of alcohol was apparently unreservedly permitted in the early years. Then offering prayers while under the influence of alcohol was prohibited. Later it is said, 'They ask you about alcohol and gambling. Say: in these there is great harm and also profits for people but their harm far outweighs their profits' (II, 219). Finally a total ban was proclaimed (V, 90–91) on the ground that both alcohol and gambling 'are works of the devil. . . . The devil wants to sow enmity and rancour among you'. This shows the slow, *experimental* legal tackling of problems *as they arise*.

But the most important legal enactments and general reform pronouncements of the Qur'ān have been on the subjects of women and slavery. The Qur'ān immensely improved the status of the woman in several directions but the most basic is the fact that the woman was given a fully-pledged personality. The spouses are declared to be each other's 'garments': the woman has been granted the same rights over man as man has over his wife, except that man, being the earning partner, is a degree higher. Unlimited polygamy was strictly regulated and the number of wives was limited to four, with the rider that if a husband feared that he could not do justice among several wives, he must marry only one wife. To all this was added a general principle that 'you shall never be able to do justice among wives no matter how desirous you are (to do so)' (IV, 3, 128). The overall logical consequence of these pronouncements is a banning of polygamy under normal circumstances. Yet as an already existing institution polygamy was accepted on a legal plane, with the obvious guiding lines that when gradually social circumstances became more favourable, monogamy might be introduced. This is because no reformer who means to be effective can neglect the real situation and simply issue visionary statements. But the later Muslims did not watch the guiding lines of the Qur'ān and, in fact, thwarted its intentions.

The case of the Qur'ānic treatment of the institution of slavery runs parallel to that of the family. As an immediate solution, the Qur'ān accepts the institution of slavery on the legal plane. No alternative was possible since slavery was ingrained in the structure of society, and its overnight wholesale liquidation would have created problems which it would have been absolutely impossible to solve, and only a dreamer could have issued such a visionary statement. But at the same time every legal and moral effort was made to free the slaves and to create a *milieu* where slavery ought to disappear. 'Liberating the neck' (*fakk raqaba*) is not only praised as a virtue but is declared, along with feeding the poor and orphans, to be that 'uphill path' which is absolutely essential for man to tread (XC, 10–16). Indeed, the Qur'ān has categorically told the Muslims that if a slave wants to purchase his or her freedom by paying off in instalments a sum that may be decided upon according to the situation of the slave, then the owner of the slave must allow such a contract for freedom and may not reject it: 'And those of your slaves who wish to enter into freedom-purchasing contracts, accept their proposals if you think they are any good and give to them of the wealth that God has given you. And do not compel your slave-girls to resort to a foul life when they want to be chaste, seeking thereby petty gains of life; but if they act under sheer compulsion, God is forgiving and merciful' (XXIV, 33). Here again we are confronted by a situation where the clear logic of the Qur'ānic attitude was not worked out in actual history by Muslims. The words of the Qur'ān 'if you think they are any good' when properly understood, only mean that if a slave cannot show any earning capacity, then he cannot be expected to stand on his own feet even if freed and therefore it may be better for him to enjoy at least the protection of his master.

These examples, therefore, make it abundantly clear that whereas the spirit of the Qur'ānic legislation exhibits an obvious direction towards the progressive embodiment of the fundamental human values of freedom and responsibility in fresh legislation, nevertheless the actual legislation of the Qur'ān had partly to accept the then existing society as a term of reference. This clearly means that the actual legislation of the Qur'ān cannot have been meant to be literally eternal by the Qur'ān itself. This fact has no reference to the doctrine of the eternity of the Qur'ān or to the allied doctrine of the verbal revelation of the Qur'ān. Very soon, however, the Muslim lawyers and dogmaticians began to confuse the issue and the strictly legal injunctions of the Qur'ān were thought to apply to any society, no matter what its conditions, what its structure and what its inner dynamics. One clear proof that, as time passed, Muslim legists became more and more literalists is reflected in the fact that sometime during the 2nd/8th century the Muslim legal doctrine began to draw a very sharp distinction between the clear wording (*naṣṣ*), the text and what was deducible therefrom. There is a good deal of evidence to believe that in the very early period the Muslims interpreted the Qur'ān pretty freely. But after a period of juristic development during the late 1st/7th and throughout the 2nd/8th century (the prominent features of which – as we shall see in Chapters III and IV – were the rise of the Tradition and the development of technical, analogical reasoning), the lawyers neatly tied themselves and the Community down to the 'text' of the

Holy Book until the content of Muslim law and theology became buried under the weight of literalism.

Throughout the centuries, Muslims have not only written innumerable commentaries on the Qur'ān from different points of view and with different, indeed, conflicting tendencies, but have evolved a science of Qur'ānic exegesis (*'ilm al-tafsīr*), with its auxiliary branches of learning, including Arabic grammar, lexicography, the Prophetic tradition, the circumstantial background of the verses of the Qur'ān, etc. Indeed, it is claimed by Muslim scholars with a good deal of justice that all the sciences in Islam which are not absolutely secular owe their origin to the Qur'ān. The Qur'ān has also exerted an incalculable influence on the growth of Arabic literature and literary style, and continues to exert it up to this day. The doctrine of the 'inimitability' (*i'jāz*) of the Qur'ān, not only in content but even in literary form, is common to almost all Muslim schools, and has attained a cardinal status and found expression in various treatises specially devoted to this topic. Muslim orthodoxy had strenuously resisted any attempt to produce a translation of the Book in any language without the Arabic text. This has contributed not a little to the unity of Muslims who, throughout the world, recite the Qur'ān in their prayers five times a day in Arabic. Only recently in Kemalist Turkey the Qur'ān was translated and produced in Turkish without the original Arabic, although the Arabic text continued to be used in prayers. But even in Turkey, there has been a return to the Arabic text even for ordinary reading. For the purpose of understanding the text, accompanying translations in local languages are allowed.

Commentaries on the Qur'ān

During the lifetime of the Prophet the Qur'ān had been committed to memory by many people and recited in prayers. It was also written down on leaves, bones, parchments and such other material as was available. The entire Book was collected together by the first Caliph Abū Bakr. The commonly accepted text, however, the Vulgate edition, dates from the time of the third Caliph, 'Uthmān, who, on the recommendation of a committee appointed for the purpose and headed by Zayd ibn Thābit, the faithful servant of the Prophet, also effected the present arrangement of the Qur'ān, which, as opposed to the chronological order, is based more or less on the length of the Sūras.

Whereas there is some evidence that in the earliest generation after the Prophet people were shy of, and even opposed to, any interpretation of the Qur'ān, this attitude soon gave way to all books of interpretations which were more or less coloured by the faiths and old ideas of the new converts. Such interpretations, which probably sometimes diverged markedly from the obvious meaning of the text and had an arbitrary character, were severely attacked as 'interpretation of arbitrary opinion (*tafsīr bi'l-ra'y*)'. The rôle of opinion or personal opinion in early Islam we shall discuss a little more fully when we come to treat of law in Chapter IV.

The need was thus felt to develop some scientific instruments whereby to control the progress of the science of Qur'ānic commentary (*'ilm al-tafsīr*). First of all, therefore, the principle was recognized that a knowledge not only of the Arabic language but also of the Arabic idiom of the times of the Prophet was requisite for a proper understanding of the Qur'ān. Hence Arabic grammar, lexicography and Arabic literature were intensively cultivated. Next, the backgrounds of the Qur'ānic revelations called the 'occasions of revelation' were recorded as a necessary aid for fixing the correct meaning of the Word of God. Thirdly, historical tradition containing reports about how those among whom the Qur'ān first appeared understood its injunctions and statements was given great weight. After these requirements were fulfilled came the scope for a free play of human reason. A monument of traditional commentary, based on reports from earlier generations, was compiled by al-Ṭabarī (d. 310/922) in his extensive work. In course of time, as various schools of thought and converts of intellectual and spiritual life developed in Islam, commentaries came into existence. Indeed, it is quite true to say that whatever views Muslims have wanted to project and advocate have taken the form of Qur'ānic commentaries.

The language and the style of the Qur'ān have also exerted a most powerful influence on the growth and development of Arabic literature. The Muslims early developed the doctrine of the literary and artistic 'unsurpassability' of the Qur'ān, but even for the non-Muslim Arab it remains an ideal of literary production even to this day. The Qur'ān strenuously rejected the epithet 'poet' flung at Muḥammad by his opponents and never allowed that it be called poetry. Yet in its depth of feeling, in its telling expressiveness and in its effective rhythm the Qur'ān is not less than poetry of the highest order. Indeed, Muslims have developed a special art of its recitation (called *tajwīd*), and when the Qur'ān is chanted in this way it does not fail to affect even a hearer who does not know Arabic. In translation, of course, it is impossible to keep its artistic beauty and grandeur. We quote below three passages from different dates, not because they will convey to the reader its artistic excellence but to illustrate the development of its content stage by stage. The first passage, belonging to an early Meccan Sūra, reads:

As for man, whenever his Lord trieth him by honouring him and is gracious unto him, he saith 'My Lord honoureth me'. But whenever He trieth him by straitening his means of life, he says 'My Lord despiseth me'. Nay, but (this is because) ye honour not the orphan. And urge (others) not on the feeding of the poor; and ye devour heritages with devouring greed and are attached to wealth with excessive attachment. Nay, but when the earth is ground to atoms, grinding, grinding and thy Lord shall come with angels, rank and rank (LXXXIX, 15–22).

The following verses belong to the later Meccan period:

Successful, indeed, are the believers who are humble in their prayers; and who shun vain conversation; and who pay up the welfare tax; and who guard their modesty – save their wives or the (slaves) that their right hands possess (for them they are not blameworthy) – but whoso craveth beyond that, such are transgressors; and who guard their pledge and fulfil their covenant; and who pay heed to their prayers. These are the heirs who will inherit Heaven. There they will abide (XXIII, 1–11).

This passage is from a Medinese Sūra:

(Here is) a Sūra We have revealed and enjoined and wherein We have revealed plain tokens, that haply ye may take heed. The adulterer and the adulteress strike ye each one of them with a hundred stripes. And let not pity for them withhold you from obedience to Allāh, if ye believe in Allāh and the Last Day. And let a party of believers witness their punishment. The adulterer shall not marry save an adulteress or an idolatress, and the adulteress none shall marry save an adulterer or an idolater. All that is forbidden unto believers. And those who accuse honourable women (of unchastity) but bring not four witnesses, strike them with eighty stripes and never accept their testimony – they, indeed, are evil-doers – except those who afterward repent and make amends (XXIV, 1–5).

CHAPTER THREE

ORIGINS AND DEVELOPMENT OF THE TRADITION

Preliminary – The State of Western Scholarship – The Nature of the Prophet's Authority – Ḥadīth and Sunna, or the Verbal and Practical Tradition – Classical Opposition to the Ḥadīth – Development of the 'Science of the Ḥadīth'

Preliminary

So long as the Prophet was alive, he provided the sole religious and political guide for Muslims both through the Qur'ānic revelation and by his extra-Qur'ānic words and behaviour. With his death the Qur'ān remained, but his religiously authoritative personal guidance was cut off. The first four Caliphs met the ever-arising new situations by applying to these their judgments in the light of the Qur'ān and what the Prophet had taught them.

The next century (from about 50–150/670–767), which saw the rise of early theological sects, to be described in Chapter V, and the first stage of development of law, which shall occupy us in the next chapter, was most remarkable for the growth of a phenomenon which may perhaps best be described as religious methodology in the absence of the living guidance of the Prophet and of the earliest generation of his Companions. The first manifestation of this phenomenon is known as the Ḥadīth or the Apostolic Tradition, subsequently compiled in a series of works six of which, composed in the 3rd/9th century, came to be accepted as the authoritative second source of the content of Islam besides the Qur'ān. Whereas the vast majority of Muslims still uphold the view that the Ḥadīth genuinely represents the sayings and deeds of the Prophet, Western Islamists are generally sceptical; some indeed have recommended a wholesale rejection of the Ḥadīth as an index not only of the Prophetic example but also of the religious attitudes and practices of the Companions. We shall subsequently note the existence of a small group of contemporary Muslims who also seek to reject the Ḥadīth, but not on the grounds of any scholarly study of the development of this discipline.

The State of Western Scholarship

Before we attempt to portray a positive picture of the methodology of religious discipline in the earliest period of Islamic history, which proved decisive for the subsequent religious development of Islam, a brief critical review of the treatment of the subject of Ḥadīth by the leaders of modern Western scholarship in this field is necessary.

In his *Muhammedanische Studien*, until now the most fundamental work on the subject, I. Goldziher declares that it is hardly possible to sift, with any confidence, from the vast material of the Ḥadīth, a portion that may genuinely be referred either to the Prophet or to the early generation of his Companions and that the Ḥadīth is to be regarded rather as a record of the views and attitudes of early generations of Muslims than of the life and teaching of the Prophet or even of his Companions.[1] Goldziher, however, maintained that the phenomenon of the Ḥadīth goes back to the earliest times of Islam and even conceded the possibility of the existence of 'informal' Ḥadīth records contemporaneous with the Prophet, although he voiced his scepticism about some of the alleged records (*ṣaḥīfa*) of that period. But, his argument runs, since the corpus of the Ḥadīth continued to swell in each succeeding generation, and since, in each generation, the material runs parallel to and reflects various and often contradictory doctrines of Muslim theological and legal schools, the final recorded products of the Ḥadīth, which date from the 3rd/9th century must be regarded as being *on the whole* unreliable as a source for the Prophet's own teaching and conduct.

A concept the understanding of which is fundamentally important for our understanding of the development of the Ḥadīth and which, at least throughout medieval Islam, has been identified with the practical norms or the model behaviour contained in the Ḥadīth, is the concept of the Sunna. Sunna literally means the 'trodden path' and was used by the pre-Islamic Arabs to denote the model behaviour established by the forefathers of a tribe. The concept in this context has therefore two constituents, (a) an (alleged) historical fact of conduct and (b) its normativeness for the succeeding generations. In the Qur'ān the word 'Sunna' is applied in the same sense where the opponents of Islam are rebukingly referred to as upholders of the exemplary behaviour of their forefathers as against the new teaching.[2] The Qur'ān also speaks of the Sunna of God, i.e. the behaviour of God with reference to the pattern or fate of societies – a behaviour which is unalterable.[3] Here the same two constituents are to be found, i.e. past conduct (in this case of one Being only) which ought to (here 'shall') be operative in the future.

Now, Goldziher holds that, with the advent of Islam, the content of the concept Sunna changed for Muslims into the model behaviour of the Prophet, i.e. the practical norms that flow from his reported actions and sayings.[4] This is in line with medieval Muslim theory itself. For Goldziher, therefore, as for medieval Muslim theory, the Ḥadīth and the Sunna (in its Islamic, as opposed to the pre-Islamic usage) are not only coeval but also consubstantial (i.e. they are not two separate things but one). The difference between the two is that whereas a Ḥadīth as such is a mere report and something theoretical, the Sunna is the very same report when it acquires a normative quality and becomes a practical principle for the Muslim. But Goldziher notices at the same time that in early Muslim literature there is evidence of a difference between the two, such that they can sometimes even mutually clash and are admitted to do so. Hence Goldziher also defines the Sunna as the *actual* (*as opposed to the normative*) living practice[5] of the early Muslim Community.

But this raises a grave issue of which Goldziher does not show a full awareness. How could the Sunna be both normative and actual when the normative and the actual conflict? Or, how could the Ḥadīth and the Sunna conflict if they are coeval and consubstantial although one Ḥadīth may contradict another or, one Sunna another Sunna? No systematic attempt has been made since Goldziher to explore the various possible methods of resolving so fundamental an issue for an understanding of the development of Islam in this early period. Indeed, even the issue has not been clearly formulated by subsequent specialized scholarship and much ingenuity has been directed to discrediting the totality of the Ḥadīth corpus as it finally took shape in the 3rd/9th century. We shall presently essay a plausible picture of this obscure period for which there are very scanty records and hardly any direct source.

After Goldziher a series of scholars developed one of the two lines of thought put in juxtaposition by him, but since the issue was not clearly kept in mind, both sides of the contradiction noted above suffered violence. D. S. Margoliouth, in his *Early Development of Islam*,[6] maintained (1) that the Prophet had left no precepts or religious decisions – i.e. had left no Sunna or Ḥadīth outside the Qur'ān; (2) that the Sunna as practised by the early Muslim Community after Muḥammad was not at all the Sunna of the Prophet but was the pre-Islamic Arabian usage as it stood modified through the Qur'ān; and (3) that later generations, in the 2nd/8th century, in order to give authority and normativity to this usage, developed the concept of the Sunna of the Prophet and forged the mechanism of the Ḥadīth to realize this concept. H. Lammens, in his *Islam: Beliefs and Institutions*,[7] expresses the same view and declares tersely that the practice (Sunna) must have preceded its formulation in the Ḥadīth.

Neither of these two writers asks, or decides the question whether this early Sunna of the Islamic Community was regarded as Sunna because of its status as pre-Islamic Arabian usage or because the Qur'ān, after introducing modifications into it, approved the rest tacitly. For, if the latter be the case, it, in religious theory (and it is the theory that is here in question), cuts the connection between the pre-Islamic usage and the Islamic Sunna. Further, there are two objections to this account of the Sunna, one logical, the other historical. The logical objection is that, as we have seen, the notion of normativeness is an integral part of the concept of the Sunna and, indeed, these authors define the Sunna as 'the normative practice' of the early Muslim Community. We see here that the two juxtaposed but inconsistent descriptions of the Sunna given by Goldziher, i.e. the 'normative conduct' on the one hand and 'actual, living practice' on the other, have been blended in a self-contradictory whole. Now, if the actual practice of the Community was the Sunna i.e. the normative practice, what sense does it make to say that the normative quality was sought to be conferred on the actual practice by *making* it the Sunna of the Prophet? The historical objection, which shall be elaborated presently, is against the thesis put forward explicitly and at some length by Margoliouth and assumed by Professor J. Schacht, whose views we shall discuss next, that there was hardly any extra-Qur'ānic legacy of the Prophet.

Professor J. Schacht has been led to assess the general character of the Ḥadīth more systematically through his scholarly studies in Muslim law and the development of legal theory in Islam. But his views on the character of traditions in general are essentially the same as those on legal traditions.[8] We are not concerned in this chapter with the development of law in Islam but only with the findings of Schacht on the character of the Ḥadīth, which occupy the author in a major part of his *Origins of Muhammadan Jurisprudence*. Schacht claims that his enquiry fundamentally confirms what his predecessors, Goldziher and Margoliouth, had concluded concerning the concepts Ḥadīth and Sunna in the first century and a half of the Islamic era, and that he goes beyond them only in finding that when for the first time the Traditions began to find currency they were referred not to the Prophet but, in the first instance, to the 'Successors' (i.e. the generation after the Companions), then, in the next stage, to the Companions and finally, after a time, to the Prophet himself.[9] His views are fairly summarized in the following quotation:

One of the main conclusions to be drawn from Part I of this book is that, generally speaking, the 'living tradition' of the ancient schools of law, based to a great extent on individual reasoning, came first, that in the second stage it was put under the aegis of Companions (i.e. after the Successors more or less), that traditions from the Prophet himself, put into circulation by traditionists towards the middle of the second century AH, disturbed and influenced this living tradition, and that only Shāfi'ī (150–204 AH) secured to the traditions from the Prophet supreme authority.[10]

Schacht in fact follows and seeks to complement the views of Margoliouth and Lammens and does not seem to realize that, as we have endeavoured to make clear above, there is a fundamental difference between Goldziher on the one hand and these two authors on the other: the former maintains that essentially the Traditions and the Sunna (in Islamic time) were of common origin and consubstantial whereas, according to the latter, the Sunna or the practice (of the Muslim Community, based on pre-Islamic usage) was temporally anterior to the Traditions by nearly a century. Schacht has also taken over from these authors the expression 'Normative practice of the Community' to characterize the Sunna or living usage, and we have seen in connection with our criticism of Margoliouth and Lammens the logical contradiction that this concept contains.

Schacht's argument about the character of the Ḥadīth is in two parts. First, on the basis of evidence he finds in the works of Muḥammad ibn Idrīs al-Shāfi'ī (150–204/767–819), he concludes that Traditions from the Prophet did not exist at all until about the middle of the 2nd/8th century; that the usage or the Sunna until that time was regarded not as the Sunna of the Prophet but as the Sunna of the Community (although the Sunna in Medina, for example, differed from that in Iraq), for it was mainly the product of the free reasoning of individual lawyers; and, finally, that the natural resistance of the lawyers to the Traditions from the Prophet was broken by the efforts of al-Shāfi'ī, who, for the first time, systematically introduced into the legal theory of Islam the concept of the Sunna of the Prophet. Secondly, by a comparison of some earlier and later versions of Traditions, he finds that either in the succeeding period there exist Traditions which did not exist in the preceding period and hence that these are forged, or that the succeeding versions are fuller than the earlier ones and that therefore the later ones had been expanded by forgeries. As regards the first part of the argument, which constitutes a more detailed and scholarly corroboration of Margoliouth's hypothesis (which for the first time used al-Shāfi'ī), we shall, in constructing our own thesis, endeavour to show that it gives too simple an account of the situation and instead of illuminating the early development of Islam makes it more obscure by unnecessarily creating insoluble problems for the religious history of Islam.

The second part where, to my knowledge, Professor Schacht is the first scholar to have undertaken an extensive and systematic comparison of legal traditions in their historical sequence, is unassailably scientific and sound in method and one only wishes that it were practised thoroughly in all fields of the Ḥadīth. But it is equally important that the method be used carefully and that we must be quite clear as to what precisely it can accomplish, prove or disprove. Thus Professor Schacht (*Origins*, p. 141) contends that no Traditions of a dogmatic nature existed in the time of Ḥasan al-Baṣrī's composition of the dogmatic treatise which will be discussed later in this chapter. This he seeks to prove by the fact that Ḥasan does not mention any Traditions. Now, as we shall see later, Ḥasan explicitly speaks of the Sunna of the Prophet in this connection. But he says expressly that there is no *actual transmission* (*riwāya*) from the Prophet or his Companions *about the question under discussion*, viz. the problem of the freedom of the human will and action *vis-à-vis* theistic determinism, and that he himself (and probably others who had similar views) has *originated* discussions concerning the thesis of human freedom. The Sunna here simply means that neither the Prophet nor the Companions *behaved* in a way that could be compatible with the doctrine of divine determinism which, Ḥasan also tells us, 'is a new invention of the people'. In this connection, therefore, the question of an explicit verbal Ḥadīth does not arise although the term Sunna has a valid meaning as Ḥasan has employed it. What this proves is that, *on this problem* what later Tradition attributes to the Prophet does not verbally belong to the Prophet and must be considered a later formulation, although it will still be perfectly legitimate to say that the anti-deterministic Ḥadīth represents the Sunna of the Prophet and of the early Companions. But to say that there was no dogmatic Ḥadīth *of any kind* is quite a different proposition. How can we assume that there was *no* tradition, e.g. about the importance of the Unity of God and about a hundred other matters?

Other cases of such historical comparative study may be cited but we have given only one example to illustrate the point at issue. Another fundamentally inalienable difficulty that besets the historical critic in this field is to assume the truth of certain statements and on their strength to try to judge others. This difficulty becomes accentuated beyond all proportion both in the case of a naïve and credulous historian and in that of an excessively sceptical mind. An inevitable subjectivity follows which may lead to a contrary conclusion. A person with a sympathetic understanding may challenge both the credulous and the aggressive sceptic by his conclusions. Let us illustrate this with an example. There is a story that the Umayyad Ibrāhīm ibn al-Walīd came once to the famous Traditionist Ibn Shihāb al-Zuhrī with a book and asked the latter that he transmit as Ḥadīth on his authority the statements contained in this work. Al-Zuhrī (d. 124/742) thereupon, without any scruple, said to Ibrāhīm: 'But who else (besides me) could have related to you these Traditions?' The image of al-Zuhrī in the Muslim Tradition is that of a very pious man and a reliable Traditionist. But unlike most other pious men of the day, he had good relations with the Umayyad rulers. Can this story be true? Goldziher accepts it as true and regards it as one of his major proofs to show that the Umayyads influenced the Tradition in their own interest. Goldziher also admits that al-Zuhrī was a pious man but explains that al-Zuhrī did not collaborate with the Umayyads in the forgery of Ḥadīth from any impious motive but for reasons of the stability of the state and that although 'sometimes he did have qualms about this, he could not gainsay the official circles' pressure indefinitely' (*Muhammedanische Studien*, II, p. 38).

That opposing political parties tried to influence public opinion through the medium of the Ḥadīth and used the names of great authorities of Tradition is a fact no one conversant with the early history of Islam may deny. That al-Zuhrī may have even given his support to such official views, out of 'consideration for the State', as he might have considered in keeping with the spirit of Islam, may well also be admitted. The piety of al-Zuhrī and his reliable knowledge of the Ḥadīth is not an image built up over the years, but a man of the stature of Mālik ibn Anas (b. between 90–97/709–15, d. 179/795) quotes Traditions directly from him. Under these circumstances one is more tempted to believe that the above story about his unscrupulous circulation of the Umayyad Ḥadīth is a legend put out under 'Abbāsid rule to blacken the Umayyads. Or, what is perhaps even more likely, that certain pupils of al-Zuhrī (the story actually goes back to a pupil of al-Zuhrī) put this anecdote into circulation in order to enhance the prestige of al-Zuhrī as the pan-Traditionist without whose authority no Ḥadīth was regarded as valid in his time.

On similar considerations we must use with some caution and reserve the fundamentally sound principle that an earlier report must be true or at least truer than a slightly later version of it, thus condemning the relative fullness of the later versions as being necessarily forged additions. Our reserve about the validity of this principle should apply more especially to the very early period when the Ḥadīth was being 'gathered' and put together. It is perfectly possible and indeed logical that in this earlier period the first reports of a given Ḥadīth had not been able to mention all the relevant facts and details and that these were supplied by wider contacts with the Companions and their immediate followers. On the whole, a healthy caution rather than outright scepticism is likely to lead to reliable and constructive results.

The Nature of the Prophet's Authority

The Qur'ān incessantly couples Muḥammad with God when speaking of authority, and in a large number of verses the Faithful are commanded to obey God and the Prophet of God.[11] Muslims, *at least* since the turn of the 1st/7th century, and the majority of orientalists, take this to mean that this authority of Muḥammad refers to the verbal and preformative behaviour of the Prophet outside the Qur'ān. In fact, for Muslims, the Qur'ānic authority is something above the authority of the Prophet himself, who, standing under its commands and judgments, is himself only its transmitter. There is also little doubt that the Prophet himself carefully distinguished between Qur'ānic pronouncements and his own quotidian speech and action, even though the Qur'ān itself appeared in a historical context and a considerable part of it is related to specific events.

Margoliouth, however, has contended that wherever the Prophet has been coupled with God in the Qur'ān, this refers only to the context of the Qur'ān itself: that the authority of God and the authority of Muḥammad, the human instrument of divine revelation, are both indistinguishable and one and the same, and have only an intra-Qur'ānic reference. From this it follows that Muḥammad had no extra-Qur'ānic Sunna which *could* have been recorded in any 'tradition'. This view seems untenable on the basis of the Qur'ān itself. While in many cases, where the Qur'ān speaks of the authority of God and the Prophet, this may be interpreted in general terms as referring to the injunctions of the Qur'ān itself, there are cases where this is obviously not so. There is, for example, the case where the Qur'ān refers to a dispute (which, the commentators say, arose over a decision of the Prophet with regard to the distribution of booty after a certain expedition) and says, 'And what the Prophet giveth unto you take it, and what he prohibiteth desist from it'.[12] In another verse the Qur'ān says, 'Nay, by thy Lord, they shall not have faith, until they bring their disputes under thy judgment and then feel no misgiving in their souls about thy judgment but submit (to it) completely'.[13] This warning also refers to a specific case of an internal dispute in the Community, and there are other similar instances in the Qur'ān. The point here is that these and other specific cases have been dealt with in the Qur'ān only because certain acute troubles arose in the Community threatening above all the authority of the Prophet as the judge. If, as in normal cases, the Prophet's authority had been accepted willingly by all people without bickerings in certain quarters, the Qur'ān would not have intervened. It follows necessarily from this that the Prophet had, and, indeed, normally exercised, an unchallenged authority outside the Qur'ān in giving judgments and moral and legal precepts. The Qur'ān, indeed, also speaks of the 'exemplary conduct of the Prophet of God'. There was, therefore, an exemplary conduct, i.e. a Sunna of the Prophet, besides the Qur'ānic revelation. Obviously, the basis for Margoliouth's thinking that the only moral and legal precepts and precedents left by the Prophet were those recorded in the Qur'ān is the conversation recorded by al-Shāfi'ī in his works between himself and certain Mu'tazilite ('neutralist') adversaries of the Ḥadīth who claimed to accept only the Qur'ān as authoritative. But we shall show in the next section the true character of this controversy and bring out the fact that the *Ahl al-Kalām* ('rationalists') or the Mu'tazila in fact accepted much more than the Qur'ān.

But if our reasoning has been at all correct, another conclusion follows from this argument to make the situation intelligible. This is that the Prophetic Sunna, outside the fundamental matters touching the religious and the social and moral life of the Community, could not have been very large, let alone being of such titanic inclusiveness of all the details of daily life as medieval law and Ḥadīth literature make out to be the case. The evidence as a whole strongly suggests that the situations where the Prophet was called upon to decide or pronounce authoritatively, or where he felt compelled to do so, were *ad hoc* situations. Normally, the Muslims carried on the business and social transactions of daily life by settling their minor differences among themselves. This view is also in accord with the general character of Muḥammad as Prophet-statesman: he was not primarily a lawyer but a religious and political reformer. Indeed, nobody who reads the Qur'ān itself carefully can fail to notice the gradual character of Islamic reform. Wine-drinking, for example, was allowed for a period of many years after the opening of the Prophet's mission. Then came measures introducing restraint in drinking, and finally a ban on all consumption of alcohol. Further, on most, perhaps all, measures of important political and legal action and reform, the Prophet consulted informally with his senior Companions and sometimes consulted the Community publicly. The Qur'ān bears unequivocal testimony to this.[14] Sometimes the advice that was forthcoming conflicted, and indeed at points it conflicted so much that (since it had the character of group-functions) it culminated in challenging the Prophet himself.[15] In the Prophetic Sunna indeed democracy and religious authority were balanced with a *finesse* that defies description.

But as to the religious and religiously binding character of the outcome of the process of the arrival by the Prophet at a decision, the Qur'ān repelled every shadow of doubt for the potential dissident. Further, the life and character of the Prophet himself were permeated with a religious spirit. Even if we may *theoretically* suspect each individual statement in the medieval Muslim records about him, the nature of the case forbids us concluding otherwise than that to his Companions his life was a religious paradigm and as such normative. Any suggestion that this was not the case until about nine or even fifteen decades later, when formal Ḥadīth was developed as a neat and perfected medium of transmitting information about the Prophet, must be rejected as a shallow and irrational 'scientific' myth of contemporary historiography. But the myth itself arises from and singles out a crucial enigma in the situation. If the Prophet's speech and conduct were regarded as religiously normative for the Muslims, it is extraordinary that there should be no contemporary records of these Sunnas preserved as the Qur'ān has been recorded and preserved, except for certain documents relating to pacts, etc. Besides, despite agreement on general and fundamental points of law, we find that the practice in detail differed in the early schools on most points and each regional school, for example the Medinese and the Iraqi, defended its practice by calling it 'Sunna'. If the ultimate reference of the Sunna is the Prophet's example then, so the argument runs, differing Sunnas cannot be called '*the* Sunna' and must, therefore, be regarded as the practice of the local Muslim communities. As for the Prophet, it follows either that he had left hardly any precedents relating to such points in his conduct, or that if he had, they were not regarded as Sunna or as binding.

As for the 'practice' of the Muslims in the early post-Prophetic period and the concepts with which they worked out this practice, we shall analyse these more closely in the next section of this chapter. As regards the two alternatives offered theoretically about the Prophet which have been partly tacitly, partly expressly accepted by modern writers on the Ḥadīth and the Sunna, our investigation so far has led us to reject them both. This must be done in order to bring the requisite reasonableness into the situation. To solve the enigma, however, two important points must be made. First, there must have been the fear that if the extra-Qur'ānic speech of the Prophet were formally recorded, it could easily have been confused with the text of the Qur'ān which was also delivered by the Prophet. Confusion could have worked in both directions. Either the Qur'ān, in the course of time, might pass as the word of the Prophet and not as the Word of God, in whole or in appreciable part; or, the word of the Prophet might have passed as the Word of God. Historical evidence suggests that some confusion in certain quarters did nevertheless take place. There is, for example, the report that the famous Companion of the Prophet, 'Abd Allāh ibn Mas'ūd (d. circa 32/653) did not regard the first and the last two

Sūras of the Qur'ān as part of it. Ibn Qutayba (d. 276/889) explains that since the Prophet often recited the last two Sūras over his grandsons as prayers and that Ibn Mas'ūd frequently saw him do this, he concluded that these were not part of the Qur'ānic text.[16] We have already mentioned that the Prophet himself distinguished between his own utterance and that of the Qur'ān and that it was only at special critical points that his decisions had to be supported by the Qur'ān itself.

Secondly, we have already referred to the *ad hoc* character of the Prophetic decisions and precepts. As for the precepts, they were usually occasioned by a particular situation and were informally proclaimed in the presence of such Companions as happened to be there. The most formal pronouncements were made in a sermon (*khuṭba*) but these also usually grew out of immediate phenomena and situations, religious or political. The same holds true of decisions legal or otherwise. Each case was decided as it presented itself, taking into account both general and specific factors. Now, the informal and *ad hoc* nature of these procedures naturally argued for not being formally recorded. It also meant that similar but always somewhat different cases were decided in a similar but at the same time somewhat different manner, and there is little doubt that the Prophet used his discretion, even though on major issues he consulted his senior Companions. Let us illustrate this variation from the case of the religious rite of prayer, the most fundamental of all obligatory religious duties. Among other minor details, controversies raged in the early Muslim legal schools about certain physical postures, for instance, the position of the hands – are these to be left loose in the standing posture or are they to be folded? If folded, whether on the breast or below the breast? Similarly, controversies existed about variations in the exact times of prayers. Those who reject the Sunna-tradition from the Prophet will have to say that this reflects variations in a generation after the Prophet. But this is surely ridiculous – for the Prophet regularly offered prayers in public for a good many years, and the only explanation that would make sense is that he used slightly different postures at different times and that those who happened to observe a particular posture regarded it as normative. Just as in the ritual sphere, so variations in the field of positive legal decisions of the Prophet probably explain in part the differences in the legal schools of Islam, although here, in view of the ever-increasing complexity of the legal situation in a rapidly expanding empire, the individual interpretations of legists played a fundamental rôle, as we shall see.

Ḥadīth and Sunna, or the Verbal and Practical Tradition

Ḥadīth (which literally means a story, a narration, a report) as we know it, being a unit of that discipline which bears the same name, is a narrative, usually very short, purporting to give information about what the Prophet said, did, or approved or disapproved or, of similar information about his Companions, especially the senior Companions and more especially the first four Caliphs. Each Ḥadīth falls into two parts, the text (*matn*) of the Ḥadīth itself and the transmissional chain or *isnād*, giving the names of the narrators, which supports the text. Both the classical and the modern historians agree that at first Ḥadīth existed without the supporting *isnād* which probably appeared at the turn of the 1st/7th century. This is also roughly the date when the wholesale appearance of the Ḥadīth as a formalized written discipline begins. There is, however, strong direct and indirect evidence that before becoming a formal *discipline* in the 2nd/8th century, the phenomenon had existed at least since about 60–80/680–700.

The first point to be made in this connection is that a highly developed system with two parts, the text and the *isnād*, could not have appeared on the scene all of a sudden without a period of growth in which it had not only developed technically but expanded materially as well. An informal tradition is, indeed, naturally to be postulated during the lifetime of the Prophet himself who was the pivot of the Muslim Community. But after the Prophet's death, the Ḥadīth passed from a purely informal condition into a semi-formal state. By this I mean that whereas during the lifetime of the Prophet people talked about what he said or did as a matter of course, after his death this talk became a deliberate and conscious phenomenon since a new generation was growing up for whom it was natural to enquire about the Prophet's conduct. But it must be remembered that the natural religious orientation of a Ḥadīth – a verbal transmission – was towards a corresponding Sunna, a religious norm of practice. This practical orientation, rather than primarily intellectual curiosity, especially in a community that was expanding and growing more complex at an astonishing and unprecedented speed with the assimilation of new elements, argued for the fact that the 'transmission' be less of a verbal nature and more of the character of a 'silent' exemplification *in actu*. This non-verbal transmission, the 'silent' or 'living' tradition, was called the 'Sunna'.

We must, therefore, distinguish between the two, but closely allied, meanings of the word Sunna. We said above that to the later generations the Sunna meant (as it originally did mean) the conduct of the Prophet, from whom it acquired its normativeness. But to the extent that the tradition continued to be largely 'silent' and non-verbal, this word was applied to the actual content of the behaviour of each succeeding generation in so far as that behaviour claimed to exemplify the Prophetic pattern. It is clear that the second usage is a derivative from the former and the two are related *secundum prius et posterius*. 'Sunna' literally means 'a trodden path' and just like a path, each part of it is a Sunna whether it be near the starting-point or remote from it. In regard to content, as we shall see, it was not so much like a path as like a river-bed which continuously assimilates new elements; but the *intention* of the term Sunna was always directed towards the Apostolic model. It is this very confusion which has led several modern writers to assert that until well into the 2nd/8th century, the Sunna meant *not* the practice of the Prophet but that of the local Muslim communities in Medina and Iraq.

But the tradition was not entirely 'silent' and non-verbal. That this could not have been the case is in the first place *a priori* deducible from the *fact* of the living tradition itself. Men do not merely act and follow (and innovate) but also talk and report. There was, therefore, at least an informal verbal tradition. But, further, this informal tradition seems to have become a deliberate activity in the hands of the younger generation of the Companions. A letter written by the Umayyad Caliph 'Abd al-Malik (65–8/684–8) to Ḥasan al-Baṣrī (21–100/642–728) and the latter's answer[17] shed important light on the subject when analysed carefully. This letter from the Caliph, who disapproved of Ḥasan's views in favour of human freedom and responsibility, states:

> The Commander of the Faithful has been informed of your views on human freedom (*qadar*) such as he never heard before from anyone else from among the bygone generation: the Commander of the Faithful does not know of anyone whom he has met from among the Companions holding any view with regard to this such as he has been told about you. . . . So write to him about it – whether it is a *verbal transmission* (*riwāya*) from anyone of the Companions of the Prophet of God, or your own considered opinion (*ra'y*) or anything that may be confirmed by the Qur'ān. . . .[18]

The essential point here is that the Caliph demands, among alternative forms of evidence, a *verbal transmission* from any one of the Companions. The Caliph could have demanded this only if he thought that verbal transmissions existed and were authoritative. In his reply, Ḥasan al-Baṣrī refers to the 'Sunna of the Prophet of God', but is unable to quote any verbal transmission from the Prophet or his Companions on *this specific point* (although he goes on to quote the Qur'ān profusely). But this is not because there was no verbal transmission or Ḥadīth of any kind – as Professor Schacht holds[19] – but because Ḥasan al-Baṣrī goes on to admit that the debate about the human freedom of choice versus the theistic determinism is new:

> There was none among our (Muslim) predecessors who rejected this (viz., that human beings are free to choose); nor did anybody dispute with regard

to this since they were (tacitly) agreed and unanimous about it. *We have introduced* this theological discourse (*kalām*) on the point since (some) people have *innovated* a rejection of it. . . .[20]

In an enclosed note, the officer who forwarded Ḥasan al-Baṣrī's letter to the Caliph says, 'None remains among those who learned (*akhadha*) from the bygone generation of the Companions of the Prophet, more versed in knowledge about God . . . than Ḥasan'.[21] The word used for 'learning' in this quotation has remained a technical term for formal study with a master.

The conclusions we have arrived at so far are first that the Sunna and the Ḥadīth were coeval and consubstantial in the earliest phase after Muḥammad and that both were directed towards and drew their normativity from him. Secondly, we have also noticed that the concept Sunna, since it meant the 'silent' living tradition, came perforce to have the meaning of the living tradition in each succeeding generation. Therefore, although the Sunna as a concept referred to the behaviour of the Prophet, its *content*, nevertheless, was bound to change and derive largely from the *actual* practice of the early Community. But the actual practice of a living community must continuously be subject to modification through additions. In a rapidly expanding society such as the early Islamic one, new moral issues and legal situations, including the almost entirely new administrative system, constantly arose. These moral issues had to be answered and these legal situations resolved. As the legal situations and the consciousness of moral and religious issues became more and more complex, controversies arose on most points, and in the theological and moral sphere especially there were foreign influences. But the concept of an ideal Sunna was retained: whatever new material was thought out or assimilated, it was given as an interpretation of the principles of the Qur'ān and the Sunna. The interpretation, as we shall see in the next chapter, was at first based on free and considered individual opinion which was replaced in the second century by the concept of systematic analogy (*qiyās*).

The term Sunna itself was at first probably not formulated as a conscious concept until differences arose over religious issues. The 'silent' living tradition implies that it was not *ab initio* described by any term, and that this description and formulation came only when different and indeed opposed interpretations were put forward. Then one was led to oppose the concept Sunna to innovation (*bid'a*). The occasions of religious controversy had most probably political implications. This is suggested by the controversies between the Shī'a (the followers of 'Alī), the Khārijites and the Umayyads. The above account of Ḥasan al-Baṣrī illustrates this: it clearly shows that the Sunna was being explicitly formulated not only in respect of its content but also in the concept of Sunna itself, after extreme predestinarian views were put forward. And the ethical controversy about human freedom and determinism had also definite political implications, since the anti-determinists would favour the reform or displacement of the worldly-minded rule of the Umayyads.

From the fact of individual interpretations of what had been handed down from the Prophet, both through living tradition and through the meagre amount of verbal transmission (Ḥadīth or *riwāya*), there followed a third meaning of the Sunna – that is to say, in relation to the content, because the *intention* of the concept still remained directed to the Prophet, besides the two noted above and again closely allied to these. This is that from a Ḥadīth or a Sunna-report several points of practical norm were *deduced* by interpretation and all these points were called Sunnas because they were seen to be *implicit* in the Sunna. This process of interpretation undoubtedly began both tacitly and explicitly with the Companions themselves. For the generation after the Companions, all the sayings and deeds of the Companions also began to be regarded as Sunna since, it was argued, the Companions, especially when they agreed, but even when they disagreed, were in the most privileged position to know and interpret the Prophet's conduct. After the period of the Companions (and in some cases of the following generation of the 'Successors') the Sunna could not be deduced from actual practice but only from the expressly transmitted Ḥadīth. But it is most significant and remarkable that deductions by interpretation from a Ḥadīth in *any* period were called Sunnas. Thus Abū Dā'ūd (d. 275/888) after relating a Ḥadīth remarks, 'There are five Sunnas in this Ḥadith', i.e. five points with the character of practical norms can be deduced from this Ḥadīth.

The three categories of the content of the Sunna outlined above – the Sunna of the Prophet, the living tradition of the earliest generation, and the deductions from these – created a wealth of material, especially through individual interpretation of the law and the dogma, which although it was generally uniform in its essentials, except for certain extreme doctrines of the Khārijites and other sects, conflicted in its details on most points. This material was, in the next step, brought under the concepts of 'the agreed practice' (*al-'amal*) and the 'consensus' (*ijmā'*). These terms were used equivalently and the concept of the 'consensus' was destined, as we shall study more closely in the next chapter, to play the most fundamental part in the paraphernalia of Muslim methodology throughout the religious history of Islam. There is a certain affiliation between the concepts Sunna and *Ijmā'* in this early period: just as the former was formulated to check innovations, the latter was formulated against arbitrary individual and sectarian opinions. But there is a conceptual difference as well: the Sunna is the Sunna of the Prophet in its primordial intention and thus innovation is that which contravenes the Prophetic model, while the *Ijmāʿ* is the consensus either of the Community or of the doctors of religion and thus arbitrary opinion is that which contravenes the *communis opinio* of the Community. But since the *materials* of the Sunna, as distinguished from its conceptual intention, included, as we have seen, also the interpretation of the Prophetic model, *in fact* Sunna and *Ijmāʿ* come close to one another, and so do their opposites.

Classical Opposition to the Ḥadīth

We have seen above that verbal transmission (*riwāya*) concerning the Prophetic model of behaviour started early in Islam. The contemporary statement about Ḥasan al-Baṣrī given above, that 'the most learned surviving person of those who learned from the bygone generation of the Companions of the Prophet', implies that this process of transmission had started earlier than Ḥasan's career as a student (he was born in 21/642). But, as we have seen also, the work of interpretation of the Prophetic Sunna had also begun with the Companions themselves, a fact upon which the nature of the case bestows intelligibility of the highest order. This is because the Companions were not 'students' of the Prophet, even though this impression is sometimes created by later Ḥadīth literature, but his followers and disciples. A disciple does not only 'learn' and write from his master but tries to live, and so embody, the master's teaching. It was therefore inevitable that in the minds of the Companions the *actual* dicta and facta of the Prophet were often imperceptibly intertwined, and even more so in the minds of the succeeding generations, with their own behaviour. This fact must be borne in mind because it explains why it became difficult for the formal traditionist at the turn of the century and for subsequent generations to disentangle the strictly prophetic element from the alleged dicta and facta of the Companions. It also explains in part why the Ḥadīth, when it first began to be codified by the traditionists, was referred to the Companions rather than to the Prophet. But only in part, because the major burden of this explanation must be borne by the fact that in this early phase there had not yet developed the technique of the transmissional chain (*isnād*) and thus a Ḥadīth was referred to the immediate reporter in his reportative capacity or to the source of the actual transmission, although the Ḥadīth itself claimed to go back to the Prophet himself. While in the pristine period, as we have seen, the Ḥadīth and the Sunna were coeval and consubstantial, the inevitable expansion we have described of the *content* of the Sunna in the categories of the living tradition and individual interpretation complicated the situation and there emerged a disengagement of the Ḥadīth from the Sunna. The concept of *Ijmāʿ* or consensus was still nebulous and failed in practice to standardize or render normative the actual and conflicting living practice. In order, therefore, to bestow normativity on the actual views or practice, the traditionists launched a wholesale and mass campaign to standardize the living Sunna and to try to codify the practice that would conform to the Prophetic model and to reject the more extreme interpretations of both the dogma and the law. That is how the mass codification of the Ḥadīth as a discipline began towards the end of the 1st/beginning of the 8th century. This led to the introduction and subsequent perfection of the chains of transmitters. A typical chain of transmitters runs like this: *A* (the last narrator) says he heard it from *B* on the authority of *C* who said this on the authority of *D* that the Prophet of God said . . . , etc.

The mass introduction of the Ḥadīth in its new formal phase represented a genuine and basic need for some kind of canonization of the earliest interpretative-assimilative experiences of the Community which had undoubtedly derived much of its basic teaching from the Prophet. The process of the living tradition could not go on indefinitely by itself because in the long run the religious ideological fabric of the Community would be endangered by chaos for want of a sufficiently authoritative point of reference. It was indeed against an already emergent extremism and arbitrary interpretation that the Ḥadīth invaded the field on this massive scale. But there were dangers in this process of canonization too, against which warnings, sometimes also couched in extreme terms, came from some law schools and theological circles, warnings which were partly justified by the subsequent development and growth of the Ḥadīth. These anxieties essentially consisted of drawing attention to two undesirable alternative developments that would ensue: first, by referring every theological, dogmatic or legal doctrine to the authority of the Prophet as was demanded by the logic of the Ḥadīth phenomenon, the free and creative process of interpretation would almost come to an end. Or, secondly, if the creative process is to go on then a massive and incessant fabrication is necessary. In fact, both fears interacted. But the traditionists attempted to safeguard against both extremes by producing two principles, both of which are probably fictions generated by the Ḥadīth itself. According to the first, the Prophet was reported to have said that whatever of good sayings there be, it can be assumed to have been said by him and can be accepted[22] on his authority. According to the second principle, the Prophet was alleged to have pronounced: 'He who tells a deliberate lie about me should be prepared for his seat in Hell'.[23] Up to about the middle of the 3rd/9th century theology and law continued to develop under the aegis of the Ḥadīth and so did the selective activity of the 'genuine' Ḥadīth from the 'weak' and the false. This, as we shall study further in the following chapters, was also the period of the formation and consolidation of the orthodoxy. When the climax of this formulative process was reached, the Ḥadīth was finally codified and accepted and at the same time the activity of creative interpretation in any major sense came almost to an end.

The earliest extant record of the warnings against and opposition to the Ḥadīth is contained in the works of the jurist al-Shāfi'ī (d. 204/819). These are highly instructive about the situation obtaining in the 2nd/8th century. The opposition varied from that against an individual Ḥadīth to that against almost all Ḥadīth. Al-Shāfi'ī was the arch-protagonist of the acceptance of the Prophetic Ḥadīth in the field of law on a mass scale and *as a principle of law*, while his opponents in the legal schools claimed that the basis of law shall be the Prophetic Sunna as it was living actually in the practical tradition. They did not deny the Prophetic Ḥadīth as such but claimed that the Prophetic teaching was to be found in the practice of the Community. By that time the concept of the *Ijmā'* or consensus had emerged, and they argued that the agreed practice was more entitled to represent the legacy of the Prophet than an obscure Ḥadīth which claimed to go back to the authority of the Prophet but had in fact no basis in the practice. Such Ḥadīths, they contended, if accepted would in fact open the door for wholesale fabrication of the Ḥadīth in the name of the Prophet. Their argument ran as follows: 'The Companions of the Prophet generally and *as a whole* knew best and were the only and reliable bearers of the Prophetic tradition. The younger generations of the "Successors" saw the Companions in action and also learned from them, even if they could not have access to the Prophet himself, and therefore, were the best immediate source for the Prophetic teaching. Even if a few of the Companions did not know the Sunna of the Prophet on certain points, they could come to know such Sunna from the general practice of the Companions and *so by the time of the next generation the Prophetic Sunna can be taken to have been firmly established.*[24] This is *Ijmā'* or consensus and against this we cannot accept the testimony of one or two stray narrators of a Ḥadīth that may now claim to go back to the Prophet.' This argument is clearly brought out in a conversation between al-Shāfi'ī and one of his opponents:

Al-Shāfi'ī: 'If a report reaches us from any of the Caliphs of the Prophet (i.e. the first four Caliphs) and another report reaches us from the Prophet himself contrary to the first, then surely we shall accept the report from the Prophet? For, everything has a final object of pursuit and such object in knowledge is the Book of God (the Qur'ān) and the Sunna of the Prophet. Do you agree that the Sunna (of the Prophet) as long as it is with us allows nothing else to take its place?'

The opponent: 'Yes; and I have heard you say – of which I am also not ignorant – that sometimes an opinion is related from more than one of the Companions of the Prophet which is contrary to the Sunna of the Prophet. But if these Companions become aware of this Sunna, they accept it (and reject their own opinions) or if their Successors come to know of the same Sunna, they come back to it (so that by now the Sunna of the Prophet can be assumed to have become accepted). . . . In Medina there were about thirty thousand, if not more, of the Prophet's Companions, but you transmit perchance a single report not even from six of them but from one of them – or may be from two or three or four, wherein either they agree or disagree – and in most cases they do disagree. What becomes of the *Ijmā'* then?'[25]

Especially cautious towards such solitary Ḥadīths was the attitude of the lawyers in Medina which claimed a unique position as the depository of the living Sunna. They did not reject the Ḥadīth as such but only solitary Ḥadīths in certain cases. In such cases they claimed to rely on the 'agreed practice' even though al-Shāfi'ī ceaselessly pointed out that their practice was in fact not agreed on all points. But in Medina too were many of the most eminent and prolific of the traditionists and al-Shāfi'ī accused his fellow jurists of lagging far behind these in relating traditions.[26] Al-Shāfi'ī's success was, however, ensured by the nature of the controversy itself. Given the need for an anchoring point which would bestow normativity on legal practice and theological opinions, once the name of the Prophet was associated by the Ḥadīth with these, there could hardly be two predictions about the issue of the controversy. Gradually but surely the whole of the living tradition was reflected in the Ḥadīth, and the Ḥadīth and the Sunna once more became completely consubstantial in content. Once the formalized Sunna of Medina was enshrined in the Ḥadīth, most of which also arose out of Medina, the position of that city as the home of the Prophetic Sunna was established beyond question, although Iraq, with its practice interacting with that of Medina but retaining something of its own entity even in tradition, remained the second major region of the Sunna, and independent in law with its Ḥanafī interpretation.

The emergence of the Ḥadīth as an all-engulfing discipline led some of the Mu'tazila, the rationalistic theologians who will be discussed in Chapter V, to take up a sceptical attitude to the Ḥadīth *as a whole*. One should guard against the mistake of regarding the Mu'tazila as a second group of Ḥadīth opponents *separate in kind* from the legists who have been spoken of in the last paragraph. This impression arises from the fact that the Mu'tazila, or rather some part of them, doubted the formal Ḥadīth as a whole and the impression is strengthened by the fact that al-Shāfi'ī reported about them as a separate category from the normal legists. As a matter of fact, the Mu'tazila were not only theologians, which they were primarily, but also lawyers and jurists as is evident from al-Shāfi'ī's writings themselves.[27] Their general doubt about the Ḥadīth is rather elliptical and indirect and is fundamentally inspired by the fact that the anthropomorphisms of the Ḥadīth put formidable impediments in the way of their rational understanding of the religion. In actual fact, there was a whole range of warners against the wholesale cultivation of the Ḥadīth, with this wing of the Mu'tazila at the extreme end. The second point to be made in this connection is that *none* of the Mu'tazila in their arguments against the Ḥadīth says that the Ḥadīth is a new-fangled phenomenon appearing in the first half of the 2nd/8th century. Their basic argument was essentially the same as that of the other legal schools noted above, that the Ḥadīth, since its essence is transmission by individuals, cannot be a sure avenue of our knowledge about the Prophetic teaching, unlike the Qur'ān about whose transmission there is a universal unanimity among Muslims. Here is what they say to al-Shāfi'ī:

'You are an Arab and the Qur'ān has been revealed in your language. You have preserved it in memory (i.e. verbally). God has deposited in it certain obligatory duties such that, if someone were to doubt about a single item (literally: letter) in it you would ask him to retract from his doubt. If he retracts, well and good, otherwise you would execute him. . . . How then can you permit yourself or someone else to say (on the basis of the Ḥadīth transmissions) with regard to the Qur'ānic obligatory duties that these are sometimes general and sometimes specific and sometimes that a certain command therein is clear obligation and sometimes that a certain other command is only an indication (which is to be clearly worked out in the light of the Ḥadīth and does not provide a clear direct obligation). If some person, under the influence of his own whims, were to carry this dissection of the Qur'ān further (what would you say?).

'You have a solitary Ḥadīth transmitted to one person from another and to him from another, or maybe two Ḥadīths or three, until you reach the Prophet. But we find that you and other people who are like you (protagonists of the Ḥadīth) do not acquit any one of the transmitters you have met and whom you regard as being foremost in truthfulness and reliability of memory . . . from (the possibility of) error, forgetfulness and making mistakes in the Ḥadīth. . . . We also find you saying that if someone were to say concerning a Ḥadīth by which you make things lawful and unlawful . . . "the Prophet did not say such a thing; you either lie or are mistaken or those who have transmitted this to you" – in this case we have found that you do not ask such a person to retract (from his doubt, as you do in the case of one who doubts the Qur'ān) and you accuse him of nothing more than saying something bad. Is it permissible that the injunctions of the Qur'ān – which is apparently uniform throughout to whomsoever listens to it – be dissected on the basis of reports transmitted by people whose position we have described according to yourselves (i.e. who cannot be absolutely relied upon)?'[28]

While most of the Mu'tazila were originally sceptical of the Ḥadīth on the above grounds, they nevertheless accepted the Sunna and the consensus and indeed they interpreted the Qur'ān in the light of both these principles, as is attested by al-Shāfi'ī.[29] This occurred in the legal field. It may well be that their reluctance to accept the Ḥadīth resulted primarily from theological motives which forbade them to accept anthropomorphisms. This is further corroborated by the fact that when they gradually accepted the Ḥadīth as such they were content either to reject specific Ḥadīths or even to accept these but to interpret them in rationalizing terms. Ibn Qutayba's work entitled *Ta'wīl Mukhtalif al-Ḥadīth* (i.e. 'Interpretation of the apparently inconsistent Traditions') is specifically devoted to answering these *specific* charges of the Mu'tazila against inconsistencies and anthropomorphisms in the body of the Ḥadīth.

Development of the 'Science of the Ḥadīth'

By the middle of the 3rd/9th century the Ḥadīth had taken definite form, had established almost all its detailed content, and had completely won the field. So far as the content is concerned, it patently reflects the growing and conflicting mass of religious (including political) views and opinions of the Muslims in their first two centuries. In order to collect, sift and systematize this massive and amazing product, a number of eminent scholars began to travel throughout the length and breadth of the then Muslim world. This powerful movement is known as 'Seeking of the Ḥadīth'. Eager seekers went from place to place learning from man to man. By the end of the 3rd/beginning of the 10th century several collections had been produced, six of which have since then been regarded as being especially authoritative and are known as 'The Six Genuine Ones'. Foremost among these is the *Ṣaḥīḥ* (the 'Genuine') of Muḥammad ibn Ismā'īl al-Bukhārī (194–256/810–70) acclaimed later by Muslims as being next only to the Qur'ān in authority. The *Ṣaḥīḥ* of Muslim ibn al-Ḥajjāj (d. 261/875) comes next, close to that of al-Bukhārī. The four remaining are the works of Abū Dā'ūd (d. 275/888), al-Tirmidhī (d. 279/892), al-Nasā'ī (d. 303/916) and Ibn Māja (d. 273/886).

By this time also the criticism of the Ḥadīth, such as Muslims have known it, was perfected into the 'Science of the Ḥadīth'. This criticism is exclusively directed towards the *isnād* or the transmissional chain of the Ḥadīth. A systematic and complex inquiry was undertaken into the biographies of the transmitters of the tradition and their bona fides and this is known as 'the Science of Justification and Impugnment'. An attempt was made to assess the good character and the reliability of the memory of transmitters. The transmitters were thus divided into different categories such as 'completely trustworthy', 'truthful', 'weak', 'mendacious' and 'unknown', etc., although there remained differences of opinion among scholars about several transmitters. Another classification was adopted concerning the continuity or otherwise of a chain of transmission and as to the stage of transmission at which the link is 'broken'. The third line concerned the *number* of simultaneous transmitters at each stage. On the basis of these investigations, the Ḥadīths were classified into various categories such as 'genuine', 'good', 'weak', 'not well-known', 'continuous', 'discontinuous', 'discontinuous at the source' (*marfū'*, i.e. where the connection with the Prophet is indirect), etc. The lines of criticism intersect: e.g. a Ḥadīth may be regarded as 'genuine' even though a link is missing. A Ḥadīth which at every stage of transmission has found numerous narrators is called *mutawātir* or inductively so certain that doubt is almost *logically* excluded.

A very large proportion of the Ḥadīths was judged to be spurious and forged by classical Muslim scholars themselves and was excluded from the six canonical collections, and al-Bukhārī and Muslim included in their works only those Ḥadīths which they judged to be 'genuine'. These men sifted out only a few thousand from hundreds of thousands of current Ḥadīths and some self-confessed forgers are reported to have been executed. Al-Bukhārī especially, the ablest and most acute of Ḥadīth critics, showed extraordinary scrupulousness in judging traditions. But it must be remembered that this historical criticism was not the only principle of selectivity used by canonical collectors. This very period in which the Ḥadīth discipline reached its full fruition was also the period during which, from a massive interaction of different and indeed often opposed religious doctrines and views, an 'orthodoxy' was emerging and coming to the surface. The 'people of the Ḥadīth' (*Ahl al-Ḥadīth*) were actively involved in this great drama. They were indeed the vanguard of this orthodoxy, people who *crystallized* it in their works even though its *formulation* was to be achieved by men like al-Ash'arī (c. 300/913). There was indeed, as we have shown in the last section, a fierce battle between the rationalist *Ahl al-Kalām* and the traditionists from the very beginning, a battle in which the former relied, besides their rationalism, on the living tradition. By the middle of the 3rd/9th century the ground had slipped from beneath their feet because the living tradition had by that time been translated into the Ḥadīth form. But they continued to attack individual Ḥadīths on the grounds of inconsistency and on the basis of reason. The extent of the intensity of this struggle may be gathered from an example. According to a Ḥadīth, 'Ā'isha, the Prophet's wife, is reported to have said that just before his death a verse of the Qur'ān was revealed ordering the stoning to death of adulterers. During the shock and the disturbance at the Prophet's death, so the report goes, the piece of paper containing this verse was devoured by a stray goat. The *Ahl al-Kalām* are shocked at the suggestion that a part of the Qur'ān – the consummate Word of God – be obliterated in this manner. Ibn Qutayba[30] replies to this by saying that there is nothing astonishing in the fact that a part of the Qur'ān be verbally destroyed provided it survives in the living practice (*al-'amal*).

Thus, quite apart from the historical criticism of the transmissional chains, and much more fundamentally than this type of criticism, another intuitive principle of selection was at work *e silentio*. This principle was that of conformity to the Sunna. But this intuitive principle of selectivity was not primarily historical, but doctrinal. Its historicity must have been in the first place a very indirect one, dictated by the exigencies of the form of the discipline itself. The justification of this historicity was furnished by the same type of reasoning whereby the content of the living Sunna was earlier regarded as being the Sunna of the Prophet, i.e. as being deduced from it in spirit and hence being entitled to the name Sunna. This makes us realize the full import of the so-called Ḥadīth according to which the Prophet said, 'Whatever of good speech there be, you can take it to have been said by me'. How much truer this dictum should be about a body of teaching which the incessant and prolonged experiences of the earliest generations had established as expressing the spirit of the Prophet's message. On no other hypothesis than this can we explain the fact that palpably post-Prophetic developments – the theological positions with regard to human freedom, Divine Attributes, etc. – were verbally attributed to the Prophet himself, and indeed the fact that the Shī'a, the major sect of Islam, which differs from orthodoxy *doctrinally*, also has an entirely separate body of Ḥadīth.

But further, between the personality of the Prophet and the Qur'ān on the one hand and the development of the Sunna-Ḥadīth phenomenon on the other, there exists a relationship of public historical continuity which is unique in the major religions of the world. The Prophet founded not merely a religion but a developing large-scale Community, and this in the broad daylight of history. Indeed, this public continuity between the Prophet and his Community is the real guarantee of the Prophetic Sunna differentiating it from the parallel case of early Christianity. The existence of shadows does not deny but merely confirms this basic fact. Much of its light may *actually* radiate from the media on the historical path, but so long as the media are homogeneous, they do not distort and conceal but illustrate and reveal the source. Surely this is the deeper reason why also the intelligent orientalist regards this major river-bed of Islam as orthodoxy! For this fact cannot be explained merely on the basis of the number of followers or on the latter's claim to be orthodox. It is this double connection, of spirit and of historical continuity, that rendered the Ḥadīth, despite a lack of strict historicity on the part of much of its contents, impregnable to all attacks in classical Islam. In its turn, it bestowed continuity and stability on the career of the Community for centuries, even though this stability was preserved in later medieval times at the expense of fresh creativity and originality.

Modern Islam yearns for creativity and in the interests of new progress certain groups have arisen[31] which, if their utterances are taken at their face value, wish to reject all Ḥadīth and rely on the Qur'ān. But in these groups there is hardly any awareness of the issues that are at stake. It is not clear whether they wish to deny historical or doctrinal validity to the Ḥadīth. This confused position (and virtually no appreciation of the nature of the Ḥadīth development) is considerably similar to that of the *Ahl al-Kalām* in classical times. But there is one major difference. The *Ahl al-Kalām* wished to reject the verbal tradition (the Ḥadīth) in favour of the living tradition. But now the only tradition is the verbal one, since the living Sunna, in so far as it is there, now derives its validity from the Ḥadīth through which lies the only avenue of our contact with the Prophet and fundamentally also with the Qur'ān as it was delivered to and understood by the Community. For, if the Ḥadīth *as a whole* is cast away, the basis for the historicity of the Qur'ān is removed with one stroke. But the present unrest is equally genuine and expresses a vital need. This need for new vitality and fresh interpretation neither can be nor ought to be suppressed, but the orthodox guardians of the tradition have so far displayed an uncompromisingly conservative attitude and a lack of judgment both of the new situation and of the actual development of the Ḥadīth. They do not realize that this attitude, far from maintaining stability, which was the real reason behind the Ḥadīth system, would destroy it with violence. But the Modernist also must realize that although the Ḥadīth in part does not represent the verbal and pure Prophetic teaching, it has certainly an intimate connection with the Prophet and especially represents the earliest development of the Community's understanding of that teaching. He may certainly reinterpret the Qur'ān and the Prophet's Sunna, in so far as it can be disentangled – and in this he would be only following the practice of the earliest generations – but he cannot disregard, even if he tries, the *ethos* of the Ḥadīth and of the institutions which it guaranteed: no interpretation can take place in a vacuum. For the Qur'ān did not come in a vacuum. Hence the well-known paradox that even the thoroughgoing sceptics about the Ḥadīth cannot resist supporting their views by it whenever it suits them.

The disentanglement of the historical Prophetic elements is perhaps incapable of complete achievement for want of early enough sources. But a candid and responsible investigation into the development of the Ḥadīth by the Muslims themselves is a desideratum of the first order. Whatever can be achieved in this way will be a sheer gain, for it will reveal the intimate connection between the Community and the Prophet on the one hand, and between the doctrinal and the practical evolution of the Community and the growth of the Ḥadīth on the other. It will illuminate the relationship between these three and will clear the way for proper future development.

CHAPTER FOUR

THE STRUCTURE OF THE LAW

Preliminary – Early Developments: Qur'ān and Sunna; Qiyās; Ijmā' or Consensus – Al-Shāfi'ī and After – The Law and the State – Formation of the Legal Schools – Conclusion

Preliminary

According to the medieval Muslim theory of jurisprudence, the structure of Islamic law is built on four foundations, called 'the roots of law'. These are the Qur'ān, the Sunna of the Prophet, the Ijmā' (consensus) and *Qiyās* (analogical reasoning). The mutual relationship of these four principles is highly confusing and it is not at all easy to make it fully clear. Perhaps, as a rough parallel, the famous Aristotelian scheme of analysis will be helpful. Pursuing this analogy, the Qur'ān and the Sunna are the material principles (or the 'sources'), the activity of analogical reasoning (*qiyās*) the efficient cause, and the Ijmā' the formal principle (or the functional power). To complete the picture of the Aristotelian scheme, the purpose of the structure is to enable man to live under the sovereignty of God and in accordance with His will. In this chapter we shall outline the history of the development of these fundamental principles into a juridical structure and briefly describe the history and content of the structure itself. As for the place of the discipline of law as a whole in Islam and the history of that place, it will be discussed in Chapter VI which will deal with the most central concept of Islam, the Sharī'a.

Early Developments

QUR'ĀN AND SUNNA

At the very root of the Muslim conception of law lies the idea that law is inherently and essentially religious. That is why, from the very beginning of Islamic history, law has been regarded as flowing from or being part of the concept Sharī'a (the divinely ordained pattern of human conduct). It must, therefore, have its basis in the Divine Revelation. The Qur'ān, the most consummate and final revelation of God to man, must be made the primary and indeed the sole director of human life and the source of law.

Now, the Qur'ānic body of statements is both universal and concrete enough to inculcate a definite attitude to life: it enunciates not only eternal spiritual and moral principles, but also guided Muḥammad and the early Community through their struggles against the Meccan and Jewish enemies and Hypocrites and in the constructive task of the nascent society and state. These struggles and constructive instructions were of a specific nature. But still the strictly legislative portion of the Qur'ān is relatively quite small. Besides the detailed pronouncement on the law of inheritance and laying down punishments for crimes such as theft and adultery, which are not defined legally, there is little in it that is, properly speaking, legislative. As for the specific injunctions about the Muslims' struggles against and relationship with the non-Muslims, these varied according to situations and were too specific to be termed 'laws' in the strict sense. These different but also similar responses of the Qur'ān to different but also similar situations had to be brought together for a comparative study. But, further, it had to be set out as to which specific command was earlier in time and which later.

The only natural method to be adopted in this comparative and interpretative procedure for a fresh application of the Qur'ān to any given new situation was to see it as it had been actually worked in the lifetime of the Prophet, who was its most authoritative factual exponent and to whose conduct belonged a unique religious normativeness. This was the Sunna of the Prophet. As we shall see presently, the doctrine of the sinlessness of the Prophet was formulated considerably later, but it was only the formal outcome of the inner logic of a process which goes back to the starting point of Islamic history. As we have seen in the last chapter, despite the fact that the Prophet consulted his Companions, despite the fact that his decisions were sometimes challenged in some quarters and despite the fact that the Qur'ān itself sometimes criticized him,[1] his religious authority was binding. While he was alive, this authority was sufficient for and at any given point of time; the future remained open until it became present and was filled with decisive content by the Prophet bringing his authority to bear upon it. But after his death, that living authority was no longer available and had to be transformed formally into a doctrine of infallibility. This means that whatever decisions or pronouncements of the Prophet were authoritative during his lifetime became *infallible* after his death. This is the specific legal ground of the Prophetic infallibility. There is also a theological ground for a different, more general doctrine of infallibility, embracing all the Prophets, which is based on the consideration that a human who is a recipient of divine revelation cannot be expected to err grossly, especially in moral matters. The theological doctrine, therefore, covers only bigger and serious errors and not small slips of judgment as does the specifically legal theory.

In the early period of Islam (up to about 150/767), there is little trace of the formal doctrine of the Prophet's infallibility although a pragmatic notion of his absolute authority was certainly assumed. This is shown clearly by the fact that the first Caliph, Abū Bakr, in his inaugural address after the election, spoke of 'God and (the example of) His Prophet' as deserving obedience and binding upon him.[2] Some modern scholars have raised doubts as to whether the Prophet in his farewell speech on his last pilgrimage included his Sunna, alongside of the Qur'ān, as guidance for posterity on the grounds that in a somewhat earlier version the words 'my Sunna' do not occur. But this is immaterial and does not gainsay the fact that after his death his authority continued as it had been in his lifetime. Indeed, after his death, and especially immediately after it, there was the added reason that no one person could claim authority except under the Prophet's aegis.

But, as we have seen in the last chapter the Sunna was subsequently materially expanded to include the precedents of the first four Caliphs (the 'patriarchal Caliphs' as they are sometimes called by modern historians) and the agreements of the Companions or of a large number of them. These are known as the Sunna of the 'rightly-guided Caliphs', and that of the Companions respectively. But as we have also seen, these precedents were called 'Sunna' in the derivative sense, i.e. in the sense that the Companions were regarded as the living embodiments of the Prophetic Sunna. The application of the term was not extended to subsequent generations (except in the sense of deducing 'Sunnas' from the Ḥadīth) which rather came under the aegis of Ijmā' or consensus. Indeed, the agreed practice of the Companions is also known as the Ijmā' of the Companions, and their generation is unique in the sense that with them *the term Sunna ends* (*including them*) *and the term Ijmā' begins* (*including them*) *at the same time*. But although no new generation as such was thought capable of engendering new Sunna, the point of liaison between the Companions and the next generation, that of the 'Successors' or followers, produced the bulk of the actual material, by direct deduction and application by individual thinkers, to which the term Sunna and Ijmā' both applied. But the term Ijmā' gradually gained ascendency *for the work of this generation* until the advent of the wholesale development of the Ḥadīth transformed much of this material into the Sunna of the Prophet under the aegis of Ijmā'.

In this early period, the question as to whether the Qur'ān was more primary than the Sunna as a source of law was not yet explicitly discussed. True, the Qur'ān was regarded as the Word of God and the doctrine of the infallibility of the Prophetic Sunna was not yet formulated, but since, with a few exceptions noted above, the Qur'ān had only an indirect relationship to law, from the very beginning the Sunna was coupled with the Qur'ān as the source of law. Further, the small body of Qur'ānic legislation itself had also arisen within the context of the usages and practical norms of the Arab Community. But by the end of the 1st/beginning of the 8th century so much massive material had been brought within the field of the Sunna from different sources that to the Sunna the further adjective of 'agreed upon' was affixed.

QIYĀS

The term *qiyās*, according to the Muslim jurists, means analogical reasoning, i.e. concluding from a given principle embodied in a precedent that a new case falls under this principle or is similar to this precedent on the strength of a common essential feature called the 'reason' (*'illa*). Later on in Muslim philosophy the same term was employed to mean a syllogism or syllogistic reasoning. The common element between the two usages is the movement of thought from the explicitly known to the explicitly unknown. The term, as consciously formulated, most probably shows foreign influence, but the doctrine itself shows unmistakably a consistent internal development.

The earliest predecessor of this conscious analogical reasoning is called 'personal judgment' or 'considered personal opinion' (*ra'y*). This term has a strong subjective note and in the first person singular present means 'I think', 'I opine'. It was so intensively cultivated that many scholarly groups were nicknamed 'Do-you-think-ers'. This type of thinking was relatively very free and produced a wealth of conflicting religious and legal opinion. But a rudimentary and almost unconscious analogical method was, of course, always present; when faced with a new or refined and complicated issue, wherever the Qur'ān and the Sunna gave no clear and unequivocal decision, a verse of the Qur'ān or a general principle or a specific case in the Sunna was taken and a decision was made on its strength with regard to the present issue. But in both the choice of the model and the discernment of the point of resemblance almost unbridled liberty was taken and the results varied between sound analogy on the one hand and almost complete arbitrariness on the other.

After several decades, the unregulated products of this pure 'personal opinion' produced a strong and bitter reaction against itself and in the first half of the 2nd/8th century more systematic thought arose both in Medina and Iraq. In Medina, Mālik (d. 179/795) continued to use the term *ra'y*, but the procedure had become more systematic, helped no doubt by, and further strengthening, the fact that a more or less uniform doctrine had by this time emerged in Medina, characterized by the concept 'agreed practice' or Ijmāʿ. But in Iraq, Abū Ḥanīfa – the exemplar of logical thought in Islamic law – and his early followers formulated expressions like 'this is in the category of', 'this is similar to'. At the same time the concept *ijtihād* or 'systemic original thinking' which, from its narrower beginnings in the first half of the 2nd/8th century, bloomed into a powerful principle of original thought in the later 2nd/8th and 3rd/9th centuries, swallowing up *qiyās* as its method.[3]

From its beginnings as *ra'y* and other informal expressions, *qiyās* seems to have been established in the second half of the 2nd/8th century. Later on, in the 3rd/9th century, a minority school of jurists called the 'literalists' (*ẓāhirī*) under the leadership of Dā'ūd (d. 269/882) rejected this principle. But the difference is rather formal because this latter school substituted for *qiyās* the principle of 'evident interpretation' (*mafhūm*). Although al-Shāfiʿī (d. 204/819) – the first jurist to have written on the foundations of the law – is generally credited with having established *qiyās* as a principle, his manner of referring to it clearly shows that it was already accepted. Indeed, as we have already hinted, and as we shall describe presently under Ijmāʿ, the development of personal opinion into *qiyās* was a link in that process of securing uniformity and solidification that logically ended in Ijmāʿ. To this we must now turn.

IJMĀʿ OR CONSENSUS

After the period of the first four Caliphs, the multitudinous differences in legal and dogmatic opinion on details began to appear. The secular administration of the Umayyad Caliphate left the task of legislation to the recognized religious leaders and jurists of different regions, especially eminent of which was Medina with its lion's share of the legacy of the early Islamic piety. The jurists, in their turn, exercised their minds mainly employing the method of personal opinion on the materials of the Qur'ān and the Sunna (both living and verbal traditions). But alongside this free, individual legislative activity, which, as has been said above, produced an uncoordinated body of opinion, went another balancing and complementary movement of coordination and unification. The development of individual opinion into systematic analogical reasoning was a step in this direction. But even before the doctrines of *qiyās* and *ijtihād* ('original thinking'; see further below) were formally adopted, a large measure of 'agreed practice' had been achieved, thus enabling the jurists and traditionists of the 2nd/8th century to project the doctrine of *qiyās* backwards into the earliest generation of Islam. This is clearly brought out in al-Shāfiʿī's conversation with a group of Medinese jurists:

Al-Shāfi'ī: 'Shall we say that you, taking, for example, Ibn al-Musayyib to be the authoritative scholar of Medina, 'Aṭā' to be that of Mecca, Ḥasan that of Baṣra and Sha'bī that of Kūfa – all among the "Successors" – regard that as Ijmā' what these men are agreed upon?'
The opponent: 'Yes.'
Al-Shāfi'ī: 'But you assert that they have never met together in any assembly you knew of. You, therefore, infer their Ijmā' from reports about them, and, indeed, since you have found these men making statements about matters which you do not find dealt with either in the Qur'ān or in the Sunna you infer that they have exercised *qiyās* on these matters and you argue that *qiyās* is that established and true body of knowledge on which the scholars have agreed?'
The opponent: 'This is what I say.'[4]

Further, in this early period, the interaction between *qiyās* and Ijmā' was regarded not as a static principle but as a natural dynamic process of assimilation, interpretation and adaptation. This is brought out in another passage in al-Shāfi'ī which, although somewhat lengthy, is the most comprehensive on the subject and reveals the true nature and the all-comprehensive character of Ijmā':

The opponent: 'Knowledge comes about in several forms. First, what the total community relates from the total community of the previous generations (constitutes knowledge) with a certainty that I can swear upon it by God and His Prophet: this is exemplified by the obligatory religious duties. . . . Secondly, that part of the Qur'ān which admits of different interpretations must be accepted in its direct and commonsense meaning: it cannot be given an "inner" or allegorized sense – even though it may admit of such a one – unless it be by a consensus of the people. . . . Thirdly, that knowledge upon which the Muslims agree and have related a previous agreement upon it. Even if this latter may not come from the Qur'ān or the Sunna, for me it has the same status as the *agreed upon* Sunna. This is because the agreement of the Muslims cannot be reached merely by "personal opinions" (but only through *qiyās*) for "personal opinion" leads to disagreement. . . . Fourthly, there is the knowledge of the specialists,[5] which does not constitute a conclusive argument unless it is transmitted in a way immune to error. Lastly, the *qiyās*. . . . No disagreement can enter into knowledge in the forms I have described and all things remain rooted in their principles unless the general community agrees to dislodge them from their principles. Ijmā' is the final argument on everything for it is immune from error.'
Al-Shāfi'ī: 'As for the first kind of knowledge you have described, viz. the transmission of the general body of the community from the previous generations of the general community, it is granted. But do you know and can you describe the second type with regard to which you assert that the general community is agreed upon it and transmits similar general agreement with regard to it in the previous generations? And what is this general body of

the community. . .? Does it include both scholars and non-scholars. . .?' *The opponent:* 'This is the Ijmā' of scholars only . . . for they are the ones who alone can know and agree about it. Thus, when they agree, this becomes authoritative for those who do not know (i.e. for non-scholars); but if they do not agree, their opinions have no authority for anyone and such matters must be referred back to a fresh *qiyās* (analogical reasoning) on the basis of what has been agreed upon. . . . It is immaterial whether their Ijmā' is based on a verbal tradition reported by them or without a tradition . . .; and even when they disagree it is immaterial whether there exists a verbal tradition which agrees with what some of them hold or not. For I do not accept any Ḥadīths except those on which there is agreement. . . .'[6]

The first point to be noticed is that not only both these passages link *qiyās* or systematic reasoning with Ijmā' as being a preparation for it, in the eyes of the early schools of law, but they both distinguish between the Sunna on the one hand and Ijmā' on the other, both in the eyes of the early schools and in the eyes of their opponent, al-Shāfi'ī. Sunna, therefore, cannot be identified with Ijmā' as such. The former is restricted to the teaching of the Prophet and is extended to the Companions inasmuch as they are the source for its transmission; the latter begins with the Companions and is extended to subsequent generations.

But further, and far more important, the principle of Ijmā' is given an overriding and absolute authority, is made 'the final and conclusive argument on everything', by the representative of the early schools of law. This certainly does not mean that *no* differences were allowed; indeed where it was felt that relatively minor differences had come to stay, they were all incorporated into the Ijmā'. But Ijmā' was regarded as absolutely authoritative not only for discerning the right at present and in the future, but also for establishing the past: it was Ijmā' that determined what the Sunna of the Prophet had been and indeed what the right interpretation of the Qur'ān was. In the final analysis, therefore, both the Qur'ān and the Sunna were authenticated through Ijmā'.

The common denominator between these two different operations – on the past on the one hand and on the discovery of the right for the present on the other – expresses the essence of Ijmā'. This is the idea of authority or 'working security' from error. One must distinguish between authority and infallibility in this context. Many modern writers on the subject and pre-eminently Snouck Hurgronje[7] have sought to draw sustained parallels between Ijmā' and the *ex cathedra* declarations of the Catholic Church. What is regarded as infallible by the early Muslim scholars, an infallibility more assumed than expressed, is the Ijmā' *as method and principle* rather than its contents which are regarded as authoritative, not infallible. The Muslim doctrine of Ijmāʿ has a strong practical bent and there is no talk of absolute truth-value of its content, but only of a practical rectitude-value. But rectitude-values change. And certainly this is the only view compatible with the practice and theory of the early schools according to which Ijmāʿ was an on-going process, thanks to the fact that the activity of 'original thinking' (*ijtihād*), carried on through systematic reasoning, intervened between the Sunna and the Ijmāʿ. It is true that these schools, against attacks by al-Shāfiʿī on their Ijmāʿ, projected the contents of this Ijmāʿ back to the early generations, thus giving the impression that they thought of Ijmāʿ as tradition, but this was, in part, only a device to defend themselves against attacks.

Because of its very nature, Ijmāʿ is the most potent factor in expressing and shaping the complex of belief and practice of the Muslims, and at the same time the most elusive one in terms of its formation. It is an organic process. Like an organism it both functions and grows: at any given moment it has supreme functional validity and power and in that sense is 'final' but at the same moment it creates, assimilates, modifies and rejects. That is why its formation could not be vested in any institution. The body of scholars and lawyers that grew rapidly in the 1st/7th and 2nd/8th centuries and thence onwards could discuss and formulate the results of their thinking which were very influential, especially when they agreed (or rather concurred – this is known as the Ijmāʿ of Scholars), but the formation of Ijmāʿ could not be achieved in the schoolroom. It was more akin to an enlightened public opinion in whose creation the formulation of schools was the most potent factor but which, as we shall see, gradually vetoed many schools of law and theology even out of existence and discredited or modified or expanded the validity of others.

Al-Shāfiʿī and After

In the development of the foundations of Muslim law portrayed so far, the Qur'ān had its own identity, but the other three 'roots' or principles – Sunna, *qiyās* and Ijmāʿ stand in a very intimate relationship to one another. Sunna and Ijmāʿ especially, although distinct, pass into one another. The bridge, the inalienable link, is the *qiyās*. This principle of systematic reasoning, which not only interpreted the Prophetic Sunna into law but also integrated the new social and administrative institutions and practices with the Sunna into 'living tradition', had by virtue of its activity, embedded itself in the Sunna. On the other hand, the results of *qiyās* activity, by conflict, compromise and adjustment, gradually crystallized into Ijmāʿ which had the ultimately decisive authority.

By the middle of the 2nd/8th century, however, a large body of Ḥadīth, claiming to emanate from the Prophet, had appeared on the scene. Al-Shāfi'ī, who is credited with being the first jurist to have propounded the foundations of the law in the latter half of the 2nd/8th century, attacked the existing methodology and made a vigorous plea for the acceptance in law of the Ḥadīth materials on a mass scale. His programme, though he did not perhaps see it quite in those terms, was to attack the doctrine of Ijmā' of the law schools and to restrict it to essential religious obligations and practices. Thereby he would do away with the 'living Sunna'; and the Ijmā' having been made quite innocuous, i.e. reduced to the essential and broad religious duties embodied in the verbal Sunna of the Ḥadīth as well, he would fill the whole vacuum with the Ḥadīth. In other words Ḥadīth and Ḥadīth alone would represent the Sunna, not the living tradition or the Ijmā'. One all-important result of this would be to dislodge *qiyās* or the reasoning element from its intermediary position between the Qur'ān and the Sunna on the one hand and Ijmā' on the other.

That the large body of 'isolated' Ḥadīths (i.e. traditions transmitted verbally and later on in writing in the 2nd/8th and 3rd/9th centuries, through only one or two channels) opposed Ijmā' is the one outstanding lesson taught by al-Shāfi'ī's controversies. Against these Ḥadīths, the law schools upheld their Ijmā' or 'agreed practice'. Al-Shāfi'ī argues against them that, in fact, outside the main religious duties, there had been no Ijmā', that the Ijmā' which the schools attribute to the early authorities and scholars is not a real consensus but at best a concurrence and that on several details there was still conflict. But his chief argument is to point out that if there were an Ijmā' on a question, it could only be transmitted through certain channels of narration, a fact which the schools disallowed as basis for the Ḥadīth. Al-Shāfi'ī comes back tirelessly to this argument whereby he seeks to turn the tables on the old schools. But his conception of Ijmā' was that of a neat and precise 'event' if not of an institution, whereas the schools' conception of it was that of the elusive but potent process of gradual crystallization and stabilization of opinions. In their zeal to defend themselves, however, they projected Ijmā' back to earlier generations in many matters.

Largely because of al-Shāfi'ī's efforts, the verbal tradition or Ḥadīth presently supplanted 'living tradition' as the vehicle of the Prophetic Sunna. As we have also pointed out in Chapter III, some such solution was inevitable because 'living tradition' could not go on indefinitely and had in some way to be standardized. According to al-Shāfi'ī's proposal, the four foundational principles of law were to be reached in this order: first the Qur'ān, then the Sunna of the Prophet as communicated in the Ḥadīth, next the Ijmāʿ of the Community, and last the effort at original thought (*ijtihād*) of scholars to be exercised through *qiyās*. It is quite clear that *ijtihād* or *qiyās* instead of being at the service of Ijmāʿ, and preparatory to it, as was the case in the old schools, is put outside it. Indeed, al-Shāfiʿī contends insistently that disagreement not Ijmāʿ or agreement, would be the necessary result of *ijtihād* and that the claims of his opponents to reach Ijmāʿ through original thinking were vain pretensions. But, on the other hand, not much scope for *ijtihād* and disagreement would be left, thanks to the wholesale development of the Ḥadīth.

Ijmāʿ, however, finally accepted Ḥadīth but on its own terms and without losing any ground whatever. This result also, despite al-Shāfiʿī's efforts to the contrary, was inevitable. For, what other authority besides Ijmāʿ could there be to discriminate between the Ḥadīth representing the true Sunna from that bearing the false? Or, who could finally decide what the teaching of the Ḥadīth is? (We have pointed out in the preceding chapter that the criticism of the transmissional chains to establish the genuineness of a Ḥadīth was more a formal criticism than a real one.) Thus, even in order to establish Ḥadīth, Ijmāʿ was needed. In the middle of the 3rd/9th century when the Ḥadīth had virtually conquered the field, even a crusading defender of the Ḥadīth such as Ibn Qutayba gives priority to Ijmāʿ over it: 'We hold that Ijmāʿ is a surer vehicle of truth (or the right) than the Ḥadīth for the latter is subject to forgetfulness, neglect, doubts, interpretations, and abrogation. . . . But Ijmāʿ is free from all these contingencies.'[8]

But in the subsequent development, *ijtihād* or *qiyās* fared differently. Although the Ḥadīth materials were once more reinterpreted to obtain new legal norms through *qiyās*, this largely remained a scholastic activity. Shorn of its function as leading to Ijmāʿ, it gradually lost vitality until, when at the end of the 3rd/9th and beginning of the 4th/10th centuries, both the dogma and the law had taken a definite shape, the Ijmāʿ arrived at by that time was declared final and the door of *ijtihād* was closed. In other words, once Ḥadīth had been established by Ijmāʿ, it ousted Ijmāʿ by its very logic. Islamic law and dogma have developed but little since. One of the most creative and brilliant epochs of all intellectual history came to a sudden close. Why did this happen? Many answers may be adduced to solve this important question of the religious and cultural history of Islam. We shall essay our main answer in Chapter VI where we shall give a historical analysis of the concept of the Sharīʿa, the central religious concept developed in Islam. A partial answer is that Islam had passed, during the preceding three centuries, through a period of great conflict of opinions and doctrines and had finally attained stability, through the emergence of an orthodoxy, only towards the end of the 3rd/beginning of the 10th century. When that point was reached and a difficult and stormy formative period had ended, the results were given permanence. But, as we have just noticed above, the mechanism of development was disturbed just before this point of fruition was reached. The body of the Ḥadīth, sanctioned by Ijmā', relegated *ijtihād* to a subsidiary place cut off from Ijmā'; in its turn, Ijmā', which was originally a function of the 'living tradition' dislodged from fresh thought or *ijtihād*, could not continue its function for the organism needed both for its growth. A stabilizing principle without a principle of expansion necessarily becomes a static tool of oppression. Now a theory of the infallibility of the Ijmā' was developed whereby the early concept of a *pragmatic authority* of the Community's consensus was changed into a theoretical absoluteness of the Community in terms of truth-values. A Ḥadīth was circulated according to which the Prophet said: 'My Community shall never agree on an error'. Thus, Ijmā' became a theoretically founded mechanism of traditional authoritarianism.

Actually, Ijmā' did continue to function in some form or another even after the 3rd/9th century, which was also inevitable in face of the ever changing circumstances of the religious attitudes and the fortunes of the Community. A striking example is the acceptance into orthodox Islam of Ṣūfism after a series of Muslim orthodox Ṣūfīs (Muslim mystics; see Chapter IX), culminating in the great al-Ghazālī (d. 505/1111) who won for it recognition among the 'Ulamā'. Again, the gradual change in the constitutional theory of Islam supplies a no less striking instance. Early in Islam, because of internecine wars, the Ijmā' adopted the principle that fanaticism and war in the Community was unlawful, and that the ruler, despite his failings and even positive injustice ought to be obeyed. Al-Māwardī (d. 450/1058) quotes a Ḥadīth that a sinful ruler should be obeyed provided he does not give a sinful command.[9] Indeed, later the idea had fully gained ground that even an unjust ruler may not be rebelled against. And subsequently the ruler was described as the 'shadow of God'.[10] For the 'Ulamā' this meant a point of cohesion against chaos and lawlessness,[11] but in the popular belief, influenced by the old Iranian ideas of kingship, this phrase assumed literal truth. But in all these cases Ijmā' followed rather than led: instead of being a moulding principle acting formatively on circumstances – through *ijtihād* – it became a passive follower, a mere recognizer of the brute force of circumstance.

The qualifications for *ijtihād* were made so immaculate and rigorous and were set so high that they were humanly impossible of fulfilment. The pictures of the early religious leaders of the Community during the formative period were accordingly idealized more and more and fiction mixed with facts. The power of 'absolute *ijtihād*' was completely abolished; a 'relative *ijtihād*' was allowed. This meant either that one was allowed to reinterpret law *within one's own school of law* or, and this was the highest point of the original legislation, one could carry on an eclectic and comparative study of law of different schools and thus find some scope for limited expansion in details. Some rare, bright and bold spirits such as Ibn Taymīya (d. 728) claimed the right of absolute *ijtihād* for themselves, but their recognition in this matter remained limited during the medieval period. We shall see subsequently in the present work how the question has been reopened in modern Islam with vehemence by modernist thinkers. But throughout the medieval centuries the law, definite and defined, was cast like a shell over the Community.

The Law and the State

During the period of the first four Caliphs (up to about 40/660), the Muslim state and government was headed by the Caliph but was indistinguishable from the public body thanks to the large number of Companions in Medina, especially the senior members who advised on, controlled and participated in both legislative and executive functions. Indeed, at this stage, law can hardly be separated or even distinguished from administration. Legislation in this period can, therefore, mainly by courtesy be attributed to the contemporary Caliphs, for it was the joint work of the Community or its senior members. With the Umayyads, however, the government became vested in the ruling autocracy which became distinguished from the public. The Umayyad rulers carried on their administration from Damascus, largely guided by the Qur'ān and the Sunna, but these were interpreted by their advisers and officers on the principle of expediency and in the light of local practices in different provinces. In face of this lay authority, the leaders of the religious community centred in Medina began to construct the body of Islamic law. The local practice of the Ḥijāz was indubitably a factor in their body of laws. Soon the religious legislative activity also arose in Iraq, in Baṣra and Kūfa. The Umayyad state was influenced by this legislative activity and the Caliph 'Abd al-Malik (d. 86/705) was himself educated in Medina. But the first Umayyad Caliph to take the application of the Sharī'a law seriously and systematically was 'Umar ibn 'Abd al-'Azīz around the close of the 1st/early 8th century and tradition credits him with sending out emissaries to all the outlying provinces to teach people the Sharī'a law and to record traditions from the Prophet.

The state was thus the executive institution which applied in different provinces the Sharī'a law as it had been formulated by local legal authorities. But this body of law (*fiqh*), although uniform in its essentials, differed largely in details both because of the different local practices and because of variations arising out of *ijtihāds* of several scholars. The scholars even of a single town differed in detailed legal opinion. After the Umayyads were ousted, Ibn al-Muqaffa' (d. 140/757), a Persian convert to Islam, an eminent man of letters and a Secretary of State, wrote a treatise advising the Caliph that he should systematize the law and exercise his own *ijtihād* on the Qur'ān and the Sunna. Ibn al-Muqaffa' was probably the first man in Islam to advocate state legislation, advice (apparently not followed) which was probably motivated both by the chaotic differences in legal practice at the time and the Persian background of his ideas of rulership.

The 'Abbāsid Caliphs gave full recognition and validity to the Sharī'a law and perfected the machinery for its application. But several new developments took place. Not only did the Caliphs (or later when the Caliphal power became weak and titular, the powerful sultans owing only nominal allegiance to the Caliphs) begin to enact special laws of their own from time to time to cope with exigencies, a new, although small, body of law emerged devised by the lay authorities to supplement the Sharī'a law. The later Muslim lawyers (*fuqahā'*) attempted gradually to integrate this new body of laws into the Sharī'a law, but the fact that it had originally arisen outside the Sharī'a was a significant development.

But large-scale lay legislation by the state was effected by the Ottomans who assumed the title of the Caliphs in the 10th/16th century. This lay body of law was called the *qānūn* (canon) and Professor Sir Hamilton Gibb has remarked with perfect justice that canon law in Islam means the exact opposite of what it means in Christianity.[12] Among the Ottomans, however, the two functions of Sultanate and Caliphate were separately invested in the same ruler, and Caliphate never returned to its original state. The function of *ijtihād* which all the later constitutional theorists had been attributing to the Caliphal office was never used, and the Ottomans, in so far as they functioned in the field of positive law, functioned only as Sultans. The *qānūn*-law was a product of the Sultanate, not of the Caliphate. We shall see later on in this work, when we discuss modern Islam, how the challenge of the modernization of law is being met by Muslims in modern times.

The administration of the law was carried on in the courts by the *qāḍīs* appointed by the state. These were drawn from the ranks of the 'Ulamā'. Thus appointed by the state, the *qāḍīs* could be used as instruments of the ruler's will and in every age, beginning with the early Umayyad times, we read recurring condemnations of the *qāḍīs* by pious 'Ulamā' and jurists (but later on above all by Ṣufīs), many of whom refused to accept governmental offices holding that their integrity was thereby in danger of being compromised. Besides these law courts, the Caliphs held special courts called the *maẓālim* courts (and similarly various sultans had their *dīwān* courts) for the redress of personal wrongs. Very often these functioned like courts of higher appeal against the decisions of lower courts and officials of the administration. Here the head of state personally decided cases and dispensed justice according to his judgment. Between these two, a third moral-judicial department of 'moral practice' was instituted called *iḥtisāb*. Its function was to keep an eye on public morality and to decide 'obvious' cases on the spot such as defective scales, counterfeit money or adulterated commodities, etc.

The task of specific interpretation of law and its application to individual cases was vested in the *muftīs* who could be either official or private. The verdict given by a *muftī* on a specific case or point of law is called *fatwā*. In course of time, a large body of case-law was built up comprising the collections of *fatwās* of authoritative 'Ulamā'. These were in turn used by *qāḍīs* in deciding cases that came before the courts. The *muftī* was thus a jurisconsult, a *qāḍī* a judge. The *fatwā*-collections provide for us the best source for the knowledge of the development of Islamic law throughout the Middle Ages and in the different regions, and reveal to us that long process whereby local customary laws were gradually Islamized and integrated into Islamic law.

Formation of the Legal Schools

It is an evidence of the characteristic freedom of legal thought in early Islam that during the 1st/7th and 2nd/8th centuries a host of accumulations of legal opinion grew up in different centres in Iraq, the Ḥijāz, Syria and Egypt. These were centred on or attached themselves to an eminent legal personality. The differences in these bodies of legal thought were largely due to the various ways in which the Qur'ān was interpreted, in the light of local customary law, i.e. in the different ways in which *qiyās* and *ra'y* were applied to the Sunna. The body of law that resulted from such application of rational activity in different regions was also called Sunna. Hence the local Sunnas differed in detail in the different provinces.

But slowly, with the development of the concept of Ijmā', these particular centres merged into one another by mental interaction and the accumulations of legal opinion gradually crystallized into schools in the 2nd/8th and 3rd/9th centuries during which the schools themselves came closer to one another, thanks to the wide measure of agreement not only on principles but even on major details. In Iraq, the school associated with the name of Abū Ḥanīfa (d. 150/767) called the Ḥanafī school, developed and was systemized by his two disciples Abū Yūsuf (d. 181/797) and Muḥammad al-Shaybānī (d. 189/805) and ousted that of Sufyān al-Thawrī (d. 161/778) and others. This school, favoured by the 'Abbāsids whose capital was in Baghdad, was most characterized by the exercise of free opinion and became the favourite object of the bitter invectives of the Ahl al-Ḥadīth in the 2nd/8th and 3rd/9th centuries, since these latter strenuously rejected free opinion.

The Syrian school of al-Awzā'ī (d. 157/774), whose reliance on the 'living tradition' was greater than on legal Ḥadīth, in contrast to Sufyān al-Thawrī, was overcome by that founded by Mālik ibn Anas (d. 179/795) in Medina. Mālik himself resembled al-Awzā'ī in that at bottom he placed his reliance on the 'living tradition' (*Sunna*) of Medina, but was equally anxious to support or vindicate this tradition through Ḥadīth. He collected a body of legal traditions and, testing them in the light of the living practice of Medina, constructed a system of juridical opinions into a famous work called *al-Muwaṭṭā'* – 'the levelled path'. The Mālikī school, the second surviving one after the Ḥanafī, takes its name from him.

The third major surviving school is called the Shāfi'ī school, after Muḥammad ibn Idrīs al-Shāfi'ī (d. 204/819), references to whom have figured prominently in the present and the preceding chapters of this book. A pupil of Mālik, he formulated the principles of Islamic jurisprudence in the form that these have retained ever since, wherein, as we have described before, the verbal tradition was regarded as the sole vehicle of the Prophetic Sunna and *ijtihād* was thrown outside Ijmā'. The influence of al-Shāfi'ī has been incalculable on the development of Islam.

In the 3rd/9th century arose two new schools and at least one attempt at a school. The first and only successful one of these continued to push the logic of al-Shāfi'ī's insistence on the Ḥadīth in law to its extremes. The founder of this school, called the Ḥanbalī school, was the famous doctor and arch-traditionalist Aḥmad ibn Ḥanbal (d. 241/855) whom we shall meet again in the next chapter as the orthodox opponent of the rationalist school. Ibn Ḥanbal's teaching was systematized after him by his disciples but after a widespread following was commanded by this school up to the 8th/14th century, the numbers suffered a continuous diminution although a series of brilliant and sensational representatives of the school appeared across the centuries. In the 12th/18th century the Wahhābīs – the puritanical movement in the Arabian Peninsula – derived their doctrine and inspiration from

Ḥanbalism as it had been expressed by the celebrated doctor and theologian Ibn Taymīya (d. 728/1328).

Dā'ūd Khalaf (d. 269/882), called al-Ẓāhirī – 'the literalist' – established the literalist school in the 3rd/9th century. It sought to reject *qiyās* altogether and even restricted the Ijmā' to the consensus of the Companions only. Acceptance of the literal interpretation of the Qur'ān and the Ḥadīth was the keynote of their doctrine. But on closer analysis, they were not as literalist as they claimed to be because the rejection of the reasoning element in jurisprudence freed them to extend the acceptance of the Word to include what the Word 'assumes' or 'implies' (*mafhūm, faḥwā*). But the restriction of the mechanism of interpretation that they advocated found little support among the large body of Muslims although their point of view has from time to time found eminent champions. Al-Ṭabarī (d. 310/922), whose voluminous and monumental works on the exegesis of the Qur'ān and history are full of information about early Islam, attempted to found a new school of law, but not only was this attempt unsuccessful, even the work in which he laid down its principles does not seem to have survived.

By Ijmā' the four schools, or *Madhāhib* (pl. of *Madhhab*), as they are called, were accepted, and accepted one another as equally orthodox. A detailed history of their mutual interaction still needs to be written. But there is not only no fundamental difference of jurisprudence between them, even the difference in detail has been largely turned into a remarkable unity thanks to the limited *ijtihād* that continued to be allowed and exercised by the scholars. At present the Ḥanafī school is predominant in Western Asia, lower Egypt, Pakistan and among the Muslims of India. The Mālikī rite holds sway in North and West Africa and in Upper Egypt, the Shāfi'ī in Indonesia, and the Ḥanbalite in Northern and Central Arabia.

Conclusion

As indicated at the beginning of this chapter, the place of law in Islam, and consequently its nature, will be treated more fully in Chapter VI where we shall attempt both an analysis of the concept of Sharī'a and a history of it, but a general characterization of it may be in place here. It will have become clear by now that the real basis on which rests this whole structure is religious, the idea of God as the sovereign and 'the Ordainer Whose Will is Law'. Man must discover, formulate and execute that Will of which the final index is the Qur'ān and Muḥammad the most perfect commentator. Accordingly, Islamic law, in its first intention, is a system of 'oughts' and 'ought-nots' rather than a specific legal code. That is why every book of Islamic law starts with a discourse on religious duties. That is also why actions are ethically classified into five categories: (1) obligatory, (2) recommended, (3) permissible or indifferent, (4) reprehensible and (5) forbidden. Indeed, the trans-legal religious and moral state of the agent's heart (faith, intention and will) is demanded by this system to be present in all behaviour. Nothing illustrates this trait better than the fact that most actions classified in the above categories and especially (2), (3) and (4) are made subject to a general rule known as the law of 'resoluteness and relaxation ('*azīma* and *rukhṣa*)'. These categories which primarily apply to the agent's will, whereby he should regard, under special circumstances, the permissive actions to be unpermitted and vice versa (because of moral considerations), are erected into a quasi-legal enactment. This trait of the *fiqh* system is further evidenced by the fact that frequently religious penalties (known as *kaffāra*) run concurrently with strictly legal sanctions. A further example of this translation of the spiritual into legal terms is the verbalization, in many cases, of the act of intention by uttering 'I intend. . . '. Such considerations should warn us against applying the term 'law' in its ordinary denotation to a system which, in its primary intention, is trans-legal but which can undoubtedly constitute the raw materials for a properly legal system.

CHAPTER FIVE

DIALECTICAL THEOLOGY AND THE DEVELOPMENT OF DOGMA

The Early Phase – The Mu'tazila – Ash'arism and Māturīdism – Philosophy and Kalām

The Early Phase

The Qur'ān is essentially a religious and ethical document aiming at the practical goal of creating a morally good and just society composed of religiously righteous men with a keen and vivid awareness of a God who enjoins good and forbids evil. Consequently, pure theory is minimal. Perhaps the nearest it comes to speculation is in its exhortations to contemplate the vastness and regularity of the universe, but even this argument from design is used not to establish the theoretical existence of God but to depict His living majesty and full-blooded purposive beauty. The emphasis is on faith-in-action. For this, the necessary moral and psychological factors and tensions were supplied. Human pride was emphatically humbled beside God's majesty and omnipotence. On the other hand, those who sought to escape action, taking refuge in divine omnipotence, were repudiated, and the essential freedom and responsibility of human action was vividly portrayed. Together with the repeated condemnation of human arrogance and conceit, despondency was categorically rejected as being characteristic of the devil and his followers, the infidels. Human nature was criticized as weak and fallible but the sense of urgency of human initiative was patently maintained.

This simple but effective and practical attitude inculcated by the Qur'ān and the Prophet was first shocked into reflection by the upheavals during the Caliphates of 'Uthmān and 'Alī. But when, under the Umayyads, the unity of religion and state was disturbed, it led to widespread and deep heart-searching. The Umayyads, fully aware of the fact that it was Islam that had engendered unity among the Arabs and brought them success and glory, retained the Caliphal form and as such the religious basis of the state and accepted the Sharī'a as giving it constitution. But not only was their administrative law not consciously based on the Sharī'a, they used the state primarily as an instrument of personal power. Their personal lives were not wholly un-Islamic but were certainly far removed from the pious ideals of the early Caliphs and fell far short of the expectations and demands of the religious leaders of the Community. Under 'Umar ibn 'Abd al-'Azīz, in c. 99–101/717–20 they tried to remedy the situation, but it had by then become too late to save the dynasty.

The first question that was raised in Islam was: does a Muslim remain a Muslim after committing a grave sin? Or, is faith alone sufficient or must it express itself in works as well? The extreme sect of the Khārijites (the 'Seceders') maintained that a grave sinner no longer remains a Muslim and turned the fury of their *jihād* (holy war) against the established rule and the Community in general in the name of a transcendent and extreme idealism which they combined with uncompromising fanaticism. 'Decision (rule) belongs to God alone' was the watchword of these tribesmen, who were strong in Iraq and Persia. The pious leaders of the Community in Medina were largely dissatisfied with the Umayyads; but a major part of religious opinion, in its powerlessness, slowly acquiesced in the régime of the Umayyads and declared that the possession of faith alone was sufficient for a person to be defined as a Muslim and that works were not essential. For them 'Decision belongs to God alone' came to mean that political power, seen as having been established by God's will, ought not to be disobeyed. These people, called the Murjites (*Murji'a*, i.e. those who 'postponed' judgment on people until the Last Day) recommended that one should desist from passing judgment on a grave sinner whose fate will be decided by God.

In their first appearance during the time of 'Uthmān and 'Alī, the Murji'a represented the mild and moderate opinion against the strong factions for and against 'Uthmān and 'Alī. During the Umayyad period, however, this moderate attitude slowly sank to the level of pure determinism, thus falling in line with the popular moral laxity and becoming an instrument in the defence of the Umayyad régime which, in turn, encouraged the dissemination of their views. Thus the Murji'a of the early period of 'Alī, who took a neutralist position in the political quarrel between 'Alī and his opponents and were therefore also called Mu'tazila (the 'neutralists'), came to be called Jabrīya, 'pre-determinists'.

The true tradition of these early political neutralists and religious moderates, who comprised the majority of the Companions and the Medinese in general, was during the Umayyad ascendancy located in Medina. The religious leadership at Medina, although shocked at the violent jolt that the Islamic state had received at the hands of the

Umayyads, and generally dissatisfied with the latter, nevertheless refrained from active rebellion and concentrated instead on the elaboration of the religious sciences of law and Ḥadīth. The ethos of piety, practicalism and moderation of Medina – which, being the true home of the religious development of Islam in the early centuries, occupied a central and paramount place – set the tone for all subsequent development of Islamic orthodoxy whose central character, as we shall presently see, is the gradual assimilation of extremism into moderation. It was to win the day, and came to full fruition in the 'Abbāsid Caliphate.

The Mu'tazila

Outside the Ḥijāz, however, and especially in Iraq, this attitude of practical religiosity was soon to be subjected to stormy philosophical speculations by outside influences. Iraq was already, before Islam, a battle-ground of ideas and theories which came from different directions. Hellenism, Hellenized Christianity, Gnosticism, Manichaean dualism and Buddhistic elements provided the stock ideas for philosophical, religious and moral speculation. And although, as said above, the initial reflexive impulse to moral issues was generated by events within Islam, these were soon to be transformed in the great cities of Iraq into speculative issues.

The first tangible figure that we meet in Baṣra in the 1st/7th and early 2nd/8th century is that of the famous Ḥasan al-Baṣrī (d. 110/728), who is to be regarded as representative of Medinese piety. He strongly rejected the deterministic interpretation of Islam (see Chapter I), and regarded man as responsible for his actions. But it is abundantly clear from his writing that he was motivated by pietistic morality rather than speculative curiosity. For we do not find in him a purely philosophical discernment of the issues. He sometimes argues (on the basis of the Qur'ān) that *all* actions emanate from man who is responsible for them; at other times that all good is to be attributed to God while all evil is to be referred to the devil and to man (again on the basis of the Qur'ān). Thus, two different motives are in play here: to save the goodness of God and to make man responsible *especially for evil deeds*. The purely philosophical question of whether God or man is the productive agent of *all* acts does not concern him at all.

But the more systematically thinking minds could not accept this pietistic rejection of determination and voiced their opinion in favour of an unequivocal authorship of man of his own acts: only thus could praise and blame, reward and punishment for man and the justice of God become intelligible. This thesis they pushed to its logical conclusions with regard to the nature of God and the destiny of man. Similarly, on the question of the relationship of faith to deeds, whereas the Khārijites regarded a grave sinner as an outright infidel and the main body of Muslims considered him a 'sinner-Muslim', the Mu'tazila held that he was neither a Muslim nor a non-Muslim. This doctrine is known as that of the 'intermediate state'.

It is probably this doctrine of the 'intermediate state' of a grave sinner that gave the new movement its technical name of Mu'tazila, 'neutralists', and which distinguished them from the old political neutralists. It is not, however, certain when this name was given to them. According to the generally accepted Sunnī tradition, they were given this name when their founder, Wāṣil ibn 'Aṭā' (80–131/699–749) 'broke off' (*i'tazala*) from the circle of al-Ḥasan al-Baṣrī. Many orientalists have, however, denied this and attempted different surmises. Goldziher thought that the name (the Arabic root means 'to abstain from', 'to be neutralist', 'to be aside from') refers to their abstemiousness and piety.[1] But although the pious character of the early Mu'tazila cannot be doubted, they were not more pious or abstemious than al-Ḥasan or many other people. Nor can they be regarded as a continuation of the old political neutralism, as H. S. Nyberg holds.[2] On the contrary, while the bulk of the thinking elements of the Community were political neutralists, the Mu'tazila were by and large (including their leaders) pro-'Alī although some of them did not declare for either party in the earliest civil wars. In any case, their break with al-Ḥasan and the practical piety of the Medinese branch was of far greater consequence for the future development of Islam.

Thus, in their origins, the Mu'tazila were not 'free-thinkers' as they have been sometimes called. They were not pure 'rationalists' (despite their claim that reason is an equal source, with Revelation, of moral truth), although the impulse to a *systematic thinking out* of dogma, unlike traditional Islam, was certainly an activity which made them pursue their ratiocination further and further as time went on. Indeed, the deterministic doctrine which the Mu'tazila were fighting at home was also shaped early into a systematic doctrine at the hands of such men as Jahm ibn Ṣafwān (put to death in 128/746) who advocated, in all probability under foreign influences, an uncompromising and absolute determinism. But, above all, as newer researches have shown,[3] they waged a relentless and successful struggle in defence of Islam against outside attacks of Manichaeism, Gnosticism and Materialism. In doing so, they perforce produced the first systematically thought-out creed for Islam, but, inside Islam, they had gone too far beyond the limits which traditional Islam could recognize as valid. The outside dangers having been quelled, they struggled inside Islam on the twin platforms of the 'justice and unity of God' wherein they increasingly showed themselves as rigid and intolerant advocates of Hellenistic rationalism, and were finally defeated with their own weapons.

The doctrine of the freedom of the human will as advocated by the Mu'tazila came soon to be a part of the wider theological concept of the 'Justice of God' and overshadowed its original aspect, the freedom and responsibility of man. From among the various constituents of the Qur'ānic concept of God, power, mercy, will and justice, they isolated this last one and carried it to its logical conclusions that God *cannot* do the unreasonable and the unjust. In this connection they developed their doctrine of the 'Promise and Threat' according to which God can neither pardon the evil-doer (and therefore violate His Threat) nor punish the good-doer (and violate His Promise). Taking the Qur'ānic statements about the promise of reward and threat of punishment as categorical statements of future *facts*, they deduced that God would not only be unjust if He did not carry out His promises and threats, He would be a liar. Consequently, the Qur'ānic dicta concerning the mercy and grace of God were interpreted by them in terms of necessity and duty: God *must* do the best for man; He *must* send Prophets and Revelations to mankind. If He did not do the best for man He would neither be just nor God. These doctrines were developed patently under Hellenistic influence and more especially under the influence of Stoicism, as indeed Stoical influences have been established beyond doubt in other doctrines of later *kalām*.[4] In the eyes of the orthodox, this freedom for man was bondage for God. They accused Mu'tazilism of extreme humanism and they insisted that God is above the human concepts of justice: that it is not just for God what man considers as such for Him, but that which He does for man appears at the human level as just and rational. Thus, whereas the Mu'tazila subsumed the idea of God under that of human justice, the orthodox subsumed the idea of justice under that of God.

As with the problem of justice, with that of the Divine Attributes, the Mu'tazila went to extreme limits. Starting with a genuine anxiety to safeguard the idea of Divine transcendence, they explained away all expressions of Scripture and the Ḥadīth that contained anthropomorphism in a rational spirit and ended up by negating all the Divine Attributes. God is pure Essence having no eternal names and qualities, affirmation of which, according to them, was tantamount to a form of polytheism. This was their version of *tanzīh*, 'divine transcendence', which according to the orthodoxy rather consisted in the absoluteness of His attributes, Power, Knowledge, Will, etc. Consequently, the Mu'tazila were branded as *mu'aṭṭila*, i.e. those who denuded God of all content and rendered Him unsatisfactory for religious consciousness.

And although the Mu'tazila, in their turn, accused orthodoxy of *tashbīh*, i.e. 'likening God to man', so far as religion was concerned, there could be hardly any doubt about the final issue. As Professor Gibb has put it: 'The orthodox rightly rejected these pretensions (of the Mu'tazila) for in religion anthroposophy is a more insidious solvent than anthropomorphism'.[5]

Indeed, the Mu'tazila carried their rationalism so far as to claim parity for reason with revelation in the discovery of religious truth. They were not content only with a declaration of the superiority of reason over tradition, but put it on an equal footing with the Word of God as religious guide. The implications of this went even further: since they could not accept the Speech of God as an Attribute of God, they declared the Qur'ān to be a created word. On the subject of the Attributes and especially with regard to the Word, they were undoubtedly influenced by Hellenistic ideas especially in their Christian formulations about the Logos. But since they held reason to be the essential constitution of God, a purely Greek idea, the net result was to put reason above revelation. The orthodox held the Qur'ān to be the eternal Word of God, and the Mu'tazila, when their doctrine temporarily became the state-creed in the Caliphate of al-Ma'mūn and his successors, persecuted their representatives, especially Aḥmad ibn Ḥanbal (d. 241/855), who was flogged and imprisoned for resolutely refusing to believe in the Mu'tazila dogma.

It is, however, undeniable that the Mu'tazila movement did a great internal service to Islam not only by attempting to erect an edifying picture of God for refined minds but, above all, by insisting on the claims of reason in theology. This attempt, as we shall presently see, did leave a legacy which was, to some extent, taken up in subsequent developments. But while the Mu'tazila movement itself lasted, its excessive emphasis on formal rationality, indeed on an apotheosis of reason (in its later development), created a severe reaction in the orthodoxy. Orthodoxy, while maintaining in spirit its original ethics of integrative, broad and stabilizing catholicity, was nevertheless, in its actual formulas, pressed into a reaction under the aggressive attitude of this proud and hollow rationalism. While the Mu'tazila stuck rigidly to 'Reason and Justice of God' and the freedom of the human will, traditionalist orthodoxy, in order to save vital elements in religion, put almost exclusive stress on the formulations of Divine Power, Will, Grace and determinism. In its definitions, therefore, orthodoxy fell in danger of losing the comprehensiveness of the original simple faith. Henceforth Islam was launched on a career where its dynamic formulations had only a partial and indirect relationship to the living realities of the faith.

Ash'arism and Māturīdism

The right wing of orthodox traditionalism was represented by Ibn Ḥanbal and his school. But the truly broad catholic spirit of Islam was crystallized by the compilers of that unique phenomenon in Islam, the Ḥadīth, described in Chapter III. By a fairly broad-minded exercise of their 'orthodox' insight, these men allowed to fall within the scope of the acceptable Ḥadīth a body of authoritative material that allowed for latitude and integration of points of view and opinions that could not be fitted into one mould. It exhibits no external or superficial wisdom but an impeccable scrupulousness and an inner and genuine insight into the spirit of the Prophet's teaching and the early Community's understanding of it. The Ḥadīth was opposed by the Mu'tazila who nevertheless slowly lost ground by the latter half of the 3rd/9th century; on no other hypothesis than this can we really understand the absolute success of the Ḥadīth in that century.

Yet, the success of the Ḥadīth was not due to the fact that it was, in its formulations and content, a possibly valuable amorphous mass, but because at bottom it expressed a definite spirit of religious realism that had characterized both the Qur'ān and the early Community. It brought under the aegis of the Sunna all the necessary religious elements that were implicit or explicit in the Qur'ān. Side by side with the coming to fruition of the Ḥadīth, a widespread movement of dissatisfaction had started with the *clichés* of the rationalist school. Their newer views began to shape on the basis of their acquaintance with tradition and their gradual acceptance of it.

The most celebrated name in this newer movement, which turned the tables on the Mu'tazila by their own dialectic, is that of Abu'l-Ḥasan al-Ash'arī (d. 330/442) who broke from his Mu'tazilite master al-Jubbā'ī in maintaining that Divine Justice could not be defined in human terms. The following oft-quoted passage celebrates this *coup de bouleversement*:

'Let us imagine a child and a grown-up person in Heaven who both died in the True Faith. The grown-up one, however, has a higher place in Heaven than the child. The child shall ask God: "Why did you give that man a higher place?" "He has done many good works", God shall reply. Then the child shall say, "Why did you let me die so soon so that I was prevented from doing good?" God will answer, "I knew that you would grow up into a sinner; therefore, it was better that you should die a child". Thereupon a cry shall rise from those condemned to the depths of the Hell, "Why, O Lord! did You not let us die before we became sinners?" '[6]

Al-Ash'arī's formulation of dogma essentially represents an attempt at a synthesis of the hitherto largely unformulated orthodox position and that of the Mu'tazila. This is, as we have pointed out before, the very ethos of orthodoxy. But his actual formulas unmistakably show the character of a reaction of orthodoxy to the Mu'tazilite doctrine, a reaction from which he was unable to escape completely. The net result is therefore a partial synthesis and a partial reaction. On the question of human free will he erected, on the basis of certain Qur'ānic texts, his doctrine of 'acquisition'. According to this doctrine, all acts are created and produced by God but attach themselves to the will of man who thus 'acquires' them. D. B. Macdonald[7] has seen in this formula an attempt to do justice to the psychological fact that man has the consciousness of owning his voluntary acts. But, to begin with, man has the consciousness not merely of owning his deliberate acts but also of producing them; and both the Mu'tazila and their opponents were aware of the argument from direct consciousness. Secondly, the problem that al-Ash'arī set out to resolve was not so much a psychological as a moral one: how to reconcile Divine Omnipotence with human responsibility. And if man's consciousness of owning his acts is itself created by God, as al-Ash'arī believes, then man 'acquires' neither the one nor the other. The principle that seems to be at work here is that all power is referred to God while responsibility must remain with man. The principle itself, although it has a metaphysical form, is religious and moral in its essential character.

Similarly, on the problem of the Unity of God, al-Ash'arī taught that God has real, Eternal Attributes, but attempted to safeguard against anthropomorphism. God knows by virtue of His Attribute of Knowledge, wills by virtue of His attribute of Will, etc. These are neither identical with His Essence nor different from it. They are real although we do not know their 'how', and in this connection al-Ash'arī makes use of the negative dialectic of the Mu'tazilites which ultimately comes from Neoplatonism. As to rewards and punishments, he emphasizes both the absolute Power of God and His absolute Mercy and Grace: He may punish or reward as He will. This is done not to uphold any caprice and arbitrariness on the part of God but again in order to express the religious attitude of humility and fear. Like all Attributes, God's Speech is eternal and uncreated. But the Qur'ān as we know it, a definite text of a certain length, etc., is only *an expression although an expression par excellence* of the Eternal Speech of God which in itself is a 'Mental Word'.

Thus, al-Ash'arī confirmed the absolute Power and Grace of God as orthodoxy had maintained it. All acts take place by the Will and 'Good Pleasure' of God, whether good or evil. As said before, al-Ash'arī was strongly under the influence of the orthodox reaction against the Mu'tazilite doctrine which seemed to restrict God's power.

And, indeed, he made no secret of the fact that he did not want to deviate from the teaching of Aḥmad ibn Ḥanbal. This absolute Power of God was further supported by an atomistic theory of nature denying causation and potentialities in natural bodies and providing for the direct efficacy of God for the production of events, whether physical or mental.

Another theological system which grew up almost contemporaneously with that of al-Ash'arī is that of Abū Manṣūr al-Māturīdī (d. 333/945) of Samarqand in Transoxiana. Māturīdism is very similar to Ash'arism in basic outlook, but differs from it in certain important points. Al-Māturīdī, like al-Ash'arī, holds that all acts are willed by God, but unlike him, maintains that evil acts do not occur 'with the good pleasure of God'. More important, Māturīdism, while emphasizing the Omnipotence of God, allows the efficacy of the human will and, in some of its later developments, the absolutely free human production of acts was unequivocally stated. In these later developments, indeed, there is a free interaction between the two systems, and the doctrine of the absolute inefficacy of the human will generally lost its force although the Ash'arite dogma, backed by some important Ḥadīth, still retained it.

An important problem discussed widely by Muslim dogmatists and theologians was that of the 'degrees of faith'. This was connected with the question of faith and works, and subsequently came to be connected with the idea of the Omnipotence and Grace of God under the influence of speculative theology. Those who held, like the Mu'tazila and the Khārijites, that acts were an essential part of the faith, also held that faith increases and decreases, is quantitative – and could reach a zero degree, despite the profession of the faith by the agent. The Murjites, on the other hand, believed that faith was something qualitatively unanalysable and simple, not admitting either degree or measurement. The Sunnī *kalām*, as expected, was between the two in principle, but on the whole inclined to the tenets of the Murjites. This was undoubtedly in order to check fanaticism and persecution, and the Sunnīs, accordingly, maintained that, with a genuine profession of faith, an irreducible amount of faith came into existence which was incapable of being eliminated by almost any external behaviour, although it could increase or decrease beyond that point. The Qur'ān repeatedly affirms the increase of faith (e.g. III, 167, and elsewhere) and incessantly urges acts born of genuine faith; and the Ḥadīth speaks of intimate connection between acts and intentions, although certain Ḥadīths, which apparently counselled moderation and were to the effect that none shall be eternally damned with a 'grain of faith', were seized upon by theologians in this connection.

Indeed, the 'Ulamā' henceforth limited their function of the 'tendence of the soul' to the formulas of belief and issuing *fatwās* (authoritative legal opinions) on external legal matters. This fundamentally explains the subsequent tide of the largely anti-orthodox Ṣūfī movement which claimed exclusive right to cater for the inner, spiritual welfare of individuals. But in the meanwhile, a split occurred within orthodoxy itself. The main continuation of the old traditional school of Medina, the 'People of the Ḥadīth', not only opposed Ash'arite solutions of dialectical theology but rejected the dialectical theology itself. The Qur'ān and the Sunna, they contended, must not be defended by a 'reason' that lies outside these, but the true 'reason' is to be found rather within them. They accused the Mu'tazila, in effect, of betraying the true spirit of the Qur'ān and the Sunna in the process of defending them by rational formulas. Nevertheless, Ash'arism, as a system of dogma, slowly overcame opposition and finally won recognition in the East in the 11th/17th century through the efforts of the great Seljūq wazīr Niẓām al-Mulk and the brilliant theologian and religious reformer al-Ghazālī. But the friction between the religious spirit of the Ahl al-Ḥadīth and the rationalizing tendencies of the Ahl al-Kalām continued and culminated in the 7th/13th and 8th/14th centuries in a vigorous reassertion of puritanical activism in Ibn Taymīya and his school. But before that the *kalām* had to face a more thorough-going rational movement of the Muslim philosophers.

Philosophy and Kalām

The Islamic philosophical movement, to be studied in Chapter VII from the point of view of its amplification of Islamic doctrine, was an outgrowth of the Mu'tazila *kalām*. Against the rationalist systems of the philosophers, al-Ghazālī (d. 505/1111) represented the first great reaction, monumental in the depth and durability of its influence. A truly searching religious spirit (he has often, with justice, been compared to Augustine), he went through a series of spiritual crises. Early in life he became disillusioned with the traditional *kalām*-theology because of its formalism and externality. In his search for truth, he studied philosophy but found it not only far from orthodox Islam in its teachings but above all lacking in certainty in its proofs. In religious convictions he searched for a type of mathematical certainty. This, as the balance of religious forces in the structure of Islam stood at that time, he found only in Ṣūfism (Muslim mysticism).

This explains why, after refuting the philosophers' theses in his famous work, the *Tahāfut al-Falāsifa*, al-Ghazālī did not attempt an alternative philosophical system. The answer is that no metaphysic, purely rationally constructed, would satisfy the religious need of certainty. Nevertheless, despite his rejection of Greco-Islamic philosophy in general, he adopted certain beliefs from it. Thus he finally adopted from the philosophers the view, which was in harmony with the Ṣūfī ethics, that man is soul alone to the exclusion of the body.

But if the need for religious certainty impelled al-Ghazālī to mysticism, his mysticism led him back to a rediscovery of the Qur'ānic conception of God as formulated in the Ash'arite *kalām*. He was thus destined to prove the first and greatest reformer of Ṣūfism for which at the same time he secured a place in the structure of Islamic orthodoxy. And, what is even more important, he brought the formal, dogmatic formulation of the orthodox *kalām* into contact with the living religion, thereby revitalizing them and infusing into them the original spirit of the Revelation. He thus dealt a powerful blow to pure scholasticism, softened the dogmatic character of the creed and established a vital nerve between the inner and the exterior aspects of religion. Armed with this, he wrote his great work *The Revivification of the Sciences of the Faith.*

Al-Ghazālī has puzzled many a modern writer. Some have wondered whether he was essentially a mystic or a theologian, although he is described as both. In some quarters, which have dared to be more decisive on the matter, his mysticism has been rejected with the thesis that he is really a *mutakallim* ('declaimer') who devised a purely *psychological* method of concentration on the dogma, the two being linked purely mechanically. To us it appears a capital misunderstanding of al-Ghazālī. Fundamentally, al-Ghazālī affirmed an agnosticism about the ultimate and absolute nature of God and maintained that He was knowable only in so far as He was related to and revealed Himself to man. This revealed and relational nature of God is constituted by the Divine Names and Attributes. Mysticism reveals these to man in their true nature. He, therefore, rejected the extreme Ṣūfī claims of absorption, union and incarnation. He was in pursuit not of religious aesthetics and artistry but of religious *morality*. The religious certainty he sought did not consist of security, safety and calm repose, but of moral purification and the war against vice that degraded man. Thus it was that he came to substitute for the 'Prime Mover' of the philosophers and the 'Essence of Essences' of the Ṣūfīs, the ultimate 'Commander' of the Qur'ān. The *kalām* formulates that Command: mysticism reveals it to man in a way that his whole being is transformed into its receptacle and organ. And although there may be found unconcealed contradictions in al-Ghazālī's intellectual aspect, the spiritual integrity and organic unity of his personality is beyond a shadow of doubt.

The synthesis thus achieved by al-Ghazālī between Ṣūfism and *kalām* was largely adopted by orthodoxy and confirmed by Ijmā'.

Its strength lay in the fact that it gave a spiritual basis for the moral practical *élan* of Islam and thus brought it back to its original religious dimensions. But the balance was delicate and could be maintained only within the limits of a strictly moral ethos. Within orthodoxy, there were two groups which did not adopt al-Ghazālī's synthesis. One of these, which actually opposed al-Ghazālī, was the right-wing Ahl al-Ḥadīth, the traditionalists who considered both parts of the synthesis, the *kalām* and Ṣūfism, as foreign and therefore suspect elements, and actually attacked al-Ghazālī for using weak and even forged traditions to support his Ṣūfic interpretations. The other, the more intellectualist Mutakallims, could not accept the plea for a reduced and purely practical *kalām* which did not satisfy demands of formal intellectualism. They thus expanded the theses of the traditional *kalām* to reckon with the new philosophical challenge and reinforce the Islamic creed. Their main doctrines we shall study presently.

But unexpected developments took place about a century after al-Ghazālī, which used the *kalām* in quite a new direction with a purpose wholly alien to it. Ṣūfism, which we shall study in Chapter VIII, when developed into a speculative system, turned the moral doctrine of the Unity and Omnipotence of God of the *kalām* into a monistic pantheism of mystic philosophy on the basis of the philosophical doctrine of emanation. In this theory, the scholastic-Ghazālian Names of God are transformed into a network of hierarchical manifestations or epiphanies of the Divine Essence through which the mystic progressed to be united with the Being of God.

The main stream of *kalām*-theology, however, could not reject reason in favour either of pure mysticism as al-Ghazālī had done, or of simple traditionalism like the majority of the Ahl al-Ḥadīth. The rationalist challenge, whose first phase began with the Mu'tazila, became far more systematic and formidable with the advent of the philosophical movement, and left a permanent legacy. The Islamic dogma, therefore, had to be restated equally systematically and with a corresponding vigour with the same logic as the philosophers had used. The greatest and most incisive formulator of the new systematic theology is Muḥammad ibn 'Umar, known as Fakhr al-Dīn al-Rāzī (d. 606/1209). At first a pure rationalist and almost indistinguishable from the philosophers in his theses, even a vindicator of certain philosophical doctrines (e.g. that of the eternity of the world) against al-Ghazālī, he gradually embraced the Ash'arite creed and undertook to defend its tenets. Later, the results of this systematic theology were set forth by al-Ījī (d. 756/1355) in a work entitled *al-Mawāqif* which attracted commentators for several centuries.

All the relevant philosophical disciplines were studied and elaborated by the new systematic theology. Greek logic, especially its theory of knowledge, was assiduously cultivated. This together with physics (theories of nature) and metaphysics, formed the basis for theology. In each of these fields, the theories of the philosophers were elaborated, modified or rejected according to what was seen as implicit in the dogma. In the theory of knowledge, cognition was declared to be a non-essential, external relation between the knowing mind and the known object. This was the Islamic answer to the philosophical epistemology which, at the level of pure cognition, declared the identity of the subject and the object in the act of cognition and which, despite the efforts of Ibn Sīnā (Avicenna) to safeguard it against any pantheistic suggestion, or incarnationism, was, nevertheless, being manipulated by many Ṣūfī theorists in terms of a final identity between God and man.

In the field of natural philosophy, controversies continued between the atomism of the *kalām* and the Aristotelian, philosophical theory of matter and form, which was the basis of the philosophers' theory of causation. The Mutakallims rejected the Aristotelian doctrine of matter and form as a prerequisite for rejecting natural causation and restated the early Ash'arite atomism with fresh arguments until affirmation of atomism and denial of natural causation came to be looked upon as almost a cardinal religious dogma regarded as a necessary step to prove the temporal creation of the world and the Islamic eschatology.

The most patent and cherished subject for systematic theology, however, was the most widely discussed problem of Being which had started with early *kalām* but which was erected into the most fundamental theological doctrine of his system by the philosopher Ibn Sīnā (see Chapter VII). The philosophers had attempted to draw a distinction between God and the world, a distinction which was to be adopted by St. Thomas Aquinas in the West as the foundation of his theology, on the basis of a theory of essence and existence. All created things, according to this theory, were composed of an essence and a fact of existence or actual being which was conferred upon them by God who is simple Being without any essence and whose only real attribute is being: God is existent *per se*; everything else exists through God. Hence God is the Necessary Being while all created things are contingent *per se* and necessary-by-God.

The philosophers had, by this doctrine, sought to distinguish fundamentally between God and the world: at no point can a created being *become* Necessary Being. But by allowing existence to be a common attribute of all created things, bestowed by God, it was tempting to argue that all things 'shared' in the Being of God, especially in view of the fact that the philosophers' God had no essence. This was, in fact, argued vigorously (see Chapter VIII) by thinkers such as Shihāb al-Dīn al-Suhrawardī (put to death in 587/1191) and by the great Ṣūfī thinker Ibn al-ʿArabī (d. 638/1240). The systematic theology emphatically rejects the distinction between essence and existence, affirms that essences are created at the time of their existence, attributes an essence to God, which, as in the case of created beings, is indistinguishable from Divine Existence. Thus, by making existence unique in the case of each being, it eradicates even the slightest tendency to pantheism and develops into a form of existentialism.

The systematic theology of Islam, as it developed after al-Ghazālī, has not been adequately studied by modern scholarship. But an extreme doctrine wherein systematic theology corroborated the philosophers' teaching was that of an uncompromising determinism and a flat rejection of human freedom. Fresh arguments were put forward, with the help of the philosophical stock of ideas, to strengthen determinism. In the doctrine of Fakhr al-Dīn al-Rāzī, there appears no scope even for al-Ashʿarī's doctrine of the 'acquisition' of the act by the human agent. The Muʿtazila, in their attempt to establish human freedom, had appealed to direct consciousness of freedom on the part of the agent. This psychological approach was now resumed, deepened and turned the other way round. A theory of human motivation was developed to show, on the one hand, that while a specific motive holds sway, action (or non-action) becomes absolutely necessary, and, on the other, that we are not the authors of our acts but God is, on the ground that we are never fully aware of the details and consequences of our actions. For an agent to own an act properly it is necessary for him to know exactly and completely the empirical conditions and consequences of the action. This principle of quantitative correspondence between knowledge and action led to the conclusion that only an omniscient being can, strictly speaking, act.

This limpidly systematic and excessively logical body of doctrine imposed itself henceforth on the educational institutions of Islam throughout the Middle Ages. It undoubtedly touched in its subtleties and logical *finesse* the lofty pinnacles of reasoning. But it is truly scholastic both in its spirit and its content: with all its subtle reasoning, it expressly formulated and, in the very process of this formulation, exhibited a fundamental lack of confidence in human reason. While nobody need quarrel on grounds of religion with its doctrine of Being and its theory of knowledge, wherein it performed a real service for Islam, it is difficult to defend its solution of the problem of freewill on religious grounds. On this central problem of religious consciousness, with which the very history of religious thought started in Islam, it had moved far beyond any reasonable distance from the spirit of the Qur'ān and the ethos of the early Community. Even with al-Ashʿarī and his early followers, the problem had retained its original moral urgency, but in the hands of the systematic theologian it became a purely doctrinaire pedantry.

There is a fairly common view among modern scholars, according to which this uncompromisingly transcendentalist picture of God, entailing a denial of trust in natural properties and the immanent processes of nature, and freedom of the human will, is to be based squarely on the Qur'ān or is, at least, the most logical development of its teaching. This judgment, examined in the light of the Qur'ān itself, seems considerably less than a half-truth. In the religious history of Islam, however, there were genuine factors for concern over the transcendence of God being compromised. In particular, the Dualist challenge seems to have been persistent in one form or another. Manichaean Dualism was combated and overcome in the early centuries, but was not destroyed. Then came the philosophical doctrine of the eternity of matter, which the Iranian Manichaean thinkers, like al-Suhrawardī, were not slow in interpreting in the spirit of their own ancient doctrine. But even after this challenge was no longer a living danger, the new challenge of pantheistic Ṣūfism prevented the *kalām*-orthodoxy from re-thinking its formulation of the dogma. The result was that on the question of freewill, the balance of forces was overwhelmingly weighted in favour of determinism in the Middle Ages. The philosophers argued for a pure rational determinism; Ṣūfism, on the basis of both the philosophical teaching and a peculiar interpretation of the theological doctrine of the Unity of God, advocated a monistic determinism, and *kalām* itself began to teach a complete theistic determinism. Together, these forces constitute the giant theoretical wheel of Medieval Islam revolving around the axis of Determinism. Further, for this theoretical conspiracy, a strong enough basis was provided in the concrete realities of life by the political situation where increasing despotism both sustained and was sustained by this theoretical attitude.

The Ahl al-Ḥadīth, enemies of philosophy and suspicious both of Ṣūfism and *kalām*, were the only group that remained outside this great wheel of Determinism. The vicissitudinous and multilateral relationship between this group, the *kalām* and Ṣūfism, with their uneasy alliances and tensions is what henceforth gave vitality to Islam as a religion and constitutes its story until the modern period. Before describing this interplay, however, we must study the development of the most central religious concept of Islam, that of the Sharī'a, which will put the developments we have examined so far into perspective and render subsequent history more intelligible.

CHAPTER SIX

THE SHARĪ'A

Preliminary – Development of the Concept of Sharī'a – The Traditionalist Reform: Ibn Taymīya – The Sharī'a and the Law

Preliminary

The most important and comprehensive concept for describing Islam *as a function* is the concept of the Sharī'a or 'Shar''. This word originally means 'the path or the road leading to the water', i.e. a way to the very source of life. The verb *shara'a* means literally 'to chalk out or mark out a clear road to water'. In its religious usage, from the earliest period, it has meant 'the highway of good life', i.e. religious values, expressed functionally and in concrete terms, to direct man's life. It differs from the term 'Sunna' in that the subject of the Sunna 'leads the way' by actual example and, therefore, his action as such is of the same kind as those who follow him in accepting the example, whereas the subject of Shar' shows or ordains the way and is, therefore, none else than God, the source of religious values.

The correlate of Sharī'a is Dīn, which literally means 'submission', 'following'. Whereas Sharī'a is the ordaining of the Way and its proper subject is God, Dīn is the following of that Way and its subject is man. It is in this correlative sense that the Qur'ān says: God 'hath ordained for you a Way-to-be-followed',[1] and again 'Do they, then, have any partners of God who have ordained for them the path-to-be-followed?'[2] But if we abstract from the Divine and the human points of reference, Sharī'a and Dīn would be identical as far as the 'Way' and its content are concerned. One may, therefore, so far as the Qur'ānic idiom goes, speak of Sharī'a and Dīn interchangeably so far as the content of religion is concerned. But since the basic mood of the Qur'ān is moral exhortation to man, i.e. to follow, submit and seek, assuming that the 'Way' for a genuine seeker 'is there', the terms Dīn and its almost equivalent Islam are used far more frequently in it than the term Sharī'a. For the Muslim Community, however, which had so submitted, the primary task was to explain the Sharī'a – the 'Way' or the 'Command of God'.

Development of the Concept of Sharī'a

From the very beginning, a definite practical intent was part of the concept of the Sharī'a: it is The Way, ordained by God, wherein man is to conduct his life in order to realize the Divine Will. It is a practical concept having to do with conduct as such. But it includes all behaviour – spiritual, mental and physical. Thus it comprehends both faith and practice: assent to or belief in one God is part of the Sharī'a just as are the religious duties of prayer and fasting, etc. Further, all legal and social transactions as well as all personal behaviour, is subsumed under the Sharī'a as the comprehensive principle of the *total way of life*. But the problem is: how is the Sharī'a *to be known*?

In the earliest period after the Prophet, two sources or methods were recognized for the explanation of the Sharī'a. On the one hand was the traditional source, the authoritative 'given' – i.e. the Qur'ān and the Sunna of the Prophet which must serve as the base. But since the 'given' could obviously not suffice for the developing needs of succeeding generations, the second principle of human intelligence and understanding was recognized almost from the outset. The first principle was called 'learning' (Arabic: *'ilm*, not 'knowledge' as it has been sometimes rendered); the second was called 'understanding' or 'comprehension' (Arabic *fiqh*).

Texts are not infrequent from this period drawing this contrasted but complementary distinction between 'learning' and 'understanding' and one often meets with such passages as 'so-and-so is good in *'ilm* but not so good in *fiqh*', or 'so-and-so excels both in *'ilm* – i.e. in his learning in traditions and the Qur'ān – and in *fiqh* – i.e. in his capacity to understand the traditional "given" and draw further deductions from it'. Now *fiqh* in this period is nothing other than the *ra'y* or the 'personal considered opinion' that we discussed in Chapter IV. This brings out the contrast between the *'ilm* and the *fiqh* in another form. For whereas *'ilm* is something unshakeably given and objective, *fiqh* is something subjective, since it represents the personal understanding of a scholar. This gives us one further point of contrast: whereas *'ilm* is both a process of learning and refers to an objective, organized and disciplined body of data, *fiqh*, at this stage, is not the name of a particular discipline or objective system, but only the name of a *process* or activity of understanding and deducing.[3]

But although *fiqh* and *'ilm* are thus distinguished as ways or avenues of knowledge, they are not distinct as regards their subject-matter which is identical. They are indeed applied universally to the entire range of knowledge. Thus, there is an *'ilm* of the Arabic language (i.e. learning of the traditional philological material) as well as an *'ilm* of religion;

and equally, there is a *fiqh* or appreciation of this *'ilm* as well as a *fiqh* of religious matters. Gradually, however, as the study of religious matters became preponderant, *fiqh* came to be restricted to the religious field. But still the whole range of religious thought was *fiqh* – belief as well as practice, dogma as well as law. Thus, a book attributed to the founder of the Ḥanafī school, Abū Ḥanīfa (d. 150/767), entitled *The Greater Fiqh*, is devoted entirely to dogmatic and theological questions.

In this early phase, which roughly extended to the middle of the 2nd/8th century, the *ensemble* of traditional learning and the exercise of free, individual reasoning upon it produced religious knowledge. But it is both interesting and important, to note that the term Sharī'a was seldom, if ever, applied to the result of this activity which was most usually called Dīn and the sum of knowledge in which it was established, 'knowledge of the Dīn'. And this is the case not only with reference to the dogma but also with regard to the law. The term Sharī'a (used in this period especially in the plural) is very rare and then it is used concerning certain specific injunctions of the Qur'ān. This contrasts strikingly with the overwhelming preponderance of the term Sharī'a in later Islam. This could, of course, be a pure accident and in so far as the concrete content of both Dīn and Sharī'a, as we have indicated above, is identical, may even seem unimportant. But there are two significant considerations which probably furnish the answer, one religious and the other, allied to the former, historical.

As for the religious factor, we have noted at the outset that the Qur'ān, anxious to regulate the attitude of the believer, speaks much more of Dīn, Imān (faith) and Islam than of Sharī'a. So long as the impulse of the Qur'ān was fresh and lively, the Muslim was more likely to stress his effort to submit to and follow God's guidance. Under this attitude, whatever the Muslim 'understood' of God's Sharī'a, he would naturally regard as his attempt at Dīn rather than claim it as Sharī'a from God. For it is up to God to know whether it is really Sharī'a, i.e. His Will, or not. Secondly, as a historical fact, as we have reiterated, *fiqh* or 'understanding' was a process rather than a consolidated body of knowledge and it was personal, free and somewhat subjective rather than an objective discipline. It would be impossible for any single person to claim that the result of *his* thought was the unique content of the Sharī'a. The task of spelling out the Sharī'a should rather devolve upon the Community as a whole, through the guidance of the 'Ulamā'.

In the next phase, which may be taken to begin around the middle of the 2nd/8th century, this is precisely what happened. We have outlined in Chapters III and IV the rise and development of that mechanism which constitutes the methodology of Islam. We have pointed out that in this mechanism for 'understanding' the Word of God and the exposition of that Word in the Sunna, the place of over-riding paramountcy is occupied by the institution of Ijmā' or the consensus of the Community. Our present argument gives the rationale of the historical fact of this development and shows that this development occurred by the necessity of an inner logic of the religious history of Islam. This does not deny the influence of foreign elements and especially the influence of certain precepts of Roman Law, much discussed by scholars, but insists that essentially the genesis and the structural character of Islamic methodology are to be explained on internal Islamic grounds rather than on the basis of foreign influences.

With the establishment of Islamic methodology (i.e. interrelationship of Sunna, *ijtihād* and Ijmā') a radical change took place in the nature of *fiqh* which passed from being a personal activity to mean a structured discipline and its resultant body of knowledge. This body of knowledge was thus standardized and established as an objective system. *Fiqh became an 'ilm.* Whereas in the first stage one used to say 'one should *exercise fiqh* ("understanding")', the proper thing to say now was 'one should "learn" or "study" *fiqh*'. But what was the content of this *Fiqh* (which, as a discipline or science, we write here with a capital 'F')?

At the same time when the system of Islamic methodology was fully developed, it seems to have become restricted to law and jurisprudence. *Fiqh* became identified with the science of law. It does not seem to the present writer that the explanation sometimes advanced[4] – viz. that the term *fiqh* was adopted to correspond to the *jurisprudentia* of the Roman Law – explains this change adequately. The change, indeed, was so far-reaching and affected the future development of religion so profoundly that a purely philological explanation such as the one suggested seems utterly trivial. Let us, therefore, seek an answer in the events that occurred in Islam itself.

We have noticed earlier in this chapter that in the first stage *fiqh* and *'ilm* both applied to the whole of the religious field and that dogma, morals, law were all embraced by these two terms. From the very beginning, however, there is to be seen a preoccupation with law rather than say theology. It may be said that this was because curiosity in theological and purely moral issues was not yet fully aroused as it became in the 2nd/8th century. But there is also the fact that the actual state of affairs required legal thinking as an immediate desideratum. And although this legal thought has, from the outset, a school-room character, there is little doubt that the material on which it operated was the concretely given situation of legal practice in a real administrative and judicial environment.

But besides these factors, perhaps the most crucial was the native tendency amounting almost to reticence towards purely theological issues. An unconscious type of reasoning lies behind this attitude which looks upon discussions about the nature of God as being at best foolhardy adventures. It is to be noted that the Qur'ān itself contains only a modicum of theological doctrine, the minimal essential for religion. It is certain that those traditions which positively discourage theological speculation such as 'Do not cogitate on God but on the creation of God' or 'Earlier communities perished because they plunged into discussions of *qadar* (Divine Will)' express the most ancient attitudes of Muslims, even if they do not verbally go back to the Prophet. It is almost sinful to exercise human reason on God. This attitude, as we have seen in the previous chapter, was kept intact by the Ahl al-Ḥadīth throughout the ages. But when the throbs of moral and theological speculation were generated with full energy within the body of Islam, *fiqh* and Sharī'a were isolated from rationalism as such, which came to be denoted by the term *'aql*.

In the pre-speculative and pre-controversy period, reason (*fiqh*) and tradition (*'ilm*) were regarded as complementary and there is no doubt that in the ancient Muslim attitude reason and revelation or reason and Sharī'a were not distinct. But in the later 2nd/8th and 3rd/9th centuries, the Mu'tazila rationalists introduced an opposition between *'aql* (reason) and *sam'* (tradition or authority) or Sharī'a. By this time law had been fixed by Ijmā' and the methodology of legislation had been established. It had, thereby, become a part of authority or tradition, bringing about a change in the concept *fiqh*, as we have seen. The Mu'tazila, in general, accepted this legal structure, together with such moral precepts and maxims as it contained as part and parcel of the established authority (*sam'* or *shar'*). But they declared both theology and basic moral principles to be fit objects for the human reason to investigate; Good and bad, they held, was not *shar'ī* or ordained by Divine law but *'aqlī* or rational (cf. the Stoic distinction between that which is 'by nature' [*φύσει*] and that which is 'ordained' [*Θέσει*]. God has forbidden killing because it is bad; it is not bad because God has forbidden it.

The Mu'tazila did not, then, question the binding and divinely ordained character of the law but restricted the concept of the Sharī'a to it and in a real sense isolated it from the basic moral principles of right and wrong and from theological metaphysics wherein they advocated almost untrammelled freedom for human reason. The right wing of the orthodoxy opposed this. They exerted themselves to keep ethics and theology as well as law within the concept of the Sharī'a. As for reason, they accentuated the Power and Will of God as opposed to the Muʿtazilite idea of Divine justice, as outlined in the last chapter. They did not defend the thesis that God's actions are irrational or non-rational but that what God ought to do cannot be dictated by human reason and that from a religious point of view it is wisest to attribute God's actions to His Will. The Muʿtazilite offensive forced the extreme wing of orthodoxy, therefore, to change the pre-controversial attitude of ancient Islam and explicitly to reject human reason.

In the synthesis of the orthodox Ashʿarite *kalām* which emerged in the 4th/10th century, a compromise was undoubtedly attempted from this point of view. All the *practical* issues, including law and ethics, that impinge on actual, concrete life were given to the authority of the Sharīʿa or the Divine Commandment, but all purely theological and metaphysical issues were given to *ʿaql* (reason). One very fundamental result of this development was the isolation of theology from law and morality. This produced a sharp distinction between Sharīʿa and Dīn which in the beginning were identical, as we have argued early on in this chapter. Theology was installed as 'Principles of the Religion' (*Uṣūl al-Dīn*), moral and legal precepts as the Sharīʿa. This is clearly brought out by the following passage from al-Ashʿarī:

[The early generations] have discussed and disputed about such matters as arose at that time concerning Dīn from the side of the Sharīʿa (i.e. law) . . . like the legal duties . . . such as punishments and divorce which are too numerous to mention here. . . .
. . . Now, these are legal matters which pertain to details of life and which they (i.e. the early generations) brought under the Sharīʿa which concerns itself with the detailed conduct of life (*furūʿ*) and hence can never be comprehended except on the authority that comes from the Prophets. But as for the matters that arise in the field of the principles for the determination of questions (of Faith) every intelligent Muslim must refer these to the general and agreed principles founded upon reason, sense-experience and immediate knowledge, etc. Thus the questions of details of the Sharīʿa (i.e. law), which are based on traditional authority, must be referred to the principles of the Sharīʿa whose source is traditional authority, whereas questions arising out of reason and experience must be referred to their own bases, and authority and reason must never be mixed up.[5]

The re-inclusion of morality under Sharīʿa, against the Muʿtazila, was based on an attempt to show that reason, in fact, yielded no universal moral principles. The state of natural rationality, in a contention not unlike Hobbes, led to a state of *bellum omnium contra omnes* wherein each individual regards that as 'good' which is in conformity with his own desires and the opposite of this as bad.[6] Even the so-called universal proposition of rational ethics, e.g. 'Telling lies is bad' was said to derive its pseudo-universality from the fact that this dictum is applicable in *most*, not all cases.[7] The Mu'tazila strongly protested against this denial of universality of rationalistic ethics:

Your discourse comes to this: that (rational) 'good' and 'bad' are reducible to being conducive to and thwarting desires. But we see that a rational being regards as good that wherein he does not (necessarily) see any benefit and (sometimes) regards as bad that wherein he may find benefit. . . . If someone sees a man or an animal on the verge of perishing, he regards it as good to save him . . . although not believing in the Sharī'a and even when he does not expect any benefit from this in this world, and even though this may occur in a place where there is nobody to see him and praise him for doing so. We may indeed suppose the absence of every (selfish) motive. . . . It is clear then that 'good' and 'bad' have a meaning other than what you have described.[8]

In his reply, al-Ghazālī vigorously defends his utilitarian account of rationalist ethics by undertaking a psychological analysis of motivation. The rescuer, he insists, is primarily led to save a living being in danger, because if he does not do so this would hurt his own natural strong feelings of compassion: he is thus satisfying himself by rescuing the person in danger. Further, he thinks that if he himself were in danger and a person capable of rescuing him did not do so, he would not like this. And so on.[9] But if pure reason in its natural state is incapable of yielding moral principles, still less is it capable of producing positive obligations (*wājibāt*). Both must flow from the Sharī'a or the divinely ordained Path and al-Ghazālī concludes decisively, 'No obligations flow from reason but from the Sharī'a'.[10]

Thus, morality and law constitute Sharī'a. But what about theology? Here, as described in the previous chapter, al-Ghazālī, following an earlier development of orthodox Ṣūfism, struck a synthesis. Dissatisfied with the logical formalism of the *kalām*, he sought to integrate the Ṣūfī method with the formulations of the *kalām* and strongly advocated the 'living through' or 'interiorization' of purely rational beliefs which he regarded as being unworthy of a living faith. Further, this synthesis, worked out into a programme of inner, spiritual purification culminating in the single-minded love of God, he declared to be the true meaning of the Sharī'a. This inwardness of the faith he called Dīn. The Dīn is then the essence of the Sharī'a, its inner life. The Sharī'a without the Dīn is an empty shell and the Dīn without the Sharī'a obviously cannot exist.

But although al-Ghazālī established a necessary and intimate connection between the two, the Dīn and the Sharī'a still retained a certain duality and the pristine and original identity of the two was not restored. Indeed, it is significant that he entitled his *magnum opus* on religion *Revivification of the Sciences of the Dīn* rather than of the Sharīʿa. After him, a new type of religious literature grew up, viz. 'the science of the inner meanings of the Faith (*ʿilm asrār al-Dīn*)' which undoubtedly performed a great service in grounding the Sharīʿa on enduring spiritual bases or, as al-Ghazālī himself put it, on 'the subtle and difficult middle course between the utter free-lancing [of the pure rationalists] and the stolidity of the Ḥanbalites'.[11] But the dualism of the inner and the outer was not exorcised and the precarious balance was disrupted by subsequent developments characterized by a conflict between Ṣūfism and the Sharīʿa.

Henceforth, theology itself split into two distinct types: the dogmatic and formally rational theology of the *kalām* and the speculative theology of Ṣūfism. As for the latter, it developed on lines completely its own under the auspices of its sharply formulated cleavage between the Sharīʿa and the mystic 'truth' as we shall study subsequently. The dogmatic theology, whose course and content we have described in the previous chapter, continued to defend the credal structure of the Sharīʿa with rational weapons re-invigorated by the new philosophical material. But as soon as this happened, the scope of the science of theology came under question. Some advocated a separation of theology and metaphysics, the former restricting itself to the defence of the creed, the latter investigating the ultimate problems of philosophy *proper*.[12] But the majority of theologians feared that this would set up a branch of knowledge beyond and above the Sharīʿa and rejected this view. Thus although they adopted a good deal from the doctrines of the pure philosophers, including the philosophical doctrine of the natural development of the (Prophetic) intellect,[13] they insisted that the task of theology is merely to *defend* by rational arguments the *tenets* of the creed and not to *investigate* and *interpret* by rational methods.[14] The result was that whereas the religious dogma remained the same in form as well as in content, without any substantial reinterpretation, the complicated and sophisticated formulas and arguments borrowed from philosophy became inaccessible to the common man.

Theology thus monopolized the whole field of metaphysics and would not allow pure *thought* any claim to investigate rationally the nature of the universe and the nature of man. It thus claimed for itself the title of the 'highest science of the Sharīʿa' as the formulator of the 'Principles of the Faith' (*Uṣūl al-Dīn*).[15] The Sharīʿa thus became once more identical with Dīn. But in the meantime the law had developed apart from theology and although the legists had recognized all along the validity of the *kalām*-theology as defender of the Faith, the authorities of the law now dictated to theology what problems it should deal with and what its scope should be.

The jurist al-Shāṭibī (d. 790/1388), who belongs to the generation immediately succeeding that of the theologian-philosopher al-Ījī, wrote a work entitled *Kitāb al-Muwāfaqāt* on the philosophy of law and jurisprudence. He not only advocated the separation of strict matters of Faith from the science of law but condemned outright theoretical and purely intellectual discussions as being anti-Sharī'a and thus outside the scope of theology:

Every problem in jurisprudence on which law may be based but controversy over which does not lead to difference in actual legislation, it is entirely superfluous to defend or refute any definite view concerning it. . . . Thus . . . the controversy [between the orthodox and the Mu'tazila] is a credal one based on a principle established in theology, although it finds *expression* in juristic terms also, viz. Are obligatoriness and prohibition . . . referable to qualities of things themselves [i.e. are they discoverable by natural reason?], or do they originate in the Sharī'a commandments?. . . .[16]

And, again, pronouncing not on law but on the Sharī'a as such: 'Investigation into any question which is not a basis for an action is not recommended by any proof from the Sharī'a. By acts I mean both mental and physical acts' (vol. I, p. 46). 'The philosophers assert that the essence of philosophy is to investigate the existents in general. . . . These are, then, the proofs for an absolute recommendation of all knowledge in general. The answer is . . . that this general recommendation is really specific' (p. 52). 'And so is the case with every branch of learning that claims a relationship with the Sharī'a, but does not (directly) benefit action, nor was it known to the Arabs' (p. 54).

Al-Shāṭibī goes on to contend that it is useless and 'outside the pale of the Sharī'a' to search for scientific definitions which ought to be as direct and practical as possible – not only for law but in general. It is much better to define a star as 'that (shining object) which we see at night' rather than as 'a simple circular body whose natural place is the heaven', etc.

The points made so far are (1) that in the beginning although the term Sharī'a or Shar' was relatively little used, its use is commensurate with that of the term Dīn according as whether the point of departure is God or man; (2) that the crucial point at which the word Sharī'a becomes common is characterized by the controversy as to whether it is reason or the Sharī'a that yields moral principles and practical norms; (3) that, therefore, Sharī'a began to be applied rather to law than to theology, which, making use of rational arguments, was termed Dīn rather than Sharī'a; (4) that in its later development, theology came once again within the scope of the Sharī'a and indeed claimed to be the highest and ultimate science of the Sharī'a; but, finally, (5) that law in fact had developed independently of theology and not only was it difficult to forge a real, living link between the two but that the legists in fact claimed the law was the manifestation of the Sharīʿa *par excellence* and even positively discouraged theological and other allied and auxiliary studies and sciences.

The Traditionalist Reform: Ibn Taymīya

The four major currents characterizing religious life in Islam and, to an ever increasing extent, dividing it among themselves from the 4th/10th century onward, viz. rationalism, Ṣūfism, theology and law, could only be synthesized and integrated under some comprehensive *religious* concept like that of the Sharīʿa. This concept, however, as our foregoing historical account has shown, was, from the very moment that it came into common use, used by the rationalists in opposition to reason and identified with the law. Next, it was used by the Ṣūfīs in opposition to the mystic 'truth' (*ḥaqīqa*) and applied to the law. The theologians themselves, as we have just seen, at first used it to distinguish law from theology although gradually it came to be applied to the latter as well. The discord between Sharīʿa *thus used* and reason, and between Sharīʿa and the mystic truth, as used by the rationalists and the Ṣūfī adepts respectively, is obvious. But, within orthodox circles, the discord between the *kalām* theology and the bases of law is not less deep, although it may not be so obvious because it was claimed that this theology had been expressly evolved to defend the law.

In his orthodox synthesis of the Muʿtazila doctrine of human freewill and the traditionists' stand in favour of the Omnipotence of God, as we have seen in the last chapter, al-Ashʿarī had accentuated the Will of God and His creation of the human act, although he had sought to retain human responsibility. Al-Ashʿarī, on close examination, cannot be called a theistic determinist because he expressly distinguished between the voluntary and involuntary actions of man.[17] Indeed, al-Ashʿarī's doctrine of God's creation, through His Will, of all human actions (and, indeed, any event whatsoever) has nothing to do with the question of determinism and free-will. His assertion is simply that nothing whatever occurs without the Will and Power of God. Nevertheless, both al-Ashʿarī and his successors, when pressed to explain their doctrine of the 'acquisition' by man of his acts (created by God), treated the problem as though man and God were rival powers in the production of acts, capable of being substitutes for one another: and thus they came to deny the efficacy of the human will in favour of God's and defined the production of acts as being simply 'occasioned by' or being 'conjoined with' human volition. As we have also seen, this doctrine, corroborated both by the philosophical doctrine of natural necessity and the Ṣūfī doctrine of God as the Sole Existent, developed, during the next two centuries, into a veritable doctrine of rigorous fatalism. This was made worse by two other Ash'arite doctrines. First, in order to raise God above the human categories of 'purpose' and 'justice' which were central themes of the Mu'tazila, the Ash'arites rejected the attribution of either to God. Secondly, in their doctrine of atomism, the Ash'arites denied causation and along with it the idea of potentialities or capacities latent in things.

But no law worthy of the name can be based on these concepts. Law requires that the human being be both free and efficacious. It requires that man be possessed of objective powers and capacities. Further, the concept of Divine Law, which the Sharī'a is, requires that both purpose and justice be attributed to God or else the whole idea of Divine Command and Prohibition falls to the ground. And, indeed, the collaboration of *kalām* and Ṣūfism (and philosophy) in *substituting* the Will and Efficacy of God for His Sharī'a or Command, constitutes the greater part of the religious history of medieval Islam.

We have briefly described above al-Ghazālī's attempt at the synthesis which constitutes the first landmark of the religious integrative capacity of Islam. But al-Ghazālī's impulse being essentially of personal purity and piety, his synthesis has a decisively personal character. His reform of theology and law consists fundamentally in giving them a personal meaningfulness and depth. Without his work, it is no exaggeration to say, Ṣūfism and philosophic rationalism might well have made a clean sweep of the Islamic ethos. Against the philosophers' First Cause and the Prime Mover, al-Ghazālī brought to the fore the 'Command' of the Qur'ān. Against the formulas of the theologians and the pantheism of the Ṣūfīs, he resuscitated the living God who demands and fulfils, who inspires genuine hope and fear.

Al-Ghazālī's work may be described as a bilateral synthesis between theology and Ṣūfism on the one hand and law and Ṣūfism on the other. Ṣūfism stands in the centre, which is in perfect consonance with the personal character of al-Ghazālī's reform. But al-Ghazālī did not reform the content of orthodox theology. Nor did he bring theology into a genuine contact with the law, again because of his preoccupation with personal piety. Indeed, he does not seem to have taken the law seriously. For, the Sharī'a cannot remain personal, even though it must be grounded in a personal understanding and acceptance. Indeed, law is essentially a non-personal phenomenon. And we may recall the fact with a fresh realization of its force that al-Ghazālī's *magnum opus* is devoted not to the Sharī'a but to Dīn. On the balance of the religious forces as they existed in the 7th/13th century, the traditionists (Ahl al-Ḥadīth) were the only group who were not in any of the currents we have described but who stood observing and waiting. And, just as they had appeared at an early religious point in Islam in the form of these forces which were behind al-Ashʿarī, now from their ranks emerged the dynamic personality of Taqī al-Dīn ibn Taymīya (661–728/1263–1328).

It is, indeed, a curious and striking fact about the religious history of Islam that at each critical point of its career the force that comes to the forefront and takes over the situation is not the then formalized established 'orthodoxy' but rather something that presents itself at every juncture as the 'raw material' of the orthodoxy subsequently to be formed. In itself this force is something nondescript and for want of a better designation is called by such terms as 'Ahl al-Ḥadīth' or 'Ahl al-Sunna' by the Muslims themselves and identified as 'conservative' or 'orthodox' by modern Western scholars. But the Ahl al-Ḥadīth or the Ahl al-Sunna is not the name of any particular group, sect or party; and if there is an 'orthodoxy' or a 'conservatism', this is surely the one that is an 'orthodoxy' or a 'conservatism', this is surely the one that is in ascendancy at the point of time concerned. To some extent, of course, this happens with all developing religions. But whereas in Christianity, or even in as little 'reified' a religion as Hinduism, there is something that runs through it like a wave with the new elements riding on its crest, Islamic orthodoxy seems to develop in recreated formations of quanta that issue from time to time from the very heart of Islam. It is characterized by an indistinguishable blend of reinvigorated fundamentalism and progressivism: it develops not by self-propulsion, so to say, but by watching, adjusting and absorbing within itself that which moves within it. It is a synthetic activity and this very character it is that signifies 'orthodoxy' as we remarked in Chapter V.

Ibn Taymīya's programme fundamentally consists of a restatement of the Sharīʿa and a vindication of religious values. Sharīʿa is a comprehensive concept and includes the spiritual truth of the Ṣūfī (*ḥaqīqa*), the rational truth (*ʿaql*) of the philosopher and the theologian, and the law. This 'inclusiveness' is not formal and 'aggregative' but points to a religious quality which is the source of these three. 'Traditional authority' and 'reason' may, indeed, be distinguished and even opposed, but Sharīʿa and 'reason' cannot be meaningfully opposed: 'The fact that a proof is rational or is based on authority is not in itself an object of condemnation or appreciation, or itself a guarantee of truth or falsity. "Authority" and "reason" are only avenues of knowledge although "traditional authority" can never be divorced from "reason". But the fact that something is a Sharīʿa-value cannot be validly opposed to something being rational. . . .'[18]

Similarly, the concept of the Sharīʿa as being a collection of purely external legal precepts and decisions, divorced from their inner bases, must be rejected. This dichotomy was rendered popular by the Ṣūfī movement. On the contrary, the Sharīʿa is that which makes law possible and just and which integrates the legal and the spiritual into one living religious whole. Commenting on different opinions concerning the execution of the Ṣūfī al-Ḥallāj (see the Chapter on Ṣūfism), Ibn Taymīya has an important and interesting passage which clearly shows that contrary to the opinion generally held, he was not only not inimical to Ṣūfism as such, but considered it as necessary, a part of religion as law:

These people (who regard al-Ḥallāj as having been unjustly slain) are two parties. One party says that he was unjustly killed . . . and they regard the Sharīʿa and its protagonists as their enemies. . . . Some are against all lawyers and scholars believing that they have killed al-Ḥallāj. These are the kind of people who say, 'We have a law (Sharīʿa) and we have a "truth" (*ḥaqīqa*) which contradicts that law'. People who talk in this way do not understand clearly the distinction in the meanings of the word Sharīʿa as employed in the Speech of God and His Apostle (on the one hand) and by common people on the other. . . . Indeed, some of them think that Sharīʿa is the name given to the judge's decisions; many of them even do not make a distinction between a learned judge, an ignorant judge and an unjust judge. Worse still, people tend to regard any decrees of a ruler as Sharīʿa, while sometimes undoubtedly the truth (*ḥaqīqa*) is actually contrary to the decree of the ruler.

The Prophet himself said: 'You people bring disputes to me; but it may be that some of you are able to put their case better than others. But I have to decide on evidence that is before me. If I happen to expropriate the right of anyone in favour of his brother let the latter not take it, for in that case I have given him a piece of hell-fire'. Thus, the judge decided on the strength of depositions and evidence that are before him while the party decided against may well have proofs that have not been put forward. In such cases the Sharīʿa in reality is just the opposite of the external law, although the decision of the judge has to be enforced. In many cases the inner truth is contrary to what appears to some people. . . . In this case if it is said that the inner truth is the opposite of the externals, this will be true, but to call the inner 'the Truth' and the externals 'the Sharīʿa' is a semantic question.

But there are people according to whom 'the Truth' is the 'inner' absolutely and the Sharīʿa concerns only the externals. This is just as 'Islam', when it is juxtaposed to 'faith', means external acts, whereas by 'faith' is meant that which is in the heart. . . . Thus, by a juxtaposition, one speaks of the 'Sharīʿa (laws) of Islam' and the 'truths of faith', which distinction may be (technically) valid. But when each is used by itself alone, a person possessing only the law, without the inner truth, cannot be called truly a man of faith, and, similarly, a person possessed of a bare 'truth' which is in disagreement with the Sharīʿa . . . cannot be even a Muslim, let alone being a pious saint of God.

> Sometimes by 'Sharī'a' is meant that which the lawyers of the Sharī'a say on the basis of their own effort of thought, and by the 'truth' is intended what the Ṣūfīs find by direct experience. Undoubtedly, both these groups are seekers of truth; sometimes they are right and sometimes wrong while neither of them wish to contravene the Prophet. If the findings of both agree well and good, otherwise neither of them has an exclusive claim to be followed, except by a clear proof from the Sharī'a.[19]

Having formulated the concept of the Sharī'a in this comprehensive spirit, it is necessary to establish a real and living contact between theology and law lest the former become arid formulas and the latter an empty, rigid and lifeless shell. But in order to do this it is necessary to reformulate theology. Ibn Taymīya does not even use the term *kalām* for his theology which he more usually calls 'science of the Unity of God'. A radical re-orientation of theology is, indeed, needed, for the doctrine of the Divine Will (*qadar*), accepted and one-sidedly developed by the 'official' theology, undermines the religious moral life. A sharp distinction is required between the omnipotent Will of God and God's function as the Commander. If the former is needed by religious *belief*, the latter is the pivot of religious *action*: 'The Divine Power and Will is not an argument for anyone over against God and His Creation. . . . Thus, the *qadar* is an object of faith, but cannot be the premise of an argument, he who does not believe in *qadar* is like the Magians (i.e. the Dualists), but he who argues from it (in the sphere of action) is like the polytheists (who argued against Muḥammad that if God had willed they would not have been polytheists).'[20]

Especially guilty of the furtherance of moral laxity is the Ṣūfī doctrine which states that 'he who witnesses the Will of God feels no longer bound by the Command of God'. It is an infidelity which the Jews and the Christians also reject and which is impossible both rationally and religiously.[21] But the conceptual groundwork for this negative philosophy has been provided by the 'official' theology itself which, having regarded God and man as rivals, so to say, gave the entire field to God. Thereby theologians shut themselves off from the Divine imperatives which are the spring of religious life. Ibn Taymīya praises in this connection the Mu'tazila who at least kept the idea of good and evil, of Divine Commands and Prohibitions as a live religious force.[22] This is characteristic of Ibn Taymīya, who, contrary to the general belief about him, shows an extraordinary lack of prejudice and an open-mindedness to all opinions and constantly makes such pronouncements as 'the truth does not belong to one party exclusively but is divided among all groups'.

Accordingly, Ibn Taymīya reinstates into Muslim theology the doctrine of the purposiveness of the Divine behaviour, a doctrine so strenuously denied by Ash'arism, Māturīdism and Ẓāhirism as compromising the omnipotence of God's will and His dissimilarity to His creation. This purposiveness is God's involvement in the destiny of man and from this he directly deduces the idea of God as the Commander or the Sharī'a-Giver. He next strives to distinguish the planes at which the Will and Wisdom of God are respectively meaningful. The Will and Power of God are the efficient cause, but His Command or the Sharī'a is the final cause of His activity.[23] The omnipotence of God must not be denied for whatever comes to be, is through His Power, but to explain events in this way, to affirm the efficient cause is to look backwards 'towards the beginning'. But the Sharī'a, the Wisdom and the Command of God, is forward-looking, 'towards the end and the purpose'.[24]

Ibn Taymīya bluntly points out the discord that exists at bottom between the Sunnī orthodox theological formulas and the presuppositions of the law: 'You will find many jurists involved in self-contradiction. Thus, when they think along with the theologians who affirm the sole Power of God by saying that the (human) power and efficacy (does not precede) the act (but is created by God) together with the act, they agree with this. But when they think in terms of law, they have to affirm a preceding (and free) human power which is the foundation of the Command and the Prohibition.'[25] The human power and the Divine Power are not, indeed, mutually exclusive rivals to determine and produce the human act. The Sharī'a, in order to be possible at all, requires free human agency. If what is possible is coextensive with the actual, then the Qur'ānic saying, 'Fear God as much as is possible for you' must be translated as 'Fear God as much as you do fear', and the Prophet's dictum, 'When I command you something, act upon it to the best of your ability' should be rephrased as 'When I command you something, do what you do', a senseless proposition, indeed.[26] Certainly, what is possible cannot be coextensive with what is humanly possible but it would be absurd to conclude from this that nothing, in fact, is humanly possible.

The influence of Ibn Taymīya remained restricted to his immediate disciples and did not issue forth into a movement. In the long run, however, it seeped gradually through the religious intelligentsia and the 12th/18th century Wahhābī movement was only one, if the most organized and spectacular, of its manifestations. We shall see in Chapter VIII, while dealing with Ṣūfism, how similar movements subsequently grew within Ṣūfism, which brought Ṣūfī thought and practice closer to orthodox Islam. There is visible, in fact, a widespread trend, of which Ibn Taymīya's is the most forceful example, which ultimately resulted in those reform movements of various shades that characterized Islam immediately before the impingement upon it of modern Western influences. This explains why many modern Western scholars have observed on more than one point that the influence of Ibn Taymīya is a major signpost for the accumulation of forces that we shall describe in the chapter on the pre-modernist Reform Movements (Chapter XII).

The Sharī'a and the Law

The religious developments that took place from al-Ghazālī to Ibn Taymīya visibly affected legal science. The legal theory whose history we outlined in Chapter IV was exclusively devoted to the task of establishing and elaborating the mechanism for creating laws and deducing particular legal enactments from the Qur'ān and the Sunna. The 'Principles of Law' (*Uṣūl al-fiqh*) were just this mechanism. But now a philosophy of law developed which discussed and elaborated the moral-religious bases of the law – 'the objectives of the law' (*maqāṣid al-Shar'*) or 'the intentions of the Sharī'a obligations' (*asrār al-taklīf*). A series of brilliant scholars and thinkers from the 8th/14th to the 12th/18th century sought to work out the rational, moral and spiritual foundations of the legal system of Islam. Thus, Abū Isḥāq al-Shāṭibī speaks of his philosophy of law as infusing 'spirit into the dead body and real substance into the external shell (of the law)'.[27] As we have seen in the case of Ibn Taymīya, a central problem also of all these philosophies of law is to prove how moral obligation is related to Divine Omnipotence and Will and how the former in fact necessarily flows from the latter.[28]

The Sharī'a itself is defined as comprising both 'the acts of the heart as well as *overt* acts'.[29] It is indeed the assembly of Divine imperatives to man, imperatives which are frankly admitted to be primarily of a moral character. The Sharī'a is thus not an actual formal code of particular and specific enactments but is coterminous with the 'good'. But, surprisingly, little attempt was made to *rethink* and reformulate the actual body of the *fiqh* – the earlier attempts at actual legislation by the representatives of the four schools of law. For this the main reason seems to be that this law was looked upon as flowing necessarily from the principles of the Qur'ān and the Sunna and was further *consecrated* by Ijmā'. The Ijmā', as we have said in Chapter IV, was considered final, the 'gate of *ijtihād*' (original thinking) was closed and, therefore, no thinker, however bold, dared to touch it.

As we have also hinted in Chapter IV, the *motivation* behind the acceptance of the Ijmā' as final in the 4th/10th century was to ensure permanence and stability to this legal system since it had passed through great conflicts and controversies through its formative period. But in course of time it became rigid, its rigidity being softened only by casuistries which, however, further tended to make it ineffective. It was mainly also because of this hardening process that in the Middle Ages the secular authorities produced the body of secular law known as the *qānūn* which at times supplemented and at others supplanted the Sharī'a law. Once the *concept* of the Divine Law was thus restricted, a grievous blow was dealt to it and to the prestige of the Sharī'a legists themselves.

The fact that no real and effective boundaries were drawn between the moral and the strictly legal in Islamic law (a fact which we observed at the end of Chapter IV) must have also contributed to the fact that law was regarded as immutable. But this argument can be pushed too far and would not hold good for the early, creative phase of Islamic law. Indeed, the Muslim law books are full of moralizing themes and discuss at length, for example, the concept 'intention' not merely from a legal point of view but from the deeply religious ethical angle. But this has, in general, kept the moral fibre alive with a keen sensitivity to right and wrong. And a living moral sense is in any age better for humanity than an expediently clever and effective law. Indeed, it will become clear from our treatment of Modern Islam (Chapter XIII) that the real charge of the practitioners of the Sharī'a against modernist reformers is not so much that the latter contravene the law of the Qur'ān and the Sunna, but that the secularist has no ethic beyond the expedient and the utilitarian (even though much of the time neither side correctly understands the other).

CHAPTER SEVEN

THE PHILOSOPHICAL MOVEMENT

The Philosophical Tradition – Orthodoxy and Philosophy – Philosophic Religion

The Philosophical Tradition

Early scholastic theology, under the influence of 2nd/8th century Arabic translations of works of Greek philosophy and science, branched off and developed into a vigorous and brilliant movement of scientific and philosophical thought which produced works of great value and originality from the 3rd/9th to the 6th/12th centuries. Our object here is not to describe this thought as such, nor to assess its influence on medieval European scholasticism, but to trace its powerful impact on Islamic thought and its development both by way of absorption and reaction. Instead of giving the individual philosophical doctrines of several philosophers (who may be studied in works on Islamic philosophy), we shall find it convenient to consider their overall conclusions which, so far as the Islamic creed is concerned, are generally uniform, and came to fruition in the comprehensive system of Ibn Sīnā (370–428/980–1037) generally known to the West under the Latinized name of Avicenna.

The materials with which this philosophical system was constructed were either Greek or deduced from Greek ideas; in its material or content aspect, therefore, it is Hellenistic throughout. But the actual construction, the system itself, has an indubitably Islamic stamp: all along its metaphysical frontiers it reckons with the corresponding religious metaphysics of Islam and consciously tries to create points not only of contact but of coincidence with the latter. But this it does only in so far as the rational Greek character of the material would allow. Herein lies both its brilliant originality and its tragic fate in Islamic history; for, having failed to satisfy orthodox requirements, it was denied the passport to survival.

Over against the orthodox dogma of creation, it upheld the doctrine of the eternity of the world. But in order to do justice to religious consciousness, it affirmed that the world was an eternal effect of God *vis-à-vis* whom it had a unilateral relationship of absolute dependence.

In the making of this doctrine, it sought the help of the monistic Neo-platonic doctrine of emanation and discarded the Aristotelian theory of the dualism between God and Matter. Matter, therefore, instead of being an existent *per se* independently of God, was derived ultimately from God at the end of an emanation process. It further sought to draw a fundamental distinction between God and the World, to soften even the rigours of emanation, with the categories of necessity and contingence: God is the Necessary Being, this world is contingent. Orthodox theology accepted this distinction and built upon it its other doctrines but rejected the doctrine of the eternity of the world.

On the basis of the Plotinian idea of the ultimate ground of Reality, the One of Plotinus, as interpreted by his followers and endowed with a mind that contained the essences of all things, the philosophers re-interpreted and elaborated the Mu'tazilite doctrine of the Unity of God. According to the new doctrine, God was represented as Pure Being without essence or attributes, His only attribute being necessary existence. The attributes of the Deity were declared to be either negations or purely external relations, not affecting His Being and reducible to His necessary existence. God's knowledge was thus defined as 'non-absence of knowable things from Him'; His Will as 'impossibility of constraint upon His Being'; His creative activity as 'emanation of things from Him', etc. In the framework of the Greek theories of Aristotle and Plotinus, it was impossible that God should know particulars: He could cognize only universals since a cognition of the particular would introduce change in the Divine Mind both in the sense of a temporal succession and a change of different objects. But this theory could hardly be accepted by any religion for which a direct relationship between the individual and the Deity forms the core of interest. Accordingly, Avicenna devised a clever theory which would do justice both to the demands of religion and the requisites of his philosophy. God, according to this theory, knew all the particulars since He, being the ultimate cause of all things, necessarily knew the whole causal process. Thus, God knew from eternity that, for example, a solar eclipse would occur, with all its particular characteristics, at a particular point of the causal process.[1] This type of knowledge would require no change in the Divine knowledge since it removes the necessity of perceptual knowledge which occurs at a definite time and place.

From Greek epistemological and metaphysical theories, again, the Muslim philosophers acquired the idea of a radical dualism between body and mind, which under Greco-Christian influences had also developed into an out-and-out ethical dualism between the material and the spiritual. This affected the Muslim philosophers' eschatological teaching very fundamentally. The philosopher al-Fārābī (d. 339/950) held that only the soul survived in an individual and, further, that only the souls of thinkers survived, 'undeveloped' minds being destroyed at death.[2] Ibn Sīnā held that all human souls survived, body being unresurrectible, although he allowed that souls, after being separated from their bodies, especially those that are 'undeveloped' but morally virtuous, felt a kind of 'physical' pleasure since they were incapable of experiencing purely mental states. But in general he taught that the resurrection of the body was an imaginative myth with which the minds of the Prophets were inspired in order to influence the moral character of the unthinking masses.[3] Ibn Rushd (Averroes, d. 594/1198), the Spanish Arab philosopher who introduced medieval Europe to Aristotle in his own interpretation, came nearer to orthodox Islam with his doctrine that although the same body could not be identically resurrected, a numerically different but qualitatively identical body, a *simulacrum*, would be supplied.[4]

Having thus reached a stage of consciousness where the entire philosophical metaphysic seemed to correspond, point by point, to theological beliefs of religion but never exactly tallied with the latter, a general problem was raised before the philosophers about the nature of religion and philosophy and their mutual relationship. Either there was a double truth, one apprehended by philosophy, the other by religion, or the truth was unitary but appeared now in rational, and again in a metaphorical, imaginative form. The first alternative, that of two truths, did not seem possible rationally and so the philosophers decided to pursue the latter line of thought. Religious truth is but rational truth, but instead of being expressed in nakedly rational formulas, manifested itself in imaginative symbols – a fact which was responsible for its widespread acceptance by, and effectiveness among, the masses. Thus, religion is but philosophy for the masses, and, once accepted, is philosophy *of* the masses, having as its primary function their moral education and purification.

In order to make this view possible, an intricate and brilliant theory of Prophetic Revelation was constructed to do justice to the Islamic phenomenon as the philosopher saw it. Basically, nothing new was imposed on the Greek system of thought: the materials were those of late Hellenism, but these were pressed into a new direction so that a novel, original pattern emerged from them. The Greek theory and psychology of cognition were internally manipulated to yield the idea of a unique type of human intellect which intuitively apprehended the Reality in a total sweep and then clothed this truth, through an inner impulsion, into figurative symbols to make them accessible to the common man. Thus, instead of saying, 'If you pursue moral good, your mind shall attain the real spiritual freedom which is bliss', the Prophet said, 'If you are virtuous and perform these *specific acts*, you shall enter Paradise and will be saved from the flames of Hell', etc.

The philosophical system, thus constructed, was a magnificent creation of the Islamic civilization. In itself it was an impressive achievement, and both in the ethos of its *Weltanschauung* and in its actual structure it represents a genuine landmark in human thought as it stands on the threshold between antiquity and the Modern Age. But *vis-à-vis* the religion of Islam it created a perilous situation for itself. It was not so much in the actual doctrines professed by it taken severally that the danger lay, but in its overall judgment on the nature of religion and its implications for the Sharī'a. For its individual doctrines – the eternity of the world, the nature of eschatology, the nature of God, etc. – could be controverted or modified by criticism, but the status that it assigned to religion and to the Sharī'a could not fail to be rejected if religion was not to be reduced to a kind of spiritual mockery.

Orthodoxy and Philosophy

The natural theology of the philosophers, then, posed a patent threat to the revealed content of Islam. The very points of its original achievement in religious thought became the target for orthodoxy's suspicion and attack, i.e. the points where it had sought deliberately and consciously a liaison with orthodox dogma and had hoped for acceptance as a valid interpretation of Islam.

The orthodox refutation, formulated by al-Ghazālī in his classic work 'The Incoherence of the Philosophers' (*Tahāfut al-Falāsifa*), argued against the philosophers' position with regard to religious doctrine point by point and revealed both its self-contradictions and its insufficiency from the religious point of view. The doctrine of the eternity of the world was shown to be impossible even rationally apart from the fact that it denied the God of creative activity in the real sense of the word. For the philosophical doctrine of the necessary emanation of the world from God was substituted God's voluntary activity. The rational constitution of God, operating by an inherent rational necessity, was replaced by the Ash'arite concept of the Will of God. Similarly, the purely spiritual character of the philosophers' eschatology was rejected.

But the most crucial basis of the orthodox dissatisfaction with the philosophers' religion concerned the nature of religion itself. It was here that the most sensitive nerve of Islam was to be located. The philosophical theory of the Prophetic Revelation, which saw in the Prophet an immensely endowed intellect and spirit, capable of coming into contact with the Universal Intellect or the Archangel, was not completely rejected; on the contrary, some of its new elements, especially the intellectual perfectionism of the Prophet, were incorporated into the *kalām* doctrine. But the character of the Revelation, as being essentially intellectual, was rejected and especially the idea that religion is but a symbolic form of this intellectual truth. The nature of the ultimate Reality for orthodox Islam could not be solely intellectualized, but directly inspired moral activism. The net result of this was a revindication of the primordial and absolute status of the Sharī'a which the philosophers had declared to be mere symbolism adequate only for the masses. But the most important legacy which this philosophical teaching left for Islam and which the orthodoxy unhesitatingly adopted was the division of Being into necessary and contingent. Henceforward, this constituted the burden of the *kalām* proofs for the existence of God: the created world as contingent effect requires the existence of God, the Necessary Being, as its cause.

Henceforth, two ways were left open in which philosophy could operate, and it pressed itself through both these channels. One was that philosophical speculation should continue despite the strictures of orthodoxy and should seek for itself a heterodox medium. This medium was found in philosophical Ṣūfī thought, a fact which was undoubtedly facilitated by the mystical tendencies in the thought of the Muslim philosophers themselves, especially in that of Ibn Sīnā. We shall describe this important career of philosophical thought in Islam below. The other alternative was to give up the idea of producing a rival system to theology as far as religious dogma was concerned and rather to work within the orthodox system. This is what made possible the expansion of the *kalām* into a systematic body of thought comprising epistemology and metaphysics, an expansion which first appears in the work of the theologian-philosopher Fakhr al-Dīn al-Rāzī (d. 606/1209).[5] Within this system, however, an astonishingly wide scope was offered for the exercise of speculative reason, an activity which had a very lively and rich career for several centuries but which has been little studied by modern scholarship which seems so far to stop at al-Ghazālī's refutation of philosophy.

The orthodox *kalām* had accepted the philosophical doctrine of the necessary and the contingent but, as we pointed out above, they rejected an objective distinction between essence and existence. Ibn Sīnā had taught that God gave existence to essences which were in themselves non-existent. God bestowed existence thanks to the fact that He is pure Existence, possessing no other nature than Necessary Being. On this view, existence was 'added to' essences in some sense. The orthodox rejected this doctrine because of the fear that if Being was regarded as univocal, i.e. had the same meaning when applied to

God as when applied to the world – then this would result in pantheism and that despite the fact that God's Being was thought to be necessary whereas the Being of the world was considered to be contingent. Accordingly, the orthodox *kalām* declared Being to be equivocal, i.e. it had different meanings when applied to God and the world.

The protagonists of the philosophical tradition developed their doctrine by introducing further distinctions and held that 'being' had two different applications. In one sense, it denoted the particular being of a thing (the 'haecceity' of Duns Scotus in Western scholasticism), and in this sense the term was equivocal because everything is unique in this respect. And, consequently, God's peculiar Being, far from flowing into other existents, was unknowable. But in another sense, being is an abstract idea, generalized from actual existents. This abstract concept must be univocal if it is to be applied to God and to creatures. Being in this latter sense, it was argued, is the proper object of metaphysical inquiry[6] which should deal with its general properties (*umūr 'āmma*). Indeed, a group, notably among them the philosopher-theologian Qāḍī Abu'l Thanā' al-Urmawī (d. 684/1285), contended that the doctrine of God should be separated from this doctrine of Being which should constitute the proper domain of *kalām*-metaphysics. This was, however, rejected by the theologians, jealous of their preserves, on the ground that this would create a super-science over *kalām*.[7]

Thus the tension between philosophical thought and dogmatic theology continued down the centuries even within orthodox Islam which had transported within its own theological systems a great mass of philosophical and metaphysical ideas. The protagonists of philosophy within this liquid atmosphere gave up certain of the more extreme of the anti-dogmatic conclusions of the classical philosophers. This neo-philosophical activity came to life especially since the 7th/13th century when the *rapprochement* between philosophy and theology had been set on a definite footing and had recovered a certain balance, after al-Ghazālī's total rejection of philosophy, through the work particularly of al-Rāzī, which henceforth becomes the centre of controversy. In the 7th/13th century itself there arose a number of eminent philosophical writers and critics who, while defending philosophy in general, nevertheless accepted orthodox positions on the most critical and sensitive points of the dogma. For example, Naṣīr al-Dīn al-Ṭūsī (d. 672/1273), an acute and clear thinker, rejects the doctrine of the eternity of the world and defends Islam on this point.[8]

But the tension between the traditionists – the Ahl al-Ḥadīth – and the philosophers remained more basic and permanent. From time to time it erupted into fierce outbursts of the traditionist attacks on intellectualism. To the right wing traditionists, *kalām*-theology itself had become suspect because of its very *rapprochement* to philosophy. This traditionism found its monumental expression in the 8th/14th century in the prolific work of Ibn Taymīya, which was destined to be of lasting import. Especially in his important work 'The Harmony between the True Tradition and Evidence of Reason', he severely criticized the thesis both of the philosophers and the theologians. But the struggle continued. In the famous religious university of al-Azhar in Egypt, philosophy was extradited from the syllabus during the later centuries and was only restored after the dawn of Muslim Modernism towards the end of the nineteenth century by the efforts of the reformer-revolutionary Jamāl al-Dīn al-Afghānī and his disciple Muḥammad 'Abduh. A 13th/19th century author of note in India, 'Abd al-'Azīz Pahrārawī (Pahrāra is a village near Multān, where he died before the age of forty in 1239/1824), from the circle of the Ahl al-Ḥadīth, wrote a bitter satire on philosophy. It begins:

'O 'Ulamā' of India! . . . you hope to attain bliss by the cultivation of rational sciences, but I fear lest your hopes should be frustrated'.

The satirist goes on:

'You have adopted the sciences of the infidels as your Sharī'a as though the philosophers of Greece were your Prophets',

and ends with an appeal for the study of the Ḥadīth.[9]

Philosophic Religion

While the purely intellectual philosophical tradition survived in the form of commentaries or handbooks with different rhythms either as an instrument of theology or as its critic, philosophy after al-Ghazālī developed in a new and important direction which may be called a purely religious philosophy or philosophical religion. This development, although profoundly influenced in its course by Ṣūfism and its modes of thought, is, nevertheless, to be distinguished from the latter (which is the object of our study in the next chapter). For, the phenomenon we have termed philosophical religion, although it often identifies its doctrines with those of the Ṣūfīs, especially of speculative Ṣūfism, is characterized by rational argumentation and purely intellectual and logical thought-processes while Ṣūfism relies exclusively on gnostic experience or intuition and uses poetic imagination rather than purely rational processes.

In assuming a religio-centric character, this new movement was undoubtedly helped by the fact that the philosophy proper, described earlier on, had itself a strong religious nature in that, on the basis of purely naturalistic and rational principles and using these as its point of departure, it had built up and culminated in a world-view which is undeniably religious. But the new philosophy was also under the spell of Ṣūfī spiritualism which diverted its interest from the field of natural philosophy except in so far as it could use the general concepts of natural philosophy for its own religious ends.

This new philosophical tradition begins with the work of Shihāb al-Dīn al-Suhrawardī, the 'martyr' (executed at Aleppo in 587/1191) founder of the 'philosophy of illumination', and reaches its final formulation, deeply influenced by the Ṣūfī thought of Ibn al-'Arabī, in the monumental work of Ṣadr al-Dīn al-Shīrāzī (d. 1050/1640), entitled 'The Four Journeys', which has not yet been properly studied. The fundamental doctrine of this tradition is the principle of the 'grades of Being', i.e. a doctrine of pantheism built and elaborated on the basis of the Neoplatonic theory of emanation (the most important single source used by them is the so-called 'Theology of Aristotle' consisting of passages from the *Enneads* of Plotinus with a Neoplatonist commentary). Another grand theory, closely allied to the principle of the 'grades of Being', is that of cognition which asserts the identity of thought and being. From these two arose the third important doctrine which came to play a central rôle in its religious world-view, the essential contribution to the development of which was made by Ṣūfī thought, is the doctrine that affirms a 'Realm of Similitudes (*'Ālam al-Mithāl'*), i.e. an ontological world of images where the spiritual reality from above assumes the form of concrete images and where the gross bodies from the material realm from below change into subtle bodies and images.

The first two doctrines were developed by al-Suhrawardī. He criticized the Avicennian thesis of the distinction between essence and existence and removed the basis of the philosophers' distinction between God and man. Correspondingly, he negated the distinction between possibility and necessity and declared these distinctions to be purely mental and subjective. Further, he attacked the idea of duality between matter and form and formulated a doctrine of pure existence which tolerated the only distinction within itself of 'more or less' or 'more perfect and less perfect'. Indeed, al-Suhrawardī denounced all Aristotelian categories as pure subjective myths. His whole trend of thought led to the impossibility of any definition whatsoever, for definitions presuppose absolute distinctions in reality, and it was on this function of definitions that the Aristotelian-Avicennian system was built. Consequently, for al-Suhrawardī, reality was one, homogeneous continuum punctuated only by 'more or less' or 'grades of Being': 'the whole of God is Being and the whole of Being is God'.

Beside this monistic picture of reality, al-Suhrawardī developed a theory of knowledge according to which cognition came about not through the 'abstraction' of forms as the philosopher had taught, but by a direct awareness or immediate presence of the object. He upheld the phenomenon of self-awareness as the primordial characteristic of all knowledge and declared, resurrecting the old Zoroastrian concept of 'Light', this awareness to be the fundamental self-luminosity of Being. Thus, as the stream of Being processes from the ultimate Reality by emanation, so does the stream of Light or immediate consciousness from its ultimate source. Consciousness itself is, therefore, a continuum differentiated at various points by the only category of 'more or less'.

This trend of thought profoundly influenced the whole subsequent development of metaphysical thought in Islam, both Ṣūfic and philosophical: its importance and depth cannot be over-estimated. It produced in Islamic speculative thought a characteristic quality of what might be termed a subjective humanism with regard to the universe and its constitution. The human cognitive faculties are projected into the ontological structure of the Reality which appears as a person. Just as man has sense-perception, imagination, rational thought and spiritual intuition, so is the universe objectively invested with these faculties. Especially favourably was this line of thought cultivated by the Ṣūfīs whose methods of personal experience of Reality peculiarly predisposed them towards it. Thus, the mystic Ibn al-'Arabī (560–638/1165–1240) was the first to develop the idea of the universe as the 'macro-anthropos (*al-insān al-akbar*)' or 'macro-persona (*al-shakhs al-akbar*)'. Man is called 'micro-anthropos (*al-insān al-ṣaghīr*)'. This doctrine is the reverse of the idea of the macrocosm and microcosm. Where the former patterns the Universe on man, the latter patterns man on the Universe.

In this many-tiered homocentric structure of Ibn al-'Arabī's reality, a very prominent rôle was played by the 'realm of similitudes' which is the ontological counterpart of the human faculty of creative imagination. It is a vast, unlimited realm indeed – quite as infinite as the human imagination which, in fact, does nothing but reflect the Images in the 'realm of similitudes', just as the faculty of sense-perception only represents perceptual images of the material world, or the intellect only mirrors the ideas objectively existent in the Intelligible World. This world of similitudes or images was specially invoked to explain the living symbols, neither purely spiritual nor purely material, which were the objects of mystic and religious visions and experiences. In these experiences, the purely spiritual reality, the object of spiritual experience, also clothed itself in the quasi-material form of an image directly apprehended by the faculty of imagination. This is the realm wherein the Prophets saw angels in human form; and, finally, this is the place where the events so vividly portrayed in religion concerning the Day of Judgment do occur.

This doctrine of the multi-level reality with the world of imagination in the middle is a peculiar development in medieval Islam and was accepted by an overwhelming majority of the orthodox Ṣūfīs. It gave to much of Islamic mysticism its characteristic ethos. Finally, it reacted back on philosophy and found its rational grounding and philosophical formulation in the 11th/17th century in the work of Ṣadr al-Dīn al-Shīrāzī, the architect of the last great philosophical system in Islam.

Mullā Ṣadrā (as Muḥammad Ṣadr al-Dīn is commonly known), having accepted from al-Suhrawardī the monistic doctrine of the grades of Being in terms of 'more or less', develops his own doctrine of cognition and the nature of the human soul. The human soul is not a single-level entity having different faculties of cognition, but is of different levels (*nasha'āt*) corresponding to those of the ontological reality. The powers of the mind are not mere powers but are literally constituents of reality. The soul, therefore, not merely 'knows' reality but participates in it and is identified with it: it is not merely receptive but creative. It follows that at higher levels of experience, the mind experiences and becomes whatever it wills and thus attains absolute freedom from the finite existence of the material world.

This doctrine of phenomenological idealism asserts a complete identity of thought and being, of mind and reality. Knowing is the ultimate and primordial form of being and, therefore, that theory of knowledge is completely rejected which declares that cognition is a process whereby the mind *conforms* itself to reality. Originally a form of Neoplatonism, this philosophy takes on a new character through the phenomenology of Ṣūfī intuitionism as developed by Ibn al-'Arabī and his followers. Based on spiritual empiricism, it is essentially personal. The truth is that its theoreticism is only apparent and formal. At bottom it sought to cater for the religious need of refined minds in the later Muslim Middle Ages: the need on the part of the individual to live in peace with the universe in a society that was fast becoming subject to internal decline and disintegration.

Thus, philosophy in Islam did not die with the orthodox attack of al-Ghazālī as is commonly supposed by modern scholarship. It had, on the contrary, a vibrating life down to the 11th/17th and 12th/18th centuries. But its character was radically changed through the influence of mysticism. From a rational endeavour to understand the nature of the objective reality, it became transformed into a spiritual endeavour to live in harmony with that reality. This it achieved through an intellectual romanticism by an identification of the human mind with reality, of thought with being. This was an easier task than solving the difficult questions that reality imposed on the mind if the two *confronted* one another. It gave comfort at a time when the external situation was far from comfortable. At a popular mass level the same need was being answered by a total spread of Ṣūfism in Muslim society, a subject to which we must now turn.

CHAPTER EIGHT

ṢŪFĪ DOCTRINE AND PRACTICE

Rise and Early Development of Ṣūfism – Beginnings of Institutional Ṣūfism – The Ṣūfī Way – The Emergence of Orthodox Ṣūfism – The Ṣūfī Theosophy

Rise and Early Development of Ṣūfism

Muḥammad's Prophetic consciousness, which issued in his mission, was founded upon very definite, vivid and powerful mystic experiences briefly described or alluded to in the Qur'ān (XVII, 1; LIII, 1–12 and 13–18; LXXXI, 19–25). It is interesting that all these descriptions of experiences and visions belong to the Meccan period; in the Medina era we have a progressive unfolding of the religio-moral ideal, and the foundation of the social order for the newly instituted community but hardly any allusions to inner experiences. This is in consonance with the orientation of the Prophetic consciousness for which the spiritual experience is not to be dwelt on and enjoyed for its own sake but is primarily meaningful for action in history. (From this point of view, the claims of later Ṣūfīs, that in practising mysticism they are only following the spiritual legacy of the Prophet, is not altogether fanciful even if it may be questioned on historical grounds.) Indeed, even the allusions in the Meccan period are not made by the Qur'ān for the sake of pure description but to support the truth of the Prophet's mission: 'The heart has not lied in what it saw; will you, then, dispute as to what it witnessed?' (LIII, 11–12), and again, 'Your Companion is not infirm of mind; indeed he has witnessed him (the heavenly figure) on the clear horizon' (LXXXI, 22–23).

But when action began and the Community came into being, the need for this kind of remonstrance disappeared and so did allusions to experiences; mysticism was fulfilled in prophethood. Nor did the majority of the Companions ask many questions about the nature of these spiritual experiences. For one thing, they were being trained for a moral purpose on a religious basis and their activism probably made them disinclined towards an inquiry into the metaphysical secrets of spiritualism. They were interested in divine commands, not in the Ṣūfic mysteries. Besides, they must have thought that these spiritual flights were characteristic of the Divine Messenger and that their duty lay in believing and in carrying out what they believed (which itself was, as history knows so well, a formidable task) with an intensity of faith and a deep sense of purpose.

What Islam generally inculcated among its early followers, in varying degrees, was a grave sense of responsibility before the justice of God which raised their behaviour from the realm of worldliness and mechanical obedience to the law to a plane of moral activity. The keynote of this piety is '*Fear of God*' or responsibility to the moral ideal. Among the Companions, there were some with whom this sense deepened into a special degree of inwardness of actions, or the interiorization and introspection of the moral motive. This is exemplified by men like Abū Dharr al-Ghifārī, who formed the nucleus of Medinese piety after the Prophet. This became the foundation stone of Muslim asceticism that developed rapidly during the later 1st/7th century and the 2nd/8th centuries.

This ascetic pietism received a further stormy impulse from two sides: the environment of luxury and worldly enjoyment that came generally to prevail in the Muslim community with the establishment and consolidation of the vast new empire, and especially as a sharp reaction to the secular and none-too-pious life and attitude of the new ruling dynasty of the Umayyads at their court, the majority of whom behaved in strange contrast to the simple piety of the four early Caliphs. At this stage, the protest of the pious nucleus of the Community is still undifferentiated; the 'Ulamā' and the ascetics are identically the same persons, with varying degrees of emphasis on personal piety and abstinence. This protest asserts that the ruling group should accept, observe and enforce the religious law of the Sharī'a rather than make their own will and expediency the law of the state. Should this come to pass, the pious hoped that the original spirit of Islam would be reinforced to its true life. Thus, the trend in this period (late 1st–early 2nd/early 8th century) is purely ethical with a deepening of the inwardness of the ethical motivation. Among the more prominent representatives of this ethical piety, the most famous is al-Ḥasan of Baṣra (d. 110/728) who not only won the recognition of his contemporaries but who exerted after his death one of the most powerful influences in the whole spiritual history of Islam down the ages. Secondly, the Ṣūfic impulse undoubtedly fed on that isolationism which set in as a tremendous reaction to Khārijism and the political controversies that it raised. This isolationism, which is preached side by side in Ḥadīth literature with Ijmā', teaches that men should desist not only from politics but even from administration and public affairs, and much Ḥadīth seeks, indeed, to preach that a person should retire to a cave and leave others alone.

During the course of the 2nd/8th and the 3rd/9th centuries, the Muslim religious intelligentsia tended to become divided into two groups: the 'Ulamā' or pure theologians and legists on the one hand, and those who gave to religion a more personal basis in religious devotion on the other. Among the sciences of the religion, the first to develop was the law (see Chapter IV). The legists themselves endeavoured to give to their system as much of inner life as possible; we drew attention to this fact while discussing the peculiarly religious character of the Islamic law: how it tried to fuse the moral and the legal into *fiqh*. The legal life must, however, by its very nature, remain impersonal. It was as a reaction against this legal formulation of Islam – which was also its first formulated expression – that the early pietistic asceticism changed definitely into what is technically known as Ṣūfism with its proper ethos. The Qur'ānic concept of trust in God (*tawakkul*), as already stressed by pietism in an ethical sense, was developed in certain circles into an extreme doctrine of renunciation of the world and a vindictive independence from natural 'causes', although on its precise meaning difference of opinion has always existed among the Ṣūfīs, typified in the following story: Mālik ibn Dīnār and Muḥammad ibn Wāsi', two Ṣūfīs of the 2nd/8th century, differed over the question of possession of means of subsistence. Mālik would prefer to have a piece of land on which he could live and be independent of men, while Ibn Wāsi' would rather be a man who, if he had a meal, knew not whence his next repast would come.[1]

This development of the doctrine of *tawakkul* directly led to the central Ṣūfī concept of the relationship between man and God – the twin concepts of love and grace fused into one sentiment. The famous woman saint, Rābi'a al-'Adawīya (d. 185/801), sings of this pure love and grace in the oft-quoted verses:

> I love Thee with two loves, love of my happiness,
> And perfect love, to love Thee as is Thy due.
> My selfish love is that I do naught
> But think on Thee, excluding all beside;
> But that purest love, which is Thy due,
> Is that the veils which hide Thee fall, and
>   I gaze on Thee.
> No praise to me in either this or that,
> Nay, Thine the praise for both that love and this.[2]

Ma'rūf al-Karkhī (d. 200/816), is reported to have said, 'Love is not to be learnt from men, it is a gift of God and comes of His grace.'[3]

Such was the Ṣūfī challenge of love and pure devotion to the legists' concept of obedience and observance of the Law. There was as yet no open friction except for an uneasiness on the part of the legists who contended that the *law* of Islam could only legislate for external behaviour and could not deal with the inner tribunal of Conscience or the state of the agent's heart: a worry that harked back to the old Khārijite doctrine which drew perilous conclusions about a man's inner faith on the basis of external acts; only now it was the other way round: whereas the Khārijites made a man's faith suspect because of his actions, the Ṣūfīs called actions into question on grounds of the quality of faith, something which it was impossible to handle legally.

Considerable ink has been spent by modern scholarship on the 'origins' of Ṣūfism in Islam, as to how far it is 'genuinely' Islamic and how far a product, in the face of Islam, of outside influences, particularly Christian and Gnostic. So far as the ideas of trust in and love of God are concerned, our analysis of the situation has led us to believe that their rise to prominence is a result of the developments within the intellectual and spiritual life of the community. The idea of 'trust in God' is prominent in the Qur'ān, although there it does not exclude, and is not opposed to, God's working through 'causes'. Similarly, the ideal of love of God, if necessary, at the sacrifice of all worldly possession, is put forward by the Qur'ān repeatedly, although again, love is there not the name of a pure emotion, only inwardly cultivated, but has a decisively activist tendency. In the new Ṣūfi context, on the other hand, both have shifted their emphases remarkably. But this purely introverted attitude of emotional idealism is a response to an inner situation, viz. a this-worldly realism, political activity, civil wars, and the development of legalism. Outside influences must have played an accessory rôle and these no one may deny, but they must have supervened upon an initial native tendency. Nor is this the only phenomenon of this type in the early development of Islam. This case, within its own special terms, bears a striking resemblance to the early theological controversy between the Mu'tazila and the Ḥanbalites. Just as there the Mu'tazila espoused the justice of God to the exclusion of His omnipotence and were diametrically opposed by the Ḥanbalites, so here Ṣūfī 'inwardism' arises as a direct challenge to the external political and legal developments in Islam. The point of peril is reached in modern scholarship when, on the basis of this division, one is tempted to characterize the pre-differentiated Islam, and pass one-sided judgments on the Prophet or the early Community. The situation resembles an undifferentiated central nucleus which expands and develops new cells, but does not and cannot exclude outside factors although it cannot be intrinsically explained in their terms.

One fact stands out plainly in the life of the Prophet: that he practised rigorous realism with (and we believe that this was *because of*) an intense spiritual life. Devotional prayers and solitary nocturnal vigils were a normal part of his life. It would be astonishing indeed – even if there were no historical evidence – if this had not affected his followers in varying degrees. This point of view must throw light also on the Islamic attitude to the much discussed question of celibacy which certain Ṣūfīs began to practise in the 2nd/8th century (although married life remained the normal practice of Ṣūfīs down the ages). The Qur'ān had undoubtedly encouraged marriage but it has not left it for an exceptional intelligence to guess why it did so. Man's nature normally seeks sexual companionship and, indeed, the Qur'ān declares this law to be true of the universe in some sense: 'And of everything we have created pairs' (LI, 49). The Qur'ān recommended matrimony, either for the protection of women (III, 3) or for the general purpose of chastity (*taḥaṣṣun*), i.e. to avoid an unregulated sexual life. It follows therefore, that *the Qur'ān discourages celibacy* as an *institution.* In its critique of monasticism (LVII, 27), it does not condemn it morally, but criticizes it *as an institution that failed of its purpose.* Of monks individually the Qur'ān is full of praise at several points as embodiments of saintliness and as the opposites of conceit and pride.

Beginnings of Institutional Ṣūfism

For the first two centuries Ṣūfism remained a spontaneous individual phenomenon but, with the development of the formal disciplines of Islamic law and theology, and the gradual emergence, with them, of the class of 'Ulamā', it rapidly developed into an institution with a tremendous mass appeal. The beginnings of this movement are connected with the activity of a class of people who themselves had arisen from the ranks of earlier ascetics variously called 'ascetics' (*zuhhād*), 'reciters' (*qurrā'* – *scil.* of the Qur'ān) who 'wept' as they recited and preached (*bakkā'ūn* 'weepers'). These popular preachers, also known as *quṣṣāṣ* or 'storytellers', exerted a powerful influence on the masses by enlarging Qur'ānic stories with the aid of materials borrowed from all kinds of sources, Christian, Jewish, Gnostic and even Buddhist and Zoroastrian, indeed, anything that would make their sermons persuasive and effective. As the Ṣūfī way of life became common as a recognized type, the term Ṣūfī slowly replaced the older names '*zuhhād*' and '*nussāk*' applied to this class of men (and women). The name 'Ṣūfi' seems to be originally derived from *ṣūf* or wool, the coarse material these people used for clothing as a sign of ascetism and renunciation. Other etymologies suggested either by later Muslim writers, for example, that 'Ṣūfī' comes from the root *ṣafā*, 'to be pure', or from *Ṣuffa*, i.e. the raised platform in the Prophet's mosque in Medina where poorer people used to sit and exercise devotion, or as suggested by some modern authors, that the word is derived from the Greek *sophós*, have little reliable foundation.[4]

The earliest beginnings of Ṣūfī organization are indicated by informal and loose gatherings for religious discussions, and spiritual exercises, called 'circles' (*ḥalaqa*). The repeated recitation of a religious formula, called *dhikr*, can take place anywhere, including mosques, which fact shows that still at this stage (first half of the 3rd/9th century) Ṣūfī practice was not, and was not regarded as, a rival growth challenging the formal disciplines of Islam. But later on, as we shall see, this simple practice developed into elaborate spiritual concepts with the introduction of music and dancing and threatened the position of the mosque as the centre of religious service.

Through the activity of the popular preachers and the pious mass orators, a number of ideas were introduced into Ṣūfism and thence into popular Islam. These ideas, as we have said, originated from heterogeneous sources, but the chief impact made on Ṣūfism seems to come from the Shīʿite sources which themselves were under the influence of Christianity. The most important of these importations is the eschatological doctrine of the Mahdī ('The guided one of God'), a spiritual personage who will appear at the end of time and restore the supremacy of justice and Islam over ungodly forces. The Shīʿa, already sometime during the latter half of the 1st/7th century, had developed the idea of the 'awaited Mahdī', after their attempts failed to control the course of Muslim political life.[5] Among the 'orthodox' or Twelver Shīʿa, this personage was identified with the 'hidden Imām' who would effect the victory of the Shīʿa political faith. The fusion of this Messianic doctrine with the Christian doctrine of the Second Advent of Christ was a natural development. In Sunnī Islam itself, where a deep-seated consciousness existed of the failure of political and public life to meet the standards of the Islamic ideal, such ideas found a ready place in the hearts of the frustrated and disillusioned public through the effective mediacy of the preachers. And although the doctrine of the Mahdī was never formally included in Sunnī theology, it has always weighed heavily with popular orthodox Islam. To this field of activity also belongs the overwhelming influx of late Jewish and apocryphal Christian ideas that found their way into the commentaries on the Qur'ān and against which later Muslim critical theologians and doctors raised their protests (carried on into modern Islam as well), stigmatizing them as 'Isrā'īlīyāt' or 'of Jewish lore and legend'.

With the growing inner rupture between Ṣūfī practice and its implicit ideology on the one hand and the emerging orthodox system on the other, a new body of Ḥadīth (cf. Chapter III) also comes into existence. The Ṣūfīs, in order to justify their stand, formulated (i.e.

verbally invented) statements, sometimes quite fanciful and historically completely fictitious, which they attributed to the Prophet. These exaggerate the frugality of the Prophet into extreme renunciation and asceticism (very soon this was also applied to 'Alī, through the mediacy of Shī'ī propaganda). The anti-Ṣūfī Ḥadīth in general reproves excessive asceticism, and especially monasticism and withdrawal from the world, besides emphasizing the superiority of a scholar to an ascetic. But although both sides of this type of Ḥadīth may be regarded, in so far as their verbal formulations are concerned, as inventions, there is no reason to reject either side as being substantially untrue in the sense that they attribute to the Prophet things that were entirely foreign to him. The so-called this-worldly Ḥadīth, stressing the actual implementation of the moral ideal realistically in a social context, belongs patently to the spirit of the Qur'ān. But the Ṣūfī Ḥadīth also, once divested of its excessive and fanciful drapery, equally exemplifies the life of the Prophet and the teaching of the Qur'ān in stressing the purity of the heart and inner life.

The disturbing feature, however, was the exclusive character implicit in this situation which once more compellingly reminds us of the Mu'tazilite-Ḥanbalite dichotomy in theology. Especially unacceptable to Islam was the negative attitude to this world that seemed to develop among the Ṣūfīs with alarming alacrity. Hence it rightly deserved the rebuke administered to it in the famous Ḥadīth, 'there is no monasticism in Islam' with the further commentary, 'the monasticism of this Community is the Holy War'. These efforts saved Ṣūfism from the further step of establishing completely monastic orders; otherwise, with its popular character and mass appeal, the whole fabric of Islam would surely have been destroyed.

As the rift threatened to widen, however, a number of eminent representatives of orthodox Islam set themselves the task of saving the situation. From the 3rd/9th century onwards there arose a whole series of important orthodox Ṣūfīs who both by their practice and teaching sought to integrate orthodoxy and Ṣūfism and from then on the central spiritual history of Islam can be viewed as a continuous tension between these two streams and progressive attempts at integration and the resolution of this tension. This was because Ṣūfism, on its side, continued to absorb ever novel ideological modes and heterodox elements while formal religious disciplines continued as before.

The first great name among this succession of orthodox Ṣūfīs is that of Ḥārith al-Muḥāsibī (d. 243/857) who, after a moral conversion from rational theology to Ṣūfism, devoted himself to establishing orthodox religion on an intense inner life of the conscience. Like al-Ghazālī, two and a half centuries later (for whom he seems to have served as a model), he summed up the pietistic legacy of the early Ṣūfīs in order to base upon it and enliven the external life of religion with its law and ritual. The essence of his teaching consists not in the renunciation of the outer life but in a ceaseless vigil on the purity of motive and in perpetual self-criticism, especially with regard to self-deception and inner self-righteousness and pride. This concentration, he taught, generates a succession of moral 'states' of conscience, progressively deepening the purity of motive.

The Ṣūfī Way

But Ṣūfism could not stay content for long with its simple piety and its gospel of love. Once it won converts to its general point of view from among the respectable members of the orthodoxy, it soon evolved the methodology of its 'inner way', its 'spiritual itinerary' to God. Its impulse to do so probably quickened with the charge of the 'Ulamā' that, should the Ṣūfī claims be granted, a door would be opened to spiritual anarchy because of the impossibility of regulating, controlling, and indeed, predicting the course of the 'inner life'. Dhu'l-Nūn of Egypt (d. 245/859), who is generally credited by the Ṣūfis with having classified the 'stages' of spiritual development, was actually charged with heresy at Baghdad in 240/854. Besides, the Ṣūfīs themselves were in need of developing some method of control and criticism in order to standardize and, as far as possible, to objectify their experiences.

If this doctrine of the stages or 'stations' (*maqāmāt*) of the Ṣūfī itinerary was generally stated in religio-moral terminology, borrowed on the whole from the Qur'ān [it usually includes such terms as 'repentance', 'abstinence', 'patience', 'gratitude', 'trust' and 'pleasure' (in God's Will)], it also elaborated a theory of psychologico-gnostic 'states' (*aḥwāl*) through which the Ṣūfī passed. By the middle of the 3rd/9th century this development became definite, and led to the doctrine of 'absorption' or 'annihilation' (*fanā'*), i.e. replacement of the human attributes by the Divine. This doctrine is traditionally associated with the name of the famous Ṣūfī Abū Yazīd al-Biṣṭāmī (d. 260/874), to whom are attributed certain ecstatic utterances such as 'Praise be to me; how great is my majesty', 'I am your Lord' and 'my banner is greater than that of Muḥammad'.

Such ecstatic statements, which multiplied among the Ṣūfīs and were called *shaṭaḥāt*, were explained away as 'non-responsible' utterances spoken in the 'state of intoxication'. But the whole method of the Ṣūfīs created a problem of the utmost gravity for Islam. With the emergence of the Ṣūfī doctrine of the spiritual itinerary, there arose the problem of the Ṣūfī goal defined in terms of 'annihilation' of the human into the Divine attributes and qualities. With this the concept of sainthood, *wilāya*, was elaborated with an appeal to the use of the term *walī* ('friend of God') in the Qur'ān, but with a peculiar Ṣūfī content borrowed from the mysticism of Eastern Christianity, Gnosticism and later on from Neoplatonism. The question then arose as to how sainthood is related to Prophethood and the saint to the Prophet. That in the concept of sainthood Ṣūfism saw a parallel to prophecy, and a rival to the religion instituted by the Prophet, became clear already in the 3rd/9th century when, in contradistinction to the concept of the 'Seal of the Prophets' (a term applied by the Qur'ān to Muḥammad indicating the fulfilment of prophecy in him), the idea of the 'Seal of the Saints' was introduced. In a book by the Ṣūfī al-Ḥakīm al-Tirmidhī (d. 285/898), the greatest Ṣūfī authority on doctrine and systematizer of the 3rd/9th century, such questions are treated as: 'who deserves the title of the Seal of the Saints?' and 'how is a saint related to a Prophet?',[6] etc.

Sainthood also brought with it the doctrine of a hierarchy of 'preserving' saints, most probably a Ṣūfī parallel to the Shī'a doctrine of the Imām. The beginnings of this teaching were in the 3rd/9th century, but it became a definite part of Ṣūfī doctrine in the following century. According to this doctrine, the world is kept intact, thanks to the existence of a network of invisible saints of different ranks. The successive rungs of this ladder are constituted by 'successors' (*abdāl*, plural of *badal* 'a substitute' or 'a successor'), 'pegs' (*awtād*), 'pillars' (*'amā'id*), etc., and end in a 'pole' or 'axis' (*quṭb*) around which the whole universe rotates. But for this spiritual structure, the universe would go to pieces. A special place in the Ṣūfī hagiarchy is occupied by an invisible figure called al-Khaḍir or al-Khiḍr (literally 'the Green') who, like the Phoenix, ever recreates his youth, is immortal and whose chief function is to guide those who lose their way in the wilderness (both physical and spiritual). Many eminent Ṣūfīs claim direct discipleship of al-Khiḍr from whom they have received investiture for the spiritual guidance of mankind. (The orthodox identify him with the 'Servant of God' on whom, according to the Qur'ān, XVIII, 65, God bestowed special knowledge and who is represented there as a spiritual guide of Moses.)

So much for the invisible realm. In the visible world, Ṣūfīs or rather those among them who were credited with sainthood, were invested with miracles or special divine graces and favours (*karāmāt*) which constituted signs of their sainthood. Special theories were constructed to distinguish scrupulously between these miracles and those of the Prophets, lest the two should be regarded as rivals. When thus qualified, orthodoxy felt no qualms about accepting the doctrine into its system.

But from the 4th/10th and 5th/11th centuries onward there emerged a new doctrine, completely opposed to the spirit of orthodox Islam, but which nevertheless became the first article in the constitution of Ṣūfism as it launched itself in an organized fashion. In this respect the contrast, not only with orthodox Islam but even with the early Ṣūfī practice, is remarkable. Whereas during the first three centuries, seekers of the Ṣūfī path displayed a striking independence of spirit, resourcefulness and creativity, later on a rigorous discipline was imposed and an absolutely unquestioning submission to the spiritual dictatorship of the Shaykh or the master. And whereas in the 3rd/9th century Junayd of Baghdad taught that a seeker should behave, *vis-à-vis* God, as a puppet, it was now said that he should be in the hands of his preceptor as 'a dead body in the hands of its washer'.

In the meantime, efforts had already begun in the 3rd/9th century within the Ṣūfī fold to bridge the gulf between orthodox Islam and Ṣūfism and to keep the latter within reasonable limits. We have already studied the case of al-Muḥāsibī. After him came al-Kharrāz (d. 286/899) and that great critical spirit in early Ṣūfism, the formulator of orthodox Ṣūfism, Junayd of Baghdad (d. 298/911), who is said to have been a pupil of al-Muḥāsibī. The result of this movement, the development of an orthodox Ṣūfism, we shall study below. We end by mentioning the price Ṣūfism paid in the execution of one of its great representatives in the 3rd/9th century, al-Ḥusayn ibn Manṣūr called al-Ḥallāj ('the wool-carder'). Al-Ḥallāj, who had been a disciple of Junayd but who was expelled by the latter from his circle, was charged with having identified himself with God in his saying, 'I am the Truth' (*anā 'l-Ḥaqq*) and with deceiving people by sorcery, and was condemned to death with the approval of eminent jurists of Baghdad. He was flogged in public, mutilated, hung on a gibbet, decapitated and burnt. Islam never forgot this event (although the Ṣūfīs themselves later devised formulas both to exonerate him from heresy and to excuse his opponents) and the name of al-Ḥallāj has become a legend across the centuries not only with Ṣūfīs but in popular folk-literature throughout the Muslim world.

The Emergence of Orthodox Ṣūfism

The emergence of a Ṣūfī reform movement aiming at integrating mystic consciousness with the Prophetic Sharī'a has its origins in Ṣūfism itself and started in the last half of the 3rd/9th century with the activity of men like al-Kharrāz and Junayd. Al-Kharrāz introduced the concept of 'subsistence' or 'survival' (*baqā'*) to amend and amplify Bisṭāmī's doctrine of 'annihilation' (*fanā'*) On account of the paucity of resources, it is not easy to say what 'subsistence' meant fully to al-Kharrāz, although it is generally said that he meant by it something positive: whereas 'annihilation' destroys (the human defects), by virtue of 'subsistence' man 'subsists in' or 'survives with' God. What seems certain from the scanty words of the author of the doctrine is that 'subsistence' is a spiritual development whereby God bestows upon man a recovery of his self.[7] By the 4th/10th century, the doctrine had come to be accepted by Ṣūfism and al-Kalābādhī (d. 385/995) quotes a Ṣūfī authority (probably al-Ḥallāj himself) as saying:

'Subsistence is the station of the Prophet (in contradistinction to saints) who are invested (by God) with peace and integrity *(sakīna)*, for, whatever comes to them (by way of ecstatic developments) does not prevent them from carrying out God's duties'.[8]

Junayd subjected Ṣūfī claims to an acute criticism both in terms of their experiences and their external practices. He thus disallowed to the Ṣūfī 'states' any objective validity and declared that Ṣūfīs, including Abū Yazīd al-Bisṭāmī, had died prisoners of their imagination.[9] He also sought to counteract the antinomian and latitudinarian trends in Ṣūfī practice by enunciating the principle that 'knowledge (*'ilm*) has a priority over gnosis (*ma'rifa*) and prohibition has a priority over permission'.[10]

As a result of this process, the Ṣūfī doctrine evolved a multitude of partly antithetical, partly complementary pairs of categories to integrate and do justice to the mystic and prophetic consciousness, the inner life and experience of the spirit and the Sharī'a law as a social institution. We have already described the twin categories of 'annihilation' and 'survival'. The other major sets of categories are: (1) 'intoxication' and 'sobriety'; (2) 'unity' and 'difference'; (3) 'absence' and 'presence' (i.e. of the self before God in mystic experience). The difference between the mystic and the prophetic consciousness came to be located in the fact that whereas the mystic consciousness generally remains content with the first part of the experience described in each of the above-mentioned categories, in the prophetic consciousness it forms only a moment in the total experience which exhibits a dialectical character between the two terms. Epistemologically, this doctrine led directly to the doctrine, accepted very widely, that ecstatic statements uttered in the state of intoxication are invalid and that reliance may be placed only on statements when 'sobriety' supervenes, even though many Ṣūfīs contended that the state of 'intoxication' was the higher of the two and that the Prophet 'returned to sobriety' perforce and under the command of God.

Even though the Ṣūfīs were not able to formulate explicitly an organic relationship between their dialectical categories, nevertheless their doctrine contributed materially to salvaging their relations with orthodoxy and the disciplines represented by it. From the middle of the 4th/10th century there are visible signs of a movement for compromise between Ṣūfism and orthodox theology. A well-known Ṣūfī, Ibn Khafīf (d. 371/981), rallied to al-Ash'arī's theology and was its noted defender.[11] A curious example is offered by a brief credal exposition of strict orthodoxy, attributed to the theologian al-Māturīdī (see above, Chapter V). This work, called '*An Epistle on the Creed*' (*Risāla fi'l-'aqā'id*), though it cannot have been written by al-Māturīdī himself (he died in 333/945), nevertheless cannot, it seems, be later than the second half of the 4th/10th century, for its terminology is primitive and pre-philosophical. The Ṣūfī overtones of this otherwise strictly formal work are striking, even though these mystic traces are kept in check so that they do not fall outside the fundamental framework of *kalām*-theology. Thus, on the nature of Faith, we are told:

> Islam is the knowledge of God *simpliciter* (without asking 'how') and its seat is the breast; and Faith is the knowledge of God in His Godhead and its seat is the heart which is inside the breast; and true knowledge (*ma'rifa—gnosis*) is the knowledge of God with His attributes and its seat is the centre of the heart (*fu'ād*) which is inside of the heart; and (recognition of) the unity (of God) is the knowledge of His (absolute) unity and its seat is the 'secret' (*sirr*) or the inner being which is interior to the centre of the heart. A parable of this is what God the Exalted has said 'the likeness of God's light is like a niche wherein is a lamp', etc.[12] (Qur'ān, XXIV, 35).

From the very beginning of its formulation at the hands of al-Ash'arī the possibility of non-prophetic miracles or 'signs of the righteous' was accepted by theology. This anti-Mu'tazilite doctrine was a major concession to Ṣūfism, a concession that was made easier for the theologians by their atomic view of nature and of time. In the 4th/10th century, the acceptance of belief in the saintly miracles grew very wide and even a completely rationalist philosopher like Ibn Sīnā found a place for them in his anti-atomistic system, although he explained these miracles as 'natural' effects of the power of the mind over matter. Later orthodox text books of the creed invariably accepted the miracles of the saints, which were explained as evidence of the truth of the mission of the Prophet to whose Community a particular saint belongs – an interpretation which the Ṣūfīs unanimously accepted.

A powerful instrument in this whole *rapprochement* were the new traditions put into circulation throughout the 3rd/9th and 4th/10th centuries with the double purpose of promoting the cause of Ṣūfism and bringing it into the orthodox fold. In the last quarter of the 4th/10th century a number of men wrote books, like al-Sarrāj's (d. 377/987) *Kitāb al-Luma'* and al-Kalābādhī's (d. 385/995) *Introduction to the Way of the Ṣūfīs*, to plead the cause of a moderate Ṣūfism with a structure of ideas consistent with and even lending support to orthodoxy. This activity was followed in 438/1047 by the famous 'epistle (*Risāla*)' of al-Qushayrī (d. 465/1073), a manifesto for a synthesis of Ṣūfism and orthodox theology.

This movement culminated in the monumental life-work of al-Ghazālī, who proved to be its genuine corner-stone. This greatest figure in medieval Islam proved decisive for the future development of Islam, not so much through what he thought as through what he taught on the basis of his personal experience. Endowed with a rare religious insight (developed through a series of spiritual crises and struggles that affected him even physically) and a keen and perceptive mind, his mystic experience enabled him to transform the formulas of orthodox theology about the Divine Will, Power and Mercy into a living and moving personal reality that throbbed in his very veins (see Chapters V and VI). He called both the 'Ulamā' and the Ṣufīs to this in a philosophical language of remarkable clarity, incisiveness and irresistible persuasiveness.

The influence of al-Ghazālī in Islam is incalculable. He not only reconstituted orthodox Islam, making Ṣūfism an integral part of it, but also was a great reformer of Ṣūfism, purifying it of un-Islamic elements and putting it at the service of orthodox religion. As such he represents a final step in a long developing history. Ṣūfism received, through his influence, the approval of Ijmā', or consensus of the community. Islam received a new vigour of life and a popular appeal which won large areas in Africa, Central Asia and India to the Faith (see next chapter). Henceforth, often a great theologian and a great Ṣūfī were one and the same person, a development which, as we shall see presently, produced in due course a series of original thinkers who reconstructed Muslim theology on a new and more integral basis, than the old formal *kalām*. Two dangers, however, threatened the new synthesis from two sides, dangers which ultimately altered, to a large extent, the character of Islam between the 7th/13th and 13th/19th centuries and were responsible for much of the degrading beliefs and practices with which Muslim society became loaded. One of these dangers, the invasion of Islam by popular religion, we shall deal with in the next chapter. The second, the development of Ṣūfī theosophy, we must discuss next, for, at the intellectual level, it was this that sapped the energies and almost unreservedly claimed the minds of men of the greatest ability and creativity.

The Ṣūfī Theosophy

If the early ascetic piety, with its emphasis on the interiorization of the motive, was a reaction to the external development of the law, during the 3rd/9th and 4th/10th centuries Ṣūfism developed a doctrine of Gnosis (*ma'rifa*), of an inner experiential knowledge which it progressively came to oppose to the intellectual knowledge (*'ilm*) of theology which developed during the same period. There is evidence that in the 3rd/9th century the Ṣūfīs, on the whole, were a special class of theologians, rather than being opposed to theology. The author of the earliest extant bibliography of Arabic works, *Kitāb al-Fihrist*, treats of them as the fifth category of theologians, whereas he does not give a separate class even to the Ash'arites. To the *'ilm al-tawḥīd*, the 'science of the unity [of God]' as dialectical theology was called, the Ṣūfīs then opposed their *ma'rifat al-tawḥīd*, the 'gnosis of unity'. This 'unity' of God was then transformed under the Ṣūfī experientialism, into 'union' with God (the Arabic word *tawḥīd* means both 'regarding something as one' and 'unification of something with something else'.

The Ṣūfīs, then, soon arrived at the idea, encouraged most probably by influence from outside, that God alone is really existent and from there on to the doctrine that *God is the sole reality of everything*. When the new Sunnī theology of al-Ash'arī and al-Māturīdī came into circulation, declaring that the author of all acts is God alone (against the Mu'tazilites), Ṣūfī theosophy readily clung to this dictum but interpreted it on its own characteristic principles: nothing *exists* except Allāh. This is what the Qur'ānic doctrine of the unity of God was transformed into through the experiential method of the Ṣūfīs.

Yet, more even than any particular doctrine Ṣūfism might put forward as the content of the mystic consciousness, it was the principle of gnostic knowledge with its self-righteous intuitive certainty and the infallibility of its specially privileged deliverances that was not and could not be admitted by the 'Ulamā'. For with gnostic Ṣūfism the case was very different from that of the early pietistic Ṣūfism where it was a matter of merely emphasizing the purity of the conscience against external acts. The Ṣūfīs now claimed an incorrigible way of *knowing* which was supposedly immune from error and, further, whose content was utterly disparate in character with intellectual knowledge. The 'Ulamā' resisted this claim not only because it threatened a body of doctrine they had evolved with great effort over the four centuries, but more fundamentally because the Ṣūfī gnosis was not open to any check and control, being by definition incorrigible. Even after the revolution through al-Ghazālī's labours, the 'Ulamā' never admitted the objective validity of the uniquely privileged mystic knowledge.[13]

Similarly, the 'ecstatic statements', despite the general acceptance of the principle that these were made in the state of 'intoxication' and were not valid, were nevertheless at the same time regarded as having a peculiar cognitive nature not open to the scrutiny of ordinary avenues of knowledge. The very doctrine of the 'states' of inner experience implicitly assumed the possession of an esoteric knowledge of a unique, irreducible type posited for the unquestioning recognition of the Faithful. Here is a brief early statement of this cognitive miracle attributed to al-Tustarī (d. 283/896):

'Lordship has a secret which, if manifested, would destroy Prophethood; and Prophethood has a secret, which if divulged, would nullify knowledge; and the gnostics have a secret which, if manifested by God, would set the law at naught'.[14]

It is the same al-Tustarī who is reported to have said: 'I do not discuss the sinners in the community of Muḥammad, its evil-doers, murderers, fornicators and thieves, but I disown those who lay claims to *trust* in God, *satisfaction* with Him, *love and desire* of Him'.[15] Indeed, a peculiar mixture of extreme moral contrition (for developing which into a doctrine he was castigated by the 'Ulamā') and hold theosophic claims exists in this personality. As a matter of fact, whatever the claims to esoteric knowledge, the Ṣūfīs were coming strongly under the influence of the Greco-gnostic concepts and Christian and Manichaean doctrines.

An early example of the intrusion into Ṣūfism (later 3rd/9th century) of these Gnostic-Manichaean ideas was the doctrine of Muḥammad as the Primal Light, the penultimate constituent of ontological reality after God, a doctrine which later became a centrally 'orthodox' doctrine of Ṣūfism through the teaching of Ibn al-'Arabī (7th/13th century) who, as we shall see, made of this light God Himself. With the doctrine of Muḥammad as the Primal Light in which all the Prophets were foreshadowed, including Adam, emerged the Ḥadīth, largely accepted even by orthodoxy, which declared that 'Muḥammad was a Prophet while Adam was still (in a state) between water and earth'. Orthodoxy did not accept the metaphysical implications of this Ḥadīth but regarded it as a correct eulogistic statement of Muḥammad's position *vis-à-vis* other Prophets.

In a passage attributed to al-Tustarī but which represents probably a development of his doctrine by his followers we read: 'God created the Light of Muḥammad from His own Light and He formed it and brought it out at His own hands. This Light remained before Him for a hundred thousand years, during which time He contemplated it every day and night seventy thousand times. Then He created from it the whole creation.'[16] This philosophical trend was accelerated by the infusion of Neoplatonic ideas of emanation which exerted a powerful attraction on speculative Ṣūfism. These ideas were formulated in a famous encyclopaedia of popular character in the later 4th/10th century by an esoteric Ismāʿīlī circle calling itself 'the Brethren of Sincerity'. This religio-philosophical work, '*The Epistles of the Sincere Brethren*' which circulated widely in the 5th/11th century, and upon which later Ismāʿīlī theosophy drew as a source, held up before the seekers of the gnosis the goal of the Neoplatonic ascent or 'return' of the soul to the ultimate principle of Being and absorption of the former into the latter.

Such was the Ṣūfī gnosis. It developed a peculiar doctrine of the relationship between the Sharīʿa and what it called the *ḥaqīqa* ('inner truth'). Many Ṣūfīs came to hold that the seeker who arrives at this mystic truth goes beyond the Sharīʿa – the religious law of which he is no longer in need, and which is meant only for the masses and neophytes. Even those who held a less extreme view saw in the positive religion only a pedagogy, a ladder to be climbed and then discarded. Some, indeed, insisted that the law may not be transcended at any point. These were precisely the orthodox Ṣūfīs who developed the categories of the 'inner' and the 'outer' described in the previous section. But their reform was not enough; they did not develop any *organic and necessary* relationship between the Inner and the Outer, between the mystic experience and its cognitive content on the one hand and the Sharīʿa life and the discursive intellect on the other. If they had been able to do so, this might not only have averted the gravest inner conflict in Islam, but would have enriched it with an unprecedented creativity. As a result, these Ṣūfīs also left the impression that they were merely juxtaposing two irreconcilable currents out of hypocrisy and through fear of the 'Ulamā'.

Yet Ṣūfism exerted an irresistible pull on men's minds and during the 4th/10th and 5th/11th centuries won an increasing number of the ablest intelligentsia. The systems of the 'Ulamā' had become rigid and their legal casuistry and empty theological pedantry drove the more serious-minded men of religion and originality into the Ṣūfī fold. The 'Ulamā' scoffed at the Ṣūfī pretensions of possessing the unique cognitive avenues to God but they did not seem to understand the power and the depth of the genuinely religious demand represented by the tide of Ṣūfism, and the ground was rapidly slipping beneath their feet. The more orthodox Ṣūfīs made the effort to come half-way, but the 'Ulamā', as a whole, remained insensible. In the meantime, the more extravagant forms of theosophic Ṣūfism were gathering momentum. Immediately before al-Ghazālī, the great systems of philosophical mysticism elaborated by the philosophers al-Fārābī and Ibn Sīnā gave a fresh impetus to and were exploited by this theosophic Ṣūfism.

Al-Ghazālī's mission, therefore, was welcome not merely as a reform or rather re-orientation of orthodox Islam but equally as a reform of Ṣūfism. Philosophic enquiry into the ultimate nature of God had yielded him no results; hence he did not turn to Ṣūfism to gain this knowledge in another way. He neither wanted nor hoped for any occult miraculous knowledge. His purpose was to live through the verities of the Faith and to test those verities through the Ṣūfī experientialist method. He succeeded. The test confirmed his faith and he concluded (1) that it was only through the 'life of the heart' that faith could really be acquired and (2) (and what is of at least equal importance) that Ṣūfism has no *cognitive content or object but the verities of the Faith.* He, therefore, disallowed the pretensions of theosophic mysticism and castigated the men of ecstatic delirium.

This was a remarkable lesson taught by a great mystic spirit, one of the most remarkable lessons, we venture to think, in the whole history of mysticism – viz., that mysticism is *not* a way of finding extra *facts* about Reality but is a meaningful way of looking at it, of looking at it as a unity. Further the unity of the mystic consciousness is *conditioned* by the factual content (however much it may try to transcend that content), which it tests and transforms by new *meanings*. This was an especially reassuring discovery for the position of the Sharī'a, and it revolutionized the relationship of Ṣūfism to the orthodox faith, producing in course of time men who worked out that relationship, as we shall see, and restated their faith in new terms.

But the critical, synthetic and reforming activity of al-Ghazālī, at the same time, proved to be a great watershed in the spiritual history of Islam, and forced the currents of ideas in the Muslim community into both new divisions and new combinations. The most powerful and fateful for the future of Islam was the junction produced during the century after al-Ghazālī between philosophical currents and Ṣūfism at the level of doctrine, to which we have alluded in the previous chapter. Under the violent attacks of orthodoxy, successfully initiated by al-Ghazālī, rational philosophy did not die but went underground, and avenged itself through its new guise of theosophic Ṣūfism where it found a ready and secure home. It was, indeed, an almost unassailable citadel, for, whereas in its rational, purely philosophical form it could be criticized and its inadequacies exposed by an al-Ghazālī, under its new Ṣūfī form this theosophy claimed to be the product of infallible intuitions, immune from rational criticism. Thus, the formal structure of Ṣūfī methodology advocated by al-Ghazālī as outlined above and adopted by orthodox Ṣūfīs was set at naught by the new theosophy which increasingly attracted some of the best minds of later medieval Islam. In place of the moral, non-metaphysical mystic experience of orthodox Ṣūfism, an out-and-out philosophical intuitionism was now substituted whereby men claimed to arrive at metaphysical knowledge.

The classic formulation of the new Ṣūfī epistemology was worked out by Ibn al-'Arabī (d. 638/1240), the apostle of theosophic mysticism in Islam. At the beginning of his *magnum opus* entitled 'The Meccan Revelations (*al-Futūḥāt al-Makkīya*)' he discusses the 'ways of knowledge' and concludes that intuitive revelation (*kashf*) is the highest and the only sure source of cognition. He criticizes the philosophers for their exclusive reliance on reason but he also admonishes the religious classes in the same work that not all philosophical doctrines are to be rejected as false. What really happened in this process was that the philosophical legacy was adopted and developed by Ibn al-'Arabī and his followers into a monistic doctrine, but instead of being given out as a product of reason it was issued in the name of mystic intuition. Subsequent mystic works of theosophic Ṣūfīs are full of criticism of 'rationalists' and of disparagement of reason over against intuition, and give the impression that the Ṣūfīs are the arch-enemies of philosophy. Thus Jalāl al-Dīn Rūmī, the great Ṣūfī poet-philosopher (d. 672/1273) says:

> 'Philosophers' legs are made of wood;
> Legs of wood are infirm, indeed.'

The truth, however, is that this opposition is only methodological, and corresponds more or less accurately to al-Ghazālī's opposition to the orthodox 'Ulamā'. The content does not vary in this opposition; what is contrasted here is the form of experience with the process of discursive reasoning. Indeed, we find that later philosophers like Ṣadr al-Dīn (see the preceding chapter) also systematically adopt intuitive revelation as the highest form of knowledge in their epistemological framework.

So much for the epistemological challenge of Ṣūfism to orthodox theologians. But even more grave was the content of this theosophy which is also essentially the product of Ibn al-'Arabī's versatile and imaginative genius. His system, which, for the speculative Ṣūfīs, came to supplant that of orthodox theology, is thoroughly monistic and pantheistic, the very reverse of the teaching of orthodox Islam. Briefly, Ibn al-'Arabī taught that the Absolute Reality is transcendent and nameless and its only attribute is self-existence. But this Absolute, by a kind of propulsion or process of 'descent' and 'determination' develops a state of being wherein it becomes conscious of its attributes, knowledge, power, life, creativity, etc. These attributes of perfection, however, exist only in its mind or consciousness. But it is also these attributes which constitute the stuff from which the world is made. The 'creation' of the world is nothing but the projection of these attributes from the

Divine Mind outward into 'real existence' which is nothing but the existence of the Absolute Himself. The attributes or names of God, as they are in the Divine Mind prior to external existence, also constitute the essence of the 'created' World. The highest of these essences is the essence of Muḥammad which manifested itself in the historic person of the prophet Muḥammad but whose transcendental state is to be fulfilled not in the 'Seal of the Prophets' but in the 'Seal of the Saints'. This 'Seal of the Saints' is no other than Ibn al-'Arabī himself.

Both these doctrines threatened orthodoxy directly. The second doctrine, which was a challenge to the status of the Prophet personally, lost its force because Ibn al-'Arabī's pretensions to be the 'Seal of the Saints' were not taken seriously, but even so the old controversy of pre-Ghazālian times as to the relationship of the saints to the Prophet was revived. But the more insidious effect of both doctrines was that the position of the Sharī'a and its visible pillar, the law, was gravely endangered. A thoroughly monistic system, no matter how pious and conscientious it may claim to be, cannot, by its very nature, take seriously the objective validity of moral standards. 'All is He' (Persian: *hama ūst*) was the inevitable conclusion. Jāmī, the 9th/15th century Persian mystic poet, teaches:

> The companion, comrade and co-traveller,
> All is He,
> In the mendicant's tattered robe and in the brocade
> of the regal dress, All is He;
> Whether in the display of variety or the privacy
> of unity –
> By God All is He! Again, by God All is He!

A remarkable feature of this literature especially in its poetic form, was the development of the images of earthly love and its employment to depict the spiritual passion of the seeker of God. Ibn al-'Arabī himself had composed his lyrical *Interpreter of Desires* inspired by a lady of parts in Mecca. Later he had to comment on this poem to show that his object of desire was spiritual. In general, para-sexual symbolism abounds in his thought. Adam, he taught, was really the first female for Eve was born from his inside, an act repeated by the second Adam, Mary, in generating Jesus. In the subsequent Persian Ṣūfī poetry that blossomed so brilliantly, amorous images are employed in stark realism and many poets have been objects of controversy as to whether they were singing of spiritual love or earthly passion. This imagery became the stock-in-trade of most of Persian, Turkish and Urdu poetry, and so powerful was its charm that it is only during the present century that literary style has begun to move away from it.

We shall have occasion in the following chapter to describe the practical consequences for Islam of the monistic doctrine known as the doctrine of the 'Unity of Being' and its threatened *bouleversement* of the very concept of the Islamic Sharīʿa. We may end this chapter by noting the methods by which the orthodox forces set themselves to face this challenge. At the level of doctrine, orthodoxy, as we noted above, was unwilling to admit the objective validity of the Ṣūfī insight or intuition, although certain later figures like al-Taftāzānī (d. 791/1389) concede that mystic intuition is authoritative for the experiencing subject himself even though it cannot claim validity beyond him. At the theological level (which, unlike the creed, is not the level of the masses but of religious intellectuals), however, chiefly due to al-Ghazālī's influence, Ṣūfī intuition began to be taken seriously although its claims to infallibility were not and could not be conceded. Indeed, the monistic theosophic content of Ṣūfī doctrine was severely rejected by the majority of orthodox theologians.

It is this background which mainly set the field of activity of Ibn Taymīya (see supra, Chapter VI) and his disciples, primarily Ibn Qayyim, from the 8th/14th century onwards. As we saw in Chapter VI, Ibn Taymīya accepts the validity of the Ṣūfī experimental method although he and his school relentlessly attacked the Ṣūfī rituals and practices of tomb worship and the cults of saints. His pupil, Ibn Qayyim, showed himself even more tolerant in his language than his master. What Ibn Taymīya and his school insisted upon, however, was that Ṣūfī experience had no exclusive and infallible validity and that in fact the validity of its content is to be tested with reference to the external world. Thus, Ṣūfism might interpret and give new meaning to the Sharīʿa and the Revelation, but it cannot set them at naught. The doctrine of monism, they held, obliterates all distinctions in the real world which must serve as the touchstone for the validity of any proposition and thus destroys the Sharīʿa or the moral order. Monism not only fails to satisfy this criterion but negates the criterion itself. Hence this doctrine as a *moral* interpretation of the universe must be rejected. There is no doubt that the immediate object of Ibn Taymīya's criticism is the Ṣūfī doctrine of the Unity of Being. But he goes back and attacks the philosophers whose doctrines had prepared the way for Ṣūfī monism. And pushing his analysis back still further, the Ashʿarī doctrine of the Will of God is found to be a great milestone in this monistic development. Ibn Taymīya felt it imperative, therefore, to construct a concept of the Sharīʿa which would synthesize a double but analogous duality between Muʿtazilism and Ashʿarism and between Ṣūfī monism and the reality of the moral law.

Ibn Taymīya's teaching aroused much bitter criticism even from among the ranks of the 'Ulamā', the chief reason for which was his rejection of the unquestioned acceptance of authority (*taqlīd*) and his consequent fearless criticism of almost all Muslim sects, including the orthodox Ash'arī theology which he denounced in very strong terms as advocating anti-Islamic predestinarianism. Gradually, however, his message served as a leaven for subsequent religious developments and in the 12th/18th century burst out in the violent form of the Wahhābī reform (see Chapter XII). But the more hopeful and influential approach was to reform Ṣūfism from within Ṣūfism itself. Gradually recognized by the Ijmā' of the Community after al-Ghazālī, Ṣūfism attracted many followers from the ranks of the 'Ulamā' who realized that the only hope to rid Ṣūfism of its excesses and aberrations was to take it seriously. In the later medieval centuries of Islam, it came to be a normal procedure to combine the purificative and contemplative path of Ṣūfism with the normal orthodox disciplines of Ḥadīth, law and theology.

Criticism of extravagant intellectual and spiritual consequences of Ibn al-'Arabī's monistic doctrine had begun early even within Ṣūfism. A notable Ṣūfī, al-Samnānī (d. 736/1336), had accused him of 'confounding God with the world' by identifying the Divine and the human. This movement culminated in the teaching of Aḥmad Sirhindī (d. 1034/1625), an outstanding Indian theoretician of reformed Ṣūfism. Sirhindī, a practising Ṣūfī of the Naqshbandī order, declared that the experience of the Unity of Being, although real as an experience, does not represent the last stage of the mystic's development. He then constructed his own doctrine seeking to do justice to the reality of the moral distinctions in religion and propagated it through numerous letters to his disciples who were widely scattered throughout India and in Transoxiana. Confirming the teaching of Ibn Taymīya from the Ṣūfī side, he taught that the Ṣūfī 'Reality' (*ḥaqīqa*), which was so commonly opposed to the Sharī'a was really the life-foundation of the Sharī'a itself.

Sirhindī's movement was of very considerable influence in the subcontinent and largely successful in counteracting the antinomian tendencies within the ranks of the Ṣūfī adepts. Despite the efforts of this group, however, the attraction exerted by monism on many minds was irresistible. In India this was especially the case because of the Hindu pantheistic influences to which Islam was constantly exposed. It was partly these influences which had led the Mughal emperor Akbar to proclaim a syncretistic religion (*Dīn-i Ilāhī*) in the 10th/16th century and to attempt to impose it as state religion (to which the Sirhindī-led movement was a successful reaction). The second Ṣūfī movement, therefore, had as its objective to synthesize the monistic framework of mystic theosophy with the moral exigencies of the Sharī'a. The most prominent exponents of this type of thought were the Syrian 'Abd al-Ghanī of Nābulus (d. 1144/1731) and Shāh Walī Allāh of Delhi (d. 1176/1762). A similar reinterpretation of the Ṣūfī doctrine, breaking away vehemently from pantheism, was undertaken in the Malay Archipelago by Nūr al-Dīn ibn Muḥammad al-Ranīrī (d. 1077/1666). These Ṣūfī theologians, in their general objectives, are comparable, from the Ṣūfī side, to the synthetic spirit of Ibn Taymīya at the orthodox scholastic level. A remarkable effect of these endeavours was to change the character of Islamic theology from its traditional scholastic mould to a more genuinely intellectual and speculative one. It was achieved by men who were professional Ṣūfīs but whose orthodoxy was equally indubitable. It provides us with a shining example of that fundamentally catholic genius of Islam – a panorama of continued tensions and challenges and of equally persistent efforts to resolve these tensions and meet these challenges in a process of modification, adaptation and absorption.

CHAPTER NINE

ṢŪFĪ ORGANIZATIONS

Ṣūfism and Popular Religion – The Ṣūfī Orders – Sequel

Ṣūfism and Popular Religion

Just as the doctrine and practice of Ṣūfism arose out of early pietism and the activity of the preachers, so the movement of popular religion, which, from the 5th/11th century onward, developed with an astonishing rapidity into Ṣūfī orders throughout the length and breadth of the Muslim world, is directly associated with the doctrines of the Ṣūfī schools. The early development and formulation of the Ṣūfī ideal and its broader techniques had taken place at the hands of the individual Ṣūfīs who were centres of limited and close circles of disciples. These circles with their differing doctrines may justifiably be called Ṣūfī schools of which the chief mystic doctrines have been recorded by the 5th/11th century Ṣūfī 'Alī al-Hujwīrī (whose tomb in Lahore is an object of public veneration) in his work *Kashf al-Maḥjūb*.

In the middle of the 3rd/9th century Ṣūfism began to be publicly taught in Baghdad and elsewhere. The overwhelming attraction that it came to exert over the masses has to be explained by several factors, religious, social and political. First, Ṣūfism claimed to lead its adepts to a direct communion with God, a thesis which the orthodox 'Ulamā' rejected. The religious fascination of this ideal was so powerful that Ṣūfism, in course of time, became a religion within a religion with its own exclusive structure of ideas, practice and organization. To realize this ideal, Ṣūfism offered a neat and concrete method according to which the novice or the 'seeker' was taken from 'station' to 'station' until he shed his humanity and became divine. Despite its often genuinely professed high ideals and moral precepts, however, the popular leaders of the movement gradually became less and less sensitive to the fundamental moral peril necessarily involved in an institutionalized and professional method of 'attaining to God'. But so irresistible was its fascination that the sobering voice of the 'Ulamā' gradually lost its influence, and orthodox Islam finally capitulated after the 8th/14th century.

But the directly religious motivation was not the only factor in the spread of the Ṣūfī movement. Its socio-political function, and at times more specifically its protest function, were even more powerful than the religious one. Ṣūfism offered, through its organized rituals and *séances*, a pattern of social life which satisfied the social needs of especially the uneducated classes. This, more than anything else, explains the widespread success of the 'rustic orders' of the villages removed from the cultivated influence of the city life. This was particularly the case with those orders which freely indulged in practices of singing, dancing and other orgiastic rituals. It was through these socio-religious cults that Ṣūfism came to be connected with organized professional groups. This was pre-eminently the case with medieval Turkey where the Ṣūfī movement was associated intimately with the professional guilds and with the military organization of the 'Janissaries' (Yenicheri). All organized professions of craftsmen and artisans were connected with some saint or the other, thus deriving their spiritual patronage. Such guilds then, from this point of view, show a marked resemblance with the guilds of medieval Europe. At the same time, the Ṣūfī organizations were a kind of bulwark against the state authority, especially since the 5th/11th century when the political unity of the Islamic world began to crumble, giving place to the ever insecure masses against autocratic and ever despotic sultans whose authority was also accepted by the 'Ulamā' as being a lesser evil than chaos and lawlessness. Ṣūfism, in its organized form, therefore functioned also as a protest against political tyranny. This has been pre-eminently the case both in medieval Turkey and in modern times in North and West Africa and the Eastern Sudan. In Turkey the Ṣūfī movement has been associated with the numerous rebellions against the state from the 7th/13th century (when a certain Shaykh Bābā Ilyās rose in rebellion against the last Seljūq sultan) to the 11th/17th century. In Africa, as we shall see below, the Ṣūfī orders of various kinds have constantly put up a fierce military resistance against the penetration of the European colonial powers.

Nor must it be imagined that the aversion of the Ṣūfī movement to the 'Ulamā' was based on exclusively religious grounds. For the 'Ulamā' as a class, were intimately bound up with the state. The law which it was the state's duty to enforce was the religious law formulated by the 'Ulamā'. The 'Ulamā' were also state-functionaries since they were in charge of the execution of this law. In the popular mind, therefore, the 'Ulamā' and the Islam they stood for were necessarily 'allies' of the state. Much of the hostile attitude of popular Ṣūfism, especially in later medievalism, when analysed carefully, arose from this situation and not merely from the 'aristocratic look' that the orthodox educational system and institutions assumed in the popular eye due to their intellectual and exclusive character, although this latter factor also undoubtedly played an important rôle.

From its informal and loose beginnings in the 2nd/8th century, when men gathered privately to recite the Qur'ān aloud, this *dhikr* (literally 'remembrance', i.e. of God – certain passages of the Qur'ān are appealed to in this connection) developed into an elaborate congregational ritual during the following centuries. In the Ṣūfī orders of Africa especially, the term *wird* has normally replaced *dhikr*. *Dhikr* or *wird* thus came to mean not the recitation of the Holy Book but short religious formulas, usually containing the ninety-nine 'beautiful names' of God, and repeated on a chain of beads. An initiation ceremony was adopted which commonly betrays an unIslamic origin and in some cases had its source in Christian practices but was nevertheless transformed into an Islamic mould. Here is a brief account of the initiation ceremony (called *bay'a*) performed by a Shaykh of the Khalwatīya order:

The novice seats himself in front of the master in such a way that their knees meet. The master, who has his face turned to the south, reads the *Fātiḥa* (the opening Sūra of the Qur'ān) with his hand placed into the hand of the aspirant who entrusts his soul to the former. . . . The master says to the novice three times 'say with me: "I seek pardon of God the Great" '. He then recites the last two Sūras of the Qur'ān . . . and then the verse of 'giving allegiance' (i.e. from the Qur'ān): 'Those who pay their allegiance to thee (O Muḥammad!) are but doing obeisance to God'. Then the master prays for the novice, commends him to God and admonishes him to fulfil the obligations of his affiliation and to (try to) tread always in the right path.[1]

Still more extraneous aids to bring about the ecstatic state were presently introduced into mystical practices. Having compromised with popular religious modes and ideas, Ṣūfism now succumbed to them and a point of no return seems to have been reached by the end of the 7th/13th and the beginning of the 8th/14th centuries. Especially prominent among these new features was the introduction of music and dancing and other violent movements of the body. Music is said to have been introduced into the great Qādirīya order by Shams al-Dīn, the third descendant of the founder of the order, 'Abd al-Qādir al-Gīlānī. Another order, the Rifā'īya, indulged so exceedingly in these practices that they came to be called 'the howling dervishes'. As they chanted their *dhikr* in a circle, with each participant's hands on his neighbour's shoulders, they flung the upper part of their bodies forward and backward, and in this moment of 'ecstasy' fell upon such objects as serpents and knives, that had been put there. Still another order, that of the Jibāwīya (which originated in the 8th/14th century), danced on their right heels around the hall, with their eyes shut and their arms open, and were named 'the whirling dervishes'. In certain still more extreme orders this was accompanied by the rending of garments and other 'mystic' feats such as eating glass (practices which have been attributed to the Shamanistic influences brought by the Mongol invasion).

This phenomenon of popular religion very radically changed the aspect of Ṣūfism even if it did not entirely displace its very ideal. For practical purposes, Islamic society underwent a metempsychosis. Instead of being a method of moral self-discipline and elevation and genuine spiritual enlightenment, Ṣūfism was now transformed into veritable spiritual jugglery through auto-hypnotic transports and visions just as at the level of doctrine it was being transmuted into a half-delirious theosophy. Indeed, the doctrine and the practice interacted. By the 5th/11th century, belief in miracles of 'the saints' had become widespread. The orthodoxy cautiously accepted it. Even among the pure philosophers, though al-Fārābī in the first half of the 4th/10th century is free from miracles, Ibn Sīnā, a century later, had to devise a rational doctrine to accommodate at least such 'miracles' as could be explained by scientific psychology. Under the influence of the suggestions of al-Ghazālī himself an elaborate theory was constructed to prove the existence of the '*Ālam al-Mithāl* (the World of Symbols and Figures) as an intermediary between the spiritual and material realms, described in Chapter VII. This dream and shadow land was now to serve in theory as the proper arena of miracle-mongering. This, combined with the spiritual demagogy of many Ṣūfī Shaykhs, opened the way for all kinds of aberrations, not the least of which was charlatanism. Ill-balanced *majdhūbs* (i.e. those in perpetual trance), parasitic mendicants, exploiting dervishes proclaimed Muḥammad's Faith in the heyday of Ṣūfism. Islam was at the mercy of spiritual delinquents.

Belief in miracles was, in fact, part of a wider concept of the spiritual powers of the saints transmitted through their representative Ṣūfī adepts. These powers emanated from the spiritual leader and affected both the spiritual and material destinies of his followers. This is called *baraka* or *fayḍ* 'blessing'. The widespread belief in this *baraka* led to the veneration and worship of saints' tombs and other alleged relics. Special annual pilgrimages are still held at the graves of these saints very often accompanied by fairs that constitute a genuine outlet of social needs for the public which flocks to them in thousands from far and near. Among all these miracle-working saints a special place of veneration is occupied by 'Abd al-Qādir al-Gīlānī (see below) who has very nearly displaced Muḥammad himself in the eyes of the Ṣūfī-worshipping public.

The absolute authority, both in matters spiritual and material, of the Ṣūfī leader, called Shaykh (*pīr* or *murshīd* in Persia and India, *muqaddam* in Negro Africa), over his disciples called *faqīr* (the 'poor'), *darwīsh*, *murīd* ('disciple') or *ikhwān*, popular *khwān* ('brothers'), sometimes *aṣḥāb* ('companions') as in the Tījānī order, is a cardinal constitutional principle of organized Ṣūfism. Only rare exceptions within this movement have voiced the view that one may dispense with the living authority of a Shaykh if a worthy enough guide cannot be found. The vast majority has always insisted that a living guide, even a relatively imperfect one, is absolutely necessary. Thus Ṣūfism became virtually a cult of personalities. The term *bē-pīrā* 'guideless person' became almost equivalent to 'godless person' in the popular mind. The original reason for this view seems to have been the fear lest, for want of an objective point of guiding reference, each person should become his own spiritual criterion. Thus al-Ghazālī himself says:

The disciple must of necessity have recourse to a director to guide him aright. For the way of the Faith is obscure, but the Devil's ways are many and patent, and he who has no Shaykh to guide him will be led by the Devil into his ways. Wherefore, the disciple must cling to his Shaykh as a blind man on the edge of a river clings to his leader, confiding himself to him entirely, opposing him in no matter whatsoever, and binding himself to follow him absolutely. Let him know that the advantage he gains from the error of his Shaykh, if he should err, is greater than the advantage he gains from his own rightness, if he should be right.[2]

'Thou shalt be in the hands of thy Shaykh like a dead body in the hands of its cleanser' is the well-known aphorism summing up this teaching. And it is significant that this '*perinde ac cadaver*' philosophy gained ground upon the heels of 'closing the door of *ijtihād*' by orthodoxy itself. Actually, the letter of this law was not followed in all cases, and examples are not lacking where an exceptionally capable disciple ended up by being accepted by his Shaykh as the latter's instructor. And it is also true that the history of Ṣūfism is rich with personalities of outstanding integrity and genuine moral greatness. However, the doctrine of complete spiritual surrender to a fellow human being could not be reconciled with Islamic orthodoxy which rejected it even when orthodox 'Ulamā' cautiously joined the movement and participated in some of its moderate forms. We shall see in Chapters XII and XIII that under the influence of Muslim religious reform movements this attitude has been largely undermined.

Besides Ṣūfism's 'appeal to the heart' at the higher spiritual level, it unfolded a disconcerting tendency of compromise with the popular beliefs and practices of the half-converted and even nominally converted masses. Within its latitudinarianism, latent in it from the beginning, it allowed a motley of religious attitudes inherited by the new converts from their previous backgrounds, from animism in Africa to pantheism in India. A typically Ṣūfī Ḥadīth, according to which the Prophet said, 'God the Exalted says, "I am what My servant thinks of Me", ' was given wide currency and curious interpretations by eminent Ṣūfīs. Ibn al-'Arabī had read many a theosophic meaning into it and had emphasized the relativity of the religious truth. Rūmī expresses it very graphically in his poem 'The Shepherd's Prayer':

> Moses saw a shepherd on the way, crying, 'O Lord who choosest as Thou wilt.
>
> Where art Thou, that I may serve Thee and sew Thy shoes and comb Thy hair? That I may wash Thy clothes and kill Thy lice and bring milk to Thee, O worshipful one;
>
> That I may kiss Thy little hand and rub Thy little feet and sweep Thy little room at bed time.'
>
> On hearing these foolish words, Moses said, 'Man, to whom are you speaking?
>
> What babble! What blasphemy and raving!
> Stuff some cotton into your mouth!
> Truly the friendship of a fool is enmity; the High God is not in want of such like service.'
>
> The shepherd rent his garment, heaved a sigh, and took his way to the wilderness. Then came to Moses a Revelation: 'Thou hast parted My servant from Me. Wert thou sent as a Prophet to unite, or wert thou sent to sever? I have bestowed on everyone a particular mode of worship; I have given everyone a peculiar form of expression.
> The idiom of Hindūstān is excellent for Hindus, the idiom of Sind is excellent for the people of Sind. . .'.[3]

This strong tendency to compromise with local ideas and customs of the converts has divided Islam into a variety of religious and social cultures and militated against the forces of uniformity represented by the orthodox 'Ulamā'. This uniformity remained while Islam remained true to the early spirit of the Arab stamp. Under the rising tide, from the 6th/12th century onwards, of essentially non-Arab interpretations of Islam, the original stamp – of which the carriers were the 'Ulamā' – became submerged if not entirely suppressed. The massive catalyst of these new interpretations was Ṣūfism, which also reacted forcefully on the Arab lands. But at the same time Ṣūfism proved the greatest channel for the spread of Islam precisely by virtue of the same compromise. In India, Central Asia, Turkey and Africa, it brought millions within the fold of Islam with astonishing rapidity and is still a proselytizing force in Africa. Further, the fact that Ṣūfism came to be linked with Sunnī Islam caused a severe dimunition in the ranks of the Shī'a. What made this possible is a fascinating subject: what seems to have happened is that Ṣūfism, by helping to bestow personal affection on

'Alī and his early successors – whom it acclaimed as its central source figures, became the successful rival to Shī'ism, robbing it of its very appeal and substituting itself for it. From the 8th/14th century onward, wave upon wave of orthodox reform arose to Islamize and consolidate the gains of converts made by Ṣūfism. These we shall briefly study in the third section of this chapter. In the meantime, we shall turn to a brief survey of the more important Ṣūfī orders.

The Ṣūfī Orders

Although the Ṣūfī orders as we know them date from the 6th/12th and 7th/13th centuries, one important feature of this movement goes back much earlier. This feature is the genealogy of spiritual authority commonly called *silsila* which was probably copied from the institution of *isnād* (see Chapter III) developed by the traditionists to support the validity of Ḥadīth. In the 4th/10th century, the Ṣūfī al-Khuldī (d. 348/959) traced the genealogy of his mystic teaching to Ḥasan al-Baṣrī (d. 110/728) and thence, through the Companion Anas ibn Mālik, to the Prophet himself. Later chains start going back to 'Alī, in most cases through Ḥasan al-Baṣrī, but sometimes through the early figures venerated by the Shī'a among 'Alī's descendants. This genealogy is undoubtedly apocryphal, but it shows that probably from the 7th/13th century organized Sunnī Ṣūfism had begun to claim the Shī'a Imāms as authorities and thus cut the ground from beneath Shī'ism, which seems to have suffered a heavy blow through the spread of Ṣūfism. On the other hand, however, on some of the Ṣūfī orders of the left wing, notably the Bekṭāshī order of Turkey, Shī'ism and its esotericism have exerted strong influences. It was probably as a counter-measure against this increasing appeal to the authority of the Shī'a Imāms that the Naqshbandī order traced its genealogy to the first Caliph, Abū Bakr, and the Suhrawardīs traced their source of authority to the second Caliph, 'Umar ibn al-Khaṭṭāb.

It is also worth noting that the Islamic term *ṭarīqa* and its usual Western rendering 'order' or 'fraternity' are not entirely identical. The Western terms point to the organizational aspect of Ṣūfism whereas the word *ṭarīqa*, although in organized Ṣūfism it is closely intertwined with an organization, is really the name of the Ṣūfī 'path' claiming to lead man to communion with God. A *ṭarīqa*, therefore, can exist without a corresponding organized fraternity. Indeed before the advent of organized Ṣūfism, there existed *ṭarīqas* which were merely *schools of Ṣūfī doctrine*. The Ṣūfī orders, in their rise, are connected with this early phase of schools of mysticism and the term *ṭarīqa* has therefore retained this original meaning of being ideally a *method* or *way* with doctrinal overtones even though rites and external practices increased in importance.

The pivot of a Ṣūfī fraternity is obviously the Shaykh whose residence or place of teaching (frequently they are identical), called *zāwiya* (or *ribāṭ*) in Arabic, *khānqāh* in India and Persia and *tekke* in Turkey, serves as the centre of the spiritual activities of his congregation. The membership is normally of two kinds; besides the proper initiates or the immediate circle, there is usually a large number of associates or lay members who pay visits from time to time in order to get fresh instructions, but are otherwise allowed to carry on their normal business of life. It is this latter class from which the main financial support of the *zāwiya* comes. The initiates, again, are of various ranks according to the ability, sincerity and devotion they display or the period of apprenticeship they may have undergone. To teach and treat people each according to his capacity and individual needs is a cardinal principle with Ṣūfī Shaykhs who often show a remarkable insight into practical psychology. While an able disciple may succeed in obtaining 'the robe' (*khirqa*, the insignia of graduation) and the privilege to teach the master's methods as his *khalīfa* (successor or deputy) in a few months or even in a few weeks, other initiates, during the first stages of their apprenticeship, may be required to render prolonged services at the *zāwiya*, such as gathering fuel or collecting food-grains or cooking for the congregation, etc.

The number of the individual Ṣūfī orders throughout the Muslim world is so large that there is only space here to note the most important of them with a brief description of their salient characteristics. Apart from differences in regard to the relative looseness or strictness of cohesion around the centre and variations in rituals, the orders exhibit remarkable differences in matters of general outlook and composition of their adherents. Among the non-African orders, a broad line of division may be drawn between urban orders generally with an educated and cultured following and the 'rustic' orders of the countryside. Among the urban orders, again, there are differences in respect of being more closely associated with orthodox Islam or, on the other hand, emphasizing a pure Ṣūfī doctrinal ideal, although naturally all urban orders are liable to be influenced by the orthodox teaching to some extent at least at the practical level of observing the Sharī'a Law. In North-West and Negro Africa especially, there are variations with regard to political attitude and whether a particular order is militant or peace-loving.

The orders also interact with one another and especially in the later centuries it has not been possible, in most cases, to keep a rigid line of division. It is not only possible for a single individual to belong to several fraternities at the same time, but a certain sub-order of a parent order sometimes lays claim to a spiritual genealogy within which the spiritual figures of another parent order freely appear. Indeed, in many cases, a sub-order only keeps a titular affiliation with the parent order and launches itself on an entirely independent career, wherein it may keep certain rites of the original order but adds new emphasis and sometimes introduces an entirely new orientation. Among the very few exceptions which have been able to keep exclusive membership, if not an exclusive character, are the Tījānīya in Africa and Mawlawīya in Turkey (suppressed since 1925).

The most widespread and probably the oldest of all existing Ṣūfī orders is the Qādirīya. It overarches most of the other orders which have been related to it in terms of influence at one stage or another if they have not directly descended from it. Indeed, with regard to most of the other orders it has acted as a kind of lever, because of its looseness and adaptability and its own congregations, often autonomous or semi-autonomous, have spread from one end of the Muslim world to the other.

The order is named after 'Abd al-Qādir al-Gīlānī, a native of the district of Gīlān south of the Caspian. Born in 470/1077, he was sent to Baghdad at the age of eighteen where he studied philosophy and Ḥanbalite law. In Ṣūfism he is said to have been a disciple of al-Dabbās (d. 525/1131). In 521/1127 he began to preach in public and his audience steadily grew. In 528/1134 he was installed as head of a *madrasa*, where so many people began to be attracted to his powerful sermons that a *ribāṭ* was built for him outside the gates of the city. Thus, he began to preach both in the school and in his monastery. He died in 561/1166. His most famous work, entitled *Sufficiency for the Seekers of Truth*, contains his sermons as well as an account of Muslim sects. His writings are orthodox in character with some mystical interpretations of the Qur'ānic passages. The chief underlying traits of his teaching seem to be a dissuasion from being immersed in worldliness and an emphasis on charity and humanitarianism; he wishes 'to close the gates of Hell and open the portals of Paradise for all mankind'. But whereas contemporaries of the Shaykh speak of him with profound respect and extol the tremendous effect of his preaching, which is said to have resulted both in the conversion of many Jews and Christians to Islam and in raising the spiritual level of his congregation, later accounts actually attribute all kinds of miracles to him. His legend steadily grew until, at the popular level of unorthodox 'irregular' orders, it has supplanted the religious personality of the Prophet Muhammad himself.

The phenomenon of the attribution of miracles to the saints constitutes a very interesting chapter in the history of Ṣūfism. It must remain true that by far the largest number of 'miracles' were conscious products designed to enhance the prestige of a certain saint or of the order connected with his name. But there is also the important fact that the longer the principle of the absolute authority of the Shaykh was practised, the greater was the degree of passivity, suggestibility and susceptibility of the common run of disciples. In most cases the fact is that the disciples tended to father miracles on the Shaykhs who disowned them. It follows that the tendency to attribute miracles to a personage who lived before the immediate Shaykh was still more powerful. At this sort of miracle-attribution the immediate Shaykh often connived, for he, although not claiming any miracles for himself, stood in the relationship of either immediate or remote discipleship to this personage and thus possessed enough credulousness *vis-à-vis* him to support the attribution to him of ever new and fresh miracles. There were, of course, undoubtedly other factors, as in the case of 'Abd al-Qādir al-Gīlānī, who possessed striking piety and philanthropy and manifested a powerful sincerity in his sermons.

It is highly improbable that 'Abd al-Qādir al-Gīlānī intended to form an 'order' besides training his immediate circle of spiritual disciples. It was his sons who played a central rôle in establishing the Qādirīya order and in its initial propagation. The central nucleus at Baghdad, which is still managed by a direct descendant of al-Gīlānī, spread westward into North Africa and then into Negro Africa, eastward as far as Indo-China and northward into Turkey. The affiliation of the provincial congregations to the centre is loose and its most important financial support comes from the Indo-Pakistan subcontinent. This is shown by the fact that the leaders in Baghdad have usually a working knowledge of the Urdu language. At the turn of the present century, Qādirism was transformed into a new order in Senegal by Aḥmadū Banba, who gave it a completely new direction. The new order, known as the Murīdīya, is regarded as a typical African reaction to the spirit of 'foreign' Islam and has dispensed with such fundamentals as prayer and fasting.

The Qādirīya is among the most peaceful of the Ṣūfī orders and is distinguished by piety and humanitarianism, the ethos inculcated by the Shaykh with whom it is associated. It is on the whole orthodox avoiding the excesses of the more extreme popular orders. It is doubtful whether the originator left any rigid system of either doctrine or practice besides the basic spirit of charity and non-fanaticism. The litanies (*dhikr*-formulas) are in fact different among different regional organizations, but there is nothing unorthodox in them, composed as they usually are of passages and phrases from the Qur'ān. A representative formula is: 'I seek pardon of God the Mighty. Glory be to God, O, God! bless our master Muḥammad and his family and Companions. There is no god but God.' The first three sentences are recited a hundred times each while the last one is repeated five hundred times. There are also other longer prayers known as *wird* or *ḥizb*.

A still more refined but far less widespread order, the Suhrawardīya, grew from the mystic doctrine of 'Umar al-Suhrawardī (to be distinguished from Yaḥyā Suhrawardī, the 'philosopher of illumination' spoken of in Chapter VII), who died near Zanjān in Persia in 632/1236. This order is to be found only in Afghanistan and the Indo-Pakistan subcontinent. Through his work *Cognition of the Inner Truth* (*'Awārif al-Ma'ārif*), al-Suhrawardī has exerted considerable influence on Ṣūfism outside the order that is connected with his name. Especially celebrated is his method of *dhikr* woven around different names of God in the ascending scale of 'Lights' corresponding to the 'seven subtle spirits' (*laṭā'if sab'a*) expressed in a vocabulary that is borrowed from the Qur'ān:

1. The *dhikr* of the 'Commanding Spirit': 'There is no god but God' (repeated 100,000 times); the colour of this light is blue;
2. That of the 'reproaching spirit': 'Allāh (100,000 times); this light is yellow;
3. That of the 'inspiring spirit': 'He' (90,000 times); the colour of this light is red;
4. That of the 'quietened spirit': 'The Living' (70,000 times); this light is white;
5. That of the 'satisfied spirit': 'The Sustaining' (90,000 times); this light is green;
6. That of the 'gratified spirit': 'The Merciful' (75,000 times); this light is black; and
7. That of the 'perfected spirit': 'The Benevolent' (100,000 times); this light has no particular colour but ranges through all the preceding colours.

It was from this doctrine that the 13th/19th century founder of the Sanūsīya order derived his theory of 'sixty thousand lights'.

The Suhrawardī order did not itself spread very far, probably because of its rigorous spiritual discipline. But towards the end of the 8th/14th century it inspired an important orthodox order, the Khalwatīya, founded in Persia by 'Umar al-Khalwatī (d. 800/1398). This order, noted for its strict discipline ('Khalwatī' – seclusionist), spread into Turkey and during the 12th/18th century was introduced into Egypt and the Middle East. Towards the end of the same century, a disciple of the Khalwatī order founded in North-West Africa the new Tījānī order which we shall mention below. The Khalwatī order also gave rise to several branches within itself and especially attracted the adherence of the orthodox 'Ulamā'.

A younger contemporary of 'Abd al-Qādir al-Gīlānī, Aḥmad al-Rifā'ī (d. 578/1182), founded another important order in the district of Baṣra in Iraq, called after him the Rifā'īya. We have noted in the first section of this chapter some of the more extravagant forms of *dhikr* and other rituals practised by this order. It spread into Egypt, Turkey and some parts of South-East Asia. During the reign of the Ottoman sultan 'Abd al-Ḥamīd, the head of the Rifā'ī order in Constantinople, Abu'l-Hudā, reorganized the order more cohesively and lent his support to the pan-Islamic propaganda of the sultan. Some authorities, notably Depont and Coppolani in their *Les Confréries Religieuses Musulmanes*, make al-Rifā'ī a disciple and nephew of 'Abd al-Qādir al-Gīlānī and his order an offshoot of the Qādirīya.[4] There is no authentic early evidence, however, of a blood-relationship between the two and the legend arose most probably after both these saints came to be widely venerated in Iraq. Nor is there any evidence of the Qādirīya influence on al-Rifā'ī – indeed the former did not become an order until well after the latter's death.

In the Ṣūfī world, indeed, legend finds a congenial atmosphere and relationships become obscure, because 'discipleship' is often based on a purely spiritual experience without any actual historical fact and perhaps supported only by forged genealogical chains. Such seems to be the case with the founder of the Badawīya or Aḥmadīya order of Aḥmad al-Badawī (d. 675/1276), who has been venerated as the greatest saint in Egypt for centuries. In a vision he was 'summoned' to Iraq whither he betook himself in 633/1236, visited the tombs of various Ṣūfīs, including those of al-Rifā'ī and al-Gīlānī and founded, on his return to Egypt, his own order which has been the most popular 'rustic' order in Egypt. Al-Badawī indulged in such peculiar practices as star-gazing and abstaining from speaking to people for long stretches of time. During Louis IX's invasion of Egypt in the 7th/13th century he played a conspicuous rôle in stirring up popular resistance to the invading crusaders. Hence his greatest function in the popular mind has been that of liberating prisoners. In their practices, the Badawīya have absorbed certain elements of pre-Islamic Egyptian religion. The other two popular orders in lower Egypt, the Dasūqīya and the Bayyūmīya, are off-shoots of this order.

This is also the case with Sa'd al-Dīn (d. 700/1300) the alleged founder of the Sa'dīya (or Jibāwīya) fraternity in Damascus, whose origins are shrouded in mystery. But the order is said to have spread to Egypt and Turkey during the alleged founder's life-time. We have already alluded to some of the practices of this order, which have been described by W. Lane in his *Manners and Customs of the Modern Egyptians.*

In North-West Africa, the diffusion of Islam with political overtones among the Berbers and in Negro Africa took place in close association with Ṣūfism. In the 6th/12th century the Almohad dynasty (*al-Muwaḥḥidūn*), under the Mahdī ibn Tūmart, succeeded the earlier Almoravids (*al-Murābiṭūn*) who had led an orthodox *jihād* movement of Islamization in the 5th/11th century. Ibn Tūmart combined Ash'arite orthodoxy with Ṣūfism. The most important point of radiation for Ṣūfism in North Africa was Abū Madyan of Tlemcen (6th/12th century). The celebrated pantheistic theosoph Ibn al-'Arabī of Murcia, briefly studied in the last chapter was a disciple of a disciple of this Abū Madyan whose emphasis seems to have been on an absolute concentration on God, paying little heed to the world. The order of the Shādhilīya is associated with the name of another disciple of a disciple of Abū Madyan, Abu'l-Ḥasan al-Shādhilī (d. 656/1258).

Al-Shādhilī does not appear to have evolved any particular Ṣūfī discipline, let alone instituted any separate Ṣūfī order. The tenor of his teaching seems to have been generally orthodox (he recommended the study of al-Ghazālī) with an emphasis on devotion to God. In particular, he is said to have discouraged monasticism and forbidden his followers to forsake their worldly profession. The five points of his teaching are said to be (1) fear of God in secret and open; (2) adherence to the Prophet's Sunna in word and deed; (3) contempt of mankind in prosperity and adversity; (4) resignation to the will of God in matters great and small; and (5) having recourse to God in joy and sorrow. Although al-Shādhilī did not leave any written work, his disciple, the Alexandrian Ibn 'Aṭā' Allāh (d. 709/1309), a bitter opponent of the theologian Ibn Taymīya, compiled a collection of his 'wise sayings' (*al-ḥikam*). These sayings, which have been commented upon by Shaykh al-Rundī (d. 796/1394), constitute the main mystic text-book of this order which has been propagated also in South-East Asia. The Shādhilī order gave rise to a large number of offshoots both by itself and in conjunction with the Qādirīya. In the 9th/15th century a reformed Shādhilī order called al-Jazūlīya came into existence in Morocco. One of the branches of the latter is the 'Īsawīya with its sword-slashing ritual; another is the orthodox Darqāwīya of Morocco. The Shādhilīya, although it penetrated into the Eastern Sudan, has had no impact on West African territories.

A still more peculiarly African but a much more recent order is that of the Tījānīya, founded about 1195/1781 by an ex-Khalwatī disciple Aḥmad al-Tījānī (d. 1230/1815), at Fez. This order considerably simplified the ritual and laid greater stress directly on good intention and deeds, a fact which has contributed to its rapid success at proselytization and has also given it, at times, a more militant outlook. It makes no separation between the spiritual and the temporal. Whereas in Algeria it has been on good terms with the French colonial administration, it has resisted actively the foreign domination in Morocco. From Morocco it spread into French West Africa during the 13th/19th century, propagated by Muḥammad ibn Mukhtār (d. 1245/1830), and was carried into French Guinea by al-Ḥajj 'Umar Tall (killed in 1270/1854 in fighting). This campaign of proselytization was directed particularly against pagans but also against the rival Qādirīya. During the present century, Shaykh Hamallāh sought to reinvigorate Tījānism and organized his order on a basis of 'freedom for the individual' combining certain unorthodox elements like reduction of prayers and changing the *qibla*. He was arrested by the French administration and died in exile (1943).

Through popular Ṣūfism, Berber and African animistic beliefs and rituals have imposed their own form on Islam in Africa; the 'marabout' (*murābiṭ*) of the Berbers, the 'holy man' or 'religious leader' (the *alfa*) of the Negro Muslim is essentially a carry-over from the pre-Islamic cults of holy men and witch doctors of Negro fetishism. In its expansion through Central Asia, Islam came into close contact with the similar animistic cult of Shamanism. The history of the origins of early Ṣūfī fraternities in Central Asia that eventually spread to Turkey on the one hand and to East, South, and South-East Asia, on the other, remains obscure. Aḥmad Yasawī (d. 562/1167), a disciple of Yūsuf al-Hamadhānī (d. 534/1140), who belonged to the Perso-Central Asian Ṣūfī circle called the 'Khwājagān' (the 'masters'), laid the foundations of the oldest Turkish order called the Yasawīya. The characteristics of this order were formed in Western Turkestan, with a background of Shamanism, and were transmitted to its offshoot, the Bekṭāshī order, founded by a certain Bābā Bekṭāsh probably during the 6th/12th century. The Bekṭāshī order, the most important popular 'rustic' order in Turkey, spread into Anatolia and was fully organized and established towards the end of the 9th/15th century. A characteristic of both the Yasawīya and the Bekṭāshīya was the participation of women in the ceremonies. The Bekṭāshīya, besides conserving Shamanistic elements, developed Shī'ite trends on the one hand and certain Christian beliefs and practices on the other – these latter are said to have been imbibed by them from the already existing background of the territories through which they spread. Thus they not only believe in the twelve Shī'ite Imāms but make a Trinity out of God, Muḥammad and 'Alī. Indeed, where they absorbed Christian communities, as in Albania, a kind of mixed religion came into existence. At the reception of a new member, they celebrate with wine, bread and cheese and confess their sins to their spiritual guides who grant them absolution. Among the established orders, the Bekṭāshīya are the furthest removed from orthodoxy, caring little for the obligatory law of Islam. Through their association with the military Janissaries they acquired political power in the Ottoman Empire and from time to time rose in revolt against the secular authority. Crushed in 1242/1826 by the government, they revived towards the end of the last century but were disbanded finally in 1343/1925 by the modern Turkish state along with other orders, and now survive in Albania.

Another order which spread from Central Asia into Turkey and Eastern Muslim lands but also has a spiritual connection with the 'Khwājagān' is the Naqshbandīya founded in the 8th/14th century in Bukhārā by Bahā' al-Dīn, called 'Naqshband' (d. 791/1389). The name 'Naqshband' ('painter') is explained by the fact that the founder 'drew spiritual pictures on the heart' and, actually, the Naqshbandī disciples, when practising *dhikr*, 'draw lines on their hearts' by silent words to purify the heart. Although Naqshband was immediately a disciple of the Ṣūfī al-Sammāsī and of the latter's disciple Amīr Kulāl, he adopted the method of *dhikr* of an earlier Ṣūfī, 'Abd al-Khāliq al-Ghujdawānī (d. 575/1179), who was a disciple of the same Yūsuf al-Hamadhānī who guided Aḥmad Yasawī. This has led Depont and Coppolani to regard the Bekṭāshīya order as a branch of the Naqshbandīya, but actually the two are independent and, in fact, the former is the older.[5]

The Naqshbandīya, which spread in India, China and the Malayan Archipelago, is an orthodox order and, in general, appeals to the *élite*, forbidding the practice of extravagant forms of *dhikr*, dancing and music. It was introduced into India by Bāqī Bi'llāh in the 10th/16th century and was started afresh and reinvigorated by his important and influential pupil Aḥmad Sirhindī, known in India as 'renovator of the second millennium', who led the campaign for the purification of Ṣūfism in India, rejecting Ibn al-'Arabī's pantheistic mysticism which had found a strong ally in the Vedantism of orthodox Hinduism.

The main sophisticated or 'urban' order among the Turks, however, has been that of the Mevleviye (Mawlawīya) instituted by the famous mystic poet Jalāl al-Dīn Rūmī (d. 672/1273) from whose *mathnawī* we have quoted in this chapter. The *mathnawī*, his great poetic work of surpassing beauty and, in parts, equal depth has achieved immense popularity and has, indeed, been hailed as the 'Qur'ān of the Ṣūfīs'. The Mevleviye have an elaborate mystic ritual (described in detail by J. P. Brown in his book *The Dervishes*, edited by H. A. Rose) and are famous for their 'pirouetting' dance whence they are called 'the dancing dervishes'. Since their suppression by the Kemalist revolutionary régime, the Mevleviye are confined to the Middle East, chiefly Aleppo.

In the Indo-Pakistan subcontinent, besides the universal orders of the Qādirīya and the Naqshbandīya, the chief Ṣūfī brotherhood is that of the Chishtīya, founded by Mu'īn al-Dīn Chishtī, who died at Ajmer in 633/1236 where his tomb (*dargāh*) is a famous object of popular pilgrimage (*'urs*). The Mughal emperor Akbar made a pilgrimage to it on foot in fulfilment of a vow. Akbar's son and successor, later entitled Jahāngīr, was born at the *khānqāh* of the then representative of the Chishtī order, Salīm, and was named after him. After a long line of famous representatives, the order suffered a period of eclipse, but was revived about a century and a half ago by Khwāja Nūr Muḥammad.

Besides these orders, the Indian subcontinent teems with a host of questionable and so-called 'irregular' (*bē-shar'*) orders which are but very loosely organized and, as their name implies, are not bound either by a discipline or by the religious law of Islam. These range from lesser offshoots of regular orders, through more or less organized 'irregular' orders (the chief of which are the Qalandars) to individual mendicants, called *faqīrs* or *malangs*, who attach themselves to any saint's tomb, real or imaginary, and generally lead a parasitic and often charlatanic existence. In the subcontinent, Muslim religious life, at the popular level, has been profoundly influenced by indigenous beliefs and practices; or, rather, the local Muslim population, despite its conversion to Islam, has largely kept its pre-Islamic *Weltanschauung* alive. All too often the conversion has been purely nominal and the process of Islamization has been a painfully slow one – so strong is the influence of spiritual romanticism to which the native population has ever been a prey.

Indeed, in several villages Muslims and Hindus worship common 'saints'. The phenomenon of popular *rapprochement* between Hinduism and Islam began early after the advent of Islam in India and came to a head in the 10th/16th century in a syncretist branch of the *bhakti* movement represented by men like Kabīr and Nānak. The latter was the founder of the Sikh religion, which is to some extent a result of the influence of Islamic monotheism on Hindu religious culture. In Indonesia, where Islam reached relatively late and had little time to consolidate its impact before Western colonialism made its appearance, much of the religious culture of the Muslim population remains essentially unIslamic beneath the surface. Besides, therefore, a leavening of the Muslim orders that have made their way there, the pre-Islamic mystic attitudes remain almost unchanged.

Sequel

The heyday of the Ṣūfī movement in Western Asia lasted from the 10th/16th century to the 12th/18th century, which was roughly also the period covered by the Ottoman Empire from its establishment to its zenith. At the same time, however, forces were set in motion to control the Ṣūfī movement and check its excesses and the extravagance of its cults. These forces, as noted at the end of the last chapter, took a double form. First, Ṣūfī theosophy and practices were subjected to severe criticism by such men as Ibn Taymīya. Secondly, the close association of the orthodox 'Ulamā' themselves with Ṣūfism brought into operation forces which sought to reform Ṣūfism from within. These forces, whether rejecting Ṣūfī pantheism or reinterpreting its pantheistic theosophy in orthodox terms, resulted in bringing Ṣūfism much closer to the orthodox ideals. Further, these trends prepared the way for another development which seemed to erupt with a startling suddenness over the Muslim world, although at regional levels, and which affected Ṣūfism at its very core during the 12th/18th and 13th/19th centuries. This development is the massive onslaught on popular religion which had nearly come to displace Islam in the outlying districts of the Muslim world but which had affected its central areas as well. This onslaught on popular religion expressed itself in the form of vigorous puritanical reform movements diffused all over the Muslim world; these we shall discuss in Chapter XII. Since, however, the Ṣūfī movement was closely associated with popular religion in different Muslim countries, as we have seen, it was directly and deeply affected by the new reform movements. Besides the changes wrought in the doctrines and practices of the old established Ṣūfī orders through this new development, certain new brotherhoods with an entirely fresh orientation came to be formed in the nineteenth century, such as the Sanūsīya in North Africa and the Muḥammadīya in India, which were strictly orthodox in *spirit* and practice and differed radically from the traditional objectives of the old orders. These also we shall study in Chapter XII.

CHAPTER TEN

SECTARIAN DEVELOPMENTS

The Khawārij – The Shīʿa – Sub-sects of the Shīʿa

The Khawārij

Although medieval Muslim heresiologists undoubtedly give the impression that Islam has grown into a large number of sects (or parties, *firaq*) and, in fact, endeavour to make up the number seventy-three, basing themselves on the so-called Ḥadīth of the Prophet 'my Community shall be split into seventy-three sects, only one of which will be saved', most of these are not 'sects' but legal and theological schools, as has been pointed out by Goldziher[1] and others. Indeed, throughout the history of Islam one looks in vain for a sect based entirely on doctrinal differences. The doctrinal and theological extremes to which, for example, certain Ṣūfīs and philosophers went – let alone the Muʿtazila and even the Khawārij – are obviously incompatible with orthodox teaching, and yet this by itself has given rise to no sectarian developments. The criterion of the permissibility of a schism in Islam has, rather, been something that can perhaps be best called 'Community solidarity' and, characteristically, has, from the beginning, been concerned with practical and above all political issues.

The Muʿtazila, again, are not a sect but a theological school, which has directly influenced the formation of the 'orthodox' partly by being integrated into the latter and partly by being rejected and reacted against. The nearest point they approached to sectarianism was when, after their dogma was exalted into a state creed, they became intolerant and resorted to persecution. After being dethroned, however, they continued to exist as a theological school and their doctrines had an influence both on the Shīʿa dogmatics and on Sunnī Islam, on the question of the freedom and efficiency of the human will, notably through Ibn Taymīya (see Chapter VI).

It is this characteristic of intolerance, fanaticism and exclusivism issuing in a policy, raised to an almost credal status, and of effecting political change through desperate methods of violence that distinguishes the earliest Islamic sect of the Khawārij – (plural of Khārijī). The name

'Khārijī' has no doctrinal implications of heresy but simply means a 'rebel', or a 'revolutionary activist'. A Khārijī poet, in a famous lament on the death of an early Khārijite leader, Abū Bilāl Mirdās (d. 61/681), says, 'Abū Bilāl's (death) has rendered life intolerable and has endeared rebellion (*khurūj*) to me'. Indeed, apart from their fanaticism and desperate methods, the Khārijites were extremely pious and puritanically religious men. Both these traits are illustrated in the following quotation from a *khuṭba* (sermon) of an early 2nd/8th century Khārijite leader, Abū Ḥamza, delivered by him after his capture of Medina from the Umayyads in the year 129/747:

O people of Ḥijāz: do you seek to revile me on account of my companions, saying these are youths? Is it not the case that the companions of the Prophet were but young men? . . By God, these are young men who are old in their young age. Their eyes are closed to evil temptations; their feet loathe to tread the path of wantonness. They are emaciated by incessant worship (of God), fatigued by sleeplessness. God looks upon them in the middle of the night with their backs bent over the texts of the Qur'ān. When one of them comes upon a verse mentioning paradise, he cries out of longing for it; when he comes to a verse mentioning hell, he shrieks as though the breath of Fire were actually in his ears. Their toil is continuous – the toil of the night with the toil of the day. The earth has eaten away their knees and hands, their noses and foreheads (because of long and constant prostration in prayer). But they belittle all this by the side of God. When they see the arrows mounted upon the bow-strings, the spears brandished and the swords unsheathed, and when the squadrons thunder forth death and flash destruction, they belittle the threats of the (attacking) squadrons by the side of God's promise. One of these very youths advances forward into the pitch of battle until he reels with his feet on the neck of his horse and the beauty-spots of his face are dyed in blood. The wild beasts hasten to him and many a wild bird seizes in his beak the eye that cried at the dead of night through fear of God![2]

The occasion of the Khārijite split was the arbitration (*taḥkīm*) to which the fourth Caliph, 'Alī, after being victorious against Mu'āwiya in the battle of Siffin in the year 37/648, submitted. The Khārijites, who had been so far among the Shī'a, i.e. the party of 'Alī, denounced him for submitting to human arbitration (in which he is alleged to have been cheated by a diplomatic trick) although being in the right. 'God is sole judge and arbiter' became the Khārijite rallying cry, and henceforth these idealist and fanatic rebels fought both against 'Alī, and, after his assassination at the hands of one of them, the Umayyads. Defeated by 'Alī and repeatedly crushed by the Umayyad generals in bloody battles in Iraq and Western Persia, they carried on guerrilla warfare against the 'Abbāsids as well, although they had ceased to be dangerous.

The Khārijites were, in composition, mainly nomads and semi-nomads from the Peninsula and the borders of Iraq, but their idealism, teaching absolute equality, attracted considerable numbers of the Persian Mawālī. Absolute and uncompromising equality and answerability before the Divine Command sums up their spirit and from this spirit flowed their most cardinal tenets. In their point-blank demand for 'Commanding the good and forbidding the evil', an obligation laid by the Qur'ān on the Muslim Community, they attacked not only the ruling Umayyads but also the moderate majority of the Community whom they accused of being 'sedentary' conformists. The majority of the Community, as we pointed out in Chapter V, had exercised political moderation ever since the first troubles broke out during the time of 'Uthmān. Against the Khārijite demand, their leaders now emphasized the necessity of executing the principle of 'Commanding the good and forbidding the evil' on the moral rather than the legal plane, through education rather than civil war. Alarmed by the Khārijite blood-baths, however, the Sunnī religious leadership drifted more and more to Conformism, a process which was hastened by the rise of the 'Ulamā' class.

From the 3rd/9th century onwards, the practice of moderation and catholicity of spirit which had created the *Ahl al-Sunna wa'l-Jamā'a*, 'the people of the middle path and unity', i.e. the orthodoxy, changed into a *theoretical and doctrinal* principle, according to which although 'there can be no obedience to a sinful command', yet 'the ruler should be obeyed even though he be unjust' for 'an unjust ruler is better than lawlessness'. The charge of conformism against the 'Ulamā' as a whole seems, therefore, justified and the principle of 'obedience even to a tyrant' was often carried to its extremes. It is, nevertheless, true that this political wisdom of the 'Ulamā' has done a fundamental service to the Community which goes all too often unrecognized. For, under the cover of this principle, the 'Ulamā' exercised a stabilizing function in the political chaos especially after the break-up of the 'Abbāsid Caliphate when the adventurer sultans, who might genuinely respect or fear the Ṣūfīs, nevertheless had at least externally to observe the Sharī'a-law (whose guardians were the 'Ulamā') which checked their excesses and kept their rule generally humane.

One fundamental tenet of the Khārijites that flowed from their idealism, viz. their rejection of justification by faith alone and their making deeds an essential part of faith, we have discussed in Chapter V. A corollary of this principle, always implicit in it, viz., that man is a free and responsible agent, was inherited by the Mu'tazilites. Their other cardinal theory concerned the Caliphate. Being egalitarian, they rejected the orthodox view that the office of the Caliph must be confined to a member of the tribe of Quraysh, and held that any Muslim whose character was unimpeachable was eligible for this office even though he be 'a black slave'. This law was not only opposed to the orthodox position but even more fundamentally to the Shī'ite legitimist doctrine which held that Imāmate must be confined to the descendants of the Prophet through 'Alī. The orthodox theory was in fact, a rationalization of the realities of the situation reinvigorated by a desire to avoid chaos by confining the area of possible rival claims while, at the same time, keeping clear of the Shī'ite legitimist claims.

The forces of the Khārijites, as we have said above, were crushed out in the early centuries. They now survive in small communities in 'Oman, Zanzibar (where they spread from 'Oman), in East Africa and in North Africa. All these communities belong to the moderate sect of the Ibāḍites who do not excommunicate the main body of the Muslims and do not resort to political assassination to achieve their goals. Besides, in their outlook they have, through the centuries, come under the influence of the larger Muslim body. In recent times, there has been witnessed some literary activity on their part in publishing their classical doctrinal works and expressing their views,[3] most probably encouraged by Western academic interest in them and by a more liberal and catholic outlook generated by Muslim modernism.

Our preceding analysis has shown that it would be a mistake to apply the word 'sect' in a rigorous sense to the Khārijites. No doubt by their recklessness in taking up arms against the community they excommunicated themselves from the larger body; but there is nothing in their *doctrine* that need necessarily lead to this self-excommunication. Indeed, something of their radical spirit (although not overt influence) has been relived not only in certain outstanding individuals in medieval Islam but in several relatively recent movements inspired by radical idealism such as the Wahhābīs in the 12th/18th century, and, in a more moderate spirit and more recently the Muslim Brotherhood in the Arab Middle East. We shall also note, when we discuss modern movements in Islam, certain aspects of the similarity of the Khārijite ideal with certain aspects of the doctrine of the radical Islamic movement, the Jamā'at-i Islāmī, in Pakistan. This shows that the lines of demarcation between being 'outside' and 'inside' the Community are not at all so sharp and clear.

The Shī'a

The Shī'a constitute the only important schism in Islam. Unlike the Khārijites, who rebelled against the Ijmā' of the Community at the practical level, the Shī'a have, over the centuries, evolved a doctrine of Divine Right (both with regard to religion and political life) that is irreconcilable with the very spirit of Ijmā'.

The occasion of the Shī'a secession was also the political events of hostility between 'Alī and his opponents, the Umayyads. After 'Alī's assassination, the Shī'a (party) of 'Alī in Kūfa demanded that Caliphate be restored to the house of the ill-fated Caliph. This legitimist claim on behalf of 'Alī's descendants is the beginning of the Shī'a political doctrine. The motives that led to this curious legitimist claim on the part of the Kūfan Arabs are not very clear, except the fact that certain southern tribes, in their traditional enmity against the northerners, decided to champion the Hāshimites against the ruling Umayyads, and the fact that the Prophet had been from the Banū Hāshim came to be easily exploited. It is undoubtedly true that 'Alī was a great idealist as compared to the Umayyad, Mu'āwiya. But this was something personal, not hereditary. Was it due to 'Alī's prestige as son-in-law of the Prophet? But there is little indication at this stage of 'Alī's having the kind of prestige required for this purpose. A further real reason seems to lie only in the fact that 'Alī's rights appear to have been grossly infringed (besides the fact mentioned already that Banū Hāshim's house seemed the best rallying point against the Umayyads).

This legitimism, i.e. the doctrine that headship of the Muslim Community rightfully belongs to 'Alī and his descendants, was the hallmark of the original Arab Shī'ism which was purely political. Monuments of this Arab Shī'ism are to be found today among the Zaydīs of Yemen with their Shī'ī Imām, and in Morocco where the ruler is a descendant of the house of 'Alī but the religion is that of Sunnī Islam. But already among the earliest Shī'a partisans there are strong traces of a religious enthusiasm for 'Alī together with the political motive, although there is not as yet the dogmatic extravagance that was to develop in the 2nd/8th and 3rd/9th centuries. Abu'l Aswad al-Du'alī, a follower of 'Alī, is said to have claimed to 'seek God at the future abode through my love for 'Alī'. The poet Kumayt (d. 126/744) speaks of the light that emanates from Adam through Muḥammad in the 'holy family'.

The social struggles in early Islam, when the discontent of Persian clients (*mawālī*) was broiling against the ruling Umayyads, gave undoubtedly a further spur and quite a new turn to the socio-political activities of the Shī'a wherein the leaders may have been Arabs but the following shifted from the Arabs largely to the Persians. Thus, al-Mukhtār ibn 'Ubayd, who revolted against the ruling dynasty, mobilized the clients and the slaves and, since both the sons of 'Alī from the Prophet's daughter, Fāṭima, were dead, installed another son of 'Alī, Muḥammad ibn al-Ḥanafīya, as the Mahdī (the 'rightly-guided' one). After Ibn al-Ḥanafīya's death, a belief arose in his 'return' (*raj'a*, *παρουσία*).

Thus, we see that Shī'ism became, in the early history of Islam, a cover for different forces of social and political discontent. The southern Arabs used it as a façade to assert their pride and independence against the Arabs of the north. In the Iraqi mixed population, it claimed the services of the discontented Persians and contributed to the rise, during the 'Abbāsid period, of an extreme Persian cultural, nationalistic movement known as the Shu'ūbīya. But with the shift from the Arab hands to those of non-Arab origin, the original political motivation developed into a religious sect with its own dogma as its theological postulate. The fundamental religious impulse was derived from the violent and bloody death of Ḥusayn, 'Alī's son from Fāṭima, at Karbalā' at the hands of government troops in the year 51/671, whence the passion motive was introduced. This passion motive combined with the belief in the 'return' of the Imām gives to Shī'ism its most characteristic ethos. Upon this were engrafted old oriental beliefs about Divine light and the new metaphysical setting for this belief was provided by Christian Gnostic Neoplatonic ideas.

Exactly by what stages these different motives and ideas were fused to develop the idea of the Mahdī into a divine personage, and who precisely were the persons that wrought the amalgam or vitally contributed to it, we cannot say at the present stage of research, as the early doctrinal evolution of Shī'ism is still very obscure. In the frustration caused by repeated political defeats and successive persecutions suffered by Shī'ism in its early phase, the movement went largely underground and this subterranean activity on the one hand rendered it liable to the influence of all kinds of heterodox ideas and, on the other, it produced two principles, one practical and one theoretical, but both closely allied, that have become characteristic of Shī'ism. The practical principle is that of dissimulation of belief (*taqīya*). This principle, in its mild form, was permitted also by orthodoxy and notably by Abū Ḥanīfa, who appealing to the Qur'ān, III, 27, allowed a person to confess the contrary of his real belief under an immediate threat to life. Under the law of 'relaxation and firmness' (see Chapter IV), however, orthodoxy insisted on high moral integrity and affirmed that 'firmness is superior to relaxation'. With Shī'ism, on the other hand, it became a cardinal principle to dissimulate belief, not only under direct and express danger to life but in a generally hostile environment. Further, such dissimulation is not merely allowed, it is an obligatory duty of a fundamental order. And not only do the Shī'a practise it, but attribute such *taqīya* to their Imāms including 'Alī, who is alleged by them to have 'concealed' his firm belief in his Divine Right to Caliphate and acquiesced in the Caliphate of his predecessors.

The same attitude resulted in a far-reaching theoretical direction in the formula of esotericism. Immediately after Muslim conquests of the

Fertile Crescent and Persia, the new converts from the conquered territories began to swarm into the new Faith. By and large, however, the converts left intact their older oriental and Gnostic beliefs and even practices under an overlay of Islamic formulas. Under the surface, therefore, there continued to exist a variety of religious beliefs whose confrontation with the new religion produced a tremendous spiritual ferment and a fluidity of religious ideas. Among the existing ideas were Christianity, Manichaeism and Buddhism. This led to the formation of secret sects, and just as Shī'ism served the purposes of the politically ousted, so under its cloak the spiritually displaced began to introduce their old ideas into Islam. In order to secure room for such ideas in Islam, the principle of esotericism was brought in from the older Gnostic stock of doctrines. The principle of esotericism upholds the idea of a double or even multiple interpretation of the Qur'ānic text. Side by side with the 'external' meaning of the Scripture, there are other 'hidden' levels of meaning. God, in revealing the Qur'ān, has also operated on the principle of *taqīya*. The principle of esotericism has also affected the Ṣūfī interpretations of the Qur'ān and sometimes such 'inner meanings' are carried to a pure arbitrariness of interpretation. No group of Muslims, however, have committed such unbridled arbitrariness in applying this principle as the Shī'a on the whole. Almost in every word of the Qur'ān a reference is seen to the 'holy household of 'Alī' or to later Imāms. The idea that there must be some link between the symbol and the symbolized, which must bestow plausibility or at least, intelligibility on the interpretation, is simply not recognized.

The infallible bearer of this esoteric wisdom is the Imām around the dogma of whose authority the entire system of Shī'ite religion revolves. Yet the sanction of the Imām is purely theoretical for, as we shall see presently, the actually recognized Imāms as historical figures were more or less prisoners in the hands of the Shī'a movement which fathered these pretensions on them, while after the 'disappearance' of the last Imām, there is not even the theoretical guidance but only an expectation of his 'return'. Consequently, the Shī'a do not recognize the fundamental importance of the Ijmā' or consensus as does Sunnī Islam, and its place is taken by the authority of the Imām. Ignaz Goldziher summed up the matter with succinct neatness when he said that Sunnī Islam is a religion of Ijmā', Shī'a Islam a religion of authority.[4] For whereas Sunnī Islam vests the real religious authority in Ijmā' and recognizes in the Caliph only a political and religious executive head of the Community, the Shī'ī Imām, by contrast, is both sinless and absolutely infallible in his supposed pronouncements on the dogma and, indeed, in all matters. In fact, whereas in classical and medieval Sunnī Islam the office of the Caliph is recognized as only a practical necessity, belief in the Imām and submission to him is, according to the Shīʿa, the third cardinal article of Faith, after a belief in God and in His Apostle.

With this authoritarian concept of the hereditary Imām, his metaphysical status had to be defined more closely and his place in the ultimate scheme of things fixed. This was done with the aid of the old Zoroastrian concept of light through the mechanism of the Neoplatonic theory of emanation. The Primordial Light, God, emanates into and thus gives rise to the ultimate man, the apex of the created universe, the Imām. The majority of the Shīʿa, the Twelvers, regard the Imām as an epiphany (*Maẓhar*) of this Primeval Light and attribute to the Imām only the divine qualities rather than a divine substance. But the more extreme Shīʿa sects (see below) believe the Imām to be an incarnation of God and a bearer of the divine substance. A few, like the ʿAlī Ilāhīs, indeed, believe that the Imām is literally God and that God Himself has 'no place beside the Imām'. These extreme sects, however, are not representative of the majority of the Shīʿa, who call them extremists (*ghulāt*).

It is not yet known when this metaphysical status of the Imām as the outward working of the Primeval Light first took shape. The probable period, however, may be placed in the early 3rd/9th century. The Ṣūfīs – the school of Sahl al-Tustarī (see Chapter VIII) – adopted this theory and attached it to the person of Muḥammad rather than that of ʿAlī. The Ṣūfīs, indeed, seem to have taken certain characteristic Shīʿī doctrines and attitudes and implanted them in the orthodox setting. We saw in Chapter V how the Ṣūfīs borrowed the mystique of ʿAlī, moderated it and stamped it on orthodox Islam which the latter accepted. We also saw there that, with the wide extension of Ṣūfism, Shīʿism suffered heavy losses in its following. The Shīʿī cult of the Imām ran also counter to the Ṣūfī claim of direct access to God. All these factors perhaps jointly explain the antagonizing of the Shīʿa towards Ṣūfism.

For the rest, the Shīʿī dogmatics differ from the Sunnī creed only on one noticeable and important point. Here the Shīʿa have imbibed a more rational spirit which they inherited from the Muʿtazila school: the majority of them reject the 'official' Sunnī predestinarianism and believe in the freedom of human choice. Also, they have kept open the door of *ijtihād* – individual creative thinking and interpretation of the dogma and the law – at least theoretically, whereas the Sunnī 'door of *ijtihād*' has been at least theoretically closed since the 4th/10th century. In the matter of law, Shīʿism differs from Sunnī Islam only in certain details, the most conspicuous of which is the Shīʿī permission of *mutʿa* or temporary marriage contracted for a specified period of years, months or even days. There are also slight differences in ritual prayers. On the other hand, the visiting and worship of tombs, especially of the Imāms, and other holy places, occupies a very central place in Shī'a practical religion. Indeed, pilgrimages to Karbalā' and Mashhad are performed with such devoutness and in such large numbers that the pilgrimage to Mecca has been ousted from its position. The Shī'a masses are, on the whole, more superstitious than the Sunnīs.

Despite the centrality in Shī'ism of the doctrine of the Imām, the Shī'a groups are sharply divided concerning the persons to be identified as Imāms. As we have noted before, in the earliest period the Shī'a partisans did not turn to the descendants of 'Alī from Fāṭima, the Prophet's daughter, but to the other successors of the Caliph: the 'second advent' was, indeed, attributed to Muḥammad ibn al-Ḥanafīya. A little later, when politics created a consistent theological basis, the expectation of reappearance was attached to 'Alī himself. That the Imāmate of the Shī'a was mostly fictional appears from the fact that many of these are recognized by Sunnī Islam as learned authorities on Tradition and law. The fifth Imām of the Shī'a, Muḥammad al-Bāqir (d. *c.* 114/732) e.g. is recognized by the Sunnīs as an eminent scholar and jurisconsult of Medina, but he becomes, according to the Shī'a, a direct manifestation of God. These factors have led the Shī'a to make their own collections of the Tradition different from those of Sunnī Islam (see Chapter III).

Sub-sects of the Shī'a

The 'Twelver' Shī'a, so called because they believe in twelve visible Imāms, occupy the middle ground among the various Shī'a denominations and also constitute their largest bulk. Their last Imām, Muḥammad, born in 259/873, is said to have mysteriously disappeared, and his reappearance is awaited by them. This idea of the 'hidden' Imām is, indeed, characteristic of all the sects of the Shī'a, even though there is no agreement as to his identity. The first major external split among the Shī'a occurred over the succession of the sixth Imām, Ja'far (d. 148/765 at Medina). The majority of the Shī'a recognized his son Mūsā, because the eldest son, Ismā'īl, was regarded as guilty of the sin of drinking wine. Some, however, regarded Ismā'īl as the rightful Imām and after him his son Muḥammad. Ismā'īlīs, as this group were called, are also named the 'Seveners' since they close the series of Imāms with the 'disappearance' of this Muḥammad, whose 'return' they await as the Mahdī.

Ismā'īlī propaganda was vigorously carried on during the 3rd/9th, 4th/10th and 5th/11th centuries until, during the 5th/11th century, we find it very strong throughout the Muslim world from North Africa to India. As the basis for its political programme of enthroning an Imām-Caliph, the movement, in its early stages, sought to bring about a social revolution and, through assimilating ideas from without – especially Neoplatonic and Gnostic, constructed a philosophical system on which to base a new religion having undermined the orthodox religious structure. The beginnings of this active and aggressive Ismā'īlī propaganda are traditionally associated with the name of a certain 'Abd Allāh ibn Maymūn al-Qaddāḥ, but more recent research by W. Ivanow has cast some doubt on these accounts since the Shī'a sources themselves speak of him as an earlier personage (see the *Shorter Encyclopaedia of Islam*, s.v.).

Towards the last quarter of the 3rd/9th century, however, the Ismā'īlīs staged a revolt and a socio-religious campaign under the headship of Hamdān Qarmaṭ, after whom they came to be called Qarmaṭians (Carmathians, Qarāmiṭa). He established an entrenched post near Kūfa (*c.* 277/890) in Iraq and levied contributions on his followers. This process of taxation was soon replaced by a Communist type of society – i.e. communism of all objects of general utility, in the name of the Imām. The Qarmaṭians, however, perpetrated such terrorism and committed such atrocities that they aroused a general hatred and fear against them. They were persecuted and gradually disappeared. The Ismā'īlī propagandists for the 'house of Fāṭima' had, however, made use of the Qarmaṭian movement and upon its ruins established the Fāṭimid state in Egypt and North Africa.

It was the Ismā'īlī missionaries and intellectuals of the 4th/10th and 5th/11th centuries, especially in Iraq and Persia, that perfected the Ismā'īlī system of theosophy. This theosophy is erected squarely on an allegorical interpretation of the Qur'ān in Neoplatonic terms, especially its theory of emanation. Besides the works of Persians like Abū Ya'qūb al-Sijistānī (d. *c.* 331/943) and Ḥamīd al-Dīn al-Kirmānī (d. 410/1019), the best known monument of this theosophy is the 'Epistles of the Brethren of Purity', the work of a subterranean organization alluded to in Chapter VIII above. The Neoplatonic triad of the One, the Intellect and the Soul is translated into the Ismā'īlī triad of the Fortune (*jadd*), Esoteric Interpretation (*fatḥ*), and the Thought-Image (*khayāl*) and identified with Muḥammad, 'Alī and the Imām, respectively. H. Corbin has shown the connection between the concept of the Fortune and the Zoroastrian doctrine of the Khwarna or Kharra.[5] The idea seems to be that the Prophet received the Revelation through his 'fortune' at birth but that the real interpretation of the Qur'ān

(*Fatḥ* = opening) is the function of ʿAlī. There is, therefore, more to the Ismāʿīlī doctrine than a mere borrowing from Neoplatonism.

This picture is further complicated by the peculiar Ismāʿīlī interpretation of history. Having borrowed the idea of a cyclic Universe from older systems of thought, Ismāʿīlism construed each cycle on a septennial pattern (the idea of seven was originally derived from the doctrine of seven Imāms). These seven periods of the cycle were identified with Adam, Noah, Abraham, Moses, Jesus, Muḥammad and the Imām, and this series is called 'The Speakers' or the 'Utterers' (*nāṭiq*). The series represents a progression or development culminating in the Imām who consummates the cycle while between each 'Speaker' lies a series of seven 'Mutes' or 'Silents' who consolidate the work of the previous 'Speaker'. This doctrine destroyed the doctrine of the finality of Prophethood with Muḥammad, a doctrine accepted both by the Sunnīs and the Imāmī Shīʿa.

The esoteric principle of a 'hidden' interpretation espoused by Shīʿism was carried to its extreme limits by the Ismāʿīlī adepts. The doctrine of a graded secret teaching under the theoretical dictation of the Imām (this 'teaching' – *taʿlīm* – was attacked by al-Ghazālī), was developed and declared to be accessible only through a careful initiation process. The Gnostic, ascending through these various grades of instruction, realizes that there is but one Truth and becomes convinced of the utter inanity of the positive religions which he alone is able to interpret in a truly spiritual and universal sense.

Some Western scholars have held the view that Ismāʿīlism was a truly liberal ideology, and that should it have met with success, it would have made Islam 'rational' and 'liberal'. In the first place they are impressed by the Greek terminology that overlies the Ismāʿīlī doctrine. They forget that this system is at bottom far from being rational, and that the adoption of a degenerate Gnostic form of Neoplatonism does not represent the apogee of liberal philosophic thought. It is apparent that Ismāʿīlī doctrine of the equality of the positive religions with one ultimate Truth has inspired this attitude in these scholars. But the Ismāʿīlī dogma is not so much of the equality of all religions but of the equal inanity of their positive content. This inanity, according to their doctrine, can be redeemed only through the adoption of an authoritative interpretation offered by Ismāʿīlism. This is not liberalism but authoritarianism. (If this authoritarianism were removed, Ismāʿīlism would be reduced to nihilism pure and simple.) In our own time we have become familiar with a similar position adopted by certain Hindu apologists, whose most able and effective representative for the West has been S. Radhakrishnan. Further, the Ismāʿīlī interpretation offers itself not merely as authoritative but as absolutely authoritarian, emanating from the infallible Imām. It is true that the dictatorship of the Imām is purely theoretical, since he is 'invisible' but in that case it is the visible Ismā'īlī intellectuals who must constitute the spiritual autocracy of humanity. Add to this the subterranean character of the movement, the resort to terrorism, subversion and assassination by the Qarmaṭians and the assassins and the strict taboos on social intercourse with non-Ismā'īlīs and the picture of historic Ismā'īlism is complete.

Besides the main body of the Ismā'īlīs whose two branches – the Musta'līs and the Nizārīs – are respectively headed by Muḥammad Burhān al-Dīn in Bombay and the Āgā Khān, Ismā'īlism gave rise to two offshoots in the 4th/10th and the 5th/11th centuries, the Nuṣayrīs and the Druzes (found mainly in the Lebanon). The latter arose out of the deification of the Fāṭimid al-Ḥākim (d. 411/1020) whose 'return' they expect – and changed further the Ismā'īlī doctrine into a more extreme form, but their numbers are small. The growth of the freemasonry movement is thought to have been influenced by the Druze rituals. Towards the end of the 8th/14th century, another extreme Shī'ī sect arose under the leadership of Faḍl Allāh of Astarābād. These are called Ḥurūfīs because of the centrality in their teaching of the letters of the alphabet on whose numerical values and various combinations they build many an occult and esoteric doctrine. As distinguished from the Nuṣayrīs and the Druzes, the Ḥurūfīs are not Ismā'īlīs but are to be regarded as an offshoot of the Imāmī Shī'a since they recognize eleven Imāms in a developmental series after the Prophet Muḥammad. The series is closed by Faḍl Allāh himself who is regarded as God incarnate. Ḥurūfism was adopted by the Bekṭāshī order of Ṣūfīs in Turkey (see Chapter IX), who have generally come under extreme Shī'a influences. All those sects are castigated by the Shī'a themselves as 'extremists' (*ghulāt*), as we mentioned above in this chapter.

The conjunction of the Ismā'īlī philosophy and Ṣūfī speculation as it finally took shape in the system of the theosoph, Ṣadr al-Dīn al-Shīrāzī (see Chapters VII and VIII), reacted on Imāmī Shī'ism and brought into being late in the 12th/18th and early 13th/19th centuries the school of the Shaykhīs under the inspiration of Shaykh Aḥmad al-Aḥsā'ī (d. 1241/1826). Anti-clerical, the Shaykhīs insisted on modifying the rôle of the Shī'a traditionalism and emphasized the direct importance of the cult of the Imāms whom they regard, like the Ismā'īlī 'extremists', as immediate manifestations and hypostases of God. They taught the imminence of the occurrence of the Bāb – the 'gateway' of Divine Revelation. The term 'Bāb' was employed by the Imāmī Shī'a to designate a spiritual teacher, but was used by 'extremists' like the

Nuṣayrīs to denote a stage of propulsion in the self-manifesting of the Divine Being.

Inspired by this teaching, a pupil of this school, ʿAlī Muḥammad of Shīrāz (born 1236/1821), announced himself in 1260/1844 as the Bāb and as the 'mirror' of the Universal Intelligence. He won several converts but was bitterly opposed by the Shīʿa clerics and was finally executed in 1266/1850. After him, a split occurred in the leadership constituted by the two half-brothers surnamed Ṣubḥ-i Azal and Bahā' Allāh. The followers of the former, called Azalīs, kept intact the teaching of the master but are now very few in number. But Bahā' Allāh came under other influences and declared Bahā'ism to be an independent religion outside Islam, stressing the ideas of pacifism and universalism. In the early decades of the present century, Bahā'ism won a considerable number of followers in America, but has now apparently declined to a marked degree.

Shīʿism has also influenced orthodox Islam in more than one way. The Shīʿa veneration for the 'Prophet's House', i.e. for Fāṭima, ʿAlī and their descendants, has found strong repercussions in Sunnī Islam's feeling of praise towards them. This attitude has increased with the passage of time. The tremendous, indeed, servile respect which the Sunnī masses, especially east of the Arab lands, pay to the Sayyids, the descendants of ʿAlī and Fāṭima, is a living monument to this influence and is not to be paralleled with anything in early Islam. The genesis and development of the concept of the Mahdī in Sunnī Islam are fundamentally due to the Shīʿa doctrine of the Imām. But the influence which Shīʿism has exerted through Ṣūfism on Sunnī Islam is incalculable. To mention but one salient point, the doctrine of the esoteric interpretation of the Scripture has had a profound influence on Islam in general. It is true that Ṣūfism in general did not quite go to the excesses of Shīʿism, nor did orthodox Islam absorb all that Ṣūfism had to offer; yet still this doctrine left a powerful general leaven even on the moderate wing of the ʿUlamā'.

From the 10th/16th century, since the establishment of Ṣafavid rule in Persia, Imāmī Shīʿism has been installed as the state creed in that country, the original motivation having been provided by the Perso-Turkish wars. In the first half of the 12th/18th century, the great general and conqueror Nādir Shāh (d. 1160/1747) made efforts to bring about a *rapprochement* between the Sunnī and Shīʿa Islam; and a formula compromise was worked out whereby a fifth Shīʿa school, called Jaʿfarī (Jaʿfar al-Ṣādiq, the sixth Imām of the Shīʿa, is also recognized by Sunnī Islam as a great religious authority), would be recognized by orthodoxy alongside of its four schools of law (see Chapter IV). The effort was abandoned, however, after the death of Nādir

Shāh. Since then other sporadic efforts have been made with some positive success in certain regions, notably in Central Asia. In modern times a strong ecumenical sentiment has been generated under the political and religious influence of the West, which we shall study in Chapter XIII.

CHAPTER ELEVEN

EDUCATION

The Schools – The Character of Medieval Islamic Learning – Curriculum and Instruction

The Schools

In the foregoing chapters we have described the rise and development of characteristically Islamic religious sciences and have also alluded occasionally to their relative positions. In the present chapter we shall do this somewhat more elaborately and systematically and this shall bring us to the heart of the Islamic system of education. But before that we should say something about the external aspects concerning the form and the spread of educational institutions in Islam.

The art of reading and writing, which existed to a limited extent in Arabia before Islam, increased after the advent of Islam and especially with the expansion of the empire. In the early stages after the spread of Islam, teachers in the elementary places of instruction (*kuttāb*) were mainly non-Muslims, especially Christians and Jews. But the advent of Islam brought for the first time a definite educational instrument of religious culture, the Qur'ān and the teaching of the Prophet. This phenomenon gave rise to the controversy that persisted during the first two centuries or so of Islam as to whether one may teach or learn the Holy Book to or from a non-Muslim. The functions of teaching penmanship and of teaching the Word of God were, therefore, entrusted to different persons, a practice which continued for centuries so that Ibn Khaldūn writes in the 8th/14th century: 'Penmanship is not to be taught with the Qur'ān and religion.... Reading and writing are not taught in elementary schools and any one who wants to learn them must have recourse to professional teachers'.[1] Indeed, the emphasis even at the elementary level was on religious instruction, although reading and writing and simple arithmetic were not excluded.

Elementary education, however, was a self-sufficient unit and there was no organic link between it and the higher education. Indeed, to regard elementary education as a systematic feeding-ground for higher learning is a modern phenomenon and in the medieval system the aim was to develop as highly as possible the intellectual capacities of a select few whose educational career was different from those who were intended for an elementary education only. There were, from the early times of Islam, two other types of education besides the elementary and the higher. The one was the palace-school education instituted for princes with a view to fashioning them into future rulers. This included religious education but laid stress on oratory, literature, etc., and, above all, on 'manly virtues'. The second type of education may be called adult education as it was imparted to the masses, not so much in order to teach them the art of reading and writing as with the purpose of giving instruction in the Qur'ān and in the Faith. It was from this latter that schools of higher learning grew through the *ḥalaqas* or 'circles' of pupils gathered around a certain teacher.

The instrument of religious culture for the higher educational circles was the new legal and theological-moral body of thought which was being produced during the early centuries of Islam. Among these schools legal science was the first to mature, and the followers of Abū Ḥanīfa in Iraq, of Mālik in Medina and later on those of al-Shāfi'ī and Aḥmad ibn Ḥanbal developed a legal body of doctrine. But discussions of moral issues and controversies concerning theological problems to which the former led during the 2nd/8th and the 3rd/9th centuries also continued in a climate of ferment. These discussions and disputes were sometimes carried on in the mosques, but mostly in the private houses either of learned men or their patrons in the great cities of Iraq – Baṣra, Kūfa and Baghdad. During the 'Abbāsid period, certain Caliphs, notably al-Ma'mūn and his father Hārūn al-Rashīd, encouraged holding of learned disputes at their courts on all sorts of questions, logical, legal, grammatical, etc. Before the professional class of the 'Ulamā' generally came into being, there was a great fluidity in thought and a remarkable tolerance of different views. Al-Ash'arī, the formulator of the orthodox creed, had himself heard the lectures of his Mu'tazilī master al-Jubbā'ī in a mosque.

The steady and rapid growth of official mosque-libraries and semi-public libraries is a significant feature of medieval Islamic education. Several notable and powerful officials of the state acquired book-collections in large numbers and put them at the disposal of people of learning and sometimes even donated them for the public use. So too did the semi-independent rulers and chiefs of principalities in the later 'Abbāsid period. Towards the end of the 4th/10th century, the philosopher Ibn Sīnā obtained access to the library of the Persian ruler Nūḥ ibn Naṣr, which he describes as fabulous but which was subsequently to perish in flames.[2] The palace-library of the Fāṭimid al-Ḥākim of Egypt is said to have had forty rooms full of books. These libraries contained books on all subjects – literature, specifically Islamic sciences, natural sciences, logic, philosophy, etc. It is striking that the first state-sponsored academy set up by the 'Abbāsid al-Ma'mūn in the first quarter of the 3rd/9th century was not a venture in Islamic learning but concerned itself with systematic translations of Greek philosophy and science. The interaction of this body of knowledge with the Islamic sciences, which has had such a far-reaching effect on the character of Islamic education throughout the medieval period of Islam, will be dealt with later.

Private and public schools were also founded by individual effort and by donations for special Islamic subjects. General institutions were founded for the teaching of Ḥadīth, law and so on. Abū Ḥātim al-Bustī (d. 277/890) founded in his native town a school with a library and with allowances for non-native students. These institutions multiplied especially in the East in several places like Naysābūr, Marv, etc. We must remember, however, that the subjects taught in these schools, notably Ḥadīth, had developed a content which differed from the corresponding disciplines in the Shī'a sect (cf. Chapter III). The teaching of these subjects, therefore, was *ipso facto*, an attack on Shī'ism. The Shī'a movement, which had led a subterranean life until the middle of the 4th/10th century, having attained external political success at the hands of the Buwayhid dynasty in Iraq and the Fāṭimids of Egypt, began to propagate its cause openly. It developed its own Ḥadīth and partly its own law and placed them both at the service of its central doctrine of Imāmate. It seized existing institutions of learning and established new ones, and on the basis of its political power turned these into propaganda machines for the spread of its ideology (*da'wa*). It had already acquired a skill in propaganda work by its long underground activities. In the year 361/972 the famous mosque-school of al-Azhar was founded by the Fāṭimids in Cairo, an institution which later turned into a Sunnī institution and is today the greatest single traditional Islamic university in the world. During the last two years certain new faculties of practical science have been introduced (Agriculture, Medicine, etc.) through a law enacted by the U.A.R. Parliament in 1961. In 395/1005 the Fāṭimid al-Ḥākim founded a Sunnī 'House of Wisdom' in Cairo, but closed it down in 398/1008 and executed its two learned professors.

While, therefore, the fairly commonly held view that the orthodox *madrasa* originated as a counter-propaganda measure against Shī'ism does not seem basically correct, since Sunnī schools had already existed, it is true that the employment by the Shī'a, during their political power, of their academic institutions as propaganda tools, subsequently led the Sunnī rulers – the Seljūqs and the Ayyūbids – to lend state support, after the overthrow of the Shī'a rule, to Sunnī educational institutions. By this time, the earlier Sunnī institutions had produced a considerable body of learned scholars who were now appointed in the new *madrasas*. These, in their turn, created both a new core of text-books on various religious disciplines which resulted in a definite curriculum and, above all, the new 'Ulamā' who became a distinct class in Muslim society with their own character, ethos and social status. The first of these new *madrasas* was instituted under the Seljūqs in Baghdad and Persia by Niẓām al-Mulk (the great and wise wazīr of the Seljūq Alp Arslān and Malikshāh) who was assassinated in 485/1092 by Ismā'īlī agents. In course of time, a network of such colleges spread throughout the length and breadth of the Muslim world.

It would, however, be a mistake to suppose that Sunnī Islam emerged victorious primarily because of state-support. On the contrary, the new state-policies espoused the trends that had already taken root among the majority of the population and this is the real reason for the success of these policies. It is quite obvious that the Fāṭimids, despite their efforts to propagate, through education and otherwise, the Ismā'īlī doctrine, had failed to make any large scale impact on the populace. Nor did the majority of the people in Iraq and Persia accept Shī'ism under the Buwayhids. The Ash'arite dogmatic, however, did receive state favour but even its large-scale acceptance was due to the influence of men like al-Ghazālī who taught at Niẓām al-Mulk's college at Baghdad.

From the organizational point of view, the *madrasa* system reached its highest point in the Ottoman Empire where *madrasas* were systematically instituted, endowed and maintained under the Shaykh al-Islām's office with remarkable administrative skill and efficiency. The 'Ulamā' were organized in a hierarchy and became almost a caste in the Ottoman society. These traditional seats of learning are still functioning all over the Muslim world outside Turkey: we have already pointed to the most eminent of them, the University of al-Azhar in Cairo. But these are at present in their various stages of adjustment to the challenges and demands that modern education has brought with it. Some, indeed, are still quite outside the sphere of these influences, like Deoband in India, and have refused so far to yield an inch to modern pressures. We shall, however, discuss these in Chapter XIII; for the present we shall turn to consider the content and inner character of medieval Islamic education.

The Character of Medieval Islamic Learning

The beginning and spread of Islamic learning in the early days of Islam is centred around individuals rather than schools. The content of

Islamic thought is also characterized by individual effort. Certain outstanding personalities, who had learned the tradition and had built round it their own legal and theological systems, attracted students from far and near who sought knowledge from them. The first chief characteristic of this learning, therefore, and the one which has persisted throughout the Middle Ages of Islam, is the individual importance of the teacher. The teacher, after giving his full course, personally gave a certificate (*ijāza*) to the student who was then allowed to teach. The certificate was sometimes given in an individual subject – say *fiqh* or Ḥadīth. Sometimes it concerned several subjects and sometimes it was valid only for specified books which the pupil had read. Later, when the *madrasas* came into existence, a system of examination was often instituted. But so great was the rôle and the prestige of the teacher as an individual that, even after the organization of the *madrasas*, the biographies of illustrious men and scholars usually give the names of their teachers and it is relatively rare to find the names of the colleges at which they studied. Even the certificates were issued often in the name of the teacher rather than that of the school. Indeed, it would not be far from the truth to say that even in the later Middle Ages, the majority of celebrated savants were not the product of the *madrasas* but men who had been informal students of individual teachers. If one were to write a history of great and original thinkers in Islam, one would not find many recruits from the *madrasas*.

Connected with this central importance of the teacher is the phenomenon known as 'seeking of knowledge' (*ṭalab al-'ilm*). Itinerant students travelled over long distances, sometimes over the length and breadth of the Muslim world, to follow the lectures of famous teachers. The study of the Ḥadīth, the *putative* reports of deeds and sayings of the Prophet and his Companions, gave the earliest and the most powerful impetus to these scholastic journeys (Chapters III, V). There are reports in medieval Islam of people who had heard more than a hundred teachers. 'Making ready for the road' (*shadd al-riḥāl*) is a key-phrase aptly summing up this movement of acquisition of knowledge. The 'knowledge' or *'ilm*, as we pointed out in Chapter VI, was understood to mean, in the early stages of this movement, traditional knowledge. This was distinguished from *fiqh* or understanding, i.e. the intellectual operation on this traditional body of knowledge. Gradually, however, when the sciences of law and theology were developed, *fiqh* came to mean the legal thought, and 'knowledge' came to mean theology. We have also described in Chapter VI the perennial rivalry between law and theology for the title of the 'crown of sciences'. But the 'closing of the door of *ijtihād* (i.e. original, free thought)' during the 4th/10th and the 5th/11th centuries led to the general stagnation of both legal and intellectual sciences, especially of the former. The intellectual sciences, theology and religious thought, suffered and became impoverished because of their deliberate isolation from, and the gradual decay of, secular intellectualism, especially philosophy and from other forms of religious thought such as Ṣūfism offered.

The *madrasa* system, based to a considerable extent on state-sponsorship and state-control, has been generally regarded as the cause of the decline and stagnation of Muslim learning and scholarship. But the *madrasa*, with its restricted curriculum, was the symptom, not the real cause of this decline, although, of course, it perpetuated and accelerated intellectual stagnation. We have already said above that outstanding and even great original thinkers did continue to arise even outside of the *madrasa* system. But the real reason for the decline of the quality of Islamic learning was the gradual starvation of the religious sciences through their isolation from the life of lay intellectualism which itself then decayed. From their successful opposition to the Mu'tazila and the Shī'a, the 'Ulamā' had gained the experience of developing their own sciences and teaching them in such a way that a defence would be erected for this body of teaching. This did not have to do merely with the relatively external factor of a school-system which would be physically isolated against opposition. Even more important was the way in which the *content* of the orthodox sciences was developed so that they would be isolated from any possible challenge and opposition.

The inner constitution of these religious sciences was so created as to make them apparently absolutely self-sufficient; they filled not only their own place but the place of the entire field of knowledge. All other knowledge was superfluous, if not utterly condemnable. The statement quoted from the jurist al-Shāṭibī in Chapter VI, to the effect that pursuit of all knowledge that was not related to action directly was forbidden, is characteristic of the temper of the medieval 'Ulamā'. The judgment, when directed against unrealistic, futile thinking, is valid enough, and modern pragmatism has taken a similar corrective stand against certain types of pure thought in the West. But, as enunciated by its medieval Muslim authors, this principle excludes not only philosophy but even mathematics, except the rudiments of arithmetic. It is designed to give an absolute position to *fiqh*-law. As for dogmatic theology, while vying with law for a position of paramountcy in the scheme of Islamic learning, it erected itself as a *substitute* for rational philosophy. Since the 6th/10th century – and through the genius of Fakhr al-Dīn al-Rāzī – it expanded its scope by adopting logic from the philosophical systems, by adding its own theories of physics and natural philosophy, and by substituting its dogmatic theological theses for philosophical metaphysics. The student could, henceforth, dispense with all philosophical works since theology had produced a comprehensive rival to it. Such a theological-philosophical scheme by itself is not to be derogated: it is rather a sign of the inner fertility of Islamic thinking, and indeed Thomas Aquinas had done precisely this for Christianity in medieval Europe. But when its content is regarded as absolutely and exclusively self-sufficient, taking the place of all other rational thought, it removes the possibility of all creative challenge that might arise. By organically relating all forms of knowledge and gearing these to dogmatic theology the very sources of intellectual fecundity were blighted and the possibility of original thinking stifled.

Through this process, the curriculum of the *madrasas* was necessarily and harmfully reduced with a resultant narrow outlook as well as causing higher religious education to languish. The Turkish author, Kātib Chelebī (d. 1067/1657) bemoaned the decay of rational sciences and even of higher theology: 'But many unintelligent people . . . remained as inert as rocks, frozen in blind imitation of the ancients. Without deliberation, they rejected and repudiated the new sciences. They passed for learned men, while all the time they were ignoramuses, fond of disparaging what they called "the philosophical sciences," and knowing nothing of earth or sky. The admonition "Have they not contemplated the Kingdom of Heaven and Earth?" (Qur'ān, VII, 184) made no impression on them; they thought "contemplating the world and the firmament" meant staring at them like a cow.' [3]

In Mughal India an interest in philosophical studies was created during the 11th/17th century, but philosophy itself had become so starved that instead of dealing with the problems of real importance it had degenerated into a pedantic exercise of technical terms. There is hardly a more eloquent and pungent criticism of the narrowness of the curriculum in the later Middle Ages of Islam than the following reported speech of Aurangzeb, the last great Muslim ruler of India (d. 1118/1707), addressed to his erstwhile teacher:

What did you teach me? You told me that the land of the Franks is a small island where the greatest king had previously been the ruler of Portugal, then the king of Holland and now the king of England. You told me about the kings of France and Spain that they are like our petty local rulers. . . . Glory be to God! what a knowledge of geography and history you displayed! Was it not your duty to instruct me in the characteristics of the nations of the world – the products of these countries, their military power, their methods of warfare, their customs, religions, ways of government and political policies? . . .

You never considered what academic training is requisite for a prince. All you thought necessary for me was that I become an expert in grammar and learn subjects suitable for a judge or a jurist. . . .

> You told my father that you had taught me philosophy. It is true that for several years you worried my head about unnecessary and nonsensical questions quite unrelated to the issues of life. . . . When I finished my education, I had no real knowledge of any science or art except that I could utter certain abstruse technical terms which confuse even the brightest mind and by which claimants to a knowledge of philosophy cover up their ignorance. . . .[4]

The same attitude of aloofness was adopted towards Ṣūfism – an attitude that had been so successful from the orthodox point of view against philosophy. But the impoverishment of the soul and the mind through orthodox disciplines in the *madrasa* drove the more serious and bright spirits to the fold of Ṣūfism. In the *madrasas*, attached to the Ṣūfī *khānqāhs* and *zāwiyas*, Ṣūfī works were included in the normal curriculum, especially in India where, since the 8th/14th century, the works of al-Suhrawardī (founder of the Suhrawardī order), Ibn al-'Arabī and later those of Jāmī were taught. But in most Ṣūfī centres, especially in Turkey, the academic curriculum consisted almost exclusively of Ṣūfī works. In Turkey there were special places, called *Methnevī-khāna*, where the famous Mathnawī of Rūmī was the sole work of instruction. Further, the content of these works, largely pervaded by pantheism, was in sharp opposition to the teaching of orthodox seats of learning. There arose, therefore, an acute spiritual dualism in Muslim society, that between the *madrasa* and the *khānqāh*. Characteristic of this phenomenon are the innumerable statements of Ṣūfī converts who, 'after finding the true path', burnt their *madrasa* books or threw them into wells. Gradually, however, through the work of certain outstanding personalities, described towards the end of Chapter IX, a new *rapprochement* was developed between orthodox theology and Ṣūfī metaphysics, and a new kind of orthodox speculative theology came into existence during the 11th/17th and 12th/18th centuries. In the course of the 13th/19th century the Muslim world felt the sudden and powerful impact of European education and a new and more far-reaching dualism arose, the nature and effects of which must, however, be left till Chapter XIII.

Curriculum and Instruction

With the narrowing down of the general field of learning through an absence of general thought and natural sciences, the curriculum was naturally confined to the purely religious sciences with grammar and literature as their necessary instruments. The purely religious subjects were four: Ḥadīth or Tradition, *fiqh* or Law (including the 'Principles of Law'), *kalām* or theology, and *tafsīr* or the exegesis of the Qur'ān. In many *madrasas* of the right-wing Ahl al-Ḥadīth even theology was suspect, and the subjects were accordingly reduced to three. In certain special schools, works on Ṣūfism were added. The total number of works studied was usually very small. Indeed, certain great scholars and original thinkers that emerged from time to time were something of prodigies by themselves and did not owe much to the 'official' curriculum.

Part of the explanation of this gradual deterioration of academic standards over the centuries must lie in the fact that, the number of books in the curriculum being small, the years devoted to studies were also too few for the student to be able to grapple with tough and often abstruse materials of the higher aspects of religious sciences at a relatively young and immature age. This in turn meant not so much the grasping of the subject as such but a more or less textual study of the books. This encouraged memorizing rather than real understanding. The fact that later medieval centuries produced only large commentaries rather than basically original works is well known. This phenomenon developed fundamentally from the habit of concentrating on books rather than on subjects. There is no doubt that much ingenuity and often considerable originality lies buried in these commentaries, but fundamental originality *in a subject* is relatively rare. It is remarkable that the writings of Ṣadr al-Dīn al-Shīrāzī, written in the 11th/17th century and still displaying a relatively high quality of philosophic thought, remained the highest texts of philosophy in the subsequent centuries, but were (where philosophy was pursued) always the ideal never surpassed. And yet al-Shīrāzī is himself largely a commentator on previous thinkers, especially the philosopher Ibn Sīnā. This is the case with all the other subjects.

The custom of writing systematic commentaries was, in the beginning, combined with original works. In the 6th/12th century, for example, Fakhr al-Dīn al-Rāzī wrote a commentary on Ibn Sīnā but was also the author of several independent works. But later the habit developed of writing commentaries upon commentaries until the original works, the subjects of commentaries, were almost completely forgotten. Certain works on dogmatic theology found more than half a dozen layers of commentaries. Still later commentary degenerated into mere marginal notes, usually devoted to superficial quibbles and verbal disputes. These, together with short compendia, formed the stuff of the *madrasa* curriculum. In the 12th/18th century, e.g., a curriculum of studies was worked out in India by Mullā Niẓām al-Dīn. This course, known after him as the Niẓāmī Course (*Dars-i Niẓāmī*), had widespread acclaim and, with modifications, was accepted almost all over India. Similar courses in Persia and Central Asia also existed with somewhat different emphasis on different subjects.

However, this course, which represented, and was also accused by the right-wing of the orthodox of representing, the highest emphasis on the rational sciences, had three works on pure philosophy. All of these were later résumés, compilations or commentaries, including Ṣadr al-Dīn al-Shīrāzī's commentary on Ibn Sīnā. In Ḥadīth it had only one book, a late compilation known as *Mishkāt al-Maṣabiḥ*. In Qur'ānic exegesis it had only two medieval commentaries, one of which, called *al-Jalālayn*, is so brief that its words are the same in number as those of the Qur'ān itself. The ingenuity of writing commentaries reached such a pitch that some people used only certain letters of the Arabic alphabet (i.e. only 14 out of 28 letters) to exhibit their linguistic skill![5] A concise work of Arabic syntax, known as *al-Kāfiya*, found purely mystic interpretations at the hands of some commentators.

Usually, the curriculum was executed on the method of succession of subjects. Thus, to take one example of the serial arrangement, Arabic grammar and language; literature; arithmetic; philosophy; law; jurisprudence; theology; Qur'ānic exegesis; and Ḥadīth.[6] The student passed from one grade to another by finishing one subject and starting the 'higher' one. This system did not naturally allow enough time to be spent on each subject. But this was by no means the only method; often a student started with a compendium on a subject and in the next grade studied the same subject in greater detail and with commentaries. The job of the teacher was to teach others' commentaries as well as the text usually without any comment by himself on the subject itself. Moreover, there was no agreement as to which subjects were 'higher' than others. We have already referred to the competition of law and theology. Many regarded the Ḥadīth as the greatest of all subjects since it supplied the materials, so to speak, for other religious academic disciplines. Indeed, there were several schools where almost the only subject taught was the Ḥadīth. There was, however, a great deal of flexibility in the acquisition of learning. A person, after acquiring an elementary religious education, could enter any place of higher learning. But after having completed his course, he might go to another school and enrol in those subjects which were there receiving greater emphasis and thus he could pass from school to school. If he regarded Ṣūfism as the highest spiritual goal, he entered a *zāwiya* after graduating from institutions of conventional learning.

Whereas, therefore, one may justifiably speak of the rigidity of the religious disciplines and of the general orientation of the *madrasa* education towards these religious interests, the educational field, as a whole, was far from rigid. An eminent thinker of the eighteenth century, Shāh Walī Allāh (d. 1174/1761 – see Chapter XII) has left us his own curriculum in his autobiographical sketch.[7] This included mathematics, astronomy and medicine. The *madrasa*-system does not, therefore, represent the whole of Muslim education. Shāh Walī Allāh did not attend *madrasas* but learnt privately at home from his own father. In the middle of the same century, another Indian author, Muḥammad 'Alī al-Thānawī, wrote (1158/1745) a famous book, *Kashshāf Iṣṭilaḥāt al-Funūn*, on all branches of learning and their technical terms. In his preface to this book he writes: 'When I completed my study of Arabic and the religious disciplines from my father, I prepared myself to acquire the treasures of philosophy, natural sciences, rational theology and mathematics, etc., but I could not obtain these from any teacher. I then devoted part of my time to the study of compendia of these sciences such as I possessed.' The same author has recommended to us his own carefully thought-out scheme of the rational sciences for study with their branches – physics, mathematics (including mechanics, etc.), and rational theology.

Other prominent cases of such extra-*madrasa* learning are by no means rare. But the fundamental weakness of medieval Muslim learning, as of all pre-modern learning, was its concept of knowledge. In opposition to the modern attitude which regards knowledge as something essentially to be searched and discovered by the mind to which it assigns an active rôle in knowledge, the medieval attitude was that knowledge was something to be *acquired*. This attitude of mind was rather passive and receptive than creative and positive. In the Muslim world this contrast became still more acute because of the opposition between the 'transmitted' or traditional (*naql* or *sam'*), on the one hand, and the rational on the other. In this controversy orthodoxy, anxious to safeguard tradition, came out on the whole heavily against reason, which it wanted to keep in strict subordination to dogma. We have already pointed to the phenomenon of memory-work and learning by rote in schools. The emphasis on 'transmission' and tradition had an incalculably damaging influence in this direction, even though enlightened and intelligent men were not altogether lacking who insisted on a real understanding of the tradition. In the logical part of works on dogmatic theology, there were lengthy and sometimes incisive discussions on the nature of knowledge and even special treatises were written on the subject. But since the expansion of the *kalām*-theology had been done rather mechanically and its parts had been externally juxtaposed instead of there being any inner and organic relationship of growth among them, these endless discussions on the nature of knowledge failed, in practice, to have any effect whatever on the theological part proper where dogmatic tenets were formally supported by arguments. This is what we mean by saying that the *kalām*-system, instead of stimulating thought, came to be a *substitute* for philosophy and retarded thought in general. Ibn Khaldūn very perceptively remarks, in his discussion of the sciences in his Prolegomenon, that this later development in the *kalām* has resulted in a terrible confusion between the topics and methods of philosophy and those of dogmatic theology.

Al-Azhar, now called 'the University of al-Azhar', began as a mosque-school under the Fāṭimids of Egypt. It was taken over by the Sunnīs after the collapse of the Ismā'īlī kingdom and was devoted to the study of law according to the Shāfi'ī system. The teaching of other Sunnī schools of law was later added, but still in the 9th/15th century it was only one of several places of higher learning in Egypt, although perhaps the most eminent among them. Its fame slowly ousted other rivals, however, and with the decline, in modern times, of Ṣūfī centres of religious instruction, it has emerged as the largest and most important place of religious instruction not only in Egypt but of the entire Muslim World.

The 'supervisor' of al-Azhar, charged with the administration of the institution, was replaced by a scholar-head entitled 'the Shaykh of al-Azhar' and now its entire internal administration is vested in a body of scholars, the 'Committee of the Grand Scholars'. During the late 13th/19th and the present centuries, through a series of steps initiated by Shaykh Muḥammad 'Abduh (see Chapter XIII), its curriculum has been reorganized both in form and in content and certain modern intellectual disciplines of the humanities and social sciences have been introduced together with certain natural science subjects at the high-school level. Elementary and secondary teaching have been geared to higher instruction in contrast to the practice prevailing in the Middle Ages (see above) and a vast number of lower institutions, the *kuttābs*, have been created to prepare for the higher learning. This network of lower schools even extends beyond Egypt to certain other Arab countries of the neighbourhood. Various 'wings' (*riwāq*) represent different nationalities, a practice in several *madrasas* which influenced the growth of the 'Nations' in the medieval Western universities.

Although al-Azhar, with more than ten thousand students, is the greatest traditional institution of learning today, it is by no means the only one. The mosque-college of Zaytūna in Tunisia, and that of Deoband, near Sahāranpur in India (set up in the second half of the 13th/19th century) are important seminaries for the training of the 'Ulamā', although the former institution has, during the last few years, been turned into a kind of higher institute of Islamic studies and has been placed under the direction and control of the Tunisian government. The problem of the relationship of this traditional learning with modern education will be discussed in Chapter XIII which deals with Islamic modernism.

CHAPTER TWELVE

PRE-MODERNIST REFORM MOVEMENTS

Tensions within Pre-Modernist Islam – The Wahhābīs – The Indian Reform Movements – The African Reform Movements

Tensions within Pre-Modernist Islam

The spiritual situation of Islam in the late medieval period can be said to be broadly characterized by the tension between orthodox Islam and Ṣūfism. But a closer examination reveals not one tension but a complex of spiritual forces and cross-currents which might be overlooked in a broad analysis of the situation. Before, therefore, embarking on giving our account of the phenomenon of reform-movements that sprang from within Islam, we shall do well to pause and examine more closely the different factors in this complex of Islamic spirituality and especially their mutual relationships.

As we have endeavoured to show in our treatment of Ṣūfism, this phenomenon itself is a very complex one. Its moral, emotive and cognitive or speculative aspects can be distinguished clearly enough. The moral drive with which the Ṣūfī movement had started as a method of self-discipline to realize the religious values of Islam in their fullness, however, soon gave way to and was submerged under the strongly flavoured ecstatic impulses and the attraction of a privileged type of knowledge. The orthodox synthetic reform movement that came to a head in al-Ghazālī was a sustained endeavour to curb the ecstatic extravagances of Ṣūfism on the one hand and to limit, if not to exorcise, its cognitive claims on the other. These trends, however, broke loose again soon after al-Ghazālī, and whereas the one developed into a mass spiritual hypnotism in the form of popular orders – especially the 'irregular' ones – the other plunged headlong into metaphysical mysteries of all kinds under the iron cover of infallible intuitionism.

As for orthodoxy – represented by the 'Ulamā' – its relationship with Ṣūfism is also complex, partly because of the different strands in Ṣūfism and partly because of somewhat different strands in the orthodoxy itself, i.e. the types of 'Ulamā' themselves. Generally speaking, the enrolment of the 'Ulamā' in the Ṣūfī movement resulted in the emphasizing and renewal of the original moral factor and puritanical self-control in it, especially at the expense of the extravagant features of popular ecstatic Ṣūfism. Thus, one may say that generally the history of the alignment of the 'Ulamā' with Ṣūfism is the history of the recovery of the moral motive in Ṣūfism. But although the 'Ulamā' exerted a continuous pressure towards discrediting the purely superstitious and the ecstatic in Ṣūfism, their attitude towards speculative or metaphysical Ṣūfism is not unanimous. There were many eminent orthodox scholars on whom speculative Ṣūfism exerted a powerful attraction. This had been increasingly the case since Ibn al-'Arabī (7th/13th century).

We have shown in Chapter VIII that speculative Ṣūfism – like Neoplatonism and largely under its influence – is, in fact, a definite type of idealist philosophy, and we have spoken there of a liaison between philosophy and Ṣūfism. Ṣūfī intuitionism, therefore, in the hands of speculative Ṣūfīs is a mode of philosophic thought, except that it seeks to back itself up by a theory of *kashf*, implying some kind of infallibility. Now, the orthodox speculative Ṣūfī thinkers, while they retained the theory of *kashf*, nevertheless brought about important changes in the *content* of the Ṣūfī speculative system. The most important development is that they produced a kind of synthesis of the traditional orthodox *kalām*-theology based on the Qur'ān and Islamic doctrine with the purely speculative theology of the Ṣūfī theosophy. This strand of orthodox Ṣūfism, although primarily devoted to religious *thought*, nevertheless held fast to the concept of sainthood and the special status of saints, without which the doctrine of *kashf* would have collapsed. But so long as this doctrine of sainthood remains, involving a peculiar position for saints, it is difficult not to condone, to some extent, the popular excessive reverence for the saints and even the superstitious worship of their graves. Speculative Ṣūfism, therefore, although different from the ecstatic Ṣūfism, is always more or less indulgent towards it.

But the right wing of orthodoxy has always been suspicious of the advent of Ṣūfism – as a way of life – into Islam. These are the Ḥanbalites – followers of Aḥmad ibn Ḥanbal – and the Ahl al-Ḥadīth or the traditionists. Indeed, the Ḥanbalites and the traditionists are almost, if not absolutely, identical. Ibn Ḥanbal himself was a traditionist – so much so that the 3rd/9th century historian al-Ṭabarī refused to recognize him as a legist and insisted that he was a pure traditionist. Now although the Ḥadīth or Tradition is a composite of several strands – it includes a definite core of Ṣūfī traditions – its overall character is undoubtedly puritanical and activist. The Ḥanbalites, distrustful of uncontrolled speculation, have been outspoken enemies of both rational philosophy and speculative Ṣūfism; and ecstatic popular Ṣūfism is, for them, anathema. Over against these newer developments in Islam they have always kept alive a sense of moral dynamism and puritanical activism.

But after the Sūfī movement had captured the Muslim world during the 6th/12th and 7th/13th centuries, emotionally, spiritually and intellectually, even the pure traditionists found it impossible to neglect the Ṣūfī forces entirely and tried, in their methodology, to incorporate as much of the Ṣūfī legacy as could be reconciled with orthodox Islam and could be made to yield a positive contribution towards it. First, the moral motive of Ṣūfism was emphasized and some of its technique of *dhikr* or *murāqaba*, 'spiritual concentration', adopted. But the object and the content of this concentration were identified with the orthodox doctrine and the goal re-defined as the strengthening of faith in dogmatic tenets and the moral purity of the spirit. This type of neo-Ṣūfism, as one may call it, tended to regenerate orthodox activism and reinculcate a positive attitude to this world. In this sense, the Ḥanbalites Ibn Taymīya and Ibn Qayyim al-Jawzīya, although sworn enemies of Ṣūfism, were definitely neo-Ṣūfis – and, indeed, pioneers of this new trend. Later, some of the Ṣūfī adepts themselves – like Aḥmad Sirhindī who wanted to reform Ṣūfism – adopted a similar position. Further, the neo-Ṣūfis also allowed, to some extent, the claims of intellectual Ṣūfism: they accepted the Ṣūfi *kashf* or intuitive revelation but rejected the claim of its quasi-infallibility, insisting that the reliability of *kashf* is in proportion to the moral purity of the heart, which has, in fact, infinite grades. Both Ibn Taymīya and Ibn Qayyim, in fact, patently claim *kashf* for themselves. Thus, the deliverances of *kashf* were brought to the level of sound intellectual processes. Further, Ibn Taymīya and his disciples employ the whole range of essential Ṣūfī terminology – including the term *sālik* – the spiritual itinerant – and try to instil into it a puritanical, moral meaning and an orthodox ethos. Two types of Ṣūfism thus come to be radically distinguished: an un-Islamic Ṣūfism and an Islamic Ṣūfism.

At the level of popular religion, however, it was the brotherhoods with their mass-appeal that continued to expand and dominate the world of Islam. The form of this Ṣūfism was mainly ecstatic, with its auto-hypnotic visions, orgiastic rituals and a motley of superstitious beliefs and practices which further degenerated quite commonly into gross exploitation and charlatanism. This was the spiritual situation of Islam when, during the 12th/18th century, a sense of anxiety and urgency of religio-social reform gripped the greater part of the Muslim world, expressing itself in different areas in reform movements and schools which, allowing for differences in spiritual experiences and environment of each region, exhibit a fundamentally similar character.

The Wahhābīs

There is abundant evidence that a general orthodox revival was building up against the corruption of religion and the moral laxity and degeneration prevalent in Muslim society in the outlying provinces of the Ottoman Empire and in India – a trend which took on visible expression during the 12th/18th and the 13th/19th centuries. Its most violent outburst occurred in Arabia itself in the 12th/18th century in the form of a movement which has become famous in history as the 'Wahhābī movement'. This movement, which we shall describe now, is usually represented as a sudden emergence which took the Muslim world by surprise. But, as we have just stated, there seems to have been a general spiritual build-up for the resurgence of orthodox Islam, of which the Wahhābī outburst was a striking case. First, in India, as we shall show below, the orthodox reassertion had come to the surface much earlier – in the 11th/17th century – due to the crisis Islam faced both politically and spiritually. But in the Middle East itself, the eighteenth century witnessed an intellectual orthodox reassertion in two different forms, both represented by the great Yemenite scholars, Muḥammad al-Murtaḍā (d. 1204/1790) and Muḥammad ibn 'Alī al-Shawkānī (1172–1250/1759–1834). We mention these two names here despite the fact that chronologically their activity is a little after Muḥammad ibn 'Abd al-Wahhāb, the originator of the Wahhābī reform movement, because neither of these is influenced by the doctrines of 'Abd al-Wahhāb and yet both display different forms of an orthodox revival.

As for al-Murtaḍā, he represents the moderate orthodox revival in seeking to restate al-Ghazālī's line of thought and revindicate it. This moderate trend we shall also find in much of the Indian reform movement. Al-Shawkānī, a Zaydī scholar from Ṣan'ā' – who claimed to be and was acclaimed as a great leader of the Ahl al-Sunna – rejected the idea of simple acceptance of authority in religion (*taqlīd*) and was violently attacked by his contemporaries, including Zaydī Shī'ites. That he had been deeply influenced by the writings of the Ibn Taymīya school (whose doctrines also inspired Wahhābism) is testified by the fact that his major work in twelve volumes entitled *Nayl al-Awṭār* – 'Realization of Desires' – is a commentary on a legal work of Ibn Taymīya's grandfather, Majd al-Dīn ibn Taymīya (d. 652/1254). This work was written when al-Shawkānī was still comparatively young (he states in the preface that he is not mature enough to undertake such a work but that some of his teachers had approached him to write it) and, therefore either towards the end of the 12th/18th or the beginning of the 13th/19th century. But, further, the author states clearly in the preface that this work of Ibn Taymīya was widely resorted to by the scholars:

[This work of Ibn Taymīya] has become a source-book for the majority of the 'Ulamā' when they are in need of finding a legal proof – especially in this region and in these times; upon this sweet spring, the eyes of original thinkers collide with one another and the steps of investigators vie with one another in entering its gates. It has thus become a resort for thinkers whither they repair and a haven for those who wish to flee from the bonds of slavish and blind acceptance of authority.[1]

This shows that the orthodox revival had been developing over a period; but it appeared in the Ḥanbalite form of the extreme right-wing orthodoxy in Central Arabia around the middle of the 12th/18th century, inspired by the teachings of Ibn Taymīya. The originator of this puritanical movement, Muḥammad ibn 'Abd al-Wahhāb, had been a Ṣūfī adept in his youth, but later came under the influence of Ibn Taymīya's writings, whose bitter denunciation of Ṣūfī superstitious accretions and of the Ṣūfī intellectual doctrines – especially the doctrine of the Unity of Being as expounded by Ibn al-'Arabī – and, above all, whose moral-puritanical earnestness had a decisive influence upon him. In a small treatise, entitled 'The Book of Unity (*Kitāb al-Tawḥīd*)', and commented upon by a 13th/19th century scholar, Ibn 'Abd al-Wahhāb attacked the commonly held beliefs in the powers of the saints and pious men and the practices consequent upon these beliefs – worship of and at saints' tombs, reliance upon the intercessions of the Prophet and the saints, indeed, the whole gamut of popular religion.

In his polemic against the general moral laxity, however, Ibn 'Abd al-Wahhāb does not confine himself to the malpractices and beliefs inculcated or encouraged by Ṣūfism alone, but also attacks the blind acceptance of authority in religious matters in general and therefore comes to oppose the generality of the 'Ulamā' for whom the medieval systems of Islam had become the last word in which they allowed no independent rethinking. Since the acceptance of Ṣūfism in some form – especially the intellectual content of Ṣūfism – had become a part of medieval Islam, Ibn 'Abd al-Wahhāb, after the manner of and influenced by Ibn Taymīya, found it essential to go behind the medieval authorities to the 'Sunna of the early generations'. Ibn 'Abd al-Wahhāb, therefore, came necessarily to oppose the authority of the medieval schools and recognized only two authorities: the Qur'ān and the Sunna of the Prophet along with the precedents of the Companions. Since, however, the Ḥadīth – embodying the Prophetic Sunna – was actually authoritatively collected in the 3rd/9th century, the followers of Ibn ʻAbd al-Wahhāb had later to modify this stand and accepted the Ijmāʻ or consensus of the first three centuries of Islam as binding.

The consequences of this attitude, especially when organized, like Wahhābism, in the form of a movement, were far-reaching for the spiritual and intellectual temper within Islam, and proved, in the long run, to be much more important than what the Wahhābīs might have to say on any individual belief or doctrine that they attacked. Their insistence on the right of *ijtihād* (independent thinking) and their condemnation of *taqlīd* acted as a great liberating force, and, despite the strong opposition displayed towards them in the early stages on both the political and religious planes, has affected the temper of subsequent Islamic developments perhaps more than any other single factor. 'Wahhābism', in fact, has become a generic term, applicable not only to the particular movement initiated by Ibn ʻAbd al-Wahhāb, but to all types of analogous phenomenon throughout the Muslim world, which advocated 'purification' of the Faith from degrading accretions and insisted on more or less independent and even original judgment in matters of religion.

This is, indeed, a somewhat curious phenomenon. The Wahhābīs themselves, although they had rejected the medieval authorities, nevertheless took up a stringently fundamental position in so far as they accepted only the Qur'ān and the Sunna as the material sources of religion. They even rejected *qiyās*, the analogical method of reasoning, to interpret the Qur'ān and the Sunna following Ibn Ḥanbal. And yet this apparent rejection of the only formal means of interpretation Muslim jurisprudence provided acted ambivalently in two diametrically opposed directions. On the one hand, by emphasizing the text of the Qur'ān and the Ḥadīth, it inevitably resulted in ultra-conservatism and almost absolute literalism. On the other hand, however, by encouraging the exercise of independent reasoning (*ijtihād*) rather than merely analogical reasoning with regard to those problems which were not directly covered by the *text*, the door was opened for more liberal forces to interpret the text more freely than the principle of analogical reasoning as developed by medieval legists would allow. For, in the hands of these legists, the principle of analogical reasoning had come to be formulated very narrowly and, although it served the purpose of limited interpretation, it largely acted as a restrictive force rather than as a privilege of free expansion. In operating the principle of analogy, the ʻUlamā' had generally remained too much bound to the literal text and did not allow enough weight to the actual spirit of the text. Although the principle of *qiyās* in itself had potentialities of wider and deeper application and could have been made a real instrument of liberalism, its actual mode of operation had been restrictive to an unfortunate degree. Although, therefore, the Wahhābīs were much more fundamentalists and literalists so far as the body of the text of the Scripture is concerned, their *ijtihād*, in the long run, proved to be much less literalist and restrictive than the *qiyās* of the 'Ulamā'.

But the most important aspect of Wahhābism was its normal motivation: it was a violent reaction at the moral degradation into which the Community had allowed itself to fall gradually over the centuries during which popular Ṣūfism had become the overwhelming factor. This moral motivation survived as a general legacy of the Wahhābī revolt after its first intolerant and fanatical phase had passed, and, combined with the general liberation of the mind and the spirit, paved the way for Modernist Muslims to overcome the literalism and fundamentalism of the Wahhābīs themselves and to allow for the scriptural text itself to be treated and interpreted on moral liberal lines. This is, indeed, the secret of the success of Wahhābism and its permanent lesson which has become ubiquitous in almost all the reform-movements, whether pre-Modernist or Modernist. In this general and ubiquitous sense, Wahhābism is not restricted to the actual Wahhābī movement as history knows it, but is a kind of umbrella term – the 'Wahhābī-Idea' – covering analogous rather than identical phenomena in the Muslim world. It may be summed up as a reassertion of monotheism and equality of men combined with varying degrees of reinterpretation of the actual positive legacy of the Islamic tradition for the reconstruction of Muslim society.

Muḥammad ibn 'Abd al-Wahhāb (1115–1206/1703–92) took to extensive travels in Iraq and Persia at about the age of twenty-one, and studied philosophy and Ṣūfism and for a time even taught Ṣūfism. But, after returning to his home town at about the age of forty, he began to preach his own doctrines, which were opposed by some of his own kinsmen. He emigrated to Dair'iya where he established an alliance with the local chieftain, Sa'ūd, who accepted his religious views, and it was from there that the Wahhābī movement expanded militarily from Najd to the Ḥijāz and the Holy cities of Mecca and Medina came under the Wahhābī sway. Early in the 13th/19th century, however, the Wahhābīs were militarily crushed by Muḥammad 'Alī, the governor of Egypt, under orders from the Ottoman government. But they soon revived locally in Najd with their capital at Riyāḍ and, after being driven out from there and forced to seek refuge in Kuwait for a period of eleven years. 'Abd al-'Azīz ibn Sa'ūd returned at the dawn of the present century not only to retrieve the lost power of his ancestors but to establish his sway over the whole territory known as 'Saudi (i.e., Sa'ūdī) Arabia'.

One interesting socio-religious development during this second phase of the Wahhābī sway in Arabia may be mentioned here. This is the establishment of the cooperative type of agricultural colonies or villages where people were settled, near watering places. The settlers, called *ikhwān* or Brethren, besides cultivating the soil, were divided into categories for the purposes of waging the *jihād* when called upon to do so: some of them were regarded as the standing army which could be called up for active service immediately and on the ruler's order, while the rest could be called up only on a *fatwā* of the 'Ulamā'. The feature of combining religious training with *jihād* was present in the activity of Ibn 'Abd al-Wahhāb himself and is not an uncommon phenomenon in the pre-Modernist reform movements. Indeed, a striking feature of many of these reform movements is that while their organization is on the lines of a Ṣūfī *ṭarīqa*, their content is orthodox including military training. The Sanūsīs and the Wahhābīs also added the emphasis on work and active pursuit of ways of livelihood. It is possible that the 'Muslim Brothers' of Egypt were influenced by such precedents in establishing their cooperatives.

A certain amount of opposition to Wahhābism was undoubtedly on the basis of its doctrines which challenged the moral laxity and the superstitious cults of popular religion which even the majority of the 'Ulamā' had come to condone, if not to accept in their entirety. The Wahhābī reform was, therefore, opposed not only by the masses but in the beginning even by many of the 'Ulamā' who wished to *conserve* the heritage of medieval Islam. But the greater part of this opposition must be put to the political activity of the Wahhābīs and, especially, to their violent militarism. Among their chief opponents was the Ottoman government whose authority they had challenged and overthrown. Indeed, in the Wahhābī revolt one finds clear reminiscences of the Khārijite revolt of the early period of Islam: to seek to impose reform under the compulsion of an idealism through intolerant and fanatical methods. But the catholic tradition of Islam opposed the Wahhābī methods as it had rejected the Khārijite methods much earlier. And yet it remains one of the curious but persistent paradoxes of most ultra-right-wing reform phenomena in Islam that while their express purpose is to unite the whole Community for a reformist purpose, they are impelled to break even the existing unity and to take up arms against it. One of the cardinal criticisms, for example, by Ibn 'Abd al-Wahhāb of the pre-Islamic Arab society and, by implication, of the existing Muslim Community, was that it was not united enough[2] and that it was not willing to surrender to the ruling authority, and yet the methods adopted by this movement, in its early phase, were to resort to armed rebellion and to produce further disunity. The probable cause of this paradox is the fact that Sunnī Islam, while it has developed on the basis of catholic principles, has not created sufficient machinery to provide for the necessary reform processes. In fact, the Sunnī Islam, as it developed and functioned throughout the Middle Ages, has put almost its entire weight on the side of maintaining the already achieved equilibrium, i.e. on conservation and catholicity and has not made sufficient allowance or provision for those aspects of the society through which it exercises self-criticism and develops. Undoubtedly, the medieval concepts of Ijmā‘ and *taqlīd* are the keynotes of this stagnation. Progress, therefore, had to be achieved, through violent methods.

The Indian Reform Movements

In India the roots of the reform movement go back to the 10th/16th and the 11th/17th centuries, for the spiritual crisis of Islam in India was crystallized by the political developments and the political implications of the ruling Muslim minority over and against the vast Hindu majority. After an initial political phase, that of a conquering and ruling minority, Islam in India developed, as it was bound to, a relationship towards the Hindus on a religious and social plane. The vanguard of this approach towards proselytization were not the 'Ulamā' but the Ṣūfīs who, from the 7th/13th century onward, converted a large number of Hindu masses – especially from the lower castes – to Islam. But the latitudinarian tendencies of Ṣūfism, always prone to pass into antinomianism, soon intermingled – especially at the level of 'rustic' irregular orders – with the native antinomian trends in Hinduism itself, to produce a phenomenon of Hindu-Muslim *rapprochement* as a particular phase of the *bhaktī* ('devotion') movement which had arisen in Hinduism away from, even before, Islam. This movement culminated in the 10th/16th century in the activity of certain influential eclectic religious personalities such as Kabīr and Nānak. Nānak, preaching against organized religion, adopted monotheism and rejected much of the social implication of Hinduism although retaining its general outlook. His message was, however, developed by a series of spiritual successors into a new religion called Sikhism which became militantly active against the Muslim rule in its later stages and, through the rise of a powerful Sikh state, contributed to its collapse.

The first Islamic crisis in India came to a head during the reign of Akbar who, partly through political motives, but largely on the basis of his personal religious views and experiences and helped intellectually and encouraged by the two brothers, Abu'l-Faḍl and Fayḍī, formulated and inaugurated a new eclectic religion, the Dīn-i Ilāhī, which assigned to him the prerogative of an absolute *Mujtahid*. The new religion perished in the bud – rejected equally by Hindus and Muslims – but the leaders of Muslim orthodoxy were alarmed at the extent to which the un-Islamic spiritual forces had invaded Islam until they threatened its very existence. The chief factor within was undoubtedly the uncontrolled latitudinarianism of popular Ṣūfism, and this the orthodoxy prepared to stem. The most potent and consequential personality in this reform movement was Shaykh Aḥmad Sirhindī, who not only wrote extensively criticizing the theosophy of Ibn al-ʻArabī,[3] whose works had become the theoretical foundation of Ṣūfī relativism, but also trained a large number of disciples who spread out to teach a reformed Ṣūfī doctrine and practice. In his doctrine, Sirhindī replaced the metaphysical monism of Ibn al-ʻArabī with an ethical dualism, while in practice a strong emphasis was placed on the Sharīʻa values, reinforced through Ṣūfī techniques. Ṣūfism, far from being rejected, therefore, was given a new life and a new direction and, from this point of view, Sirhindī's reform differs materially from the later Wahhābī movement in Arabia.

A generation after Sirhindī – around the middle of the 11th/17th century – a deadly war for the throne was fought between two great grandsons of Akbar, Dārā Shukōh, a manifest champion of the type of religious ideology Akbar had started, and Aurangzeb, the express defender of Muslim orthodoxy. The latter was victorious and strove, with an iron will, to restore the power of orthodox Islam, but it was like the last glare of a torch before it is finally extinguished. His reign is a record of continuous rebellions, especially those of the rising Hindu Marathas in the Deccan and the Sikhs in the Punjab. He died in 1118/1707, and after him the Muslim power in India swiftly disintegrated. Muslims, for whom Islam and political efficacy are an indivisible whole logically, and had been so also historically, were almost literally left in a dismal wilderness, not knowing whither to turn.

During the 12th/18th century, the half-conscious search of Muslims in India for a new orientation of reinterpretation of Islam expressed itself in the works of an influential thinker, Shāh Walī Allāh of Delhi (1113–76/1702–62). While, on the one hand, Shāh Walī Allāh did not give up all hope of a simple restoration of Muslim power in India (he wrote letters to various Muslim rulers and generals to occupy the political vacuum, including the Rohilla general Najīb al-Dawla and the Afghan Aḥmad Shāh Abdālī who defeated the Marathas in a pitched battle in 1174/1761), on the other he formulated a restatement of Islam on a much broader basis than the traditional Muslim theology. Although, looking from within his thought, the various elements appear to be juxtaposed rather than integrated into a logically coherent system, nevertheless the mere fact that a conscious attempt at an 'integral Islam' was made is significant. In this system, a broad, humanistic sociological base is overlain by a doctrine of social and economic justice in Islamic terms and crowned by a Ṣūfī world-view.

Shāh Walī Allāh's brand of Islamic reconstruction and reform was not only slightly prior in time to the Wahhābī programme of reform in Arabia but materially different from it as well: he not only retained Ṣūfism but crowned his system with a definite Ṣūfic interpretation of the universe. But as his influence radiated over a large part of India, through his pupils and sons – especially his eldest son, Shāh 'Abd al-'Azīz, in the early part of the 13th/19th century, the 'purification' element in his teaching received greater emphasis from the totality of his catholic approach, although an orthodox Ṣūfistic trend was never completely alienated from it. This element of 'purification' of religion from un-Islamic beliefs and practices, and a return to the positive teaching of Islam, became still more prominent in the hands of a disciple of Shāh 'Abd al-'Azīz, the fiery Sayyid Aḥmad of Rae Bareli, who transformed this reformist school into a *jihād* movement.

Sayyid Aḥmad is generally regarded as the large-scale initiator of Wahhābism in India and it is assumed that he was influenced by Wahhābī doctrines when he visited Mecca for a pilgrimage in the year 1238/1822–3.[4] It is also alleged that he was interrogated in the Holy City by the 'Ulamā' who became suspicious of his views and that he was expelled from the Holy City.[5] In any case, the term Wahhābism as applied to Sayyid Aḥmad's views does not seem convincing on historical grounds. We have seen above in this Chapter that the Ottomans had recovered the Ḥijāz from the Wahhābīs in the years 1227–8/1812–13. By the time, therefore, Sayyid Aḥmad visited Mecca, the Wahhābī influence must have been banished from there not only politically but religiously as well. The mere fact that Sayyid Aḥmad was interrogated about his beliefs and expelled shows that Wahhābī ideas were not allowed to be present in the Ḥijāz at this time, and that anyone who professed Wahhābism was persecuted. What seems probable is that the puritanical trends which had been originally present in the Indian reform school had already become accentuated in India because of the emphasis on Ḥadīth and the struggle to rid the Muslims of superstitious cults which were seen to be an inroad of Hinduism into Islam. In the activist hands of Sayyid Aḥmad, a zealous crusader, this becomes a perfect analogue of Arabian Wahhābism. Further, the Indian Wahhābīs rejected all authority of the four orthodox schools and called themselves 'non-conformists' (*ghayr muqallid*)[6] whereas the Wahhābīs had expressly affirmed that they were Ḥanbalites.

After his return from the pilgrimage, Sayyid Aḥmad preached

strenuously against accretions and cults of saints and organized a *jihād* movement. Funds were collected and men recruited for *jihād* from a large area in northern and eastern India and much of the Frontier Province was taken from the Sikhs and occupied. Sayyid Aḥmad and his associate, Shāh Ismā'īl (a grandson of Shāh Walī Allāh), were, however, killed in 1247/1831 at Bālākot in a battle against the Sikhs. Their followers carried on *jihād* against the British from Sithana on the western border although weakened by comparative lack of funds and men. In 1287–8/1870–1 some of the pro-British 'Ulamā' issued *fatwās* dissociating themselves from the movement, but the *jihād* activity was reported across the frontiers as late as 1307/1890.

In the meantime another reform movement was founded in Bengal in the early 13th/19th century by one Ḥājjī Sharī'at Allāh. Born about 1178/1764, Sharī'at Allāh went on a pilgrimage to Mecca in 1196/1782 and stayed there until 1217/1802, during which time he was a disciple of a Shāfi'ī Shaykh. It is clear that he could hardly have come under Wahhābī influence, since the Wahhābīs first occupied Mecca only in 1216/1803 and even then had to evacuate it a decade later. Nevertheless, on his return to Bengal, Sharī'at Allāh started a movement of 'purification' known as the Farā'iḍī movement. This movement seems to be a composite of three factors: (1) an anti-Britishness evidenced by the declaration that India was no longer *Dār al-Islām* (Abode of Islam) but had become *Dār al-Ḥarb* (Abode of War); (2) a socio-economic reform directed against the rich landlords in the interests of the peasants and workers; and (3) purification of Islam from Hindu ideas and Ṣūfī excesses – Sharī'at Allāh insisted that even the Ṣūfī terms *pīr* (spiritual preceptor) and *murīd* (disciple) should not be used and should be replaced by the terms 'teacher' and 'student'. This movement was carried on after Sharī'at Allāh by his son Dūdhū Miyān who died in 1281/1864, and followers of this movement are still found in Bengal.

The general discontent of the Muslims in India expressed itself also in the Indian Mutiny of 1857 where many of the 'Ulamā' not only lent moral support to the Mutiny but actually fought in it. Indeed, in that part of British India where Muslims were influential and also where their religion and culture had become strongly rooted – in the United Provinces – the Mutiny took on the definite character of a *jihād*. When the movement failed, these 'Ulamā' – ultimately emanating from the school of Shāh Walī Allāh and his sons and disciples – set up in 1293/1876 the now famous seminary of Deoband, which from its very inception has had a dual motivation of training religious scholars to safeguard the traditional Islamic learning and values and to liberate

India from the British. A disciple of Muḥammad Qāsim Nānawtawī the founder of the Deoband seminary, Maḥmūd al-Ḥasan (d. 1921) sought *fatwās* from Arabia for *jihād* against the British but was captured on his way back from Mecca and imprisoned during the First World War in Malta.

But while the Deoband school represents the moderate orthodox reformism, the more radical group of the *ghayr muqallids* or Ahl al-Ḥadīth, who also are largely traceable to the school of Shāh Walī Allāh, through Sayyid Aḥmad of Rae Bareli, constitute almost a complete break with the medieval past and seek to resuscitate the pristine Islam of the earliest centuries. Their sole reliance is on the Qur'ān and the Sunna of the Prophet and they spurn all subsequent authority. Although they are thus theoretically more radical than the Arabian Wahhābīs, they are, nevertheless, akin to the latter in outlook who have also influenced, to some extent, the Ahl al-Ḥadīth movement in its later stages and especially during the twentieth century some of the Ahl al-Ḥadīth leaders have been active sympathizers of the Wahhābī rule in Arabia. One of their earliest leaders, Ṣiddīq Ḥasan Khān (d. 1306/1889), who was the husband of the Begum of Bhopāl State but was later exiled by the British on suspicion of being in a secret anti-British alliance with Turkey, was more under the influence of the Yemenite al-Shawkānī, of the writings of Ibn Taymīya and, indeed, of Shāh Walī Allāh than under direct Wahhābī influence as pointed out earlier. The Ahl al-Ḥadīth, who have their own schools and mosques, have their headquarters in Lahore in West Pakistan.

A revivalist puritanical movement, based on a reformed Ṣūfism, also spread in Central Asia in the 13th/19th century, and the name Wahhābī was equally applied to it by Schuyler in his book *Turkestan.*[7] Little literature is available about this movement although it is certain that it waged a *jihād* against the Russian occupation but was ineffective because of insufficient preparation in men and materials. This is another striking illustration of how a Muslim reform movement, when presented with an external threat turns itself, unlike the Wahhābīs of Arabia, against the external enemy in the first instance. We have seen this already in the case of the Indian movement which, although it started to reform Islam from within, came to grips with the Sikh power and then the British forces. The Wahhābīs in Arabia were not presented with such a situation, and we shall see below that the Sanūsī movement in North Africa, when presented with such an external challenge, reacted in the same fashion.

The second common characteristic that has emerged is the presence of a new form of Ṣūfism in these movements. The reform of Ṣūfism under orthodox pressure – both from within and from outside Ṣūfism –

resulted in a phenomenon wherein Ṣūfism was largely stripped of its ecstatic and metaphysical character and content which were replaced by a content which was nothing else than the postulates of the orthodox religion. This fact cannot be over-emphasized, since through it Ṣūfism was made to serve the activist impulse of orthodox Islam and is a ubiquitous fact in all the major forms of pre-Modernist reform movements. In the following chapter we shall sketch the consequences of this development in Modern Islam. Here we only wish to establish that this form of Ṣūfism, which may be called neo-Ṣūfism, is a characteristic of this phase of Islamic religious history. This common fact is illustrated by the term *Ṭarīqa Muḥammadīya* (the order of Muḥammad, i.e. the Prophet) by which many of these movements describe themselves. Thus, this name was adopted by the Wahhābīs in Arabia for their reform programme,[8] by Sayyid Aḥmad for his movement,[9] and also by the Idrīsī Brotherhood (which we shall mention below). This cannot be a pure accident even though there does not seem to be any visible causal connection between them. Again, this must be treated, it seems, as an analogous but ubiquitous phenomenon. It means that, while on the one hand, the medieval *Ṭarīqas* or brotherhoods are essentially rejected as aberrant, Ṣūfism is affirmed on the other and is sought to be purified by a recourse to the inner, spiritual and moral life of the Prophet. One must not conclude, however, that neo-Ṣūfism entirely displaced medieval Ṣūfism in Muslim society in the immediate pre-Modernist period: this was so only for the adherents of these movements; for the vast masses medieval Ṣūfism remained the only form of intense spiritual and religious life until modern education and the impact of Western ideas joined hands in this respect with the pre-Modernist reformism and gradually dislodged the medieval forms of Ṣūfism from their central position, a process which still continues.

The African Reform Movements

The same phenomenon of what we have termed neo-Ṣūfism, i.e. Ṣūfism reformed on orthodox lines and interpreted in an activist sense, stands strikingly illustrated by the case of the Sanūsī Brotherhood of North Africa, which arose as a branch of the Idrīsī order but then developed on independent lines and followed entirely a career of its own. The Idrīsī order founded in Arabia by Aḥmad ibn Idrīs (d. 1253/1837), a Moroccan descendant of the Prophet, also named itself after the Prophet *Ṭarīqa Muḥammadīya*. It rejected the idea of a union with God and postulated instead a union with the spirit of the Prophet Muḥammad as the only possible and legitimate goal for the Ṣūfī. We have met with this name above in connection with the Arabian Wahhābism and the Indian movement of Sayyid Aḥmad of Rae Bareli. The inner revolution this name signifies is tantamount to the assertion that Ṣūfism must follow the path laid out by the Prophet, i.e. must conform to the strict Sunna of the Prophet and give up its medieval antinomian manifestations. This means that orthodox beliefs and norms will be taught and practised under the form of a Ṣūfī organization and with the use of some Ṣūfī techniques. Aḥmad ibn Idrīs was himself not only a Sūfī but also a legist and in law he rejected the medieval Ijmā' and also reasoning by analogy *(qiās)y* just as the Wahhābīs had done, and insisted on *ijtihād.* On the basis of this doctrine, coupled with the fact that he issued a drastically reformed version of Ṣūfism, some scholars have postulated a direct Wahhābī influence upon him. But the same arguments as we advanced in the cases of al-Shawkānī and Sayyid Aḥmad would also apply against this hypothesis of a direct Wahhābī influence. Mecca had not been under Wahhābī control except very briefly at the turn of the 13th/19th century and the Ottoman authorities in Mecca would hardly allow a person there openly to entertain Wahhābī views, let alone propagate them in an organized form. Aḥmad ibn Idrīs's ideas, therefore, must be traced to the same ubiquity of a spirit of reform as was manifested in the case of al-Shawkānī and the Indian movement.

The new reformed *Ṭarīqa* of Aḥmad ibn Idrīs gave further rise to three movements besides his own in Arabia in the Province of Asīr (where his followers temporarily exercised political sway): the *Ṭarīqas* known as Rashīdīya, Amīrghanīya and the Sanūsīya. Among these three, the Rashīdīya remained restricted to Algeria and even there, was overshadowed by the larger orders. As for the Amīrghanīya, founded by the Ḥijāzī Muḥammad 'Uthmān al-Amīrghanī (d. 1269/1853), it spread into the Sudan and Nubia where it opposed the Mahdī Movement and, against the radicalism of Mahdism, adopted a moderating rôle upholding the Ijmā' of the conservative orthodox Community. But by far the most important of these three sister offshoots turned out to be the Sanūsīya order founded by the Algerian Muḥammad ibn 'Alī al-Sanūsī (d. 1275/1859) in Mecca after the death of his master Aḥmad ibn Idrīs in 1253/1837.

The Sanūsī order, both in its organization and aims, is a representative *par excellence* of neo-Ṣūfism. It is thoroughly activist in its impulse with a purely moral-reformist programme, issuing in political action. On the purely doctrinal side Muḥammad ibn 'Ali al-Sanūsī claimed the right of *ijtihād* and part of his thought was thereby dubbed as infidelity to Islam (*kufr*) by a Mālikī Shaykh at al-Azhar, and because of orthodox opposition he was forced to leave Mecca in 1259/1843. On the practical side, although he inculcated in his followers a kind of liturgical practice (*dhikr*), his overall teaching was geared to practical ends based on the orthodox tenets of Islam. He organized *zāwiyas* (places of religious devotion) – the most important ones being those at Kafra and Jaghbūb (where he died) – where people were not only instructed in the Faith but where they were also trained in arms and encouraged to engage in professional pursuits like agriculture and trade.

One practical aim of the Sanūsīs was to establish peace in the Libyan desert and, in order to control the desert tribes, they built up a militant organization besides preaching the Islamic message of equality, brotherhood and peace. This resulted in a free and smooth flow of trade to the Mediterranean, a profession in which the desert tribe of the Jabābira especially excelled. To this end, the wild and unruly tribe of Zwi, enemies and rivals of the Jabābira, was won over for peace. The Sanūsīs also rejected Ottoman sovereignty, but later, when threatened by the encroachments of Western expansionist powers, they resisted first the French advance in Equatorial Africa to the south and later under Aḥmad al-Sanūsī and Muḥammad Idrīs al-Sanūsī took up arms, as the allies of Turkey, against the Italians in Libya and the British in Egypt. They were severely defeated and ruthlessly suppressed by the Italians but revived after the latter's withdrawal.

In a letter addressed to a tribe Muḥammad 'Alī al-Sanūsī wrote:

> I ask you, in the name of Islam, to obey God and His Prophet. . . . I ask you to obey the commands of God and His Prophet, viz. that you should offer five prayers, keep the fast of Ramaḍān, pay the *zakāt* and perform the obligatory pilgrimage to the sanctuary of Allāh. (I ask you) to desist from that wherefrom Allāh has asked you to refrain – from telling lies, backsliding, misappropriation of others' property, drinking intoxicants, giving false evidence and all the other acts God has forbidden. If you will carry out the commands of God and return from that which he has forbidden, He shall amply bestow His bounty upon you and shall grant you everlasting goodness and provision.[10]

In the same letter he succinctly summarized the basic programme of his reform movement as 'awakening the heedless, teaching the ignorant and guiding those who have strayed from the right path'.[11] On his peace-establishing mission he wrote, 'O people of the Wājanja (tribe)! We want to spread peace among you and the Bedouins who raid your territory, enslave your children and plunder your property. And, in doing so we are fulfilling the command of God in His Esteemed Book wherein God the Exalted says, "Should two parties from among the faithful resort to fighting, make peace between them".'[12]

Al-Sanūsī also forbade his followers from an excessive love of worldly goods and, in fact, prohibited the hoarding of gold and silver, except what was necessary for making jewellery for women. But this step in economic and social legislation is not taken in the spirit of an other-worldly spiritual interest – as inculcated by traditional Ṣūfism – but in the interests of the moral and social weal in this world. Indeed, from the quotations given above from al-Sanūsī, it also becomes strikingly clear that this preaching is positively moral rather than theological and other-worldly: God's blessings are mentioned in general but promises of Paradise and threats of Hell are not even hinted at. There is certainly no suggestion that al-Sanūsī had given up the traditional idea of the other life; to suggest any such thing would be a preposterous error. Nevertheless, the whole tone of the reform-struggle and its programme is in terms of moral positivism and social weal rather than in terms of an other-worldly spirituality and this shift of emphasis is significant.

This trend is, indeed, visible not only in the Sanūsī movement but is common to all the reform phenomena that are the subject of this chapter, and this is precisely the trend that we have sometimes characterized as moral activism, moral positivism and neo-Ṣūfism. There are, between all these phenomena, also, marked differences of emphasis: some are more purificationist than others, some are more activist than others; and their forms also differ slightly because of the local differences and differences in regional historic experiences. But the overall picture does display a more or less definite character: a call to return to pristine Islam, to do away with the moral and social abuses and general deterioration into which the Community had been falling over the centuries of the later Middle Ages and, as a remedy, to adopt an attitude of moral and religious positivism. This does not mean that religion was completely transformed. Indeed, among the masses the older ideas of occult powers and cults of saints could not be thoroughly eradicated and even in the case of the Sanūsī leaders themselves the tribesmen began to cultivate a mythology of their supernatural powers. But the fact cannot be denied that the leaders of these movements themselves gave a fresh turn to the religious feeling geared more towards the rebuilding of a good and moral society than to securing a place in Paradise, although, of course, the two were not seen as divorced from one another. The net result of this trend among the more enlightened strata of society was an orientation towards a positive attitude to this world and its moral, social and economic problems than towards eschatological issues. It was this kind of preparation upon which the influences of modern education and life supervened and wherein they found a ready base.

The reasons why the 12th/18th and 13th/19th century reformers were so oriented in their emphasis which issued in their reform programmes are not far to seek. The reformers were personalities who were tremendously dissatisfied with the existing state of affairs. Now the existing state of affairs in question was primarily – or more immediately visibly – a social decay, a political weakness and an economic disintegration. This naturally led to a greater stress on social aspects and on strengthening individual and social morality. But a remedy of these ills was not possible unless a deeper reform of religious and ultimate beliefs and ideas and practices based upon these was undertaken. It was, therefore perfectly natural that under these conditions a more positive religious attitude should emerge. This would naturally lead to an underplaying – not, of course, negation – of the other-worldly spirituality. Now, the reformers found – and there was a great deal of truth in this – that their insights, policies and programmes had a fundamental similarity to those of early Islam, for the reformist impulse of pristine Islam was essentially a positive moral dynamism and that such metaphysical-eschatological beliefs as it had sought to inculcate were those germane to this dynamism. Thus these reformist movements in a sense both confirmed and were confirmed by early Islam. This is why the Modernist Muslim is a direct heir of these pre-Modernist reformers in all these basic attitudes, with the difference that a further shift of emphasis towards positivism took place in his hands, as we shall see in the next chapter.

Far more directly political in methods and objectives than the Sanūsīya but equally reformist in *élan* and ideology were the Fulānī and the Mahdist *jihād* movements in Nigeria in the first half of the 13th/19th century and in the Sudan in the last decades of the same century respectively. While both these movements arose with a purificationist and revivalist programme of Islamic reform, they established formally theocratic states. And although in this latter characteristic they resemble the Wahhābīya, yet whereas Ibn ʿAbd al-Wahhāb had not assumed political authority himself but chosen to work through an existing political emirate, both the Mahdī and the Fulānī ʿUthmān dan Fodio established themselves as heads of their theocretic states as did the Indian Sayyid Aḥmad. But unlike Sayyid Aḥmad and ʿUthmān dan Fodio, Muḥammad Aḥmad, the leader of the Sudanese revolt against the Egyptian-European rule, claimed the Messianic-eschatological status of the Mahdī, the Reformer, who, according to medieval Muslim tradition, shall establish justice and equity at the end of time. Muḥammad Aḥmad's claim to Mahdism seems to reflect local spiritual conditions for a belief in the imminent appearance of the Mahdī was general in the Sudan at that time. A close associate of Muḥammad Aḥmad and his *khalīfa* had already tried unsuccessfully to persuade a local governor of the Khedive Ismāʿīl to declare himself as the Mahdī, and had probably influenced Muḥammad Aḥmad in that direction. Nevertheless, the Mahdists had, in the course of their struggle, expressly construed their victories in battles as a definite confirmation of the Mahdī's divine mission. This factor, although implicitly or explicitly present to some extent in most idealist struggles, became a formal trait of the Mahdī crusaders.

The Mahdist state, after a rule of fourteen years, was ultimately defeated and crushed by the Anglo-Egyptian forces under Kitchener in 1898. As for the Fulānī reform-*jihād*, its impulse gradually weakened, and by the end of the century had decayed far enough for the situation to be ripe for the imposition of British Indirect Rule. In Africa, Muslim religious and Ṣūfī movements have usually had much stronger political connections and direct militant expressions than in the rest of the medieval Muslim world. But it will be noticed from the above account of the pre-Modernist reform movements that all the major movements from the 12th/18th century to the end of the 13th/19th century developed a political character either as a method or as an ideology or both. There are two main reasons for this. The first is the general deterioration of the Muslim political power and, in a country like India, the utter destruction of that power creating a political vacuum. But secondly, and even far more importantly, the kind of reform movements these were also determined their political, activist nature. It is the paradigm of the early Muslim history as an activist reform movement and bestowing upon Islam the character not only of religious and moral preaching, but also of religious and moral *action* leading up to the formation of a state that must influence the ideals of a Muslim puritanical movement (although any puritanical movement is liable to adopt revolutionary methods). The revival of interest in the Ḥadīth (and orthodoxy in general) – the foundation of the fundamentalist purificationist reform – is bound to accentuate the emphasis on Islamic activism. It is not merely the case that in the Ḥadīth and in the orthodox teaching the doctrine of *jihād* lies permanently enshrined, but that the actual example of the Prophet and the early Community teaches a positive participation in the direct entry into and changing of the state of affairs. This political activism was another salient feature directly transmitted to much of Modern Islam.

CHAPTER THIRTEEN

MODERN DEVELOPMENTS

Preliminary – Intellectual Modernism – Political Modernism – Modernism and Society

Preliminary

To many observers, the history of Islam in modern times is essentially the history of the Western impact on Muslim society, especially since the 13th/19th century. They conceive Islam to be a semi-inert mass receiving the destructive blows or the formative influences from the West. There is a genuine reason why things should appear in this light. Islam, ever since its inception, has faced and met spiritual and intellectual challenges and indeed, the Qur'ānic Revelation itself is partly an emergent from the challenges flung to it by the older and developed Jewish and Christian religions. From the 2nd/8th to the 4th/10th centuries, a series of intellectual and cultural crises arose in Islam, the most serious and significant of which was that produced by Hellenist intellectualism, but Islam met all those successfully – assimilating, rejecting and adjusting itself to the new currents. But the Muslims were, at that time, psychologically invincible, politically masters of the situation and, at the level of the content of religion, not encumbered by a dead weight of tradition – for it was largely the new elements and currents of thought that supplied and built up the content of the Muslim tradition itself. Very different was the case at the time of the Western impacts on Islam in the 12th/18th and especially the 13th/19th century. The first phase of this impact was in each case political and military and in each case the Muslims were vanquished and politically subjugated directly or indirectly. This was followed by religious and intellectual forms of impingement through various channels, varying in degree of directness and intensity. The most patent and direct challenges were from the Christian missionaries, the modern thought of Europe and the study and criticism by Westerners of Islam and Islamic society itself. Of these three channels, the first – the Christian missions – was a professional attempt at destructive criticism, while the last one was, intentionally or unintentionally, but in effect largely so. Not until recently has this trend shown a visible change.

The unsettlement that ensued from the political defeats and subjugation rendered the Muslim psychologically less capable of constructively rethinking his heritage, and meeting the intellectual challenge of modern thought by assimilative-creative processes and the Christian challenge that came directly to this heritage. All these diverse elements of this whole phenomenon, therefore, have left an irresistible impression on an external observer (whose observations have, in turn, influenced many Muslims also) that Islam has become internally incapable of reconstituting itself and whatever it might do by way of reconstruction, if at all it can, will be done by influences and borrowings from the West. If politically Islam had not been shaken, the story would have been very different.

That this impression is, nevertheless, palpably false is shown by the pre-Modernist reform attempts described in our last chapter. These attempts are a measure of the intensity and universality of self-criticism, the consciousness of the internal degeneration of the Muslim society and the nature of the positive lines of reconstruction. The elimination of superstition and obscurantism, the reform of Ṣūfism and the raising of moral standards is a salient common characteristic of all these movements. So is the element of *jihād* or political action in order to effect religious and social reform. We have emphasized in the previous chapter that all these characteristics are directly bequeathed to Modern Islam. It is true that the positive line of a reconstitution of society universally proclaimed by these movements was in terms of a return to the pristine Islam, to 'the Qur'ān and the Sunna', including varying degrees of content of the Ṣūfī legacy, and thereby brought about a general resurgence of fundamentalism. Now, this fundamentalism itself undoubtedly has constituted and still constitutes in one sense a problem for Modern Islam and, to a superficial view, is, in fact, *the problem* for the Modernist. We must not overlook the fact, however, that this fundamentalism is not merely an impediment in the way of modernization of society and outlook but, as a term in a tension, constitutes a basic point of reference in the process of this modernization. But this is not all. Besides being a point of reference, fundamentalism has also supplied, not the content, but the morphology for much of the rethinking done by Modernist reformers: the new ethical and social content has been worked into the Qur'ān and the Sunna by way of interpretation at various levels of generality and specificness, as we shall see presently. Thus, these earlier movements have paved the way for modern developments not only through their purificative endeavour but also by positively reasserting the overriding authority of the Scripture and the Prophetic example.

Yet the fundamental character of the modern challenge and the pervasiveness of the Western influence is also a stark fact. The channels through which this influence has come in are legion – the political structure, the administrative and judicial machinery, the army, the press, modern education, the cinema, modern thought, and, above all, the present contacts with Western society. But a list of these various media and levels of the dissemination of Western culture in the Muslim society is not a very illuminating way of gauging the depth of the new challenge or the seriousness of the character of the crisis. At a general level, the problem has been posed both by Western observers and by most modernist Muslims in terms of a conflict between Reason and Tradition or Reason and traditionalized Faith. There is undoubtedly a great deal of justification for and truth in thus formulating the problem. For even though early Western critics of Islam in particular, like Renan, were thereby also projecting much of the historic experience of Christianity into the Islamic tradition, the conflict between Reason and Tradition (though not between Reason and Revelation) has been, nevertheless, a fact in Islamic history – a fact we have sought to bring into relief in several previous chapters (V, VI, VII and XI). We shall study the solution of this problem offered by Muslim Modernists below and with what success. But it is equally true that this problem has been exaggerated and over-emphasized both by Muslim Modernists and apologists and by Western critics.

The real challenge that the Muslim society has had to face and is still facing is at the level of social institutions and social ethic as such. And the real nature of this crisis is not the fact that the Muslim social institutions in the past have been wrong or irrational but the fact that there has been a social system at all which now needs to be modified and adjusted. This social system has, in fact, been perfectly rational in the past, i.e. it has been working perfectly well, as perfectly well as any other social system. The disadvantage of the Muslim society at the present juncture is that whereas in the early centuries of development of social institutions in Islam, Islam started from a clean slate, as it were, and had to carve out *ab initio* a social fabric – an activity of which the product was the medieval social system – now, when Muslims have to face a situation of fundamental rethinking and reconstruction, their acute problem is precisely to determine how far to render the slate clean again and on what principles and by what methods, in order to create a new set of institutions.

Intellectual Modernism

Although the modern challenge was directly and primarily to the social institutions of Islam, its laws of marriage and divorce, the position of women and certain economic laws etc., it also assumed purely intellectual proportions since a change in social mores involves a re-thinking of the social ethic, which touches the foundational ideas of social justice. But quite apart from this there were also problems raised by modern Western philosophical and scientific theories about specific religious beliefs pertaining to God, His relationship to nature and man and the life hereafter, problems which had been discussed for centuries in Islam by Muslim philosophers and theologians but which assumed new proportions in the light of 13th/19th century rationalism and scientific developments. But even these specific questions apart, the whole problem was raised to a most general level as to whether religion and 'reason' can accommodate one another. The criticism against Islam came with a double force from certain Western critics like E. Renan and Sir William Muir who contended that the social and economic backwardness of the late medieval Muslim society was due to the inherently inferior character of the Islamic civilization. This, in turn, was alleged to stem from the inferiority of Islam as a religion, which was seen as a 'Bedouin' phenomenon alien to 'reason' and tolerance. At this stage of the argument, the medieval Muslim conflicts between philosophers and orthodox theologians were unreservedly identified as war between 'reason' and 'religion' and the net conclusion drawn was that Islam inherently opposes reason. This position taken up by certain eminent Western scholars of Islam in the 13th/19th century (echoes of which still continue to be heard in the West) is the necessary measure of the subsequent Muslim controversialist response. We do not intend to follow up in this chapter the controversialist trends in Islam but shall only say that our contemporary orientalists who complain against these trends do not recognize fully the inner poverty and the superficial logic of the initial Western stand.

There is no doubt, however, that the critique against the contemporary state of the Muslim society and its outward stagnation found a ready response. But this response was already prepared and conditioned by the earlier reform movements. These movements, by their rejection of medieval authorities and their insistence on *ijtihād* – original personal thought – directly contributed to the intellectual regeneration of Modern Islam. The terms of the new efforts at re-thinking no doubt changed under the new stimulus and their scope widened. For, whereas the earlier movements, while removing authority, offered little new materials to be integrated into the Islamic legacy and sought merely to go back to the pristine Islam, leaving the space or field where *ijtihād* should actually work necessarily empty, this empty space was now filled in by the intellectual products of the modern civilization.

A general summons to the Muslim Community to raise their intellectual and moral standards in order to meet the dangers of the Western expansionism was issued by Jamāl al-Dīn al-Afghānī (1255–1315/1839–97), the first genuine Muslim Modernist. Although he propounded no intellectual modernism himself, he nevertheless made a powerful appeal for the cultivation of philosophical and scientific disciplines by expanding the curricula of the educational institutions and for general educational reforms. His ultimate purpose undoubtedly was to strengthen the world of Islam politically against the West, but this does not detract from his position as a powerful and effective reformist in general. While affirming in his fiery speeches and articles that there was nothing in the basic principles of Islam that is incompatible with reason or science, he aroused the Muslims to develop the medieval content of Islam to meet the needs of a modern society. But besides a reassertion of faith in the transcendental truth of Islam, an entirely new element also appears in al-Afghānī's attitude – a type of modern humanism, a concern for man as such. Replying to E. Renan's denunciation of Islam as an incurable enemy of Reason, al-Afghānī not only refutes Renan's thesis by arguments but also appeals to the Frenchman in the name of millions of people on earth who profess the Islamic Faith and whom the French rationalist seems to denounce.[1] This humanism at the religious level is the expression of al-Afghānī's populism at the political level, a legacy which has been a powerful factor in the shaping of the political and social thought of the Muslim Modernists. And yet, although this humanism – concern for the weal of man *qua* man – is expressed here in a new form with more positive dimensions, and as such is to be regarded as a definite influence of nineteenth-century Europe, it is also intimately related to and is to be regarded as an unquestionable development from the pre-Modernist reform activity of Islam itself. In this connection, it is sufficient to recall here our observations made in the previous chapter about the focal place occupied by the problem of social uplift in the endeavour of earlier reformers, a fact which gave a decisively this-worldly, positive turn to their thought: the faith in the transcendental truth of Islam is asserted with vigour but its effect is seen not so much as a betterment of the next world (which is certainly accepted but not emphasized) but of the socio-moral life *in this world*.

If to state that Islam is not against reason and science was the task of al-Afghānī, it fell to the Egyptian Muḥammad 'Abduh and the Indian Sayyid Aḥmad Khān to prove this statement. Both these men agree that Islam, as it was actually believed in and practised by most of its adherents, would certainly be threatened by the modern advances in thought and science. Sayyid Aḥmad Khān said: 'If people do not shun blind adherence, if they do not seek that Light which can be found in the Qur'ān and the indisputable Ḥadīth, and do not adjust religion and the sciences of today, Islam will become extinct in India'.[2] But both were equally convinced that the dead weight of time had encumbered the true and original Islam with later developments that were no essential part of it and both wished to reveal the true Islam primarily to Muslims but also to non-Muslims. Again, Sayyid Aḥmad Khān wrote:

Today we are, as before, in need of a modern theology (*'ilm al-kalām*), whereby we should either refute doctrines of modern sciences, or undermine their foundations, or show that they are in conformity with Islam. If we are to propagate those sciences amongst the Muslims, about which I have just stated how much they disagree with the *present-day Islam*, then it is my duty to defend as much as I can the religion of Islam, rightly or wrongly, and to reveal to the people the *original bright face of Islam*. My conscience tells me that if I should not do so, I would stand as a sinner before God.[3]

From this point on, however, Muḥammad 'Abduh and Sayyid Aḥmad Khān go different ways. Muḥammad 'Abduh (1261–1323/1845–1905), a trained theologian on traditional lines, convinced that science and the Faith of Islam cannot conflict, argues that Faith and scientific reason work at different levels.[4] He, therefore, sees his task as consisting in a presentation of the basic tenets of Islam in terms that would be acceptable to a modern mind and would allow further reformation of it on the one hand and allow the pursuit of modern knowledge on the other. Indeed, he goes further in his actual presentation of Islam and emphasizes that Islam is not only *not* incompatible with reason but is the only religion which religiously calls upon man to use his own reason and investigate nature. In connection with this, he cites those numerous verses of the Qur'ān which enjoin upon man to think intelligently and to study nature – God's creation – as the 'signs' of God. Thus, although Muḥammad 'Abduh in the actual *materials* of his reinterpretation of Islam introduced no new ideas into the body of traditional Islamic ideas, his position, nevertheless, presents an advance on the pre-Modern reformers on two important points. One is his general emphasis on the rôle of reason in Islam, i.e. the idea that although faith and reason operate in different spheres, they must not only not conflict but must positively cooperate in human advancement. And the other – which seems to be his fundamental concern – is to restate the basic ideas of Islam in such a way as to open the door for the influence of new ideas and for the acquisition of modern knowledge in general. What gave point to this teaching and made it popular was the fact that it was issued by a man who was a great religious scholar on traditional lines in terms which were also intelligible to the 'Ulamā': it offered prospects of development while safeguarding continuity with the past.

Sayyid Aḥmad Khān (1232–1316/1817–98), although his view that the true teaching of Islam is compatible with reason concurs with that of Muḥammad 'Abduh, did not rest with that position. He did not explicitly formulate, and implicitly rejected, the position of 'Abduh that reason and faith, although they cooperate in Islam, have nevertheless distinct rôles and levels of operation. Influenced strongly by nineteenth-century European rationalism and natural philosophy (he had visited England in 1867–70), he laid down what he termed the criterion of 'Conformity to Nature' to judge the contents of systems of belief and concluded that Islam paramountly justified itself on this principle. Thus, reason with him was the overriding standard. In propounding his positive content of Islam, Sayyid Aḥmad Khān, while attempting to integrate the modern scientific world-view with the Islamic doctrine, resurrected and fell back upon, not the orthodox interpretation of Islam (as 'Abduh had done), but the basic tenets of the medieval Muslim philosophers. Thus, in order to assert the autonomy of nature and natural laws, he not only rejected the doctrine of miracles but revived the emanationist concept of the Muslim philosophers and described God in the latter's spirit as the 'First Cause'. Since the starting-point of Sayyid Aḥmad Khān is a form of Western rationalism, the result is a personal interpretation of Islam rather than a restatement of it, an attempt at integrating a given set of ideas into Islam rather than a reformulation of it – more or less on the pattern of medieval Muslim philosophers.

Yet, such individual interpretations are not to be decried. They are not only statements of personal faith and expression of the principles of liberalism but provide a leaven and fertilization of ideas for an eventual reformulation of the Faith, and in this process they are necessary moments. Also, it must be noticed that, despite the fundamental difference between the approaches represented by Shaykh Muḥammad 'Abduh and Sayyid Aḥmad Khān, there emerges a close affinity in their actual recommendations on the religious plane where it touches the concrete life and attitudes of the Community. This is illustrated by their attitude to the medieval doctrine of miracles. Both modernists are concerned to rid the Community of the ills flowing from the miracle-mongering doctrines and practices of popular Ṣūfism. But whereas Sayyid Aḥmad Khān rationally rejects the possibility of miracles on principle, Shaykh Muḥammad 'Abduh, while not wishing to disturb the traditional picture of the Prophet and admitting the theoretical possibility of miracles, declares that any given and specific miraculous claim by a non-Prophet, whenever made, may be denied with religious impunity, and condemns the auto-suggestive practices of the Ṣūfī adepts, the bane of popular religion.[5]

A very important phenomenon in this development is the new attitude to the Ḥadīth, the Tradition of the Prophet, whose growth we outlined in Chapter III. Ḥadīth, especially in its legal aspect but partly also in its moral and social aspects, embodies the medieval form of Islam. Much of this material, it was felt, would be cumbersome for the task of modernization of the structure of ideas in Islam, unless it were understood purely historically and thus reinterpreted. This task, in fact, has not been yet undertaken by Muslim modernism, fundamental as it is for any reconstruction of the framework of Islamic thought, and even the problem of Ḥadīth has not yet been intelligently formulated. What has made it difficult for the Muslims to face the issue squarely and even to formulate it explicitly is the very importance of the body of the Ḥadīth and the fear that any disturbance of it might shake the very foundations of Islam as a system of doctrine and practice. On this issue, again, the positions of Muḥammad 'Abduh and Sayyid Aḥmad Khān are highly illustrative of their attitudes. The latter, in the early phase of his modernism, insisted on distinguishing between genuine Ḥadīth from the non-genuine – in the spirit of pre-Modernist reformers; but in the later phase of the development of his ideas he, like his modernist associate, Charāgh 'Alī, rejected the Ḥadīth entirely. This has left a permanent legacy in the Indian subcontinent where a group has developed who call themselves *Ahl al-Qur'ān* and who reject Ḥadīth but exhibit little real understanding either of the historical development of Ḥadīth or of the implications of what they deem to be their position.[6] Muḥammad 'Abduh, on the other hand, wishes to bring about in effect the same results – removal of the apparent impediment of Ḥadīth in the way of modernization – by suggesting that only those Ḥadīths must be accepted on which a universal agreement of the Muslims has occurred and what is more important, that any given Ḥadīth which one does not consider to emanate genuinely from the Prophet one may reject with equanimity.[7]

These intellectual developments resulted in the further Modernist proposition that Islam produces a progressive civilization and has, in fact, been instrumental in ushering in the modern era from the womb of antiquity. This doctrine is indeed latent in the stand that Islam is rational. Already Muḥammad 'Abduh had written a book to demonstrate that Islam had brought about a progressive civilization whereas Christianity had opposed the march of reason and civilization at least in the hands of the official custodians of the Church.[8] But this point was popularized and strongly argued by the eminent Indian jurist, Sayyid Amīr 'Alī (d. 1928) in his work *The Spirit of Islam*. Amīr 'Ali also wrote *A Short History of the Saracens.*[9] The essential position of Amīr 'Alī can be summed up by saying that Islam, truly understood, inculcates certain moral-social values whose formulation by the Qur'ān and the Prophet and whose embodiment is the basic institutions of Islam, while reflecting on the one hand the contemporary situation of 1st/7th century Arabia, shows on the other, a fundamental and unmistakable trend towards modernity, but that the medieval interpreters of Islam failed to perceive their true drift and import and so fathered an incompatible structure upon it. We shall deal with Amīr 'Alī's social liberal views below. Here we only note the general trend of his argument, viz., Islam as a civilizing force. Even the specifically religious institutions of Islam like the five daily prayers Amīr 'Alī explains in terms of physical unity and social solidarity. He is, however, on surer grounds when he explains fasting as a measure of self-discipline and as being conducive to economic justice.[9]

This preoccupation with the historical and cultural import of Islam has undoubtedly a threefold motive. It is used partly for controversialist purposes against the West and partly as an apologetic measure in order to fortify the self-confidence of the Muslim *vis-à-vis* the powerful and expanding culture of the West. But this is obviously not the whole story, for basically the motivation is a reformist one. It is intended to encourage the Muslim to accept the intellectualism and the humanism of the modern West as a genuine development from the apogee of Islamic civilization itself and indeed as the true message of Islam. The argument that modern Western thought is a direct descendant of the glorious medieval intellectual culture of Islam, disseminated in the West through Spain and Sicily, has been stated at a highly philosophical level by Sir Muḥammad Iqbāl (1876–1938), especially in his *Reconstruction of Religious Thought in Islam.* At this level, then, this argument reinvigorates the earlier and more direct appeal to rationalism on the basis of the Qur'ān and Islamic teaching by asking the Muslim to accept and further develop the fruits of modern rationalism.

But there is still quite a different dimension to the Modernist claim of the rational and civilizing function of Islam in history and its rôle in human development. This is bound up with and reinforces the Muslim claim for the finality of Muḥammad's mission as Prophet. This argument, put forward in its first form by Muḥammad 'Abduh, is restated by Sir Muḥammad Iqbāl in philosophical terms. The fact of the Qur'ān being the final Revelation, so the argument runs, and Muḥammad the last Prophet, is highly meaningful for the development of mankind in the sense that mankind has reached a state of maturity where it no longer needs the help of ready-made Revelation but can work out its own moral and intellectual salvation and destiny. Further, in this development Islam played a decisive rôle by making self-conscious the rational and scientific faculties of man. Apart from the Qur'ānic Revelation, the same process is seen as having taken place in actual history: the civilization of Islam both in the intellectual and the scientific fields swung the mystery-mongering *milieu* of antiquity to the scientific and sober spirit of modernity and ushered in this modern era. This claim, when stated in these terms, has a considerable element of truth which must be recognized by an unbiased and honest historian of human civilization. But the working out of this claim in specific terms, which requires a genuine scholarly effort and a sober interpretation of history, has not yet been undertaken by the Muslims themselves. Further, a new statement of the nature of Revelation will be necessary to do justice to this interpretation of history. But on this score Muslim modernism has been so far quite silent. We shall have to touch on this problem in the next chapter.

In the meantime, more complex developments continued to take place in Muslim society. Early Islamic modernism, in advocating an integration of modern ideas and institutions with the bases of Islam, had partly encouraged the influx of Western ideas and education and partly justified the Western intellectual impacts that were already there – and were bound to come anyway. The actual incorporation of Westernism into the values of Islam was, however, a long process, and these early Modernists could do no more than provide a basis for subsequent developments on Modernist lines. But who should carry the process forward? The 'Ulamā', the conservative guardians of the Islamic doctrine and practice, were not only incapable of this task because of their education being restricted to the traditional confines, but because of this very reason they could not even perceive the problem. This is why modernism, in so far as it existed at all, has been the work of lay Muslims with a liberal education. But the lay modernist, although his services have been undeniable in keeping a psychological and moral balance between traditionalism and Westernism (i.e. the influx of Western trends into Muslim society), could speak for himself only and, his credentials from the Islamic side being always somewhat questionable, he could not lay the foundations of a new Islamic theology. Partly, of course, in a liberal situation every interpreter speaks primarily for himself. But this is not the whole story about the situation. What was required fundamentally was an integrated educational programme, but it is precisely such an educational programme that failed to develop and fructify, as we shall point out presently.

The result was that the movement inspired by the initial modernist impulse split into two developments moving in two different directions:

one in the direction of almost pure Westernism and the other gravitating towards fundamentalism or what has been called 'Revivalism'. From approximately the second decade of the present century onwards the history of the spiritual and intellectual development of Islamic society is a story of the tension between these two trends. In this story, Revivalism has had a marked advantage over the Westernists, so much so that the Modernists (i.e. those who have made an articulate and conscious effort to reformulate Islamic values and principles in terms of modern thought or to integrate modern thought and institutions with Islam) have steadily drifted towards fundamentalism and have become, in most significant cases – like that of Sir Muḥammad Iqbāl – indistinguishable from it. Or, perhaps, they have become so significant because they have so moved towards Revivalism.

There are many reasons for the power wielded by fundamentalism. First, the fundamentalist, as a direct heir of the pre-Modernist reform movements, stands in a tradition that has sprung from within Islam and is indigenous to it. Fundamentalism, when it arose as a general phenomenon in the Muslim world during the 12th/18th and 13th/19th centuries, seemed an innovation which was combated by the conservatives. But in the present century, when the society is threatened by wholesale Westernization, it has become good tradition and its purificationist programme still has appeal. Further, against the conservative 'Ulamā', it is activist and dynamic and therefore seems progressive also.

Secondly, the pressing dangers to the integrity of the Community from without and the threat of corrosion from within argued for a cohesiveness and a united stand with such a sense of urgency as was perhaps never experienced in the history of the Community, except in its nascent phase in Medina during the deadly struggle with the Meccans. In such crises, it is always some form of fundamentalism – which is able to fight both the conservative placidity and the uncontrolled adventures of pioneering liberalism – that takes over the reins. Faith rather than explanation or formulation of Faith, intuitive certainty rather than discursive thought-content becomes the cry of the hour.

Thirdly, the strength of fundamentalism was the mere weakness of Westernism itself. Westernism – the projection of Western modernity into non-western societies – did not and could not produce high level immediate results in the specifically modern fields, for it required a period of acclimatization and growth. The Westernized classes in their field could not match the maturity of the traditionalists in their own domain of culture and learning for lack of sufficient time. But the lack of sufficient time is not the whole story. The basic trouble with Westernism was its lack of morale and ethic which alone could give it strength. Only some form of effective Modernism could confer upon it the required morale and ethic and root it in the new soil. This effective Modernism it failed to develop for reasons which we shall outline while treating of modern social thought below.

But the inherent power of Westernism lay in the stark fact of the appeal of modern science and technology at the collective level and the strong attraction of liberalism, freedom, initiative and opportunity at the individual level. It is a natural process of modern history, which claims itself to be its own warrant, neither seeking nor wanting to seek any justification beyond itself. Born out of a violent spiritual break with its immediate parent, European medievalism, Western liberalism is a law unto itself and, therefore, will seek no negotiation with any spiritual system or moral ideology. Communism, in its classical statement, is only a systematic and extreme orthodox form of the absolute and uncompromising character of this Western modernity. Modern Westernism, therefore, is pure secularism. In the West, this modernity has been constantly approached by Christianity, at different levels, from different viewpoints and with varying degrees of success leading towards working syntheses or at least some form of equilibrium. But in the Muslim societies, after the initial Modernist impulse, the movement split in two opposite directions. In the Middle East, the activity of Muḥammad ʿAbduh was followed, on the one hand, by almost purely Westernist intellectual developments and, on the other, by the Salafī movement which under the leadership of ʿAbduh's pupil, the Syrian Rashīd Riḍā (1865–1935), moved steadily towards a type of fundamentalism closely akin, and admittedly so, to Wahhābism. The vacuum left by the absence of a genuine Modernism was filled by the semi-reformist, semi-apologetic activity of persons chief among whom was the Egyptian Farīd Wajdī (d. 1953). In India, again Sayyid Aḥmad Khān, yielding to the pressure of his conservative critics, allowed the teaching of theology and religion to fall into conservative hands at the Aligarh College established by him (see below) with the express purpose of developing an effective progressive Modernism, i.e., a synthesis of Westernism and Islamic values. The result of this surrender was the dissemination of pure Westernism. This, in turn, provided both a reaction in the form of apologetics and in the resurgence of revivalism, an emotional cry of 'Back to Islam'.

The Westernists have not been able to formulate their stand intellectually. Many of them are secularists at heart but have not made their viewpoint explicit to any appreciable degree. Especially in the Indian subcontinent, their intellectual performance is absolutely negligible. In Egypt, attempts have been made by 'Alī 'Abd al-Rāziq (1888) and Ṭahā Ḥusayn (1891). We shall study the former's views below, for he dealt not with general intellectual issues but advocated a secular theory of state. But the intellectual Westernist, even when a secularist at heart, takes on as a matter of necessity, as it were, the garb of a Modernist with some kind of emotional appeal to Islam either genuinely or for the sake of being heard at all. This is why it is extremely difficult to identify persons in the Westernist group in terms of secularism or modernism. This is also the main reason why whatever expression there has been by this group of their stand, it has not been very effective and it is only in Turkey that secular Westernism has succeeded, or, more correctly, been imposed, for it was through militaristic political power that the secularist programme was carried through. And that is why although Turkish cities (as opposed to the country at large) have been influenced in this direction through official educational policies, there has not been any significant intellectual expression of secularism by Turkish intellectuals since the regime of Kemal Atatürk.

The reactions to Westernism, on the other hand, assuming some form or other of fundamentalism or revivalism have often resulted in the formation of definite groups or religious parties, partly activist, partly intellectualist. They have been often very vocal, expressing their views and feelings through journals and through myriads of pamphlets and books. The Salafī movement in Egypt, through its journal *al-Manār*, propagated its views far beyond the Egyptian boundaries and has influenced Muslim opinion as far as Indonesia. Although insisting on social and legal reform of the Muslim society, its temper steadily moved towards fundamentalism and anti-intellectualism. The direct heir of its legacy was the 'Muslim Brotherhood', a purely activist movement, partly reformist and partly revivalist, which aimed at securing political power to carry through its Islamist programme but which has been suppressed in Egypt since 1956. In the Indian subcontinent a similar reaction started against the Aligarh Westernism both at the popular level, through such poets as Akbar of Allahābād (d. 1921), and at a more intellectual level, by Shiblī Nu'mānī (d. 1914) and Abu'l Kalām Āzād (d. 1959). Through their ceaseless criticisms of Westernism, although these men did not create an effective intellectual Modernism, they paved the way for the eventual emergence of a revivalist movement called Jamā'at-i Islāmī. The Jamā'at-i Islāmī, in its *élan* and purpose, exhibits the essential feature of the 'Muslim Brotherhood' of the Middle East but, unlike the latter, is not purely activist but has created a theoretical basis for its socio-political programme, which we shall deal with next.

But the tension between Westernism and Islamic fundamentalism in Indian Islam has produced one outstanding figure, that of Sir Muḥammad Iqbāl, the most serious Muslim philosophical thinker of modern times. Iqbāl (1876–1938), the *content* of his philosophy apart, is a synthetic figure in his mental veneer and basic spiritual and intellectual character. A serious intellectual and a genuinely perceptive mind, he denounced intellectualism and reason as hollow and useless and insisted on Faith as the sole guide:

> Faith gives the strength to sit in fire like Abraham:
> Faith is God-intoxication, self-expending:
> Listen, O dotard of the modern civilization:
> Worse than slavery is the lack of Faith.[10]

Thus Iqbāl stresses Faith and intuition, sometimes *rather than* reason and sometimes *at the expense of* reason, depending on the context he is speaking in and the kind of group he is addressing. There are three types of position Iqbāl takes with regard to the relationship between intuition and reason, viz. (1) that reason and intuition pull in different directions; (2) that reason is subordinate to intuition or wisdom and, in a way, leads towards the latter; and (3) that there exists between the two an organic relationship and thus neither can dispense with the other. While addressing the West and the westernized Muslim, he tends to minimize the rôle of reason and even disparages it, whereas he emphasizes it while addressing the conservative whom he desires to reappropriate Western rationalism and scienticism. Inwardly, therefore, there is a deeper unity and a sense of purpose in Iqbāl, and his condemnation of pure, unconditional and undirected rational thought is partly a critique of Western thought and indirectly a criticism of Westernism, i.e., the pure and naked acceptance of the results of Western nationalism within the Muslim community. For otherwise he recommended, indeed, a respectful and responsive but at the same time independent attitude to Western thought.[11] But if his utterances – especially in his poetry – are taken separately, then, outwardly, they constitute blatant contradictions. Nor did he make any serious theoretical attempt to formulate his basic synthetic attitude and to resolve his apparent contradictions.

The result is that in so far as Iqbāl's teaching has been influential – and it has been so deeply and far-reachingly influential that spiritually it has been the chief force behind the creation of Pakistan – it has thrown its overwhelming weight on the revivalist side and has been largely construed in an anti-rational direction. The doctrine of activism and dynamism advocated by Iqbāl has found such a tremendous response that the very considerable intellectual effort of which it was the result has been made to commit suicide in the process. Iqbāl's philosophical legacy has, therefore, not been followed, partly because of what he has said but largely because he has been both misunderstood and misused by his politics-mongering followers. His *Reconstruction of Religious Thought in Islam* has remained a purely personal statement of the Islamic Faith, and has not so far been able to function as a datum-line from which further developments could take place. In the event of such a real development taking place, the genuine insights of Iqbāl into the nature of Islam will have to be carefully disentangled from the contemporary philosophical interpretations of science, especially the excessive assimilation of the natural to the spiritual.

Political Modernism

From the very beginning of the Western expansionist impacts on Muslim lands, the Muslims, after the failures of their early military and political resistance to the West, have been preoccupied with the problem of effective political reorganization. But, just as problems which had been seen first as being purely military led to an awareness of the necessity of political reform, so political reconstruction was found impossible without social reform and economic modernization. And since socio-economic modernization could not be carried out without new legislation (besides education) which depended again on political authority, the issues of social and legal reform are inextricably bound up with political problems. Add to this the interminable confusions caused by Western political forces whose own individual interests were in a perpetual state of conflicting rivalries and who acted both as enemies (i.e. those who wished to impose themselves politically and economically) and advisers of the Muslims, and the picture is complete. The purely political developments in the Muslim world do not belong to the scope of the present work, but since they are intimately related to the questions of nationalism and secularism, they have a direct bearing on the religious history of Islam. Further, the location of authority in a modern state and especially the authority to legislate – which in the history of Islam has never been Islamically vested in the government – is of intrinsic importance for Islam as a social phenomenon.

The first modernist idea of political reform was voiced by Jamāl al-Dīn al-Afghānī. There were two salient elements in his political thought: the unity of the Muslim world and populism. The doctrine of the political unification of the Muslim world, known as pan-Islamism, is urged by al-Afghānī as the only effective bulwark against foreign encroachments and domination of Muslim lands. The populist impulse arises both from a consideration of its intrinsic justice and also directly from the fact that only popular constitutional governments can be strong, stable and a real guarantee against foreign force and intrigue. Al-Afghānī's influence contributed directly to the 'Arābī Pāshā rebellion in Egypt and the constitutional movement in Persia, but the power of its appeal was felt generally also in Turkey and India. In his zeal to appeal to the popular will against the West, however, al-Afghānī evoked not only the universal Islamic sentiment but also national or local sentiments of different countries. His actual influence, therefore, has been in both directions of pan-Islamism and nationalism, sometimes in conflict with one another. Although the pan-Islamic idealism has not been successful in concrete terms, it continues to inspire various activist groups in different lands and lives on patently, if amorphously, in the aspirations of the people.

But despite this strong pan-Islamic sentiment, nationalism has made powerful inroads into the Muslim world and has been officially incarnated, with a special emphasis, in the state-ideologies of certain Muslim countries. But the term 'nationalism' has different, though allied, shades of meaning, which it is important to distinguish if we are to gain any clarity about the Muslim situation. First, there is the essentially sociological sense of the term where 'nationalism' may be defined as a sentiment for a certain community of mores, including language, which gives a sense of cohesiveness to a group. This sense of cohesiveness may be of varying degrees of intensity. A Turkish, an Egyptian or a Pakistani peasant is a 'nationalist' in this sense and has always been so. But a Turkish, an Egyptian and a Pakistani peasant are also bound by a strong Islamic sentiment. This 'nationalism', therefore, is not averse to a wider loyalty and, in face of a non-Muslim aggressor (as we have often witnessed during this and the preceding century) the two sentiments make an extraordinarily powerful liaison. At the second level, however, this primitive 'nationalism' comes to be formulated as a political ideology and is transformed into a nation-state claiming sovereignty and demanding paramount loyalty. It is this political concept, as it has developed in the modern West, which, when carried to its logical extremes, must conflict with the ideals of Islam. So long as this extreme nationalism is avoided (and by 'extreme nationalism' I do not in this context mean Chauvinism but the principle 'Nation above everything else'), the nation-states may still allow for a real, positive cooperation or a multi-state community for the larger Islamic objectives. But extreme nationalism must, by its very nature, demand secularism. Secularism, in turn, must cut at the roots of Islam in both ways: by destroying the possibilities of the unity of the Muslim *umma* (community) externally and by relegating Islam internally to the position of a private creed and ritual as 'being something merely between a man's heart and his God', as the secularist cliché has it.

In the Muslim world, the nationalism of the first type has always existed and is, indeed, a universal phenomenon unless one culture is entirely absorbed in or superseded by a different one. But the extremer form of nationalism, i.e., the one combined with secularism (and therefore built on some such notion as that of race) has been so far officially established only in Turkey although its strong currents exist in the Middle Eastern Arab world. In Turkey, after a long debate between the nationalists and Islamists, nationalism won an official victory through a conglomeration of causes, the most immediate of which was the rebellion of the Arabs against the Turks in the midst of World War I and, above all, the personality of Atatürk himself. The most important intellectual architect of Turkish nationalism, Ziya Gökalp (d. 1924), was primarily a sociologist and not a political thinker. It is, however, clear from his utterances on the relationship of religion and state that he was no advocate of secularism: indeed he expressly rejects traditionalism and pure Western secularism and even criticizes the dualistic attitude which seeks to separate religion from state, arguing strongly for a synthesis.[12] What he rejects is what he calls 'theocracy' and 'clericalism'.[13] It cannot, therefore, be maintained that Turkish political secularism is his creation. As a sociologist, he tried to construct a Turkish nationalism from the three elements of Turkish culture, Islamic civilization and modern Western science. As for the secularist nationalist currents in the contemporary Arab Middle East, a potent factor in these is the presence of strong Christian minorities, which were the first to be intellectually influenced by the modern West and for whom the call to secularism is a safety measure in a sea of Muslims.

What was, however, envisaged by the modernist was not a unity of the Muslim world under the Caliphal institution (which was dealt a final blow by Atatürk) but a League of Muslim States. Gökalp wrote, 'In order to create a really effective political unity of Islam, all Muslim countries must first become independent. . . . Is such a thing possible at the present moment? If not today, one must wait. In the meantime the Caliph must reduce his own house [i.e. Turkey] to order and lay the foundation of a workable modern state.'[14] Commenting upon this, Muḥammad Iqbāl says, 'For the present every Muslim nation must sink into her own deeper self . . . until all are strong and powerful to form a living family of republics. A true and living unity . . . is not so easy as to be achieved by a merely symbolical overlordship. . . . It seems to me that God is slowly bringing home to us the truth that Islam is neither Nationalism nor Imperialism but a League of Nations which recognizes artificial boundaries and racial distinctions for facility of reference only, and not for restricting the social horizon of its members.'[15] The great question, however, is whether and how far, after these nations have established themselves as so many independent selfhoods, they will allow themselves to be welded into a larger unity. This is, however, undoubtedly the cherished hope of the modernist as opposed to the secularist.

But apart from the question of the external unity of the Muslim world, the most serious question for the future of Islam itself, a question the answer to which shall, indeed, decide whether Islam has a future or not, is the ideological problem of the relationship between state and religion. This controversy is between the revivalists, the modernists and the secularists. The controversy between the secularists and non-secularists is whether Islam is merely a private religion or whether it is also directly involved in social and political life. There has hardly been any open intellectual formulation of the secularist standpoint except 'Alī 'Abd al-Rāziq's work *Islam and the Bases of Rule* (*al-Islām wa Uṣūl al-Ḥukm*) over which the al-Azhar 'Ulamā' raised a storm. In practice, the secularist principle has been enforced as a political structure in Turkey by Atatürk who borrowed legal codes from the West, divested Islam of all state significance, and ruthlessly suppressed opposition. Since then, however, there have been minor changes under popular pressure from 1950 to 1959, in which year a military revolutionary government seized power and officially reaffirmed Atatürk's policy.

But although there is little explicit secularism in the Muslim world – the difficulty before the real secularist being to have to prove the impossible, viz. that Muḥammad, when he acted as a law-giver or a political leader, acted extra-religiously and secularly – the *practical* secularist trends in contemporary Muslim political life are, indeed, quite powerful. For this phenomenon there is a general and a specific reason, although the two are not divorced from one another. The general reason does not concern state-life specifically but man's changed *Weltanschauung* in general; nor does it concern Islam in particular but all religions that claim to direct human life in some sense. This problem is basically as to whether religions can shed their ancient world-views and transform themselves into spiritual-moral forces for the modern mind. The question is not merely that of an antiquated cosmology in varying degrees, for this is relatively easy, but primarily that of 'the other world' or the 'hereafter': how to transform this transcendence into some form of immanence and yet not sink into the banalities of humanism. Religion, in other words, must be secularized if the secular is to be made religious. But Islamic theology and dogmatics, like those of other religions, have not yet undergone this transformation to be acceptable to the modern mind. Such a transformation has partly taken place in the West, or rather the Western modern mind has transformed the notion of transcendence into immanence, the 'next world' into 'this world' but only partly and even that non-religiously. In Islam the question has not yet been raised: the modern educated mind, therefore, floats on sheer scepticism.

But the more specific reason that forces the modernist to behave as a secularist or a quasi-secularist is the struggle between the modernist and the revivalist. The revivalist or the fundamentalist is a type of conservative who is a direct heir of the pre-Modernist reform movements. He differs from the ordinary conservative in the fact that he does not accept as authoritative the whole gamut of orthodox beliefs and practices that have developed *throughout* the Islamic past but wishes to go back, in the spirit of earlier reformers, to the practice of the early Elders (*salaf*). Therein the modernist generally agrees with him. But whereas the revivalist wishes essentially to re-enact the past, the modernist, knowing this to be absurd, talks of reinterpretation and so on. But the crux of the matter is that the modernist, who is a product of modern universities and not a scholar of Islam, cannot interpret this past adequately and is, therefore, always on the defensive against the aggressive revivalist. The modernist is, therefore, silent almost like the secularist, a target but never an archer: one cannot name a single modernist work on Islamic political theory in modern terms. The case of Pakistan which deliberately set out (in 1947) to be an Islamic State is an illustration *par excellence* of the defensive attitude of the Modernist and the attack led against him by Abu'l-A'lā Mawdūdī, leader of the Revivalist Jamā'at-i Islāmī (the 'Islamic Party').

The upshot of this development is that a large number of the modernists gradually lose their initial moorings and gravitate to conservatism or revivalism, a fact which at least gives them social harmony and peace of mind. This is the explanation of the paradox that many self-acclaimed liberals turn out to be indistinguishable from conservatives. But the modernist who is charged with the task of running the state and is not merely a politician experiences a drift in the opposite direction. For he is responsibly aware that questions like the status of non-Muslims and bank-interest cannot be decided exactly on revivalist lines in a state that means to function in a modern society. At the same time he cannot interpret the underlying *ethos* of the classical Islamic state in modern terms beyond possibly saying that Islam requires some form of democracy today and that Islamic state is not a theocracy. He is, therefore, forced to act as though he were acting outside Islam and in some cases even his inner will might undergo a change in the secularist direction, thanks to the unthinking pressures of an unenlightened and moribund conservatism.

Modernism and Society

Alongside the problem of politico-legal modernization went the struggle for social and cultural change and adaptation to the new social ethic. Indeed, in the modern Western criticisms of the Muslim way of life, in modernist Muslim thought itself and in the subsequent apologetic, the central place is occupied by the problem of the traditional Muslim social institutions – especially Muslim laws of marriage and divorce and the place of the woman in society in general. This last issue has been so ingrained in the Western mind that almost all that a man-in-the-street in the West knows about Islam is practically summed up in the two words 'polygamy' or '*harem*' and 'purdah' (*parda*, 'curtain, veil'). The early Muslim modernist took up the challenge, argued for the 'equality' of the sexes on Islamic grounds, advocated and effected the education of women and yet the subsequent replacement of modernism by conservatism is perhaps nowhere more clearly marked than in the field of social ethics.

Social modernism, of which the most able exponent was Sayyid Amīr 'Alī in his work, *The Spirit of Islam*, argued on a basis that distinguished between the moral precepts and the specifically legal prescriptions of the Qur'ān, even if this distinction is not very explicitly formulated. Thus, although the Qur'ān legally accepted the institution of slavery, and on the legal plane prescribed certain conditions vastly ameliorating the condition of slaves (indeed, even the term 'slave' was forbidden by the Prophet), on the moral plane, it exhorted the Muslims to free slaves. This, the modernist argued with plausibility, clearly means that the Qur'ānic intention was to abolish slavery once the conditions permitted. Similarly, on the question of polygamy, the Qur'ān legally accepted the institution although here also it limited the number of wives to a maximum of four and laid down important prescriptions improving the lot of the woman, which was not, on the whole already too low in Arabia. But further, the modernist persuasively pointed out, the Qur'ān had warned that 'you shall never be able to do justice among wives' (IV, 129) and that 'If you fear you cannot do justice (among wives), then (marry) only one' (IV, 3). This, he insisted, is tantamount to a virtual ban on polygamy. Indeed, the modernist asserted an absolute parity of the sexes on the basis of the Qur'ān appealing to the verse according to which women possess rights over against men just as men possess rights over against women. Citing this argument of Muḥammad Iqbāl, Sir Hamilton Gibb accuses him of 'shutting his eyes'[16] to the subsequent words of the Qur'ān, 'but men are a degree higher than women' (II, 229).

The essential point, however, which the modernist did not clearly formulate but which the Western critic also often neglects is that the Qur'ān, although it is the eternal Word of God, was, nevertheless, immediately addressing a given society with a specific social structure. This society could, legally speaking, be made to go only so far and no more. The Prophet could have, had he so chosen, indulged in *merely* grandiose moral formulas. But then he could not have erected a society. Therefore, a legal and a moral approach were both equally necessary. The modernist therefore implies, often, of course, without being aware of the theoretical implications of this position, that not all Muslim history is 'good', i.e., Islamic, and that some discrepancy exists between the socio-economic moral ideals of Islam and subsequent history which at best failed to incorporate these ideals. He, therefore, tends to be selective about this history. At this point, however, the Western critic (especially Professor W. C. Smith in his *Modern Islam in India*, et al.) accuses the modernist of 'subjectivism' and 'romanticism' about his history. But we reserve a fuller treatment of this problem for the next chapter.

Yet the modernist stand, although in itself plausible, provoked a severe conservative reaction. The reasons for this are complex. First, the modernist sought to base himself on the Qur'ān but appeared to ignore history. The conservative stand, on the other hand, was squarely based on the historic experience of the Community (even though it appeals directly to the Qur'ān), which, for the conservative, provides the only authoritative interpretation of the Qur'ān. Further, the conservative was convinced that the modernist was really inspired by Western liberalism whence he undoubtedly drew his content which he endeavoured to support by the Qur'ān. This led to a deeper suspicion that the modernist would be ready to 'sell' any traditional Muslim values, including perhaps even fundamental principles, for Western cultural commodities. This, again, must be counted among the failures of Muslim modernism, i.e., that modernism was allowed to be identified with straight Westernism. There was actually nothing fundamentally disturbing about the modernist's borrowing of Western cultural patterns and modes, for this is what every growing civilization does and this is, indeed, what Islam also did once it expanded beyond its original Arabian nursery. But Islam did not merely 'borrow', it Islamized all that it borrowed and integrated it into an Islamic framework of values which, in turn, was expanded if it was not quite adequate, and this interpretative process occurs with every developing culture.

But the integration of new social and cultural elements into a society cannot be done by mere stray and *ad hoc* interpretations of certain fundamental texts: it calls for a much more organic activity of self-interpretation and self-expression on the part of the assimilating culture whereby its value-system is given a fresh meaning. This is what the Muslims did in their early expansionist period, but what the modernist could not do. It was essential for the modernist to create a new Islamic humanism that would give meaning and point to his social reform programme. This he did not create and, instead, allowed himself to be caught stealing from the West. But in the West itself, humanist liberalism found an ally which seemed outwardly congenial but which soon became its captor. The vast, sweeping and unforeseen changes brought by a swift growth of industrial economy and modern technology broke the back of agrarian society but also, in general, broke up the family. Industrialism took the West by storm and surprise. Under these developments, when more closely examined, the disequilibrium in Western social life radically changed the outlook of the Muslim modernist himself towards social reform, and his faith in liberalism itself greatly weakened. Of course, these developments have disconcerted also the Western reformers themselves. Besides this disenchantment, there was great pressure on the modernist from the inside: the conservative and revivalist forces never lost an opportunity of wearing down his resistance and converting him 'back to the fold'.

It is thus through this combination of its inner weaknesses, internal social forces and external factors that Muslim social modernism gave way to apologetics. Apologetics have, indeed, a useful internal function to perform and, when wielded with care and foresight, they help in controlling change and keeping a vision of the past alive. Above all, they maintain a healthy sense of self-confidence which is so essential for a changing society. But the Muslim apologist became indiscriminate. Just as the modernist had selected certain texts in his traditions and bits of his history to justify a radically new cultural pattern, so did the apologist now begin to select the darkest patches of contemporary Western society to glorify his own past. Farīd Wajdī in his work *The Muslim Woman* (*al-Mar'a al-Muslima*, which he wrote in answer to Qāsim Amīn's *The Modern Woman – al-Mar'a al-Jadīda*) and more especially Abu'l-A'lā Mawdūdī, the contemporary Pakistani leader of the Jamā'at-i Islāmī, in his work *Parda*, are eminent examples of this apologetic. The latter elaborates his argument based on the most revolting details of Western brothels supplied by Western writers and concludes that if we want to be on the safe side, then we cannot allow freedom to woman, for where otherwise, he asks, shall we stop? On exactly the same basis might one not question man's right to exist at all, in view of evil human trends and the terrible aberrations humanity manifests?

Even Muḥammad Iqbāl, the most serious and daring intellectual modernist the Muslim world has produced, issued a wholesale rejection of Western social ethics denouncing the modern Western woman as heartless and devoid of womanhood. In his work *Jāwīd nāma*, he makes a Westernized feminist address a gathering of Eastern women:

> Ladies! Mothers! Sisters!
> How long shall you live as beloveds?
> Belovedness is sheer privation:
> It is sufferance of oppression and tyranny.[17]

There is, indeed, a general reaction against Western society, wherein the central point is the figure of the woman and her relationship with the family. But while this reaction continues among the intelligentsia – i.e. both the modernist and the conservative in general – modern institutions, the most important among them being the universities and their co-educational system, continue to forge ahead producing the opposite results. The truth is that social change is inevitable and, indeed, the trends that have already set in are irreversible. The more sober and realistic elements must rise to the occasion and guide this change which otherwise surely poses a most serious threat. Most Muslim governments have, in fact, enacted laws to control the unregulated practice of polygamy and divorce within the framework of the Sharī'a, and it is only in Turkey, where the Sharī'a has been completely dethroned, that these reforms have been attempted on a purely secular basis. But even in some of those countries where the reforms have been sought on the basis of the Sharī'a, there are strong conservative dissident trends aiming at putting the clock back. There is a serious need for a constructive and bold humanism that would restate Islamic social ideals in order to back up this new legislation.

CHAPTER FOURTEEN

LEGACY AND PROSPECTS

Faith and History – The Legacy to be Reformulated: The Political Dogma; The Moral Principles; The Spiritual Ideals – The Present and the Future

Faith and History

For approximately fourteen centuries Islam has unfolded itself in history; in this long process, it has partly controlled and moulded this process – especially in the early centuries, and partly compromised with this process, especially at the political level in the post-classical period and at the spiritual level in the later Middle Ages. At the spiritual level, indeed, it not only compromised but seemed to succumb to the tide of popular religion. The story of this unfolding we have studied in the foregoing pages. During the course of its history, Islam has acquired that richness and depth of experience through which it has developed as a historical phenomenon: its initial capacity to meet challenges creatively. The basic problem now, however, is what elements in its history it may emphasize and recombine for its effective self-statement in the present challenge; what it may modify and what it may reject. At bottom, all the pre-modernist reform movements, and most Modernist attempts – which were, in effect, anxious heart-searchings – were no more than endeavours to resolve this problem. But before we proceed to attempt an answer, the formal validity of the question itself has to be established, for it has been and will be challenged by many Muslims as well as Western students of Islam.

The orientalists' criticism is almost exclusively directed against the Modernists' treatment of Islamic history.[1] These latter are accused of a subjective selectivity in the interests of furthering their own interpretations, of, sometimes, violating the principles of intellectual integrity, of arguing for a foregone conclusion and of simple 'romanticism' and glorification of the past. To some extent, these charges are correct against the classical modernists – like Sayyid Amīr 'Alī. This is, however, mostly a flaw of scholarship and thought and not basically of insight. It must be remembered that whatever elements in his history the modernist praises and emphasizes – even if these be apparently mutually disparate elements – he is not so much portraying the past but indirectly pointing to a future: in the past he is not primarily describing events but *locating his faith* in certain events. He finds Islam better embodied in certain parts of his history than others. But, of course, the objection is valid against inconsistency of thought and immaturity of scholarship and the Muslim world, on the whole, has not yet come up to the standard either of the modern West or, indeed, of the great classical and medieval Muslims *in their own milieu.*

But the right-wing Muslim objection to an objective history of Islam – even if it is attempted for not purely 'academic' but constructive purposes – stems from a very different motivation which is grounded in faith or what has become faith for it during the course of history itself. We are here primarily talking of 'orthodoxy' and not of non-orthodox developments. Among those latter, the most important are the Shīʿa who, when the current of history seemed to be set decisively against them, chose to write a meta-historical drama of Imāmism and of Messianism. Sunnī Islam also incorporated this meta-history of Messianism and, through Ṣūfism, imbibed the equally meta-historical hierarchy of saints. That history at no given point actually embodies the fullness of ideals that hope inspires may not be denied, but when the centre of belief and attention is shifted from history to meta-history, it is a sure sign of hopelessness in one's faith.

But the real orthodox story is still different. Quite early in the history of Islam, most probably around the first half of the 2nd/8th century, there appeared the idea of the *salaf*, i.e. the authority of the early generations of the Muslims (very often specified as the first three generations). The doctrine itself is quite understandable and justifiable in the sense that for a religion like Islam which must express itself in all fields of human life (that have to do with goodness and justice) through institutions, a cohesive anchoring point is necessary. But the work of the *salaf* – the first generations – came to be regarded before long not merely as an inspiring model but literally as law to be implemented without further interpretation or adjustment. A Ḥadīth claiming the authority of the Prophet was put into circulation, widely accepted and subsequently enshrined in the standard Ḥadīth works; according to this the Prophet said, 'The best generation is mine [i.e. of my Companions], the next best the following one and the next one the succeeding one . . . '.

Thus sanctified, the early generations were made part of the Faith rather than of history. This is how this development took place. The actual work of these generations was largely transferred, through the medium of the Ḥadīth, to the Prophet himself. Indeed, even certain later dogmatic and legal developments were made part of the Faith. In the literature of Ḥadīth, therefore, we do not have history but largely what might be called para-history. This para-history was then *substituted* for history. The original motivation must have been to anchor the accepted interpretation of Islam to the most authoritative point, the Prophet, based more or less on the explicit or implicit belief that the earliest generations must have thought and acted under the Prophet's teaching.

Now all the pre-modernist reformers and reform movements and their direct heirs in modern times unanimously conceive of reform as 'a return to the Qur'ān, the Prophetic Sunna and the teaching of the *salaf*'. Even such radical spirits as Ibn Taymīya who regard only the Qur'ān and the Sunna as formally authoritative and binding accept the actual authority of the *salaf* in interpreting these so that the situation remains materially unaltered. But the problem is that so far as the *content* is concerned it is impossible to draw a line – unless a severely scholarly approach of historical criticism is adopted – between the Sunna of the Prophet and the teachings of the early generations of the Muslims, thanks to the instrumentality of the Ḥadīth which absorbed all elements of any importance current in the primitive period of the Community.[2] In this connection it is interesting and instructive to note that the Wahhābīs, who in their initial phase virulently rejected all authority except that of the Qur'ān and the Prophet, were soon forced to accept as authoritative the Ijmā' (consensus) of approximately the first three centuries. This is because the Ḥadīth upon which they perforce relied as the vehicle of the Prophetic Sunna contained in itself almost all points of view on every problem, which were developed by Muslims during the first three centuries or so. The Wahhābīs, however, still rejected Ṣūfism with scorn even though an appreciable part of the Ḥadīth incorporated in the classical Ḥadīth-collections is absolutely Ṣūfī in character. This brings us to the heart of the problem which a Muslim must face and resolve if he wishes to reconstruct an Islamic future on an Islamic past: how shall this past guide him and which elements of his history he may modify, emphasize or deflate? We shall try to answer this question in the following sections.

The Legacy to be Reformulated

THE POLITICAL DOGMA

Most dogmatic and theological doctrines that have arisen in Islam are ultimately of political origin but here we are concerned with certain fundamental aspects of the political doctrine proper. This orthodox political doctrine is a direct result of the political events that occurred in the early history of Islam, viz. the internecine wars and more especially the bloody rebellions of the Khārijīs who were motivated by an extremely fanatical idealism. Whereas against the Shīʿī legitimist claims, orthodoxy put forward a democratic doctrine of Ijmāʿ and allowed in theory at least the possibility of the deposition of the Caliph, when pressed hard by Khārijī rebelliousness and the latter's demands that a person who commits a grave sin must be declared a *kāfir* and that an unrighteous ruler can under no circumstances be acknowledged, they were forced to maintain, at the collective level, an essentially, though somewhat modified, Murjite stand. This stand, which stems at bottom from a desire to avoid chaos and preserve some kind of law and order and the integrity of the Community, states, now in one form, now in another, that even an unrighteous ruler is to be obeyed although there can be 'no obedience in contravention of Allāh's commands'.

A relatively early form in which this idea is expressed occurs in a Ḥadīth which says, 'You must pray (even) behind a sinning transgressor', i.e. you should not declare even a sinning transgressor to be disqualified from the function of leading Muslims in their prayers. Since, in fact, to lead prayers, especially Friday prayers, was the function of the Caliph and was delegated by him in the provinces to governors and then, in turn, to lower administrative officers, to 'pray behind' someone was tantamount to accepting his political authority, while to desist from praying symbolized withholding one's acceptance of such authority. Thus, the alleged Ḥadīth really means that one should accept the political authority even of unrighteous men. It is interesting to note that this type of Ḥadīth is nowhere to be found in the earliest collections of Traditions – e.g. in the works of Mālik (d. 179/795) or Abū Yūsuf (d. 183/799), but appears in the later collections although it must have come into existence at an early date, when Khārijism was being doctrinally formulated and opposed. Ibn al-Muqaffaʿ (d. *c.* 140/757) complains of the two extremes, the one asserting that the political authority is, by definition, as it were, beyond criticism, while the other maintaining that obedience must be withdrawn from the political authority at the commission of a mistake or, rather, at the implementation of an error. Ibn al-Muqaffaʿ, who has no Ḥadīth to quote on either side of the extreme, condemns both.

We thus see that the Ḥadīth to the effect that one must pray even if the Imām is a sinful transgressor seeks merely to accentuate and perpetuate only one side of the extreme. This forms the essential basis of orthodox doctrine on the matter. But even much later, indeed until today, the content of the orthodox position has remained unchanged even though the original conditions of Khārijism which brought it into existence have long since disappeared. As a matter of fact, during the later centuries fresh Ḥadīth came into existence to support this doctrine of absolute obedience to the authority and total pacifism. The following statement, for example, which began as an ordinary dictum, is accepted as a Ḥadīth or, at least, a quasi-Ḥadīth by Ibn Taymīya: 'The sultan (the political authority) is the shadow of God on earth'. We have pointed out that the common view which sees in this an Iranian or some other influence upon Islam about the divine nature of kingship cannot be accepted.[3] That some circles, for example certain Shī'ī sects, and certain philosophical doctrines must have been influenced by elements of such old doctrines may be reasonably conceded. But when an orthodox thinker like Ibn Taymīya declares the sultan to be the shadow of God on earth, this can have nothing in common with doctrines of divinity of kingship except pure verbal externality. For, in conjunction with the other very commonly held orthodox view that 'even an unjust ruler must be obeyed', it leads to the absurd conclusion that 'an unjust ruler is the shadow of God on earth'. What the orthodox really mean by all such statements is that *any rule* is better than no rule or civil war, and, indeed, Ibn Taymīya immediately follows up the above-mentioned alleged Ḥadīth with the quotation, 'Sixty days of an unjust ruler are much better than one night of lawlessness' (see Chapter IV, note 10).

But the orthodoxy kept clinging to the one-sided doctrine inculcating absolute obedience to the ruler. They devised nothing to control the absoluteness of the ruler himself. The *shūrā* or the consultative body enjoined by the Qur'ān and ingrained in Arab life, could have been developed into some kind of effective institution, but *nothing* was done in this direction either by the 'Ulamā' or the popular will. The *shūrā* itself ceased to exist after the very early period and, indeed, the doctrine of absolute obedience took root in the orthodoxy after the *shūrā* had ceased to exist with the vast expansion of the empire and the rise of centrifugal forces. The doctrine of Ijmā' itself, which might have been made into a nursery of political opinion, became an instrument of tyranny by being defined practically as 'consensus in the past' rather than as a developing process of the expression of the collective will and the way of resolving problems as they arise.

It is obvious, however, that a one-sided emphasis on obedience, conformism and pacifism ultimately generates chaos and defeats its very purpose. The first formulators of this principle may or may not have seen this – since they were at grips with a real situation threatening anarchy – but the later custodians of the orthodoxy certainly did not. For an uncompromising stress on obedience creates passivity and total indifference, in the long run, on the part of the public not only towards the political authority but towards political life as a whole. Where indifference and passivity grow, they generate suspiciousness which becomes second nature (for it is really impossible to remain just indifferent to public affairs). Now, not all these ills put together equal, in their destructiveness, the evil of cynicism which cannot fail to be created by these. Indeed, many of the political troubles of instability witnessed in the Muslim countries of today – even though there must be other contributory factors as well – seem to be at bottom linked with this orthodox attitude rooted in tradition. We thus see that the very effort to create political stability and solidarity, *since it was one-sided*, ended up in creating just the opposite, and an almost incurable cynicism in the bargain.

Thus, from the 4th/10th century onward, with the increasing ineffectiveness of the Caliphate, real power passed into the hands of the Amīrs and Sultans, ambitious men of great initiative and often possessed of considerable political wisdom, who sought to legitimize their *de facto* power by a nominal 'allegiance' to the Caliph. Since every successful military and political adventurer had to pay his mercenary soldiery and fill the treasury, the burden of taxation became too heavy. Together with other causes, this directly contributed to the weakening of the merchant and professional classes, which impoverished city life. When middle classes so weaken, hardly any high-level civilization can be expected to continue, let alone prosper and expand. We thus see that the unthoughtful perpetuation of the orthodox dogma of 'absolute obedience to the ruler' contributed both directly and indirectly to the decline of the Muslim civilization itself.

The task before the Muslim in the field of politics, after a candid appraisal of his history, is to reformulate the orthodox content on this point and to create adequate institutions to ensure (1) the solidarity and stability of the community and the state and (2) the active, positive and responsible participation by the public at large in the affairs of the government and the state. Once these bases have been fully restated, some stable form of the Islamic state will emerge and much of the present controversy, often superficial and prejudiced, as to whether Islam is democratic or not, will come to a natural death. Of course, if the public are to participate with responsiblity in the affairs of the state, the state must be some form of democracy. But it is imperative that the Muslims decide the issue *from the inside*, keeping free from external pressures both direct and indirect (in the form of external propaganda), although drawing lessons from the experiences of other peoples. They will find the Islamic principles broad enough to admit a varying range of constitutions, within a democratic framework, depending on social and political climates actually obtaining.

THE MORAL PRINCIPLES

The Qur'ān is a teaching primarily interested in producing the right moral attitude for human action. The *correct* action, whether it be political, religious or social, it considers to be *'ibāda* or the 'service of God'. The Qur'ān, therefore, emphasizes all those moral tensions and psychological factors that generate the right frame of mind for action. It warns against human pride and sense of self-sufficiency, i.e. pure humanism, on the one hand, and the moral turpitude of hopelessness and defeatism, on the other. It constantly insists on 'one's being on one's guard (*taqwā*)', and 'fear of God' on the one hand and the 'mercy of God and essential goodness of man' on the other. And so on. It is obvious that a basic impulse of the Qur'ān is to release the greatest amount of the creative moral energy. The view commonly prevalent among Western and through these in other non-Muslim circles, that the Qur'ānic God is an arbitrary despot inspiring more fear than anything else, is perhaps the most puerile understanding of the Qur'ān itself, stemming partly from a long-standing prejudice but partly also from the medieval theological formulations of Islam by Muslim theologians themselves and, of course, the resultant concrete attitudes of the Muslims at large.

Now the orthodox Muslim theological formulations are almost out-and-out predeterministic, presenting a rather odd contrast to the moral freshness and fervour that the Qur'ān seeks to evoke. Once again the story is exactly the same as that we have already depicted above in the case of the political dogma: the thoughtless perpetuation of a dogmatic solution arrived at to meet a particular extreme situation. The extreme challenge in this case was that of Mu'tazilism, which in some of its formulations said that God is not the author of evil but only of good, and thus earned the title of 'Muslim Zoroastrianism' couched in Ḥadīth form. Normally, the Mu'tazila were staunch protagonists of the freedom of the human will and of human responsibility. But this stand they considered to be in conflict with the idea of the omnipotence of God, for divine omnipotence seemed to them to contradict the idea of divine justice. They were, therefore, condemned as pure humanists seeking to impose upon God the constructions of justice and goodness arrived at by certain men.

Now, the moral content of the Sunnī dogmatic theology is a direct result of this situation, and once again Ḥadīth was the vehicle used for supplying this content. Almost all, even if not absolutely all, Ḥadīth on the question of free will and determinism must be accepted as a product of this historical situation, and cannot be said to emanate from the Prophet. The famous Ḥadīth, 'The believers in the freedom of the will are the Zoroastrians of this Community', is based on a much too technically sophisticated, though suppressed, process of reasoning to go back historically to the Prophet. The bulk of the Sunnī Ḥadīth is uncompromisingly deterministic. The truth is that neither Mu'tazilism nor, in its turn, Sunnism possessed adequate philosophical concepts and intellectual tools to be able to formulate their respective positions successfully, the result being that each took the form of *an extreme*, and after a deadly struggle, Sunnism emerged victorious, while Mu'tazilism survived only in the otherwise incongruous and uncongenial dogmatic system of Shī'ism.

We have seen in Chapter IV how the orthodox interpretation of the dogma of divine omnipotence and determinism grew stiffer in course of time especially after al-Ash'arī's statement of his solution. Although al-Ash'arī wanted a compromise, his attempt was not successful, primarily because of the inadequacy of his intellectual equipment, while his moral influence, which was a continuation of Ibn Ḥanbal's, preponderated on the side of predestinarianism. We also saw that later, when the philosophical movement had supplied the Muslims with a vast fund of philosophical concepts, theologians like Fakhr al-Dīn al-Rāzī drew materials from this stock in support of predeterminism which, in fact, becomes more and more rigid with the passage of century after century. We thus see that the doctrine of the Will and Power of God – the supposed logical ground of determinism – which was accentuated by Sunnism to meet a particular challenge in history, became ingrained in the orthodox structure as a permanent part of its dogmatic furniture long after that challenge and that need had passed.

There is no doubt that a one-sided or preponderant emphasis on predestinarianism is injurious to the moral fibre: it benumbs that moral initiative and, indeed, purposiveness which is the essence of life itself. But what aggravated the consequences of determinism still further was something different, although in spirit closely allied to determinism: this was the attitude adopted officially by orthodoxy over the problem of faith and deeds, and once again we find orthodoxy suffering a reaction to Khārijism. We have come across in Chapter V the Khārijī doctrine that a grave sinner becomes a *kāfir*, i.e. an infidel, and the Khārijī attitude concerning the intimate faith-deed relationship. It was, of course, imperative to find some answer to Khārijī fanaticism; otherwise the Community would destroy itself by internal accusations of unrighteousness and misbelief and resultant internecine warfare. But the burden of defence again fell upon Ḥadīth. A Companion, Abū Dharr, is said to have related that the Prophet once said, 'He who confesses "There is no god but God" [and Muḥammad is His Prophet] will go to Paradise'. To the Companion's enquiry as to whether paradise was vouchsafed to such a person even if he committed adultery and theft, the Prophet replied in the affirmative.[4] Such Ḥadīth obviously cannot go back to the Prophet since the Qur'ān itself insistently and unfailingly couples 'good acts' with 'faith'. But this Ḥadīth performs a very fundamental function in that it provides a legal definition of a Muslim as a necessary check against Khārijism and other equivalent attitudes. The definition, however, was not, unfortunately, taken in a merely legal sense but was later also assumed to define the essence of Islam. The morally dangerous consequences of this attitude are obvious. When such a sharp cleavage is adopted formally between the inner faith and the moral behaviour, both must suffer in the smug security of formalism. The actual practice did not and could not always strictly conform to this principle, and reformers, preachers and genuinely religious and moral personalities have constantly exerted their living influence on the Community at large; but it cannot be denied that the general effect of this principle on the concrete attitudes of the people has tended to emphasize the formal and nominal aspects of Islam at the manifest expense of its moral and spiritual content.

This type of attitude on the crucial question of the relationship of faith to behaviour (of which the parallel is the Christian doctrine of 'Justification by Faith'), when combined with a preponderantly deterministic doctrine, amounts to a sure fatality of the moral sense. If moral sensitivity was not killed in Muslim society – and there is no society worthy of the name in which it is completely killed – it is not due to the official moral principles but rather despite them. Certainly, in the orthodox dogmatic thesaurus, there is little that can counterbalance these principles. In Shī'ism, no doubt, the freedom of the human will has been preserved in the dogma as a continuation of the Mu'tazilite tradition. But it seems to accord ill with the Shī'ite doctrine of the Imām and, on the whole, with the charismatic structure of Shī'ism as opposed to the democratic structure of Sunnī Islam, and seems to have been adopted by Shī'ism only as an opposition to the Sunnī dogma. If the function of a dogma is to provide a kind of constitution for a religious community so that religious developments may take place within its general and broad framework, then, so far as moral principles are concerned, the Sunnī dogma, by laying an overwhelming stress on only one side of the moral tension, is incapable of performing this function and is, in fact, a betrayal of the Qur'ān itself.

We see once again that a doctrine situationally developed in order to meet certain particular historical exigencies has been erected into a permanent orthodox dogma. In fact, as time went on, the situational background of the emergence of doctrines – of determinism and of the relationship of faith to behaviour – was completely forgotten, and the doctrine of determinism and divine omnipotence came to be looked upon either as part of Revelation itself or at least as solely and uniquely deducible from the Qur'ān. We have seen in Chapter V how uncompromising determinism continued to be developed with ever reinvigorated arguments in the post-Ghazālian period by such men as Fakhr al-Dīn al-Rāzī, thanks to the vast stock of ideas the philosophical movement had left as its legacy. But more important even than official theology, the relatively new but far more powerful spiritual movement of Ṣūfism, when it took a new, speculative turn, patently espoused determinism and, indeed, transformed it into pantheism, a doctrine which is far more injurious ethically than perhaps any other doctrine conceivable, obliterating, as it does, the very distinction between good and evil. In sum, Ṣūfism passed from the theological statement, 'All acts are created by God', through the intermediate position, 'All acts are acts of God', to the doctrine, 'There is nothing in existence except God'.

Orthodoxy certainly needs to be reformulated on this crucial point and the old emphasis on the divine power and determinism has to be integrated with and balanced by its opposite term of the tension, as was clearly envisaged by the Qur'ān and the Prophetic Sunna.

THE SPIRITUAL IDEALS

The general moral deterioration caused by the developments outlined above could not fail to manifest itself at the social level. Into the moral vacuum thus created in Muslim society there moved Ṣūfism as a mass religion. We have described the rise and development of this movement of popular spirituality in Chapters VIII and IX. Here we shall briefly examine the general tenor of this massive phenomenon and its effects on the Community's moral life as a whole, for it is obvious that any attempt to reconstruct Muslim society and to restate Islam, a task in which all important Muslim countries seem to be engaged in their own ways, must take into account the colossal moral and spiritual débris which is the legacy of Ṣūfism.

That genuine moral enlightenment and an inculcation of a true inwardness of faith must form a fundamental part of Islamic education, which was the initial motive force of Ṣūfism, none may deny, for, as al-Ghazālī taught us, an excessive stress on the 'external disciplines' of religion merely creates religious fossils. But as Ṣūfism developed it created a dichotomy between inner, spiritual development, on the one hand, and what it termed the Sharī'a on the other. Having created this dichotomy, it set itself up as a religion not only within religion but above religion. The 'purificative' movements and modernist movements in Islam have both joined issue on the point of eradicating Ṣūfism; yet two hundred years after the inception of the reformist impulse, the Muslim masses, from the shores of the Atlantic to Indonesia, are still in the grip of that Ṣūfistic spirituality which, as a whole, is no better than a form of spiritual delinquency often exploited by the clever Ṣūfī leaders for their own ends. Political leaders may put through successfully myriads of reforms – feudal, industrial and social – and will be backed by the masses and the army, but none of them has so far even begun to grapple seriously with the mass phenomenon of Ṣūfism and its various, deep, and paralysing effects on society. The reason is that in this case the masses and the army themselves would be against the reform, steeped as they are in Ṣūfistic superstitions, practices like the cult of saints and their tombs, etc.

Certain beliefs which originated from Ṣūfistic or allied sources have gradually become part even of the orthodox system of belief. Examples of this are Messianism, i.e. belief in the Second Advent of Jesus and in the Mahdī, belief in the miracles of saints, etc. That these doctrines, taken literally, are morally harmful is obvious; that they have actually caused incalculable harm to Muslim society is also a glaring fact of history. As for Messianism, it was originally adopted in Islam either by Shī'ism or Ṣūfism, but in any case it came to Sunnī Islam through the Ṣūfīs or rather through the precursors of the Ṣūfīs – the public preachers of the 2nd/8th century who consoled and satisfied the politically disillusioned and morally starved masses by holding out Messianic hopes. As we have shown elsewhere,[5] the early Ḥadīth-material which had come into existence for the quite different purpose of declaring as religiously authoritative the results of the activity of the first three generations, was later given a new twist and invested with a Messianic import. Thus, the Ḥadīth, 'Honour my Companions, then the following generation and then the next following generation . . .', came into the now famous version 'The best generation is mine, then the next one . . .'. This was then taken to mean that history must go from bad to worse and was doomed unless and until the Messiah or the Mahdī appear. But Jesus and the Mahdī are fundamentally eschatological not historical figures. History is thus condemned and an inevitable historical pessimism is the result. That such a belief, if strictly adopted, must numb the moral faculties and human initiative hardly calls for an analysis. But the doctrine both of the Second Advent of Jesus and of the Mahdī was adopted by orthodoxy, probably because it had already become part of commonly accepted beliefs.

Apart from this Shī'ī-Ṣūfī legacy which Islam adopted, Ṣūfism, as it developed in the whole of the Muslim world, is solely responsible for inculcating, spreading and perpetuating the most fantastic and grotesque beliefs in the miracles of saints. The network of superstitions such beliefs have engendered has simply enchained the minds and spirits of the credulous masses, and even the educated and the learned have fallen a prey to them in large numbers. It would hardly be an exaggeration to say that between the 7th/13th and the present centuries the actual force and efficacy of Islam in practical terms (beyond the political sphere) was reduced to a collection of superstitious beliefs and practices generated by the Ṣūfī movement. The miraculous powers of the living and dead saints – of course the dead more than the living – have ruled the masses and even a large number of the 'Ulamā'. Tomb-worship and the ills accruing from this have rendered the Muslim masses almost incapable of understanding the Islamic teaching.

But what has Ṣūfism given on the positive side? There is no doubt that it has created certain great personalities from time to time – men of outstanding moral, spiritual and, in some cases, even intellectual calibre. But these are isolated cases and even in political life where opportunism reigned it has produced great personalities and men of tremendous initiative. To the masses, the Ṣūfī spiritual ideal offered an escape from the uninviting realities of life – economic hardship, social imbalance, political uncertainties. But this it did at the expense of the Islamic ideal of a social order. Instead of this moral-social order it taught people certain techniques of auto-suggestion and hypnotism and an excessive indulgence in an altogether emotionalized religion which can be only described as a mass spiritual hysteria. It is this phenomenon – the total effect of superstitionism, miracle-mongering, tomb-worship, mass-hysteria and, of course, charlatanism – that we have described above as the moral and spiritual débris from which Muslim society has to be reclaimed for Islam. It is this challenge which no political reformist leadership in the Muslim world has yet dared to face except Mustafa Kemal Atatürk. And yet, the 'reforms' of Atatürk, especially in this field, can hardly be regarded as anything better than suppressive measures imposed by sheer force. For bold as these measures were, the community at large was simply not prepared to receive them. And this brings us to the heart of the problem of reform in this most urgent and crucial sector of the reconstruction of the Muslim society: what should this mass religion be supplanted with and how?

It is obvious that Atatürk and his colleagues did not give thought, at least certainly not adequate thought, to this problem. Elsewhere in the Muslim world, the reformist movements have more or less unanimously reacted against Ṣūfism in their social reform programmes and the impact of modern education has further discredited the Ṣūfī way of life. But there precisely lies the danger. As a result of the general reform activity, purely activist movements have arisen in the Muslim world with their various organizations, brotherhoods, clubs and similar cells. These organizations, as Professor Gibb pointed out in his *Muḥammedanism*, being devoid of the spiritual depth of the old Ṣūfī brotherhoods and, therefore, lacking catholicity, tend to become coteries, narrow and intolerant. Indeed, they borrow techniques from Fascism or Communism and often threaten the existence of the state. The new, purely activist groups, intellectually shallow and spiritually impoverished, which, at the political level, behave like any other vested interest, are, therefore, no substitutes for the Ṣūfī *ṭarīqas*.

A programme of reconstruction must be set within the basic framework of orthodoxy. For the essential objective to be achieved through reform is to imbue the masses with a moral impulse in order to rebuild the good social order. This moral base orthodoxy has kept, despite heavy pressures through the centuries. What we have said in this chapter in criticism of certain orthodox principles, that these have contributed to a lowering of moral tension, does not militate against our present assertion. What we are saying in sum is that orthodoxy has made grave mistakes by perpetuating as part of its content certain doctrines which were designed to meet certain particular historical situations, but that the basic *élan* of the orthodoxy is correct. We should add here that orthodox theology has also to be reformulated if it is to absorb the basic Ṣūfī impulse within itself and thus to render the latter superfluous so that it may not function as virtually an independent religion by itself. Most critics have described Muslim theology as extremely rationalistic and unemotional. This criticism is essentially correct and lays bare the very strength of the Ṣūfistic impulse in Islam, which feeds on religious emotion, although it must be remembered that theology in Islam does not occupy that central position which Christian theology occupies in Christianity. We may further be allowed to suspect that when a Christian critic describes Muslim theology as unemotional and praises Ṣūfism, he is not altogether a disinterested observer but makes patent insinuations. This is brought home by the fact that while on the one hand he praises the worshipful veneration of the Prophet by the Ṣūfī, on the other, he is apt to look askance at the reverence accorded to the person of the Prophet by Muslims in general. This latter (not the former!) he finds contrary to Qur'ānic teaching and probably regards as a Christian influence on Islam.

On the first point, we admit that the very existence of Ṣūfism is a critique of and a challenge to the actual content of orthodox theology. We have already argued in this chapter for a reconstitution of some of the important emphases of the orthodox content, and we believe that this must do adequate justice to genuinely religious emotion. On all these points orthodox content must be brought in line with the Qur'ān itself. Now, the Qur'ān is not just 'rational' but is also full of genuine religious emotion. In its very divinity, the Divine Word is a humane document through and through. And yet the Qur'ān refuses to compromise the moral impulse with cults of personality in any fashion whatsoever. It preaches not only the unmitigated power of God but also His limitless mercy; and yet it rejects, in the last analysis, even 'intercession' (*shafā'a*), let alone a soteriology of Christian type. But later Muslim orthodoxy did accept the doctrine of 'intercession' with which the Ṣūfī adepts ran riot and vested this extraordinary privilege in every saint. So far as the person of the Prophet is concerned, the principle of his uniqueness among humanity as the greatest organ of the Divine Will and Command lies necessarily enshrined in the Faith of which this recognition must remain a cardinal principle. The unbiased minds of the world are slowly moving towards this recognition. The honour that is due to this recognition will always be vouchsafed to Muḥammad. He claimed nothing else and severely warned against deifying man.

But the reconstituted content of orthodoxy – if this can be achieved and it can be achieved only if the 'Ulamā' once more show that instinct that discerns the religious needs of the Community and which they displayed so successfully during the 2nd/8th and the 3rd/9th centuries – will contribute only partly although very fundamentally, to the solution of the Ṣūfistic problem. For Ṣūfism, in its various manifestations, has not remained even purely religious but has also lived on quite different instincts – social, political, commercial, artistic and sexual, as has been the case with many other religions. For example, Hinduism retains certain similar strong vestiges until today. These threads have to be clearly disentangled and taken up in the respective fields of the social reconstruction programme. Should this educative and reformative programme not be executed in good time, there is every danger that the Muslim countries will be taken over, one by one, by totalitarian régimes of the Communist type, which will enforce regimentation of action and thought and will have only one end before them, an end well known to all of us.

The Present and the Future

The most fundamental fact about Islam in the present century so far is the independence from foreign rule achieved by Muslim peoples in their different homelands. To a journeyman politician this may seem a hackneyed truth for, after all, 'colonialism' is disappearing fast and all countries previously under foreign rule have either become free or are so becoming and it so happens that a part – a large part – of these countries is Muslim. What makes this fact significant, however, is that in all these countries, from Morocco to Indonesia, Islam has played a very important rôle in the struggle for freedom. In some countries, especially in Pakistan but also in Algeria, it has played a dominant and decisive rôle. The long-term potentialities, therefore, of these countries coming closer to one another into some form of a 'Muslim world' are real, for a strong initial impulse to such a goal exists in the hearts of the people. The second most important fact of the present, however, is precisely the absence of an actual 'Muslim world', not only politically but culturally and socially as well. In fact, so far as the actual present reality is concerned, the 'Muslim world' was never so absent as today, when there exist only sovereign nations and states. To what extent and in what manner the genuine sentiments of the people can reconcile themselves with the hard fact of the nation-states, only time can tell. We may only point out here that the rather naïve periodic talk of an 'Islamic Unity' must remain a dream so long as real, material bases for it are not erected.

But quite apart from this question which does face Muslim countries as a whole and whose upshot it is too early to forecast, each individual Muslim society is faced with the internal problem of how to reconstruct itself. With the exception of Turkey, where the secularist basis introduced by Atatürk still persists officially (although here also the experiences of the past decade have shown that this may not be the final solution), the generality of Muslim societies have felt (although some of them, like Indonesia, are witnessing acute internal struggles) that Islam must supply a positive referent in their internal reconstruction programmes. Some of them (as is the case with Pakistan) have based themselves squarely on an Islamic plea. The real problem of these countries, however, lies in the actual, positive formulation of Islam, of exactly spelling out what Islam has to say to the modern individual and society. The problem is fatefully crucial, indeed, for should these societies fail of an adequate answer, the only alternative left to them will be some form of secularism, and there is little doubt that this solution is tantamount to changing the very nature of Islam.

From the long history of Islam, where it met both challenges and crises of different types, spiritual, intellectual and social, one should naturally expect that Islam, given time for evolving the necessary internal equipment, can resolve the present challenge successfully. But it is absolutely necessary that the Muslims be clear as to exactly in what the present challenge lies. If a correct vision is not forthcoming of what is needed – and, judging from the overall performance of both the conservatives and the modernists to date, one cannot help questioning whether this vision has yet fully developed – irreparable damage might be done. To our mind, the challenges are basically two: one stemming from the nature of 'modern' life – materialism – and the other from the nature of Muslim conservatism. We shall see that the two questions are not entirely separate, but for the sake of clarity it is convenient to take up the nature of Muslim conservatism first.

In every growing society, conservatism represents one term in a concrete tension within which onward movement takes place, the other term of the tension being liberalism or, as we have termed it, 'modernism'. But in all situations of social growth, conservatism must seek not to conserve merely the past but what in it is valuable and essential. At the beginning of this chapter we stated that Muslims must decide what exactly is to be conserved, what is essential and relevant for the erection of an Islamic future, what is fundamentally Islamic and what is purely 'historical'. In other words, they must develop an enlightened conservatism. We also pointed out that much of history had been eternalized by a kind of religio-historic fiction and we briefly described the process whereby this was done. Fundamentalist reform movements, like Wahhābism, which could have been expected to perform the function of separating the fundamental from the accretions, have essentially failed in this task even if they have contributed a great deal to the removal of certain crass superstitions and malpractices. The main reason for their failure has been that by defining the fundamentals of Islam roundly as 'the Qur'ān and the Ḥadīth', they have really re-admitted the whole religious history for in this history almost every development has come to possess its protective Ḥadīth – from legal details to Ṣūfism, from the Ijmā' of the Sunnīs to the legitimism of the Shī'a.

Unless, therefore, the problem of the Ḥadīth is critically, historically and constructively treated, there seems little prospect of distinguishing the essential from the purely historical. But it is precisely this task which the 'Ulamā' are resolutely refusing to do. They fear that if Ḥadīth is thus exposed to a scientific investigation, the concept of the 'Sunna of the Prophet', the second pillar of Islam besides the Qur'ān, will be destroyed and that it would then be impossible to hold on to the Qur'ān as well; for that which anchors the Qur'ān *is* the Sunna of the Prophet. Some of the recent Muslim and non-Muslim wholesale and absolute rejections of Ḥadīth and the Prophetic Sunna undoubtedly strengthen these fears. Now, it seems certain that Muslims cannot dispense with the concept 'Sunna of the Prophet' and on this score the position of the 'Ulamā' is unassailable. On the other hand, a genuine criticism of Ḥadīth, no matter how sweeping of the content of Ḥadīth it may be, cannot eliminate the *concept* of the 'Sunna of the Prophet'; on the contrary, it can only help to elucidate it as we have pointed out here and elsewhere.[6] Nor, of course, is it necessary that if a certain Ḥadīth is shown not to emanate from the Prophet, or, indeed, if much of Ḥadīth is thus shown to be post-Prophetic, that it should be, therefore rejected. What is necessary is to know the genesis and evolution of a given Ḥadīth in order to reveal *what function it did or was supposed to perform and whether Islamic needs do still demand such function or not.*

The task of rethinking and reformulating Islam at the present juncture is much more acute and radical than has faced the Muslims since the 3rd/9th century, and the requisite performance is equivalent to the performance of the first two centuries and a half. In other words, the thinking Muslim has to go right behind the early post-Prophetic formative period itself and to reconstruct it all over again. And this is exactly what the conservatives, who still largely control the mainsprings of power in the Community, not only refuse to do but completely fail even to recognize the need to do. These are opposed by individuals and small groups, free-ranging 'progressivists' who are pushed into the extreme position of rejecting the Sunna of the Prophet altogether. The truth is that neither of the two parties is genuinely acquainted with the historical evolution of the Ḥadīth so that they can have a balanced view of it and, therefore, of what is to be done at the present juncture. Indeed, the need to cultivate a sound, historical thinking about Islam is the first desideratum and prerequisite of any successful process of the reformulation of Islam.

But it is this capacity for historical thinking about Islam – in the sense which has been made clear by our argument, for we do not mean by it just an historical analysis of texts in the narrow sense – that cannot be generated by our old system of education in the *madrasas*. For the *madrasas* have, almost from the beginning of their organized existence, aimed at merely imparting a system of ideas, not at creating newer systems; and therefore they have not been interested in inculcating the spirit of enquiry and independent thought. On the contrary, they could not have failed to be interested in checking that spirit for, otherwise, their *raison d'être* would be gone. Nor has this requisite spirit been adequately generated so far in our modern scholarship. Firstly, as we have previously pointed out in Chapter XI, while discussing the Muslim system of education, our modern university system of education is entirely secular, and Islamic studies and research have never formed an integral part of it. The products of our modern system of education, therefore, have no schooling in Islam. Secondly, those students from this system of education who have cared to study Islam scientifically, have invariably been pupils of Western orientalists. But the orientalists, although they have made a remarkable contribution and have been, by definition, pioneers of modern studies on Islam, have studied Islam merely as a historical datum, as a dead body, so to say, to be analysed. The result is that their Muslim pupils have become orientalists also: the fact that these are orientalists remains simply juxtaposed with and mechanically added to the fact that they are also Muslims. On the whole, the two facts have not acted upon one another and borne fruit. There have been, no doubt, exceptions here and there, but neither very frequent nor fundamentally significant. It is only recently that Islamic Studies have been introduced in certain universities, but the chief problem is the lack of adequate and competent personnel to establish these studies and to produce personnel for the future. It is still more recently, indeed, contemporaneously with the present work that certain fresh but important developments have taken place like the establishment of the Islamic Research Institute in Pakistan for the purpose of reinterpreting Islam and training creative scholars for the future, and the reorganization of al-Azhar in Cairo and especially the creation of a research body. It will obviously take time, however, for these developments to bear fruit.

But if the problem of Muslim conservatism is grave, much more grave is the challenge to Muslim society of pure secularism and materialism. In all societies, even in those that are or claim to be based directly on a religious vision or impulse, such as the Islamic society, there are always 'indifferent' or secular forces, and Muslim society has never been devoid of such classes. But this trend has become accentuated disproportionately in Muslim society in modern times because of a strange argument which has been put forward very often explicitly but which is at work even more powerfully in a more or less unconscious and silent way. The argument is that the Muslims (or the Easterners) are fundamentally and inalienably spiritual whereas the West is purely materialistic, and that all that the East has to do in order to develop is to borrow the technological (material) skills of the West and, together with the spirituality that it possesses already, all will be well. This argument has been given currency in the West also by many Westerners themselves. In the East, however, this attitude, partly no doubt assumed for propaganda purposes, has had very unfortunate consequences. For, in the East, besides creating a false sense of placidity and superiority in conservative circles, it has been responsible for the development, in the so-called Westernized classes, of a naked and frightening form of materialism which recognizes hardly any moral demands whatsoever. It is again in the ranks of these Westernized classes and as a reaction against this irresponsible selfishness and materialism that Communism develops as a form of attractive, tantalizing idealism. In either case the old spirituality is ineffective: it is by and large the secularized intellectual who talks of the 'New Society' and whenever he thinks it convenient also unhesitatingly exploits the name of Islam.

Also as a reaction against this type of lawless 'modernity', the conservative recoils and, although here and there he may make superficial and mostly verbal concessions to modernity, he is basically pushed into a much more severely conservative and intractable position. Indeed it would not be far from true to say that, in a sense, conservative 'Ulamā' of today are far more uncompromisingly and, indeed, unthinkingly conservative than were their predecessors, say, of the 11th/17th or the 12th/18th centuries. This is partly a consequence of the intellectually impoverished condition of the traditional seats of learning, since in modern times better talents have been increasingly attracted towards secular education, but undoubtedly partly also because of the strong reaction on the part of the conservatives against modern secularist trends. The secularist has pushed the traditionalist into an uncompromising position not only against secularism but, since the traditionalist is unable to analyse the situation properly and diagnose the *malaise* exactly, even against genuine Islamic Modernism. The conservative has developed a strong suspicion, without being able to make distinctions, that whatever smacks of modernity must necessarily overtly (secularism) or covertly (modernism) seek to sacrifice the religious conscience at the altar of 'progress'.

The only real remedy of the situation lies in a basic reform of the modern educational system and in imparting genuine Islamic values in schools and colleges beside other subjects. Only in this way can this modern secular education be meaningfully integrated into a comprehensive Islamic culture and be creative; otherwise it is a piece of alien matter arbitrarily grafted on to an organism. But the problem to be encountered once more is: what is Islam to impart? For, the traditional formulation of Islam in terms of *kalām*-theology is no longer either fully intelligible to the modern mind nor, even if it is understood by abstract mental effort, quite meaningful in the modern situation. The truth is that this theology was developed under quite specific conditions and in response to definite and concrete religious and moral questions. It unmistakably bears the mark of history. The answer is, therefore, once again pushed back to an adequate presentation of Islam in terms that would be acceptable to and meaningful for a modern mind. In doing so, some of the important emphases of our medieval theology will have to be changed or recast. Above in this chapter we have given certain important examples of this and indicated by way of illustration, the lines along which the new work may proceed. It is only in this way that the eternal values and the basic religious experience of Islam may be resurrected from the weight of historical particularity under which they are submerged.

In carrying out this task of reformulation one more fundamental need will have to be satisfied if Islamic theology and law are not only to meet the requirements of modern man and society but if they are to save modern man and society from the nihilistic demoralizing effects of crass secularism. It is that in the new reconstruction, the specifically moral and religious emotions must be given due place and incorporated as an integral element. It is because in our previous formulation of Islam, in the old Sharī'a disciplines, due recognition was not given to this element that Ṣūfism developed as a quasi-separate religion and, in a large measure, in opposition to the 'official' Islam of the 'Ulamā'. That Ṣūfism went at points radically wrong in the course of its development was due to certain broad and deep social factors, but that it originally and fundamentally arose from certain basic religious needs cannot be denied. The reform movements in Islam, especially in modern times, have left a general but one-sided legacy of anti-Ṣūfism. That organized Ṣūfism, with its special methods and techniques, is bound to have an asocial and antinomian trend may be admitted, and its existence as a separate quasi-religion is unacceptable both to Islam and to modern life. On the other hand, the genuine inner life of the 'heart' – the basic *élan* of Ṣūfism – must be reintegrated into the Sharī'a and can be neglected only on pain, in the long run, of succumbing to the devastating onslaughts of modern secularism.

Islam is 'surrender to the Will of God', i.e., the determination to implement, in the physical texture of the world, the command of God or the Moral Imperative. This implementation is 'service to God (*'ibāda*)'. The Muslim has certainly not lost *the conviction* that he can and must perform this service. He is, in heart-searching at present, trying to discover a fuller meaning of this service than he has ever conceived of in the past, and the degree, amplitude, accuracy and effectiveness of his vision, now being born, may affect not only his own future but much of the world around him.

EPILOGUE

Since the writing of the substance of this book about a decade and a half ago, certain important developments have taken place in the Muslim world in the political and economic fields. The sudden rise of certain Muslim countries to economic power, through oil, is an accident of history whose full consequences are impossible to forecast. At present, only Saudi Arabia is making any direct use of this new power, in strengthening various Muslim communities and countries, and in aiding countries in Africa and elsewhere in order to gain good will for the Arabs and for Islam. Time alone will tell whether this power is an apparition or a thing of substance, but meanwhile Saudi Arabia has become the center of attention for the entire non-Communist world, and for the non–oil-producing Muslim countries in particular. Certain developments in Egypt (for example, the new constitution, which declares the Islamic Sharīʿa to be the source of all law) and in Pakistan (for example, the 1974 constitutional declaration that the Aḥmadīs, who believe in the prophethood or saintship of Mīrzā Ghulām Aḥmad, d. 1909, are a non-Muslim minority) are said to have been directly influenced by Saudi Arabia. There is no doubt, however, that the oil countries are taking the problem of economic development with dead seriousness, aware that oil will not last beyond a few decades, and one must admire the common sense and sobriety of a country like Saudi Arabia, plunged all of a sudden into the vortex of contemporary technology from a situation which, in many respects, can be characterized only as premedieval.

But this commonsense practicality must, in turn, lead to the cultivation of the ability to handle concepts analytically, critically and synthetically, for in the development of scientific technology, commonsense practicality by itself cannot go very far. It is true that there is some cause to dread this ability, when it comes at the expense of a robust sense of right and wrong. The wielding of ideas is a delicate business. Nevertheless, ideas and their constant growth are the lifeline of human development and the essence of civilization; no civilization can be built or sustained without them. While the purposeless and wild growth of ideas may cause or signal moral decay, the lack of ideas starves out that same human spirit which puritanical countries like Saudi Arabia, by barring free thought, are seeking to foster.

The indifference or antagonism to ideas on the part of puritanical countries like Saudi Arabia and Libya is actually an extreme case of a general trend that began in late medieval times. Muslim orthodoxy, frightened at certain ideas thrown up by the philosophical movement within Islam, exorcised philosophy from the curricula. Philosophy, where it did survive, continued at an impoverished level (except in Iran, where it blossomed brilliantly into a new form of intellectual mysticism, known as 'Irfān).

As we have pointed out in Chapters V and VII, Muslim theologians did not create a new philosophy on the basis of the Qur'ān, which would have been equally as sophisticated as, and yet much truer to Islam than, this philosophy of the 'philosophers'; they instead substituted certain dogmatic propositions which, although superficially faithful to Islam, were, in fact, its caricature in many respects—for example, the proposition that seeks to prove physical resurrection by saying that some 'fundamental atom' (*'ujb al-dhanab*) survives physical disintegration after death, around which God will rebuild a body either identical with, or similar to, the original one.

But, as we have pointed out elsewhere,[1] the Qur'ān itself not only has a great deal of definitive philosophic teaching, but also can be a powerful catalyst for the building up of a comprehensive world view consistent with that teaching. That has never been systematically attempted in Islamic history; it can and must be done.

After the general world view, a systematic attempt must be made to elaborate an ethics on the basis of the Qur'ān, for without an explicitly formulated ethical system, one can never do justice to Islamic law. As has been pointed out in Chapter IV, Muslim legists have not clearly differentiated between the strictly legal and the moral. One advantage of this omission has been the permeation of law with living ethical values (unlike the modern secular systems of law), but the same result can be obtained by systematizing law and ethics and linking the former with the latter *organically*. Law has to be worked out *from* the ethical systematization of the teaching of the Qur'ān and the *uswa* (*sunna*) of the Prophet, with due regard to the situation currently obtaining. Thus, law will adjust to changed social situations, but ethical values or long-range sociomoral objectives will remain constant. This too has never been done before; instead, emphasis has been laid on certain dead or purely formal and extrinsic formulae.

It is for this essential and inescapable task that we most need a recultivation of ideas. In Chapter XIV we passed judgment on our medieval heritage of theology, law and Ṣūfism, and made the plea for its reconstruction. It needs to be reemphasized here that our medieval theological heritage—whether Mu'tazilī, Sunnī or Shi'ī—is essentially a product of history and bears little direct relationship to the Qur'ān and the Prophet themselves. One should perhaps say, therefore, that Islamic theology/philosophy has to be rebuilt afresh on the basis of the Qur'ān, rather than reconstructed from this medieval heritage. How does one reconstruct, for example the medieval theological doctrines of God and His attributes? It is clear enough that the Mu'tazilī doctrine of the denial of attributes was palpably influenced by the totally extrinsic Trinitarian doctrine of Christianity (with whose representatives, among others, the Mu'tazila were waging controversies). But what light can it throw on the Qur'ānic God to know how to conceive of one God out of three hypostases? The very starting point of this doctrine and the whole controversy around it is, therefore, wrong.

But the greatest desideratum of medieval Islamic thought is in the field of ethics. One cannot point to a single work of ethics squarely based upon the Qur'ān, although there are numerous works based upon Greek philosophy, Persian tradition and Ṣūfī piety. Although all these have been, to a greater or lesser extent, integrated with the Qur'ān, they cannot be regarded essentially as expressions of it. Even the Ḥadīth literature, although correct in its essential spirit, must because of its diffuse and abstract character be collated with and streamlined by the Qur'ān. Such a work of ethics will represent the essence of the Qur'ān, for the Qur'ān is primarily an ethical teaching (with a theological base), and not a book of law.

Our lawyers often went too far in simply converting rhetorical or ethical statements of the Qur'ān into legal ones, while not going far enough in deriving legal norms from verses with an obvious legal import. Thus, on the one hand, in XXXIII, 28–29, the Prophet is directed to say to his wives that if they want worldly goods, he will give these to them, but then he will 'let them go in gentleness . . . but if they want God and His Prophet . . .'. The obvious meaning of these verses is the moral one, that the Prophet's wives should not demand worldly goods, but the lawyers took them to mean that a man may make over (*takhyīr*) to his wife, at any time during his life, the choice of either remaining with him or divorcing him—as a legal procedure. (It is to be noted that this is different from another legal procedure, called *tafwīḍ,* whereby a husband may, by a clause written into the marriage contract, delegate to his wife the right of divorcing him.) On the other hand, in IV, 3, where the Qur'ān explicitly states that a man may not marry more than one wife if he fears he may not be able to do justice among them, the lawyers, instead of treating this as a law, left the question up to the husband to decide! Again, when in XXIV, 33, the Qur'ān asks that slaves be freed on payment of freedom contracts, the lawyers took it as a pure 'recommendation', without any binding legal effect. This is why it is so imperative to treat ethical values of the Qur'ān separately and then to derive law from them.

Besides the cultivation of a strong Islamic intellectual base, the creation of some adequate political order both within each country and between Muslim countries is absolutely necessary if Islam is to participate positively in the fashioning of a new world order. At the intra-Muslim level certain developments have occurred during the past decade, resulting in two Islamic summit conferences (Rabat, 1969, and Lahore, 1974) and the setting up of a permanent Islamic secretariat at Jeddah. Frequent periodic ministerial level meetings have taken place with economic-cultural agenda and deliberations on the feasibility of a Muslim news agency, while an Islamic development bank has already started functioning. These developments are undoubtedly born of the intense emotional attachment that an average Muslim feels toward Islam and Islamic unity. Generally speaking, however, for the ruling elites it is more a matter of nostalgia for the shared historic past, heightened by bitterness against Western hegemony, than a conscious vision of an Islamic sociopolitical order. This nostalgia, though, can be very powerful. Indeed, in those countries, such as Turkey, where Islam has for decades been removed as the basis of the state and of collective life and a new generation is at the helm of affairs, Islam seems to have become part of the nationalist feeling. Indeed, beginning with the 1973 elections, a political party has emerged in Turkey with a sizeable membership in the parliament (either by itself or aligned with like-minded parties and groups), which has taken its stand on an Islamic platform.

But because of the lack of any Islamic vision of an economic-political order, the orientations of many Muslim countries are simply bewildering. Islam, of course, is not the name of a monolithic economic or political system: the basic requirement of the Qur'ān, as must have become clear from Chapters I and II, is the establishment of a social order *on a moral foundation,* that would aim at the realization of egalitarian social and economic values. Any system will be Islamic that is based on these values and takes cognizance of the limits of a country's resources. (Denial of human rights and refusal of human obligations are also anathema.) Thus neither socialism nor capitalism is in itself a requirement of Islam. If all the current wealth of the entire Muslim world were to be shared uniformly by the global Muslim community (something which at present cannot even be dreamed of), there would probably be enough capital to rule out any drastic socialization of the means of production. But given the present financial conditions, one would expect Libya or Iraq to be a 'rightist', and Bangladesh to be a 'leftist', country. And yet the case is actually almost the opposite. The reason is the impact, on the minds of the ruling elites, of all sorts of 'ideologies' with which they are fascinated, irrespective both of the demands of realism and of the sociomoral imperatives of Islam.

Until the time of the third Caliph, 'Uthmān, the original Islamic impulse for socioeconomic justice remained strong, particularly thanks to certain measures of 'Umar I, and the state was seen as an instrument for such justice. But the situation changed for the worse in the latter half of 'Uthmān's Caliphate. Owing largely to the vast social revolution, which brought increasing discontent to many bedouin tribes, the Persian clients, and others, and partly to the greed of the Marwānid family of 'Uthmān, the state lost that image which was hardly ever to be effectively restored in Islamic history; even though some rulers were better than others, the organic link envisioned by the Qur'ān between the ideals of the state and economic justice was severed for good. The later ideal of justice, which came from the Persian tradition during the 'Abbāsid period and influenced the Muslim state so deeply and enduringly, applied more to the class balance within the Community than to the relation between the Community and the ruler. A tremendous gap arose between the Community and the ruler who, no matter how much allowance one makes for the inevitable differentiation of functions in the increasing complexity of state life, was in theory no more than the chief executive officer employed by the Community to carry out its will.

The Sunnī political theory, which, like the Sunnī theological doctrine emerged as a reaction to certain extremist views of the Khārijites and later of the Shī'a, was basically rooted in pragmatism. In opposition to the Khārijites, the Sunnīs asserted that it was not necessary for the ruler to be free from major errors, and, against the Shī'a, they denied the infallibility and transcendence of the Imām. Why must the ruler be infallible, asks al-Bāqillānī, if he can be advised, admonished and warned by the Community which must wrest its rights from him,[2] and which can, in theory, depose him? So far so good. Further, it is also true that the power of the ruler was limited by the Sharī'a, the constitution of the Muslim Community, and, therefore, that a 'Muslim tyrant' was a sort of contradiction in terms.

But, once again, the Sharī'a by itself is an impersonal entity; the operative persons in the political field—the military commanders, the high civil servants and, sometimes, the 'Ulamā'—may be effective occasionally but other times may be so weak that a ruler of strong will could both suppress and bypass them. And whose representatives were these personages, created mostly by the rulers themselves? There was, in effect, no link between the ruler and the Community at large, and if there is more or less cohesive Muslim Community in the world today, it is because of the 'Ulamā' and the Sharī'a, not because of rulers.

Any Islamic reform now must begin with education. Although an Islamic orientation has to be created at the primary level of education, it is at the higher level that Islam and modern intellectualism must be integrated to generate a modern, genuinely Islamic *Weltanschauung*. We have already made some remarks about this process in this Epilogue, and for a more detailed treatment the reader is referred to our *Islamic Education and Modernity*.[3] Educational reform is the only approach for a long-term solution of the current problems of the Muslim societies—mental dichotomy and unintegrated collective and individual life, resulting in confusion in all fields of human endeavor and frustration and crises that paralyze life. But educational reform can neither be accomplished nor show results overnight: it is a process which, if undertaken, will take two generations. In the meantime, certain short-term measures can be taken to create an authentic Islamic political orientation and a higher intellectualism, as an effective starting point for the Islamization of all aspects of life.

As for political life, its foundation is the Muslim Community itself. This Community is constituted by its acceptance of the Sharī'a, or Islamic imperative, as its goal; i.e., it agrees that it shall realize the Sharī'a gradually in its individual and collective life. The Caliph was nothing more than the chief executive officer who undertook to execute the Community's will, i.e., the Sharī'a. This can now be done by an elected president or prime minister who enjoys the Community's mandate for a defined and restricted period of time. The process is totally democratic, since the Commuity is freely constituted by its voluntary acceptance of the Sharī'a: that Islam can or will be imposed upon the Community by a group or a government in case it chooses to give it up for some other goal is not only Islamically absurd, it is physically impossible. This free Community, by its free will, also elects an assembly. This is also Islamically correct and democratically sound; there is absolutely no reason to believe otherwise.

The question has troubled many Muslims and Western scholars of Islam as to who is to legislate in Islam, i.e., who is to interpret the

Islamic imperative in a legal sense. The source of this trouble does not lie in Islam but in Islamic history, where while the Community at least theoretically elected an executive head, it did not elect a legislative body. But it was, surely, an accident of history that lawmakers in Islam have been private individuals who, through their personal moral and intellectual influence and that of their schools, were able to have their legal opinions accepted by large segments of the Community. Indeed, in the early years of Islam after the Prophet, the head of the state did legislate by an informal consultation with the leaders of the Community. What can now prevent a legislative assembly chosen by the people from enacting Islamic laws? Those who have qualms about this procedure think that the legal interpretation of Islam cannot be left to the people (assembly members), since they are generally 'ignorant of Islam', and that it is the function of the 'Ulamā' to enact Islam into law. This is a big and dangerous fallacy. For one thing, the Qur'ān is not such a mysterious or difficult work that one needs technically trained people to interpret its imperatives. If it were, it could not address itself to the Community at large. There is certainly a correct procedure for understanding the Qur'ān. One should study it in historical order to appreciate the development of its themes and ideas (otherwise, one is apt to be misled on certain important points). One should then study it in its sociohistorical background—this applies not only to individual passages, for which there were what the Qur'ān commentators call 'occasions of Revelation', but also to the Qur'ān as a whole, for which there was a background in pagan Mecca that can be called 'the occasion of the Qur'ān'. Without understanding this macro-and-micro background adequately, one is likely to err greatly even in assessing the basic élan and purpose of the Qur'ān and the activity of the Prophet.[4] But there is nothing technical about any of this procedure. On certain difficult matters the assembly can get expert advice.

The function of the 'Ulamā' is not to legislate but to provide religious leadership to the Community at large by their teaching, preaching and diffusion of Islamic ideas to the public. It is obvious that the legislation will be genuinely Islamic only to the extent that the public conscience and mind are both Islamic; only to that extent can the public throw up an Islamic political leadership. Neither will God immediately tell the assembly what to enact, nor can the 'Ulamā' directly dictate to the assembly—their expert advice on certain matters will be tendered through committees or councils. The 'Ulamā' 's real creative direct link is only with the public. If there is more than one opinion on a certain issue—and there is bound to be difference of opinion on most issues—let the public be persuaded through discussion and debate, for there is no other way in a democratic society.

When the assembly enacts a certain law, that law may be right or wrong (for no individual or group is inerrant), but in so far as it reflects the will of the Community, it will be both Islamic and democratic; i.e., it will represent the consensus (*Ijmāʿ*) of the Community. But this is a consensus that can always be changed, since it is always potentially possible for a minority opinion to become a majority opinion through the process of debate. The medieval juristic doctrines of *Ijmāʿ* often contend that an *Ijmāʿ* arrived at by one generation is binding upon all future generations, although some authorities hold that an *Ijmāʿ* can be changed. So there is no consensus on the doctrine of consensus! Again, jurists sharply disagree as to the points on which a consensus actually exists. According to some, there is no consensus except that there are five 'basic' duties and that the first is the profession that there is no god but Allāh; the details of the other four are still open to dispute. There is also a question as to how a consensus, if one existed, could be transmitted, i.e., whether it can be transmitted through verbal reports which are always few in number. In any case, the point here is that a decision arrived at by an assembly has nothing irreversible about it, and yet it does in an effective sense represent the *Ijmāʿ* of the Community.

Since Islam does not belong to a particular people or nation but to the world Muslim Community, it is requisite that each national legislative assembly elect certain members to represent it at an international assembly of Muslim countries. Such an assembly could meet perhaps at Mecca for two or three weeks after the Pilgrimage each year. A chairman could be elected by the assembly itself for a period of perhaps three years. The function of this body should not be legislation on issues under discussion but only advice or suggestion, which would then be enacted into law by national assemblies in the light of the local/regional differences in the physical environment and social situation in each country. At an early stage of the growth of legal schools, there were such regional differences—for example, between the schools of the Ḥijāz, Iraq and Syria. These differences, however, although due to environment, were mostly attributed by lawyers to mistakes in interpretation of the Qur'ān and the Sunna of the Prophet. Now there exists a far greater diversity in regional environments. But a bona fide attempt must be made by each national assembly to bring about a legal enactment as close to the advice tendered by the international body as possible; otherwise the whole attempt would become a farce and one could not speak of a 'Muslim world' as a coherent entity.

There is absolutely no reason why the law enacted through this procedure should not be genuinely Islamic. Indeed, in an important sense it would be more Islamic than the law of the traditional schools, for that law was the work of individual interpreters, and no matter how able and great many of them were, an individual mind cannot compete with a collective mind. The question, then, as to who is competent or 'authorized' to interpret divine law turns out to be not a serious question at all, since the physical source of all authority and power is the Muslim Community itself. It is common knowledge that Islam has neither a Brahmanical class nor any real analogue to the Christian Church. The idea of an international Muslim assembly was first broached by Muḥammad Iqbāl on the basis of a statement made by the Turkish nationalist thinker Ziya Gökalp; it was severely criticized by the late Professor H. A. R. Gibb as an introduction of papacy into Islam.[6] I fail to understand the basis of this criticism. The papal institution represents God (ex cathedra); the envisaged assembly represents the Muslim Community. The former claims infallibility, the latter by definition cannot. But if the idea is that legislation in Islam may not be enacted and imposed 'from the top' by a council or an assembly, but must remain the work of private individuals as in the past, then why not criticize the idea of a *national* assembly rather than that of an *international* assembly, since the latter, as we have said above, cannot have a strictly legislative function but can play only an advisory role, merely suggesting lines along which legislation should proceed or policy be formed? As for a national assembly whose function is to legislate, not only is it not inerrant, as we have pointed out, but its legislation is subject to change and even reversal; more importantly, it cannot impose anything from the top since it is elected by the people themselves for a given number of years.

As for the creation of a higher intellectualism, we have already described it briefly here and referred the reader for further elaboration to our monograph *Islamic Education and Modernity*. The development of a theology/philosophy, ethics, law and social science based on the Qur'ān and the model of the Prophet must, in fact, in some sense precede any actual undertaking of educational reform. For although reformed education can and does create a higher intellectualism, it presupposes a general intellectual ferment as expressed in creative works of high quality. At present Islamic intellectualism is virtually dead, and the Muslim world presents the uninviting spectacle of a vast intellectual desert in the depths of whose wilderness there hardly stirs a thought but whose deadening silence itself may sometimes resemble the apparition of a flutter. This is the

Community for whose younger generation Muḥammad Iqbāl addressed his earnest prayer about four decades ago:

> May God introduce your spirit to a [new] tempest,
> For there is hardly a stir in the waters of your sea![7]

There was, indeed, a good deal of intellectual ferment for about a century before Iqbāl's death. But why has the half-century since been so barren? One answer may be that the Muslim world has been preoccupied in this half-century with liberation struggles against Western colonialism and, subsequent to liberation, with reconstruction programs. But it is also true that when people are pressed hard by challenges and are engaged in dangerous struggles, their creativity reaches unusual heights. And what 'reconstruction' is this, of which intellectual reconstruction and spiritual regeneration form little or no part? One may also say that in the post-World War II era intellectual creativity has receded in the West itself, which is now almost blindly engaged in creating 'instruments' of a civilization which has neither goals nor much of a content. This technological explosion is, in a sense, a riposte to an earlier intellectual explosion, the period extending over several centuries that was characterized by perhaps the most brilliant and sustained intellectual creativity man has ever experienced. Unfortunately, it was also characterized by an aimless emptiness, in which man as a whole, man as a concrete entity in an existential situation presenting certain dire and concrete problems, was lost sight of. The technological frenzy that has followed is equally aimless, although it is concrete enough. Neither that intellectualism nor this technology addresses man in his concrete wholeness, including his moral or human dimension.[8] Muslims are simply imitating this technology.

The question, however, is why must the Muslims look to and imitate the West? They claim to possess a teaching which is guidance for mankind, which can create a whole civilization by absorbing necessary materials from other civilizations and cultures, and which, above all, aims at bending the flow of history toward the goal of an ethically based social order. Is this grand and fateful dream not worthy of the intellectual effort necessary to spell it out, to define its nature, its goals and something of its content? Muslims have decisively rejected both those religious dreams that make this world indifferent to its fate in history and the dream of Communism that does violence to the nature of man, shortsightedly distorts history and turns it upside down. Do not these basically correct negative claims cast some obligation upon Muslims to say something positive, if only for the sake of directing their own efforts toward a concrete enough goal?

But the most important and immediate reason, we suggest, for the Muslim world's failure thus far to regenerate itself is the ubiquitous emergence of fundamentalist attitudes and movements discussed in Chapter XIII above.[9] These represent a reaction against both the West and the earlier Muslim Modernism. Their main thrust is toward discovering certain features of Islam that would distinguish the Muslim world from the West, since their charge against Muslim Modernism was that it had identified the two too easily. The distinguishing marks of Islam are now mostly found to be an interest-free form of banking, *zakāt* (the tax ordained by the Qur'ān), and the traditional role of women (in view of the breakdown of the family that Western societies are experiencing on an increasingly large scale). Each of these demands, by itself, is salutary, except that fundamentalism is advocating them not for their own sake but for that of the distinctiveness they would confer on Muslim society vis-à-vis the West. The result is a truncated and unhealthy approach to these and other similar issues. It is sheer confusion to identify the system of *ribā* (usury) banned by the Qur'ān with that of modern banking and interest, which is a special device within the context of a modern concept of 'development economy' with an utterly different function. Nor has *zakāt* been adopted in any Muslim country, simply because they all have got used to other forms of taxation. And whether maintaining women in their traditional role can coexist with change in other social sectors, particularly education and economy, remains to be seen.

The distinctiveness as well as the practicality of Islam may be demonstrated, however, by a bona fide attempt, as described here, to found an ethically based social order on earth. If the Muslim can successfully attempt this task, he will have implemented the basic èlan of the Qur'ān and saved mankind from what seems to be nothing less than suicide. Otherwise, there is little left for him to do but indulge in a trivial and vainglorious self-satisfaction; only 'vainglory can be no substitute for Truth', as the Qur'ān has it (LIII, 28).

NOTES

CHAPTER I: MUḤAMMAD

1. Ibn Hishām (Ibn Isḥāq), *Sīra*, Cairo 1937, I, 255; Engl. transl. A. Guillaume, London 1955.
2. See e.g. F. Buhl, 'Muḥammad', in the *Shorter Encyclopaedia of Islam.*
3. Ibn Khaldūn, *Muqaddima,* Engl. transl. F. Rosenthal, New York 1958, I, 279.
4. See his *Ḥujjat Allāh al-Baligha,* Cairo 1322 AH, I, 93 ff.
5. Qur'ān, VIII, 66.

CHAPTER III: ORIGINS AND DEVELOPMENT OF THE TRADITION

1. I. Goldziher, *Muhammedanische Studien*[2], 1961, II, 5, line 14 ff.
2. E.g. VIII, 38; XV, 13; XXXVI, 69 ff.
3. XXXIII, 62; XXXV, 43; XLII, 23; XVII, 77.
4. I. Goldziher, *op. cit.*, 13.
5. *ibid.*, 12, line 6 ff., where a curious distinction is drawn between Ḥadīth and Sunna.
6. See the chapter on Tradition.
7. See chapter IV, 69, line 35 ff.
8. That J. Schacht himself does not wish to make any distinction, from this point of view, between legal and non-legal *Ḥadīth* is shown by his many observations; see especially the Preface to his *Origins of Muhammadan Jurisprudence*, Oxford 1950.
9. See *ibid.*, part I, chapter I; but also part II, 138–76.
10. *ibid.*, 138.
11. III, 32, 132; IV, 58; V, 95, etc.
12. LIX, 7.
13. IV, 64.
14. III, 159 (cf. XLVIII, 38).
15. In fact, IV, 64 has reference to such an incident that occurred over the distribution of war-booty.
16. Ibn Qutayba, *Ta'wīl Mukhtalif al-Ḥadīth*, Cairo 1326 AH, 31–2.
17. *Der Islam*, XXI, 67 ff. (text edited by H. Ritter).
18. *ibid.*, beginning of the text.
19. J. Schacht, *op. cit.*, 141.
20. *Der Islam, op. cit.*, the first page of Ḥasan's reply. This does not, however, prove that the Prophet himself had never expressed *any* views discussed by dogmatic theology, although it is, of course, true that the orthodox position, as such, was developed much later and, as a whole, has little to do with what the Prophet may or may not have said. On the point under consideration, indeed, Sunnī orthodoxy came to espouse a position directly opposed to that of Ḥasan al-Baṣrī.
21. *Der Islam, loc. cit.*, the last sentence of the text.
22. *Ibn Māja*, 4 (the preliminary section of the work is about the necessity and value of Ḥadīth, etc.).
23. This Ḥadīth exists in almost all well-known collections of Ḥadīth; see *Mishkāt al-Maṣābīḥ, Kitāb al-'Ilm*; Ḥadīth no. 1, etc.
24. Al-Shāfi'ī, *K. al-Umm*, Cairo ed., VII, 255, line 4 ff.; also bottom of p. 243.
25. *ibid.*, 244.
26. *ibid.*, 240, line 2 ff.
27. Pp. 250–4 of *K. al-Umm* are specifically directed against them.
28. *ibid.*, 250, line 16 ff.

29. *ibid.*, 252, the case of evidence in a murder case.
30. Ibn Qutayba, *op. cit.*, 397 ff.
31. There is such a group in the Indo-Pakistan subcontinent, who call themselves 'People of the Qur'ān' (*Ahl al-Qur'ān*). They have produced a considerable volume of literature, and also issue an Urdu journal entitled *Ṭulū'-i Islām* from Lahore (formerly from Delhi). This type of thought, however, is not common in the Middle East.

CHAPTER IV: THE STRUCTURE OF THE LAW

1. E.g., Qur'ān, IX, 44; LXXX, 1.
2. Ibn Hishām, *Sīra*, IV, 341.
3. With the development of systematic reasoning, the use of *ra'y* was severely condemned by the Ahl al-Ḥadīth. Every major and systematic collection of Ḥadīth contains alleged Prophetic traditions denouncing personal opinion.
4. *Kitāb al-Umm*, VII, 258, line 2 ff.
5. By 'knowledge of the specialists' is meant that knowledge which is the result of individual thought and is also transmitted by isolated channels of transmission and is not agreed upon by the Community at large.
6. *Kitāb al-Umm*, VII, 255, line 17; 256, line 1.
7. His *Selected Writings*, edited by G.-H. Bousquet and J. Schacht, Leiden 1957, 228, 275, etc., but also his *Islam*, the chapter on *Ijmā'*; see also D. Santillana, quoted by H. A. R. Gibb in *Muhammedanism*, pp. 96–7, 98.
8. Ibn Qutayba, *op. cit.*, 331.
9. Al-Māwardī, *al-Aḥkām al-Sulṭānīya*, Cairo 1356/1938, 4; indeed, all the collections of Ḥadīth containing predictive traditions about civil wars either expressly mention or imply this idea.
10. See e.g. Ibn Taymīya's *al-Siyāsa al-Shar'īya*, Cairo 1951, 173.
11. This doctrine is a direct development from the early Sunnī view contained in Ḥadīth that people must 'keep to the majority (of the Community) and their political leader'.
12. *Muhammedanism*, 90.

CHAPTER V: DIALECTICAL THEOLOGY AND THE DEVELOPMENT OF DOGMA

1. Qur'ān, VI, 57.
2. Cf. H. S. Nyberg, 'al-Mu'tazila', in *Shorter Encyclopaedia of Islam.*
3. H. S. Nyberg's edition of *Kitāb al-Intiṣār*, Cairo 1925; also his article 'al-Mu'tazila', in the *Shorter Encyclopaedia of Islam.*
4. This has been especially studied by S. van den Bergh in his edition of Averroes' *Tahāfut al-Tahāfut*, II (commentary on the first volume which consists of a translation of the Arabic text), Oxford 1955.
5. H. A. R. Gibb, *Muhammedanism*, 116.
6. S. van den Bergh, *op. cit.*, I, Introduction, p. x. The story is celebrated in Muslim religious circles in varying versions.
7. See e.g. his article 'Ḳadar', in *Shorter Encyclopaedia of Islam*; but this view is repeated in his other works also.

CHAPTER VI: THE SHARĪ'A

1. Qur'ān, XLVIII, 13.
2. *ibid.*, XLVIII, 21.
3. See I. Goldziher: *Richtungen der islamischen Koranauslegung*, chapter II; *Encyclopaedia of Islam*, articles "Ilm' and 'Fiḳh'.
4. I. Goldziher, 'Fiḳh', in *Encyclopaedia of Islam*, first edition.
5. Al-Ash'arī's *Risāla fī Istiḥsān al-Khawḍ fi'l-Kalām* in Richard J. McCarthy, *The Theology of al-Ash'arī*, Beirut 1953, 94–5 (Arabic text).
6. F. Raḥmān, *Prophecy in Islam*, London 1958, 97 (reference to al-Ghazālī's *Ma'ārij al-Quds*).
7. The clearest statement of moral relativism is to be found in al-Ghazālī's *al-Iqtiṣād fi'l-I'tiqād*, 73–80.
8. *ibid.*, 78.
9. *ibid.*, 79.
10. *ibid.*, 73.
11. Al-Ghazālī, *Iḥyā' 'Ulūm al-Dīn*, ed. Ḥalabī, Cairo 1346/1927, I, 93.
12. Al-Ījī, *Kitāb al-Mawāqif*, with commentaries by al-Jurjānī and others, Cairo 1325 AH, I, 40–9.
13. Al-Shahrastānī, *Nihāyat al-Iqdām*, 463.
14. Al-Ījī, *op. cit.*, 36–7.
15. *ibid.*, 43–6.
16. Al-Shāṭibī, *Kitāb al-Muwāfaqāt*, Cairo 1302 AH, 45.
17. Al-Ash'arī, *op. cit.* (*K. al-Luma'*), 41.
18. Ibn Taymīya, *Muwāfaqāt Ṣarīh al-Ma'qūl li-Ṣaḥīḥ al-Manqūl*, Cairo 1321 AH, I, 48 (printed on the margin of *Minhāj al-Sunna* by the same author). This whole book is, indeed, devoted to this theme.
19. Ibn Taymīya, *Al-Iḥtijāj bi'l-Qadar*, in his *Rasā'il*, Cairo 1323 AH, II, 96–7.
20. Ibn Taymīya, *Al-Irādah wa'l-Amr*, in his *Rasā'il*, Cairo 1323 AH, I, 348.
21. *ibid.*, I, 341.
22. *ibid.*, I, 334–5.
23. This is the synthesis proposed by Ibn Taymīya between Mu'tazilism and Ash'arism in his works *Muwāfaqāt Ṣarīḥ al-Ma'qūl li-Ṣaḥīḥ al-Manqūl* and *al-Iḥtijāj bi'l-Qadar*, 91; see also *Marātib al-Irāda*, in *Rasā'il*, II, 70–1.
24. Ibn Taymīya, *Al-Iḥtijāj bi'l-Qadar*, 91.
25. Ibn Taymīya, *Al-Irādah wa'l-Amr*, 361, line 20 ff.
26. *ibid.*, 361, line 15 ff.
27. Al-Shāṭibī, *op. cit.*, I, 5, line 14.
28. Shāh Walī Allāh al-Dihlawī, *Ḥujjat Allāh al-Bāligha*, Cairo 1322 AH, I, 16–19 (chapter concerning the fact that these (religious and moral) obligations flow from Divine Determinism).
29. Al-Shāṭibī, *op. cit.*, 16, last line ff.

CHAPTER VII: THE PHILOSOPHICAL MOVEMENT

1. *Kitāb al-Najāt*, Cairo 1938, 248.
2. See his *al-Madīna al-Fāḍila*, ed. A. Nadir, Beirut 1959, 118.
3. See my *Prophecy in Islam*, London 1958, 42 ff., 81 (n. 64).
4. Averroes, *Tahāfut al-Tahāfut*, Engl. transl. S. van den Bergh, Oxford 1954, I, 362.
5. Cf. his works *al-Mabāḥīth al-Mashriqīya* and *al-Muḥaṣṣil* where a comprehensive scholastic treatment of, and response to, the philosophical theses appears.
6. Al-Ījī, *Kitāb al-Mawāqif* with al-Jurjānī's commentary, Cairo 1325 AH, I, 46.
7. See Chapter VI, section II.
8. His commentary on Ibn Sīnā's *Ishārāt*, Tehran, III, 97 ff.; also his commentary on al-Rāzī's *al-Muḥaṣṣil*, Cairo 1323 AH, 53, n. 2.
9. See my article 'Post-formative developments in Islam' in *Islamic Studies*, Karachi, II/iii (June 1963), 297–316.

CHAPTER VIII: ṢŪFĪ DOCTRINE AND PRACTICE

1. I. Goldziher, *Vorlesungen*, Heidelberg 1925, 152.
2. Translated by R. A. Nicholson in his *Literary History of the Arabs*, 234; Arabic text, L. Massignon, *Recueil de textes inédits*, Paris 1929, 6.
3. *Shorter Encyclopaedia of Islam, s.v.* 'Ma'rūf al-Karkhī'.
4. A good discussion of this question will be found in R. A. Nicholson's *Literary History of the Arabs*; little essentially new has been added since.
5. See Chapter X. It is not yet scientifically established as to when the doctrine of *raj'a*, 'the return of the Imām after death', was adopted by the Shī'a and to which personage it was attached first. The title Mahdī, 'the divinely-guided one', it seems, was first applied to a step-son of 'Alī and Fāṭima, Muḥammad ibn al-Ḥanafīya. It is most probable that the 'return' was also attributed to him first and then projected back to 'Alī. See I. Goldziher, *Vorlesungen*, 216, 360, although the subject needs further investigation. Also see *Islamic Studies*, Karachi, II/i (March, 1963), article 'Sayyid Muḥammad Jawnpūrī and his movement' by A. S. Bazmee Ansari.
6. L. Massignon, *Recueil de textes inédits*, 33. Also cf. al-Tirmidhī, *Khatm al-Wilāya*, ed. 'Osman I. Yahya, Beirut 1965.
7. See the *Kashf al-Mahjūb* of Abū 'Alī al-Hūjwīrī, a very valuable work on Ṣūfī doctrines, Engl. transl. R. A. Nicholson (Gibb Memorial Series) 242 ff.; also L. Massignon, *Lexique technique de la mystique musulmane*[2], Paris 1954, 301.
8. L. Massignon, *Lexique technique de la mystique musulmane*[2], 355, quoted from *K. al-Ta'arruf* of al-Kalābādhī.
9. L. Massignon, *op. cit.*, 305: *Recueil de textes inédits*, 29.
10. L. Massignon, *Lexique technique*, 305. The interpretations of Professor Massignon, however, should be read with some care, for sometimes they threaten to become too subjective.
11. L. Massignon, *Recueil*, 80.
12. Edited with a Turkish translation by Y. Z. Yorukan, Istanbul 1953, section 22 (pp. 15–16 of the Arabic text).
13. The farthest that the 'Ulamā' have officially gone to meet the Ṣūfī position is represented by al-Taftāzānī's remark (during his discussion of Faith – *Īmān* – on al-Nasafī's famous creed) that *Ṣūfī* intuition is valid for the experiencing subject himself but not for others.
14. L. Massignon, *Recueil*, 41 (no. 3).
15. *ibid.*, 41 (no 5).
16. *ibid.*, 39 (no. 1).

CHAPTER IX: ṢŪFI ORGANIZATIONS

1. O. Depont and X. Coppolani, *Les Confréries religieuses musulmanes*, Algiers 1897, 208.
2. Quoted from H. A R. Gibb, *Muhammedanism*[2], Oxford 1961, 150–1.
3. R. A. Nicholson, *Rūmī, Poet and Mystic*[2], London 1950, 170.
4. Depont and Coppolani, *op. cit.*, 326.
5. *ibid.*, 521, 530.

NOTES

CHAPTER X: SECTARIAN DEVELOPMENTS

1. I. Goldziher, *Vorlesungen*, 188.
2. Al-Jāḥiz, *Kitāb al-Bayān wa'l Tabyīn*, Cairo 1948, II, 124–5.
3. I. Goldziher, *op. cit.*, 195.
4. *ibid.*, 215.
5. H. Corbin, Introduction to the edition of Nāṣir-i Khusraw's *Jāmi' al-Ḥikmatayn*, Paris and Teheran 1953.

CHAPTER XI: EDUCATION

1. Ibn Khaldūn, *Muqaddima*, VI. 29; A. S. Tritton, *Materials on Muslim Education in the Middle Ages*, London 1957.
2. Ibn Khallikān, *Wafayāt al-A'yān*, Cairo 1948, ed. G. M. Wickens, 420–1; (cf. A. J. Arberry, *Avicenna, Scientist and Philosopher*, London 1962, chapter I).
3. Kātib Chelebī, *Balance of Truth* (Engl. transl. from Turkish by G. L. Lewis), London 1957, 25.
4. S. M. Ikrām, *Rūd-i Kawthar*, Karachi 1958, 424–6.
5. See e.g. the Commentary on the Qur'ān entitled *Sawāṭi' al-Ilhām* by Fayḍī Fayyāḍī (d. 1004/1596), a prominent savant at the court of the Mughal emperor Akbar, published in Lucknow in 1306 AH.
6. This is the method also recommended by Ibn Khaldūn (*op. cit.*), who believes that the teaching of more than one subject simultaneously confuses the mind. This procedure was normally adopted.
7. Shāh Walī Allāh al-Dihlawī's brief autobiographical note entitled *al-Juz' al-Laṭīf fī Bayān Aḥwāl al-'Abd Ḍa'īf*, an appendix to his *Anfās al-'Ārifīn*, Delhi n.d.

CHAPTER XII: PRE-MODERNIST REFORM MOVEMENTS

1. Al-Shawkānī, *Nayl al-Awṭār*, Cairo 1297 AH, I, 2–3.
2. Ibn 'Abd al-Wahhāb, *Masā'il al-Jāhilīya*, elaborated by al-Ālūsī, Salafi Press, Cairo 1347 AH, 11–13.
3. This has been studied in my forthcoming *Selected Letters of Sirhindī*, Karachi.
4. E.g., *Indian Islam* by Murray T. Titus, Oxford 1930, 182 (re-issued as *Islam in India and Pakistan*, 1961). But while there is no evidence that Sayyid Aḥmad was influenced by the Wahhābīs (Murray Titus speaks, without any support, of Sayyid Aḥmad's 'travels through Arabia and Syria'), it is stated by Ghulām Rasūl Mihr in his biography of Sayyid Aḥmad that al-Shawkānī performed pilgrimage at the same time as Sayyid Aḥmad, and that al-Shawkānī presented two disciples of the latter with a copy of his famous work *Itḥāf al-Nubalā'*. See Ghulām Rasūl Mihr, *Sayyid Aḥmad Shahīd*, Lahore 1952, 233.
5. See D. S. Margoliouth, 'Wahhābīya', in *Encyclopaedia of Islam*.
6. S. M. Ikrām, *Mawj-i Kawthar*, Karachi 1958, 42, where the poet Mu'min (Mōmin) speaks of 'those who reject *taqlīd*'.
7. D. S. Margoliouth, 'Wahhābīya', in *Encyclopaedia of Islam*.
8. D. S. Margoliouth, *op. cit.*
9. Murray Titus, *op. cit.*, 181.
10. Aḥmad Muḥammad Ḥasanayn, *Fī Ṣaḥrā' Lībyā* ('In the Libyan Desert'), Cairo n.d., I, 51.
11. *ibid.*, 52.
12. *ibid.*, 53.

CHAPTER XIII: MODERN DEVELOPMENTS

1. 'I plead here with Mons. Renan, not the cause of the Muslim Religion, but that of men, hundreds of millions of men, who would be thus condemned to be living in barbarism and ignorance', A. M. Goichon, *Jamāl al-Dīn Afghānī, Réfutation des Matérialistes,* Paris 1942, 178.
2. *Khutabāt-i Sir Sayyid,* Badā'ūn 1931, 55.
3. [*Sir Sayyid ke*] *Letters kā Majmū'a,* (?) 1890, p. 2101; see also Muḥammad 'Abduh's Introduction to his *Risāla al-Tawḥīd,* Cairo 1956, 7–24, esp. 184. See also his *al-Islām wa'l Naṣrānīya,* Cairo 1375 AH, 156 ff.
4. Muḥammad 'Abduh, quoted in H. A. R. Gibb, *Modern Trends in Islam,* Chicago 1946, 43–4.
5. Muḥammad 'Abduh, *Risāla al-Tawḥīd,* 190.
6. See above Chapter III, n. 31.
7. Muḥammad 'Abduh, *Risāla al-Tawḥīd,* 186.
8. Muḥammad 'Abduh, *al-Islām wa'l-Naṣrānīya,* is devoted entirely to this theme.
9 Syed Ameer Ali [Sayyid Amīr 'Alī], *Life and Teachings of Muhammad or the Spirit of Islam,* 1st ed., London 1893 (in the later editions, the work is entitled simply *The Spirit of Islam*), especially Chapters XVIII and XIX; *idem., A Short History of the Saracens,* London 1899.
10. Muḥammad Iqbāl, *Bāl-i Jibrīl,* Lahore 1959, 116.
11. Muḥammad Iqbāl, *Reconstruction of Religious Thought in Islam,* Lahore 1944. Preface and especially p. 7 where Iqbāl talks of a rapid spiritual movement of Islam towards the West.
12. Ziya Gökalp, *Turkish Nationalism and Western Civilization* (essays translated into English by N. Berkes, Part III, VII, 'State and Religion', a perceptive analysis of the internal struggle in modern Islam.
13. *ibid.*; this position is bound up with the first one.
14. Quoted by Muḥammad Iqbāl, *Reconstruction,* etc., 159.
15. Muḥammad Iqbāl, *op. cit.,* 159.
16. H. A. R. Gibb, *Modern Trends in Islam,* 102.
17. Muḥammad Iqbāl, *Jāwīd Nāma,* 1959, 127.

CHAPTER XIV: LEGACY AND PROSPECTS

1. H. A. R. Gibb, *Modern Trends in Islam* (this entire work constitutes a critique of Muslim modernism); W. C. Smith, *Islam in Modern History,* Princeton 1957, especially chapters on 'Pakistan' and 'The Arabs'.
2. See above, Chapter III.
3. Ibn Taymīya, *al-Siyāsa al-Shar'īya,* Cairo 1951, 173.
4. *Mishkāt al-Maṣābīḥ, Kitāb al-Īmān,* where this Ḥadīth is quoted from the two most authoritative collections of Muslim and al-Bukhārī.
5. See my article, 'The post-formative developments in Islam' in *Islamic Studies,* Karachi, 1/iv (December 1962), 17.
6. Chapter III of the present work; but this point has been attempted more fully in the article 'Sunnah and Ḥadīth' in *Islamic Studies,* 1/ii (June 1962).

NOTES

EPILOGUE

1. This has been elaborated in my as yet unpublished monograph, *Islamic Education and Modernity,* Chapter IV.
2. *Kitāb al-Tamhīd,* Cairo 1947, 184.
3. Reference in note 1 above.
4. For further elaboration of this point see the 'introduction' to the work mentioned in note 1, and my contribution 'Islam: Challenges and Opportunities To-Day', being the last chapter in *Islam: Past Influence And Present Challenge,* Edinburgh University Press 1979.
5. Muhammad Iqbāl, *Reconstruction of Religious Thought in Islam,* Lahore 1962, 173 ff.
6. H. A. R. Gibb, *Modern Trends in Islam,* Chicago 1946, 112 ff., particularly pp. 113–4.
7. Muḥammad Iqbāl, *Ẓarb-i-Kalīm,* in *Kullīyāt-i-Iqbāl,* Lahore 1973, 544.
8. There has, of course, been a vast amount written on ethics, but almost all of it is an intellectual, analytical game.
9. Also see, particularly, this writer's analysis in the second reference given in note 4 above.

SELECTED BIBLIOGRAPHY

GENERAL WORKS

Ali, Syed Ameer, *The Spirit of Islam*, London, 1939
Arnold, Sir T. W., *The Preaching of Islam* (second edition), London, 1913
Arnold, Sir T. W., and Guillaume, Alfred (eds.), *The Legacy of Islam*, Oxford, 1931
Encyclopaedia of Islam, The, Leyden, 1913–38; new edition in progress
Gardet, L., *Connaître l'Islam*, Paris, 1958
Gibb, H. A. R., *Muhammedanism* (second edition), London, 1961
Goldziher, I., *Vorlesungen über den Islam*, Heidelberg, 1925
Lammens, H., *Islam, Beliefs and Institutions*, trans. Sir E. D. Ross, London, 1929

CHAPTERS I AND II

Ali, A. Yusuf, *The Holy Qur'ān*, Lahore, 1934, 1959
Ali, Syed Ameer, *op. cit.*
Andrae, Tor, *Die Person Mohammeds in Lehre and Glauben seiner Gemeinde*, Stockholm, 1918; Eng. trans. *The Man and his Faith*, London, 1936
Archer, J. C., *Mystic Elements in Mohammad*, Yale University Press, 1924
Bell, R., *The Origin of Islam in its Christian Environment*, London, 1926; *The Qur'ān*, Edinburgh, 1937–9
Blachère, R., *Introduction au Coran*, Paris, 1947
Bowman, John, 'Banū Isrā'īl in the Qur'ān', in *Islamic Studies*, ii/4, Karachi, December 1963
Buhl, Franz, *Das Leben Mohammeds*, trans. H. H. Schaeder, Berlin, 1930
Gibb, H. A. R., *op. cit.*
Hamidullah, M., *The Battlefields of the Prophet*, Lahore, 1948; *Le Prophète de L'Islam*, 2 vols., Paris, 1959
Horovitz, J., *Koranische Untersuchungen*, Berlin and Leipzig, 1926
Ibn Hishām, Guillaume, Alfred, *The Life of Muhammad*, Oxford, 1958
Jeffery, A., *The Qur'ān as Scripture*, New York, 1952
Levy, Reuben, *The Social Structure of Islam*, Cambridge, 1958
Muir, Sir William, *The Life of Mahomet* (abridged edition), Edinburgh, 1923
Nöldeke, T., and Schwally, A., *Geschichte des Qorans*, Leipzig, 1909–38
Roberts, R., *The Social Laws of the Qoran*, London, 1925
Watt, W. Montgomery, *Muhammad at Mecca*, Oxford, 1953; *Muhammad at Medina*, Oxford, 1958

CHAPTER III

Ali, M. Muhammad, *A Manual of Hadith*, Lahore, n.d.
Encyclopaedia of Islam, art. 'Ahl al-Ḥadīth', 'Ahl al-Kalām'

Goldziher, I., *Muhammedanische Studien*, vol. ii, Halle, 1890
Guillaume, Alfred, *The Traditions of Islam*, Oxford, 1924 (partly based on Goldziher's work)
Ibn Qutayba *Ta'wīl Mukhtalif al-Ḥadīth*, Cairo, 1326 AH
Ishaq, Muhammad, *India's Contribution to Hadith Literature*, Dacca, 1955
Lammens, H., *op. cit.*
Margoliouth, D. S., *The Early Development of Mohammedanism*, London, 1914
Mishkāt al-Maṣābīḥ, Eng. trans. J. Robson, Lahore, 1956–65
Robson, J., *An Introduction to the Science of Tradition*, London, 1953
Schacht, J., *The Origins of Muhammadan Jurisprudence*, Oxford, 1952
Saḥifah Hammām b. Munabbih, M. Hamidullah (ed.), fifth edition, Paris, 1380 AH
Al-Shafi'ī, *Al-Risālah*, Eng. trans. Majid Khadduri, Baltimore, 1961
Siddiqi, M. Zubayr, *Hadith Literature*, Calcutta, 1961 (gives the Muslim point of view)
A vast literature on the various aspects of Ḥadīth has been recently produced in Urdu in India and Pakistan, but this is not available to European readers.

CHAPTER IV

Fyzee, A. A. A., *Outlines of Muhammadan Law*, London, 1949
Hurgronje, C. Snouck, *Selected Works*, G.-H. Bousquet and J. Schacht (eds.), Leiden, 1957
Ibn Taymīya, *al-Siyāsa al-Shar'īya*, Cairo, 1951
Al-Māwardī, *al-Aḥkām al-Sulṭānīya*, Cairo, 1356 AH
Santillana, D., *Instituzioni diritto Musulmano malichita*, 2 vols., Rome, 1926–38

CHAPTER V

Al-Ash'arī, *Al-Ibānah fī Uṣūl al-Diyānah*, Eng. trans. *The Elucidation of Islam's Foundation*, Philadelphia, 1940; *Maqālāt al-Islāmiyyīn*, Cairo, 1950
Donaldson, D. M., *The Shī'ite Religion*, London, 1933
Fyzee, A. A. A., *A Shi'ite Creed*, London, 1924
Gardet, L., and Anawati, M. M., *Introduction à la théologie musulmane*, Paris, 1948
Al-Ghazālī, *Iḥyā' 'Ulūm al-Dīn*, Būlāq, 1289 AH (now several books have been translated into English and other European languages)
Goldziher, I., *Die Zahiriten*, Leipzig, 1884
Lammens, H., *op. cit.*
Lewis, B., *The Origins of Ismā'īlism*, Cambridge, 1940
Macdonald, D. B., *Development of Muslim Theology, Jurisprudence and Constitutional Theory*, London, 1903
Margoliouth, D. S., *op. cit.*
Nyberg, H. S. (ed.) *Kitāb al-Intiṣār*, Cairo, 1925
Obermann, J., 'Political theory in early Islam, Ḥasan al-Baṣrī's treatise on Qadar', *Journal of the American Oriental Society*, LV, 138–62, 1935

Salem, E. A., *Political Theory and Institutions of the Khawārij*, Baltimore, 1956
Shahrastānī, *Kitāb Nihāyat al-Iqdām fī 'Ilm Kalām*, ed. and trans. Alfred Guillaume, Oxford, 1934
Veccia Vaglieri, L., 'Le Vicende del Harigismo in epoca abbaside', *Rivista degli Studi Orientali*, xxiv, 31–44, 1944
Watt, W. Montgomery, *Free Will and Predestination in Early Islam*, London, 1948
Wellhausen, G., *Die religios-politischen Oppositions-Parteien im alten Islam*, Göttingen, 1901
Wensinck, A. J., *The Muslim Creed*, Cambridge, 1932; *La Pensée de Ghazzali*, Paris, 1940

CHAPTER VI

Klopfer, H., *Das Dogma des Imam al-Haramain al-Djuwaini und sein Werk al-'Aqida an Nizamiyah*, Cairo and Wiesbaden, 1958
Laoust, H., *Essai sur les Doctrines sociales et politiques de Taki-al-Din Ahmad b. Taimiya*, Cairo, 1939
McCarthy, R. J., *The Theology of al-Ash'arī*, Beirut, 1953
Rahman, F., *Prophecy in Islam*, London 1958
Al-Rāzī, *The Spiritual Physick*, trans. A. J. Arberry, London, 1950
Schacht, J., 'New sources for the history of Muhammedan theology', *Studia Islamica*, I, 23–42, 1953
Walzer, R., *Greek into Arabic*, London, 1961

CHAPTER VII

Arberry, A. J., *Revelation and Reason in Islam*, London, 1957
Averroes, *Tahāfut al-Tahāfut*, trans. S. van den Berg, 2 vols., Oxford University Press, 1954
Boer, T. de, *The History of Philosophy in Islam*, London, 1903
Gauthier, L., *Ibn Rochd (Averroes)*, Paris, 1948
Al-Ghazālī, *Tahāfut al-Falāsifa*, trans. Sabih Ahmad Kamali, Lahore, 1958
Grunebaum, G. E. von, *Medieval Islam*, University of Chicago Press, 1953
Hourani, G. F. (ed.), *Faṣl al-Maqāl*, Leiden, 1959. Eng. trans. *Ibn Rushd*, London, 1962
McCarthy, R. J. (ed. and trans.), 'al-Kindī's Treatise on Intellect', in *Islamic Studies*, III/2, Karachi, 1964
Menasce, Pierre Jean de, *Bibliographische Einfuhrungen in das Studium de Philosophie: 6, Arabische Philosophie*, Bern, 1948
Nasr, Seyyed Hossein, *Three Muslim Sages*, Harvard University Press, 1963
O'Leary, De Lacy, *Arabic Thought and its Place in History*, London, 1922
Walzer, R., 'Islamic philosophy', in *History of Philosophy, Eastern and Western* (ed. S. Radhakrishnan), London, 1953
Wickens, G. M. (ed.), *Avicenna: Scientist and Philosopher*, London, 1952

CHAPTERS VIII AND IX

Affifi, A. E., *The Mystical Philosophy of Muhyid Din-ibnul Arabi*, Cambridge, 1939

Arberry, A. J., *Introduction to the History of Sufism*, London, 1943; *Sufism*, London, 1950

Birge, J. K., *The Bektashi Order of Dervishes*, London, 1937

Depont, O., and Coppolani, X., *Les Confréries religieuses musulmanes*, Algiers, 1897

Hampate Bā, A., and Caydaire, Marcel, *Tierno Bokar Le Sage de Bandiagara*, Paris, 1957

Massignon, L., *Essai sur les origines de lexique ιechnique de la mystique musulmane*, Paris, 1922; *La Passion . . . d' al-Hallaj, martyr mystique de l'Islam*, Paris, 1922

Nicholson, R. A., *The Mystics of Islam*, London, 1914; *Studies in Islamic Mysticism*, Cambridge, 1921; *The Idea of Personality in Sufism*, London, 1943

Ziyadeh, Nicola A., *The Sanūsiyya*, Leiden, 1958

CHAPTER X

Al-Baghdādī, *al-Farq bayn al-Firāq*, Cairo, 1367 AH

Goldziher, I., *op. cit.*

Watt, W. Montgomery, *Islamic Philosophy and Theology*, Edinburgh, 1962

CHAPTER XI

'Abd al-Qādir al-Nu'aymī, *al-Dāris fī Ta'rīkh al-Madāris*, Damascus, 1367–70 AH

Aḥmad Fu'ād Ahwāni, *al-Tarbīyah fi'l-Islam*, Cairo, 1955

Dodge, Bayard, *Al-Azhar*, Washington, D.C., 1960; *Muslim Education in Medieval Times*, Washington, D.C., 1962

Shalaby, Aḥmad, *History of Muslim Education*, Beirut, 1954

Tritton, A. S., *Materials on Muslim Education in the Middle Ages*, London, 1957

CHAPTER XII

Depont, O., and Coppolani, X., *Les Confréries religieuses musulmanes*, Algiers, 1897 (covers the history of the Ṣūfī orders with special reference to North Africa)

Al-Dihlawī, Shāh Walī, Allāh, art. in *Encyclopaedia of Islam* (new edition) by A. S. Bazmee Ansari

Philby, H. St. J. B., *Arabia*, London, 1930 (gives full account of the Wah hābī movement)

Qanungo, K. R., *Dara Shikoh*, Calcutta, 1951

Rahman, F., *Selected Letters of Sirhindi*, Karachi (in the press)

Al-Shawkānī, *Nyl al-Awṭār*, Cairo, 1297 AH
Titus, Murray, *Islam in India and Pakistan*, Oxford University Press, 1961

CHAPTERS XIII AND XIV

Adams, C. C., *Islam and Modernism in Egypt*, Oxford University Press, 1933
Browne, E. G., *The Persian Revolution of 1905–1909*, Cambridge, 1910
Gibb, H. A. R. (ed.), *Whither Islam?*, London, 1932; *Modern Trends in Islam*, Chicago, 1947
Grunebaum, G. E. von, *Modern Islam*, Berkeley and Los Angeles, California, 1962
Hourani, A. H., *Syria and Lebanon*, London, 1946
Hurgronje, C. Snouck, *The Achenese*, Leyden, 1906
Iqbāl, Sir Muḥammad, *The Reconstruction of Religious Thought in Islam*, London, 1934
Smith, W. C., *Modern Islam in India*, London, 1946; *Islam in Modern History*, Princeton, 1957

INDEX

'Abbāsids, 4, 80, 82, 168
'Abd al-Malik, 55, 79
'Abduh, Muḥammad, 123, 192, 216–220
Abraham, 15, 26, 30
Abū Bakr, 40, 70
Abū Dā'ūd, 57, 64
Abū Ḥamza, 168
Abū Ḥanīfa, 72, 82, 102, 172, 182
Abū Madyan, 162
Adam, 14
'Adawīya, Rābi'a al-, 130
Afghānī, Jamāl al-Dīn, 123, 216, 226
Africa, 6, 8, 83, 140, 155, 211
Āgā Khān, 178
agreed practice (*al-'amal*), 57, 72
Ahl al-Ḥadīth, 99, 104, 111, 122, 123, 188, 194, 205
Aḥmad, Sayyid, of Rae Bareli, 203, 205, 206, 210
Aḥsā'ī, Aḥmad al-, 178
Akbar (Mughal emperor), 148, 165, 201
'Alī (fourth Caliph), 85, 86, 168, 171, 172, 173, 179
'Alī, Sayyid Amīr, 219, 220, 231, 235
Allāh, Shāh Walī, of Delhi, 21, 149, 190, 191, 202–204
Allāh, Sharī'at, 204
Alp Arslān, 184
America, 9
Anatolia, 6
Aquinas, Thomas, 97, 187
'aql, 104
Arabia, 83, 200, 205, 206, 231
Arabian peninsula, desiccation of, 12
Ash'arī, Abu'l-Ḥasan al-, 65, 91, 98, 109, 139, 182, 242
Ash'arism, 94, 110, 114, 147
Asia, Central, 6, 140, 155, 189, 205; Western, 83
Atatürk, 224, 228, 246
Aurangzeb, 187

Badawī, Aḥmad al-, 161
Badr (battle of), 20, 22
Baghdad, 6, 7, 82
Bahā' al-Dīn, 'Naqshband', 164
Bāqir, Muḥammad al-, 175
Banba, Aḥmadū, 159
Bandung Conference, 9
Baṣra, 79, 87
Baṣrī, Ḥasan al-, 48, 55, 56, 58, 87, 88, 129, 156
Bāṭinism, 7
Berbers, 162, 163
Bīrūnī, al-, 4
Biṣṭāmī, Abū Yazīd al-, 135, 138
'Black Muslims', 9
'Brethren of Sincerity', 143, 176
Brown, J. P., 164
Buddhism, 2, 87, 132
Bukhārī, Muḥammad ibn Ismā'īl al-, 63, 64
Bustī, Abū Ḥātim al-, 183
Buwayhids, 184
Byzantine Empire, 2, 3

Catholic Church, 74
Chelebī, Kātib, 187
China, 8

Chisti, Mu'īn al-Dīn, 165
Christianity, 2, 4, 80, 223, 247
Chou En-lai, 9
Communism, 2, 37, 223, 247, 252
Community of the Faithful, 1, 2, 7, 25, 50, 58, 59, 66, 67, 69, 77–79, 86, 200, 209, 211, 222, 227, 238, 242–244, 248, 251
Companions (of the Prophet), 43, 44, 48, 49, 51, 52–54, 57, 58, 60, 61, 69, 70, 74, 79, 83, 197, 242
Corbin, H., 176

Damascus, 3, 79
Dā'ūd, 72
Depont, O., and Coppolani, X., 161, 164
Dīn, Muḥammad Burhān al-, 178
Dīn, Niẓām al-, 189
Dir'iya, 199
Divine Revelation, 68
Du'alī, Abu'l Aswad al-, 171
Duns Scotus, 122

Egypt, 6, 81, 83, 208, 224, 227
Europe, 8, 9

Faḍl Allāh of Astaiābād, 178
Fārābī, al-, 119, 143, 153
Fāṭima, 171, 172, 175, 179
Fāṭimids, 176, 183, 184
fatwās (authoritative legal opinions), 94, 200, 204
fiqh, 101, 102, 103

Gabriel, 31
Ghanī, 'Abd al-, of Nābulus, 149
Ghazālī, al-, 7, 78, 94–96, 106, 107, 120, 122, 126, 134, 140, 141, 143, 147, 148, 153, 162, 184, 193, 196, 244
Ghifārī, Abū Dharr al-, 129
Ghujdawānī, Khāliq al-, 164
Gibb, H. A. R., 1, 80, 90, 247
Gīlānī, 'Abd al-Qādir al-, 152, 153, 158, 159, 161
Gnosticism, 87, 88, 132
Goldziher, I, 44–46, 49, 167, 173

Ḥadīth (tradition), 14, 31, 36, 43–49, 51–54, 56–67, 70, 76–78, 82, 83, 87, 91, 129, 183, 198, 211, 217, 219, 236–239, 241, 250
Ḥajj, 'Umar Tall al-, 163
Ḥākim, al-, 178, 182, 183
Ḥāllaj, al-, 112
Hall of Wisdom academy, 4
Hamadhānī, Yūsuf al-, 163, 164
Ḥamīd, 'Abd al-, 161
Ḥanafīya, Muḥammad ibn al-, 171
Ḥanbalites, 131, 203
ḥaqīqa (mystic truth), 109
Hārūn al-Rashīd, 182
Hāshimites, 171
Hellenism, 3, 5, 87
Ḥijāz, 79, 81, 199, 203
hijra (the Emigration), 18
Hinduism, 5, 201, 248
Hobbes, T. 105
Hudā, Abu'l-, 161
Ḥudaybīya, Pact of, 23
Hujwīrī, 'Alī al-, 150
Ḥusayn, Ṭahā, 172, 224

Ibn al-'Arabī, 98, 124–126, 142, 146, 162, 164, 188, 194, 197, 201
Ibn al-Ḥajjāj, Muslim, 64
Ibn al- Muqaffa', 80
Ibn 'Aṭa' Allāh, 162
Ibn Ḥanbal, 82, 90, 91, 182, 194, 242
Ibn Idris, Ahmad, 206, 207
Ibn Khafīf, 139
Ibn Khaldūn, 5, 21, 181
Ibn Māja, 64
Ibn Mas'ūd, 'Abd Allāh, 52
Ibn Mu'ādh, Sa'd, 23
Ibn Mukhtār, Muḥammad, 163
Ibn Qayyim al-Jawzīya, 147, 195
Ibn Qutayba, 53, 63, 65, 77
Ibn Rushd (Averroes), 119
Ibn Ṣafwān, Jahm, 88
Ibn Sa'ūd, 'Abd al-'Aūz, 199
Ibn Sīnā (Avicenna), 97, 117–119, 121, 139, 143, 153, 182, 189, 190
Ibn Taymīya, 79, 83, 94, 109, 111–115, 123, 147–149, 162, 166, 167, 195, 196, 197, 205, 237, 239
Ibn Thābit, Zayd, 40
Ibn Tūmart, 162
Ibn Wāsi', Muḥammad, 130
Ijī, al-, 96, 108
Ijmā' (consensus), 57–61, 68, 70, 72–78, 81–83, 103, 198, 201, 207, 237, 238, 250
Ijtihād (systematic original thinking), 72, 75, 77–80, 82, 83, 103, 115, 198, 199, 207, 215
'ilm, 101, 102, 103
Ilyās, Shaykh Bābā, 151
Imām, 172, 173, 175, 238, 243
India, 6, 83, 140, 155, 196, 201, 203, 204, 211, 223, 227
Indonesia, 83, 245, 249
Indus River, 2
Iqbāl, Muḥammad, 220, 225, 234
Iran (see Persia)

Iraq, 6, 47, 55, 61, 71, 72, 79, 82, 199
Ismā'īl ibn Ja'far, 175
Ismā'īlīs, 175–178
  Sub-sects:
    Druzes, 178
    Ḥurūfīs, 178
    Ja'farī, 179
    Musta'līs, 178
    Nizārīs, 178
    Nuṣayrīs, 178, 179
isnād, 54, 58, 64
Ivanow, W., 176

Jabrīya ('pre-determinists'), 86
Jahāngīr, 165
Jāmī, 146, 188
Java, 8
Jerusalem, 19, 20, 27
Jesus, 14, 15, 26, 245
Jews, 19, 22, 23, 28
jihād (holy war), 37, 86, 200, 203, 204, 205, 210, 211, 213
jinn, 34
jizya (poll-tax), 28
Jubbā'ī, al-, 91, 182
Judaism, 4
Junayd, 138

Ka'ba, 19, 20, 27
Kabīr, 165, 201
Kalābādhī, al-, 138, 140
kalām, 89, 93, 94–97, 99, 105–107, 109, 121, 123, 139
Karbalā', 172, 175
Karkhī, Ma'rūf al-, 130
Khalwatī, 'Umar al-, 160
Khān, Sayyid Aḥmad, 216–218, 223
Khārijism, 129, 238, 242, 243
Khārijites, 37, 56, 57, 86, 88, 93, 167–170, 200
Khaybar, 28
Khuldī, al-, 156
khuṭba, 53
Kirmānī, Ḥamīd al-Dīn al-, 176
Kūfa, 79, 171
Kulāl, Amīr, 164
Kumayt, 171
Kuwait, 199

Lammens, H., 45, 47
Lane, W., 162
Law, Islamic, 6
  ethical categories of acts, 84
  law and the state, 79–81
  'roots of law', 68
    Qur'ān, 68–69
    Sunna, 69, 70
    qiyās, 71, 72
    Ijmā', 72, 75
  schools of law:
    Ḥanafī, 82, 182
    Ḥanbalī, 82, 182, 194
    Mālikī, 82, 182
    Shāfi'ī, 82, 182, 192

Macdonald, D. B., 92
Madhāhab, 83
madrasas (theological schools), 5, 184–188, 190–192, 251
Mahdī, 133, 171, 172, 210, 211, 245
Mālik ibn Anas, 49, 82, 156
Malikshāh, 184
Ma'mūn, al- ('Abbāsid Caliph), 4, 5, 90, 182, 183
Manichaean dualism, 87, 88, 99
Margoliouth, D. S., 45, 46, 47, 50, 51
Materialism, 88
Māturīdī, Abū Manṣūr al-, 93, 139
Māturīdism, 93, 114
Mawālī, 169, 171
Māwardī, al-, 78
Malay Peninsula, 8
Mecca, 11, 12, 18–27, 36, 37, 199, 203, 204, 205, 207
Medina, 3, 18–27, 37, 47, 55, 61, 71, 72, 79, 82, 86, 87, 199, 222
Mirdās, Abū Bilāl, 168
'model pattern of behaviour', see Sunna
Mongols, 2, 6
Moses, 15, 26
mu'aṭṭila, 89
Mu'āwiya, 168, 171
muftī, 81
Mughals, 7
Muḥammad 'Alī, 199
Muḥammad, 'Alī, of Shīrāz, 179
Muḥammad, Khwāja Nūr, 165
Muḥammad ibn Ismā'il, 175
Muḥāsibī, Ḥārith al-, 134
Muir, William, 215
Mukhtār ibn 'Ubayd, al-, 171
Murjites, 86
Mūsā ibn Ja'far, 175
Mutakallims, 97
Mu'tazila, 4, 5, 51, 61–63, 86, 88–90, 92, 93, 96, 98, 104–106, 110, 131
Mu'tazilism, 147, 169, 241, 242

Nādir Shāh, 179
Nānak, 165, 201
Nasā'ī, al-, 64
Niẓām al-Mulk, 184
Noah, 15
Nūḥ ibn Naṣr, 182
Nyberg, H. S., 88, 256

Ottomans, 7, 80, 196, 199, 200, 203, 207, 208

Pahrārawī, 'Abd al-'Azīz, 123
Pakistan, 9, 83
Persia, 6, 189, 199
Persian Empire, 2, 3
pilgrimage, 19, 20, 37
Plotinus, 118, 124
Prophetic infallibility, 69
Prophet's ascension, 31

qadar (Divine will), 104, 113
Qaddāḥ, 'Abd Allāh ibn Maymūn al-, 176
qāḍīs, 80, 81
qānūn, 80
Qarmaṭ, Hamdān, 176
Qarmaṭians, 176
qibla (direction of worship), 19, 20
qiyās, 68, 71–77, 81, 83, 198, 199, 207
Qur'ān:
  language and style of, 41
  main beliefs of Islam, 36, 37
  moral emphasis in, 32–35
  prayers in Islam, 36, 220
  Qur'ānic commentary, 41
  Qur'ānic revelation, 212, 221
  social legislation in,
    alcohol, 38, 50
    polygamy, 38, 231
    slavery, 38, 39, 231
    usury, 37
  Sūras, 30
Quraysh, 11, 20, 169
Qushayrī, al-, 140

Radhakrishnan, S., 177
Rānīrī, Nūr al-Dīn ibn Muḥammad al-, 149
ra'y (personal judgment), 71, 72, 81
Rāzī, Fakhr al-Dīn al-, 96, 98, 189, 242, 244
Rāziq, 'Ali 'Abd al-, 224, 242, 244
Renan, E., 215, 216
Revelation, 31, 244
Rashīd Riḍā, 223
Rifā'ī, Aḥmad al-, 161
Rose, H. A., 164
Rūmī, Jalāl al-Dīn, 155, 164
Rundī, Shaykh al-, 162

Sa'd al-Dīn, 161
Ṣādiq, Ja'far al-, 179
Ṣafavids, 7
sam' (tradition or authority), 104
Samarqand, 93
Sammāsī, al-, 164
Sanūsī, Muḥammad ibn 'Alī al-, 207, 208, 209
Sarrāj, al-, 140
Saudi Arabia, 199
Schacht, J., 46, 47, 48, 55
'Science of the Ḥadīth', 64
Seljūqs, 183, 184
Shādhilī, Abu'l-Ḥasan al-, 162
Shāfi'ī, Muḥammad ibn Idrīs al-, 47, 51, 60–63, 72–76, 82, 192
Shams al-Dīn, 152
Sharī'a, 2, 68, 77, 79, 80, 83, 147, 148, 244, 254
Shāṭibī, al-, 108, 115, 186
Shī'a, 7, 56, 65, 170-180, 238, 250
Shī'ism, 170–175, 242, 243, 245
Shīrāzī, Ṣadr al-Dīn al-, 124, 126, 189, 190
Shu'ūbīya (the nationalists), 4, 172
Siffin (battle of), 168
Sijistānī, Abū Ya'qūb al-, 176
Sīnī, Badr al-Dīn al-, 9
Sirhindī, Aḥmad, 148, 164, 195, 202
Smith, W. C., 232
Snouck Hurgronje, C., 74
Spain, 2, 220
Stoic, 104
Stoicism, 89
Successors, the, 46, 47, 48, 57, 60, 61, 70, 73
Ṣūfi orders:
  Badawīya (or Aḥmadīya), 161
  Bayyūmīya, 161
  Bekṭāshīya, 156, 163, 178
  Chishtīya, 165
  Darqāwīya, 162
  Dasūqīya, 161
  'Īsawīya, 162
  Jazūlīya, 162
  Khalwatīya, 160
  Khwājagān, 163
  Mawlawīya, 158
  Mevleviye (Mawlawīya), 164
  Murīdīya, 159
  Naqshbandīya, 156, 164
  Qādirīya, 152, 158
  Rifā'īya, 152, 161
  Sa'dīya (or Jibāwīya), 152, 161
  Samnānī, al-, 148
  Sanūsīya, 160
  Shādhilīya, 162
  Suhrawardīya, 156, 160
  Tijānīya, 154, 158, 162
  Yasawīya, 163
Sūfism (Muslim mysticism), 6, 7, 78, 94, 95, 96, 99, 106, 107, 109, 110, 114,

123, 127, 128, 150–66, 174, 197, 199, 201–3, 205–207, 209, 211, 237, 244, 245–248, 250, 254
Sūfism,
absorption (*fanā'*), 135
inner truth (*ḥaqīqa*), 143
monism, 147
stations (*maqāmāt*), 135
way (*ṭarīqa*), 156, 200, 247
Suhrawardī, Shihāb al-Dīn al-, 97, 99, 124, 125
Suhrawardī, Yaḥyā, 160
Sumatra, 8
Sunna (model pattern of behaviour), 3, 32, 44–48, 50, 52, 54–61, 63, 65, 66, 70–72, 74–77, 79, 80–82, 197, 198, 205, 213, 250
Syria, 22, 81

Ṭabarī, al-, 41, 83
Taftāzānī, al-, 147
Ṭā'if, 24
tanzīh (divine transcendence), 89
taqlīd, 196, 198, 201
tashbīh, 90
'Theology of Aristotle', 124
Tījānī, Aḥmad al-, 162
Tirmidhī, al-, 64
Transjordania, 24
Transoxiana, 93, 148
Turks, 6
Turkey, 9, 40, 155, 205, 208, 224, 227, 228, 249
Ṭūsī, Naṣīr al-Dīn al-, 122
Tustarī, al-, 142

Uḥud (battle of), 22
Umar ibn 'Abd al-'Azīz (Umayyad Caliph), 79, 86
Umayyads, 3, 4, 49, 56, 57, 79, 80, 85–87, 168, 171
'Ulamā', 5, 6, 8, 78, 80, 81, 94, 102, 147, 148, 197–200, 203, 204, 222, 239, 246, 248, 250, 253, 254
Umma, 1, 2, 7, 25, 50, 58, 59, 66, 67, 69, 77–79, 86, 200, 209, 211, 222, 227, 238, 242, 243, 244, 248, 251
'umra (lesser pilgrimage), 23
Urmawī, Abu'l Thanā' al-, 122
'Uthmān (Caliph), 40, 85, 86

verbal transmission of Ḥadīth (*riwāya*), 54, 55, 58

Wahhāb, Muḥammad ibn 'Abd al-, 197–199, 200, 210
Wahhābīs, 82, 148, 170, 196, 198–200, 220, 223–227, 237
Wahhābism, 198, 199, 203, 207, 250
women, status of, 38
World Muslim Congress (1962), 1

Yasawī, Aḥmad, 163, 164

Ẓāhirī, Dā'ud Khalaf al-, 83
Ẓāhirism, 114
zakāt (poor rate), 15, 37, 208
Zaydīs, 171
Zorastrianism, 176, 241, 242
Zuhrī, Ibn Shihāb al-, 48, 49